GEORGIA
IN THE MOUNTAINS
OF POETRY

GEORGIA
IN THE MOUNTAINS
OF POETRY

Peter Nasmyth

ST. MARTIN'S PRESS
New York

ST. MARTIN'S PRESS

GEORGIA

Copyright © 1998 by Peter Nasmyth

St. Martin's Press, Scholarly and Reference Division,
175 Fifth Avenue, New York, N.Y. 10010

First published in the United States of America in 1998

Typeset and designed by Nicholas Awde/Desert♥Hearts
Scans by Emanuela Losi
Covers & maps by Nick Awde & Kieran Meeke
Photos by Peter Nasmyth unless otherwise credited
Printed in Great Britain

ISBN 0-312-21524-X

Library of Congress Cataloging-in-Publication Data

Nasmyth, Peter.
  Georgia : in the mountains of poetry / Peter Nasmyth.
     p.   cm.
  Includes bibliographical references and index.
  ISBN 0-312-21524-X (cloth)
  1. Georgia (Republic)—Description and travel.   2. Georgia
(Republic)—History—1991–   I. Title.
DK672.9.N38   1998
947.58—dc21   98-17593
                                                            CIP

Contents

To Emily

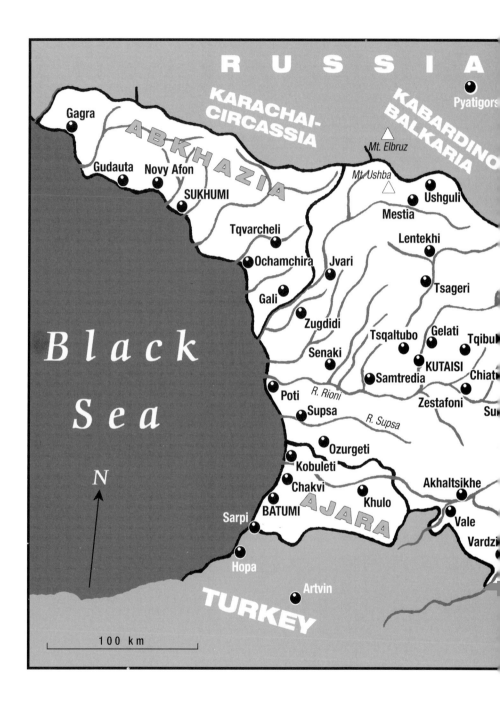

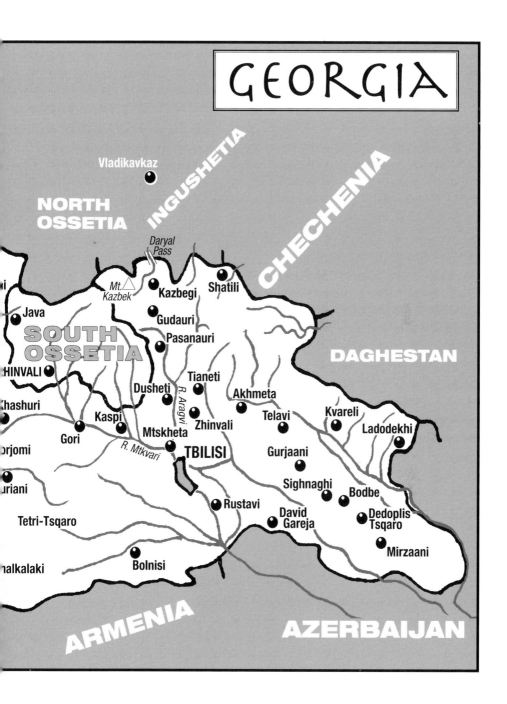

Acknowledgements

This section might better be called an 'apology' to all those who over the years assisted in this book's creation — while receiving far too little in return. It is thus addressed, with heartfelt gratitude, to the following: Marika Didebulidze, Irakli Topuria, Ilya Topuria, Gela Charkviani, Keti Dolidze, Gaioz Kandelaki and all at the GIFT office, Deda Mariam, Gia Tarkhan-Mouravi, Tamila Mgaloblishvili, Maka and Irina at GACC, Ellen Kiladze and the Caucasus Travel staff, Tamriko at the Metechi Palace Hotel, David and Keti Rowson, Madonna in Kutaisi, Maya Kiasashvili, Maia Naveriani, Teimuraz and Irina Mamatsashvili, Gia Sulkanishvili, Jonathan Aves, Stephen Nash, Michael Hancock, the British Embassy Tbilisi staff, the Wardrop Foundation, the management of British Mediterranean Airways, John Wright, Victoria Field, Jonathan Wheatley, Harry Norris, Donald Rayfield, Nino Wardrop, the late and much missed David Barrett, Adrian Roberts, Doris Nicholson, Martin Schumer, Antony Mahony, Mako Power, Kate Hughes, Rachel Clogg, Anthony Eastmond, Jonathan Cohen, Jacqui Christi, David Wilson, Bob Close, Claire Gammon, Lara Olsen, Tony Andrews, Camilla Jerrard, William Burdett-Coutts, Anthea Norman Taylor, Nick Awde and Malcolm Campbell (patient editor and publisher respectively). Additional thanks are given to the Bodleian Library, Oxford, for permission to publish pictures from the Wardrop Collection, and the National Library of Georgia and the Institute of Manuscripts in Tbilisi.

Preface

This book is the product of eleven years of ever-greater personal involvement with a surprisingly cultured nation in the heart of the Caucasus mountains. The process was launched in 1987 after a brief encounter with Georgia's drama-infected landscape and people, clearly only superficially Sovietised. It left a strong sense of the undiscovered lurking under the surface — which was then provoked back in Britain by tales of a remarkable Georgian production of Shakespeare's *Richard III* at London's Roundhouse. My informant told me the actors "had seemed to stand in both the 12th and 21st centuries," that they "offered an important lost link for Western Europe." My work as a journalist would lead to several more visits, then a book on this other land of Shakespeare (*Georgia: A Rebel in the Caucasus*) published in 1992 as a kind of psychological geography.

Now six years later, this second, more comprehensive volume brings those first impressions up to date. Certainly time has changed Georgia enormously — so much so it seemed essential to include a good section of the original book (if updated) to serve as the ground from which to discover the modern nation. The first book's period, just prior to independence, is without doubt the best psychological route map to the terrible drama that followed. At that time the whole nation shimmered on the edge of delirious 'freedom' — a volatile cocktail that, as we now know, led to a moment of dangerous and tragic intoxication.

The transformation that subsequently took place in Georgia is far greater than those in the other former Soviet republics. Some indeed claim that few countries this century have transformed so drastically, and in such a short period, as modern Georgia. Within the two years after 1991 the Soviet Union's richest republic, famous for feting visitors with champagne, caviar and gifts, became one of the poorer nations on earth, its hotels metamorphosised into refugee camps, its streets dotted with Western aid agencies in Nissan Patrols delivering aid. Politically, a fully-fledged Soviet Communist state converted into a frontier-town democracy, an All-Union, centrally planned economy flipped over into a free-for-all free market as the nation tumbled back down the ladder of wealth. The moment this drastic political coin flew into the air was late 1990 — with Georgia's declaration of independence from its overlords in Moscow.

I remember very clearly, about a year after this date, watching a television report in London on the civil war then erupting across Tbilisi. The camera panned to show the Hotel Tbilisi in flames — where just a few months earlier

Georgia: in the mountains of poetry

I had stayed — eaten dinner under the chandeliers, admired the faded Tsarist elegance of the dining room. Now it was a gun position, the classical pillars pitted by bullets. It seemed hard to believe this burnt-out bunker had so recently played host to discussions on the modern production techniques of Shakespeare.

Suddenly one felt just how delicate a thing stability is in any modern society — as indeed Shakespeare repeatedly indicates. The alarming speed with which it vanished in Georgia is a stark illustration of how the social self-image, with one slight weapons-assisted nudge, can bring a whole culture to its knees. I began to wonder about this 12th century part of the human being. What was its shape? How could it live on so irrepressibly under a cultured surface — and in our own society, as much as Georgia's?

Here was the country I had grown so much to like, with its wild mountain dances, devil-may-care dramas, prising open the fist of stone fixed around itself for 70 years — only to find it shattering. In its place out burst a thousand small fists and dances, waving and shouting louder than any before.

What were the cultural groundings of this terrible freedom? Certainly one looked for the roots of Georgia's civil war in its recent Soviet past, which showed a nationality told for 70 years they were somebody else. Georgia, the then homogenised part of the grand, Socialist, Russian-speaking Union of Peoples, had been suddenly released to be 'Georgian' again. But the wild celebrations of self and independence quickly lost focus, to be replaced by the question; what *was* Georgia? These happy-go-lucky, authority-disrespecting Georgians, rebelling so cheerfully against their Soviet overlord in the Kremlin, now had to reconstruct in a non-rebellious fashion. Where would their urge toward real-life Shakespearean drama go?

After the civil war came a period of mafia structured power. Then Eduard Shevardnadze, with some Western financial aid, slowly started reconstructing more reliable, democratic structures — in spite of two mafia-assisted attempts to remove him. As a result, today Georgia holds up a bruised but proud face to the world — Tbilisi is seeing a boom of new businesses, restaurants and investment.

From the cultural/psychological perspective, the country's slow re-construction, its inching discovery of a sense of responsibility, indicates a deeper change than just the political. The country now has a free press, a new stable currency, full embassies from most major countries, and a greater international presence than at any time in its history. It is also starting to be noticed. In October 1997, Georgia hosted its first ever International Festival of Arts (GIFT) in Tbilisi — in which I played a small part as an organiser. It was a pleasure to see the same effect Georgia first had on me, repeating itself in most of the visiting Western artists, actors, musicians, poets. Several even told me they felt an important 'lost link' here. Curiously the same optimism also found itself matched by the IMF, who in 1998 predicted Georgia would produce the world's third fastest GDP growth.

Preface

As I write, outside my window Tbilisi's main market buzzes with Armenians, Azeris, Kurds, Turks, Russians, Jews, refugees — just as it has down through the centuries. One feels again that Georgian part of Georgia, with its ability to absorb other cultures, even the latest, invading forest of tobacco ads.

On a personal level, these years of visiting and many projects (now including a bookshop), have made the story of this country a part of my own. Indeed I often shake my head remembering those first photographs of the Caucasus in the late 1980s. I would never have dreamt they would develop into a Caucasian photo-library, nor that those first tentative meetings in the Soviet House of Friendship would launch so many lifelong friendships.

As one longstanding Georgian friend recently said, holding up a glass of his country's wine now bottled in Holland: "Since your first visit we have shown you all our faces. Our childhood in Soviet times, our moment of ecstasy at independence, our political foolishness afterwards, our shame in war, now our attempts to be a free market like you. You have seen everything, now you must tell it!"

So I try again — to place this rich cultural wine into a newer, slightly more seasoned Western bottle.

Young Georgian dancers at the opening of the
1997 GIFT international festival of arts, Tbilisi,
with the Metechi Church in the background

The Caucasus

Part I

PRE-INDEPENDENT GEORGIA

Child carrying the flag of independent Georgia in 1989 — the tricolour design used during the Menshevik period, 1918-21

1

Why Georgia?

*A*ll voyages are searches in disguise, and this one to the nation of Georgia has turned out as no exception. But the discovery of this small country, in my case, must first begin with a large one — its great northern neighbour, Russia.

In 1982 I sat on an Aeroflot Tupolev jet bound for Soviet Russia — returning from seven months among the temple-towns and holy sites of the Indian sub-continent. Moscow was simply a three day stop-over before London. But it also marked the end of a youthful rite of passage — 'searching' for something in India and of course not finding it. As I pondered the next difficult step in my life a voice came over the intercom: "We are now entering Soviet airspace. Please remember it is no longer permitted to take photographs."

Those words had a strange effect on me. Suddenly the miles of indescribably white, celestial clouds outside the window took on a form of contraband. But I also noticed they bore an uncanny similarity with those I'd seen on a Tibetan poster in northern India. Was there not some bizarre similarity between myself and this statement — ostensibly concerned with aerial reconnaissance? The announcement hinted at a claim, perhaps unconscious, on that beautiful, vaporous, and constantly fluid cloudscape. A possessiveness stemming from a certainty of its own political enlightenment. Did not the culture issuing that statement, pursue a goal just as supremely idealistic as my own for spiritual enlightenment?

Within that moment a more humble beam of curiosity directed toward the giant Soviet world below and a new fascination at the psychology of motivation was born.

By chance, I also had a real mission for Moscow — a letter to be delivered to religious dissidents. It would involve a thrilling taxi ride across Moscow (escaping, so I vividly imagined, KGB surveillance), en route to God knows where — finally ending up at a strange doorway in the middle of a forest of grey tower-blocks.

I knocked anxiously. It opened a crack to reveal a pair of bright blue eyes, then swung open and suddenly I was drawn into a totally new world — a dissident flat in Communist Moscow. I sat on the floor listening to the daughter sing songs she'd written in English, learned from the BBC World Service; watched as her trembling, deep voice sent tears rolling out of her father's eyes under walls plastered with Western magazine photographs and Russian icons. At that moment I felt I'd arrived at a centre of spirituality greater than any in Asia.

Because this father and daughter boldly wore crosses in public, they suffered the punishment of unemployment for non-conformity. I was fascinated. This country, whose 19th century I'd admired through its literature, now proved in every way worthy of Dostoyevsky with his Karamazovs and Grushenkas. They still lived, walked the streets, filled flats and living-rooms with all the same contradictory demons, saints, electrified hysteria described so eloquently over a hundred years earlier.

It was five years before I returned to Moscow. By then Mr Gorbachev and his glasnost had arrived and with it a quite different atmosphere. Standing on Gorky Street that second time, the passing faces showed more curiosity, even hope. Russian friends no longer asked me to keep my voice down when speaking in public. My newest mission — to research an article on Russian avant-guard music took me to people I'd no idea existed in 1982. Heavy metal rockers, experimental jazz musicians, hippies, poets, artists, writers, even punks, throughout a large section of the former 'underground.' Seeking the new 'Notes from the Underground,' in Leningrad I was taken to see the Soviet Hari Krishnas jingling down the Nevsky Prospekt, to the graffiti covered stairway and home of Boris Grebenschikov — the Soviet Bob Dylan, to meet new pop promoters and managers, and samizdat publishers. One young writer told me: "The USSR is now experiencing the unleashing of its underground. The identity crisis amid your Western youth culture is because you've forgotten your own underground, and its energy."

Indeed the streets of Moscow and Leningrad sang out with a fashionable youth rebellion. Leningrad's Saigon Café carried the atmosphere of a Portobello café in the 1960s. People were discovering 'self,' and individuality. Only here it came with the turbulent supercharge of the Russian character.

Yet to me the purity, the sheer otherness of that first 1982 visit had faded, become tainted by something familiar. It invoked the memory of our own discovery of 'freedom' in the 1960s and 1970s in Europe. Their major event, glasnost, seemed to my 'post-Western glasnost' eye, to offer the same delirium of political and spiritual confusion, the kind set into motion a century and a half earlier amid the chaos of an industrial revolution. The dilemmas Gogol, Dostoyevsky and others had investigated so earnestly.

I'd arrived expecting to find the confident new voice of Soviet youth; but instead met the proud inferiority complex of a people forced to strain their eyes at a forbidden culture for too long. An underground where the demands on artists had been quite different to ours (or even theirs at the turn of the century). For the last 50 years the instinctive call of youth had been for the same basic freedoms as us in the West. Before the subtleties of language and art could blossom, there had to come permission to speak.

But my disappointment was about to receive a healthy crack on the head.

Toward the end of my visit to Leningrad, I bumped into a remarkably frank, well-informed man at a party, who, as so often happens at parties, disappeared into one of the eddies of faces, never to be seen again. But I vividly recall our conversation.

His words came from behind a thick black moustache, in excellent, relaxed English — from two years working in Pakistan, so he said. Placing his hand on my shoulder he appeared not so much to speak as to confide. I found myself astonished at this difference in manner from the impetuous, secretive Russians. Discovering my interest in the new directions in Soviet culture he insisted, almost to the point of arrogance, on giving me a brutally honest appraisal. He dismissed glasnost with a wave of the hand.

A Georgian dancing the Lezginka on a 19th century Russian postcard. This exotic, romanticised image of the Caucasus was common in Russia.

"It is a gallant but poor imitation of you in the West," he said.

Suddenly I felt that uncanny ability to grasp the Western perspective I'd sought for so long. But where had he learnt it? As I launched into my own ideas on "the new Soviet Revolution," he stopped me short.

"It may be new here," he said, "but where I'm from it's already 200 years old."

"And where is that?" I asked, noticing his darker features for the first time.

"Georgia," came the reply, with just a hint of pride. "The Russians colonised us at the beginning of the last century," he explained. "It's been more or less the same story since then."

Then his expression grew more serious.

"If you want to know about rebellion away from this huge imperialist power you should look at Georgia. In fact it's better you go there. When you do you'll find Georgia is not 'Soviet.' It's only a part of the Soviet Union. You'll find that when the Russians say 'Soviet' they really mean Russian. Georgia is not Russian, it's not even European. The Russians see themselves as Europeans, they think they're a modern people, they put the first dog into space . . . But to be this modern thing they're so proud of, they've had to push aside the rest of their history, forget all the lessons of the past. And do you know why?" He looked at me with the same faintly amused, hooked eyebrow. "Because it failed them."

He pronounced this verdict in such a charming, affable style I hardly noticed it as criticism at all. But I disagreed with his point on Russian culture, defending its modern literature as among the world's finest.

"Yes," he replied, "and you know why it's so fine? Because it describes the decline of the human spirit exceptionally well. It shows the way Western man is steadily losing his way, losing touch with his instinct. It shows a man so hungry for what he believes is modern he learns to ignore those who lived before this age, who still interpret their instinct."

He paused, then looked at me intently. "If you want to see a modern Asian culture, that's aware of this, or at least trying to be, then go to Georgia. You'll find a people whose past is still the most valued part of themselves . . ."

Following this line of enquiry among Russian friends bought curious correlations with his words. Nobody seemed greatly impressed by the avant-guard music of Georgia, but many expressed a liking for the Georgians and a respect for their determined desire to hang onto their culture.

The more I inquired into this southernmost republic, the more intriguing it grew. First came the discovery that a surreptitious glasnost existed there long before Gorbachev. That it even possessed official social structures — disguised within its so-called mafia. I began to hear about a nation of people with noticeably less stuffing knocked out of them from the years of Stalinism. After all, their present Soviet colonisation had been preceded by the Russians, the Turks, the Arabs, the Persians, the Byzantines, the Mongols, the Romans, the Greeks. These people regarded their current masters as just another landlord in a long succession. Furthermore as all Russians admitted, they'd learnt to preserve their culture — and much of their economic wealth — with a cheeky good humour.

I also found the name of the republic re-occurring again and again for other reasons. Georgia was the USSR's favourite holiday resort, with a landscape of exceptional beauty and variety. In Georgia, a country the size of Ireland, people could ski in the morning, swim a couple hours later in a warm Black Sea, stand with their backs to some of the world's most awesome mountains (the Caucasus have 12 peaks higher than Mt Blanc), yet face an arid, desert terrain, where former inhabitants carved towns into hillsides as the only shelter. Georgia contained one of the world's most prolific and least known wine districts with tea and tobacco plantations thriving 40km from regions too cold even to grow tomatoes.

Every Russian I'd ever met praised the Georgian wines — the most popular in the USSR, and longed to drink them at source, on Georgia's Black Sea coast, nicknamed the 'Russian Riviera.'

The more I heard about this small nation of five and a half million snuggling between mountain ranges just beyond the Turkish border, the more clearly it emerged as the richest jewel in the Soviet crown. It seemed to possess the most dramatic mountains, the most exotic agriculture, the hottest blood, strongest mafia, the most hospitable, wealthiest, religious citizens in the entire Soviet empire.

Talking to Soviet writers about 19th century literature, I then discovered that Georgia, while claiming almost no internationally known writers of its own, served as a formative inspiration to many of Russia's greatest. Pushkin, Lermontov, Tolstoy, Gorky — all visited the area, set major works there. Indeed the famous 19th century Russian critic Belinsky once had to admit: "The Caucasus seem fated to have become the cradle of our poetic talent, the source and mentor of its muse, its poetic homeland."

A particular favourite of mine, Lermontov, set his celebrated novel of the 1830s, *A Hero of Our Time* in the foothills of the Caucasus. To me, a novel strikingly more modern than many written today, and the clear forerunner to all the great 'psychological' Russian novels to follow. In it Lermontov's young hero Pechorin — a Russian officer in the Caucasian Army — attacks the decaying Tsarist society all around him with the kind of predatory boredom that now so saturates modern European and American culture.

Yet Lermontov possessed a huge romantic passion for the desolate Caucasian passes and its peoples. It is said his fascination with these chivalrous tribesmen gave him the strength to openly criticise his Tsar — for which he, ironically, found himself banished to the Caucasian Army. Thus this early hero of modern European literature sank his archetypal roots into a soil just beyond Europe. Maxim Gorky a century later also declared: "The majesty of its mountains; the romantic temperament of its people were the two factors transforming me from a tramp into a man of letters."

Tolstoy's literary beginnings also uttered their birth-cry in the Caucasus. As a frustrated young aristocrat he travelled to the area between the crucial years 1851 to 1854. Like his predecessors he was struck forceably by the Caucasian cult of honour, chivalry and hospitality. Almost certainly it was here he found the germ of his crusading sense of natural justice. His first significant stories *The Raid* and *Childhood* were written while living in Tiflis (the former Russian name for Tbilisi), and many of those Caucasian experiences of the young writer returned to haunt his later work, particularly *The Cossacks*, and *Hadji Murat*.

Not so long ago in this century Boris Pasternak described Georgia as "my second motherland," and some argue his passion for Stalin's home greatly assisted in his survival through the purges. Alas that the same passion never saved his contemporary Osip Mandelstam — who spent over a year in Georgia leaving only a few priceless impressions in letters and his *Journey to Armenia*, before dying in a labour camp during the purges of 1937.

So why did so much mighty literary talent find itself drawn to this remote area?

Picking up the few books on the Caucasus region, I made some guesses.

Possibly because the Caucasus always represented a line of mutability between the Asian and European cultures. While Georgia is one of the earliest nations to convert to Christianity (in AD 337) — second only to Armenia — its people have always liked to leave a couple of fingers, if not a whole arm, in the wilder psychic regions of Asia. Its always interesting to ask a Georgian whether he's European or Asian. More often than not he'll stop and think with his European mind, then give the answer with his Asian heart, which will depend more often than not who is doing the asking.

Men like Lermontov and Tolstoy drew in gulps of inspiration from what they saw as this healthy contradiction, between a Persian culture and Christian religion. Georgia's repeated invasion from the south (several times becoming a province of Persia) had produced a blend in character; cool mountain blood mixed with the hotter Muslim Persian and Arab cultures in the planes below. Thus Georgian culture contains many Muslim elements — like its elegant, balconied architecture, a more traditional role for women, and extravagant sense of hospitality. In many ways the Georgian character has taken some steps towards resolving the seemingly insurmountable polarisation between the Christian and Muslim religions, assisted by a hidden Sufi influence present in the region since the 12th century. However the Georgians themselves shy away from such analysis, preferring a time honoured love of drama and theatre, to ever being found out.

My frustrated quest into the awakening East had found focus again in an Asian country with European beginnings. Apart from sharing St George with England as its patron saint, Georgia also carried tantalising archaeological and mythological links with our own European background. The so-called 'Caucasian' races and Caucasoid Man, out of which European man was once thought to evolve, took their name from this area. Six entirely separate language groups also thrive here (the Georgian peoples have one to themselves and the other 50 or so peoples living in the Caucasus region share the other five).

Approached from its Black Sea side, Georgia was regarded by Greeks and Romans as "the ends of all the earth." Within it Prometheus had been chained to the flanks of Mt Kazbek, Jason found his Golden Fleece beside the mountain rivers of Svaneti in the Western Caucasus; and Medea, of the great Euripidean tragedy, reputedly lived with her father, King Medes in her Colchis home (today the Western Georgian area of Mingrelia). Most of these myths even today find many hints of authentication. Perhaps the most striking is the ongoing evidence of panning for gold through staked-out sheeps' hides in the lower Svaneti district — hence the ethnographic link with a 'Golden Fleece.'

Georgia seemed to contain more and more of the exotica I'd once fallen for in the East. But this time the East had become resiliently Christian. Added to this came the new sounds of a political awakening. Among the Soviet Republics calling for independence, Georgia shouted with the loudest voice with its population still more than 70 per cent Georgian (some of the Baltics barely managed 50 per cent). The blood of the country seethed at another crucial juncture in its history. Rising to the surface in this ancient pot of cultures, came a bubbling a cacophony of socialism, monarchism, hysterical nationalism and liberal democratic ideas, propelled with a do-or-die ambition to launch Georgia far into the future and past, at one and the same time.

In the end of course this would produce independence, civil war, refugees, followed by a slow and painful rising from the ashes. But at that time all I saw was a wide-open blank page, and I had one new mission — as the man at the party suggested — to see it for myself.

The Georgian language

The Alphabet

ა	a	მ	m	ღ	gh
ბ	b	ნ	n	ყ	q
გ	g	ო	o	შ	sh
დ	d	პ	p'	ჩ	ch
ე	e	ჟ	zh	ც	ts
ვ	v	რ	r	ძ	dz
ზ	z	ს	s	წ	ts'
თ	t	ტ	t'	ჭ	ch'
ი	i	უ	u	ხ	kh
კ	k'	ფ	p	ჯ	j
ლ	l	ქ	k	ჰ	h

Georgian is an ancient language with unknown origins. Its roots belong outside the Indo-European family, growing from the independent Ibero-Caucasian language group. Today Georgian shares the South Caucasian language family with Mingrelian (spoken in west Georgia), Laz (spoken mainly in eastern Turkey) and Svan (the oldest member, spoken in mountainous Svaneti). The modern Georgian language and script have been relatively stable and date back to the ninth century. The word 'Georgia' derives not from St George, but the Perso-Arab 'gurj', which Europeans mistakenly linked to the nation's patron saint.

2

Before the Caucasus

1989

The southernmost steppe of the Russian Federation is one of the healthiest and greenest areas in what is now the Commonwealth of Independent States. It spreads before the Greater Caucasus mountains like a luscious, grass doormat, sprinkled with spa towns and health resorts. This covering is occasionally ruffled by the odd green lump — like the five hills around the resort of Pyatigorsk.

It was up the last of these that the Intourist bus climbed, and with it my expectations. After so many months of preparation, the mighty Caucasus lay just over this ridge. The bus's intercom crackled to life as our representative from that soon to vanish institution Intourist, Viktor, prepared us with facts about the town we approached.

"Pyatigorsk was formed in 1780 as a fort to protect the Russians against the Caucasian mountain rebels to the south; its height is 530 to 630 metres about sea level; its climate 15 to 25 degrees in the summer; the number of different minerals in the waters here are 15. Today it is a model resort town, its population is 170,000, this is the 12th five year plan . . ."

The bus driver changed gear ready for the imminent descent and I knew the moment had arrived. I glued my eyes to the window, glancing up at the grey sky above, imagining those literary Russians also anticipating these mountains, just 70 kilometres to the south. The Tolstoys, Lermontovs, Pushkins, who'd been bowled over by what I was about to see. European writers never quite able to grasp the Caucasus, returning again and again to find a handle on their experience here. I remembered Tolstoy's account of their white ridges riding across the horizon in *The Cossacks* — a sight causing his character father Olenin to shake himself vigorously, quite convinced they belonged to a dream.

A dream they had remained, if a dying one, to later travellers like the American journalist Negley Farson, who arrived here in 1929 and wrote his poignant account, *Caucasian Journey* — the tale of his trek into the mountains several years before Stalin's purges in the Caucasus. An end-of-an-epoch journey up among the pre-Soviet cultures of these mountains, many of whom, as he rightly predicted, were to disappear for ever.

Then suddenly the downtown area of Pyatigorsk spread itself before us.

I strained my eyes above the treeline for the rude row of Asiatic teeth baring themselves across the horizon; the place where the Asian world bounded into the European . . . and not a cleft or snowy peak anywhere, instead drizzle. Furthermore that mean-minded, unrelenting, British variety; cutting visibility down to a few dour kilometres. Then Viktor addressed us again, his inappropriately cheerful voice announcing the weather "would be cloudy the rest of your stay."

Through the water-streaked glass I stared disbelievingly at this, my opening move into Belinsky's "cradle of poetic talent." The white hot mountains of poetry had clammed themselves up tight. In fact, as the bus wound its way down the hill, past the lounging concrete slabs of the Soviet sanatoriums, the surprisingly neat roadside verges, clean signposts — very much the model Soviet town — an uncanny feeling of familiarity began to creep over me. Bar the few Cyrillic road signs and a number of Lada cars, this overcast panorama of smart tarmac and trees could easily be mistaken for a well wooded corner of south-east England. No matter how far you push yourself across the globe, a part of you always seems to end up right back where you started. I remembered that deflating scorn Dr Johnson used to pour on all travel-romantics declaring "the use of travel is to regulate imagination with reality."

Viktor (along with the brochures) had neglected to tell us of Pyatigorsk's British climate and high rainfall — hence its abundance of mineral waters. His optimistic socialist lists of facts were, like any political statements east or west, notable more for their omissions. He'd also stretched the truth on Pyatigorsk's military garrison. According to my information it stood, not so much to protect Russia from the wild Caucasian tribesmen, as to serve as a forward base for the empire's progressive expansion southward. Pyatigorsk, like the other fortress towns on the Caucasian borders, represented the gleam in 18th century Russia's eye as it gazed on the territorial annexation it desired more than any other — the wine-rich Kingdom of Georgia.

Viktor clicked his microphone back on. "Not far from here used to be the land of Russia's most famous horsemen, the Cossacks. We now have many stud farms here." Then his voice began to swell with pride. "You know their horses are now turning into a more interesting product," he paused for effect. "Racehorses! You know in 1981 Armand Hammer bought one stallion for one million dollars and then from it he earned 35 million dollars!" One could almost hear his eyes light up.

I began to realise that in Viktor stood the good clean innocence of the idealised Soviet Man since the 1930s — as fearlessly portrayed in those Constructivist posters on sale in the bookshops along Moscow's Kalinin Prospekt. An innocence so pure it failed to notice the enormous ironies underlying it. I remembered the poster I'd bought for a few kopeks and pinned trophy-like on my wall; the sweeping image of young men and women lifting trowels, operating heavy machinery, eyes shining toward a pure and profit-free future of five year plans — and now racetracks.

Yet I told myself, Viktor would almost certainly be my last view on this traditionalised Soviet man. Within a couple of days I would stand worlds away in the Asian 'beyond' of Georgia where the Soviet ideal had never taken hold.

Later, at the Hotel bar, I mulled over these first impressions of southern Russia. Pyatigorsk, the town I knew from Lermontov's 1830s novel *Hero of Our Time*, then the fashionable nexus for numerous peoples and cultures, all milling together in the same streets and bath-houses. Cossacks, Tatars and dagger-swinging Circassian warriors all filled these streets, along with the conquistador Russian soldiers and their St Petersburg consorts, for whom Pyatigorsk served as the fashionable launching pad for Transcaucasia.

For Lermontov the town had served as the immaculate symbol of the decaying Tsarist Russia. He described it first as:

> *A small town all prim and new with the babbling of medicinal springs and the sounds of a multi-languaged throng. Beyond it stands a massive amphitheatre of mountains . . . with Mt Kazbek at one end and the twin peaks of Elbruz at the other. What a delight to live in a place like this. Every fibre in my body tingles with joy. The air is pure and fresh as the kiss of a child, the sun is bright, the sky is blue — what more can one want?*

But then a few pages later:

> *Our life here is pretty dull. Those who drink the waters in the morning are spiritless like all invalids, and those who drink wine in the evening are insufferable like all healthy people.*

He wrote these words at a time when the town came as close as Russia would ever come to a 'Wild West.' In those heady days of the early 19th century, the cult of Byronism struck deep into Russian high society and Pyatigorsk functioned as a literary foil — blending delicate St Petersburg aristocracy with war heroes from the Southern front. Lermontov liked nothing better than to watch the mingling military caps and ladies' bonnets aiming their telescopes at Mt Elbruz, declaring to himself they "didn't have a scrap of poetry in them," then sink his literary teeth into their daily social habits, through his anti-hero Pektorin.

How much had it changed? Judging from the town's trim and many over-weight Russian faces dotted round the hotel, the contingent from the capital still arrived. Before me in my glass that other well known ambassador from the south, the sweet, earthy tasting Georgian wine. As for its peoples; from a nearby table came the sound of a loud, laughing group of Georgians. But what of the other tribes? They still existed but had now intermixed over three generations of homogenising Soviet society. One made guesses at the blood lines lingering in the passing figures. Perhaps a Terek Cossack in the adroit, swarthy manner of the bartender, a Circassian in the waiter?

Georgian toasting — a Karachogeli musician speaking from the heart (regarded essential at least once in a social event) during Tbilisi's Tbilisoba festival 1997

With the second glass of wine, thoughts returned to that moment of disappointment in the bus, then Viktor's odd statement about the weather. I sensed in myself a European confusion, not so much a genuine 'disappointment,' as the pains of adjustment to this upside down world. Here people lived to be pleasantly surprised when something worked as planned, instead of unpleasantly surprised when it didn't. For Viktor drizzle came as the standard kit of life. I reminded myself I sat in a far-off corner of a land whose national character rose from foundations of appalling loss. Loss of life in World War II followed by another 20 million during the Stalinist purges and relocations; followed by a loss of initiative — withered down to an unforgiving, disciplinarian stick in the years to follow.

The Georgians at the table increased their volume. Snatches of a ragged, deep voiced, southern tongue hit me. A minute later they all suddenly stood up and raised their glasses solemnly for a long toast ending with the word "*Sakartvelo!*" — the Georgian name for Georgia.

They sat down again and the loud voices, the laughing, the back-slapping resumed. How different to Lermontov's 'Moscow dandies.' These noisy dark-haired men, with thick necks, grand-eloquent hand-gestures and standing toasts, indulged themselves careless it seemed of any political climate.

As the thicket of empty wine and cognac bottles gradually stacked up between these tragi-comic rebels, I found myself wondering how it could be possible that but one month earlier the nation of Georgia had suffered its most wounding and humiliating event of the last 30 years. Twenty Georgian protestors had been butchered by Soviet soldiers on the steps of their State Government Building in Tbilisi. An act of shameful Soviet savagery sending chills down the spines, not only of all Georgians, but every rebellious Republic in the Union. Suddenly the ugly black hand of Soviet repression had been raised again. Everybody asked themselves whether the all-powerful Soviet state would resort to its old Stalinist means of dealing with dissent — rule by terror.

Gradually the evening geared itself up, and soon the hotel restaurant chairs spread before me a delectable sample tray of the many peoples jostling for position in this new post-colonial struggle. At the front tables groups of Russians of the Party or 'official' strata — in Pyatigorsk on their All Union 'cures.' Then came various East European holiday-makers, a few odd Caucasian faces, then a good number of those mysteriously rich Georgians cropping up in expensive restaurants all across the former USSR. Before them on the white table-cloths, some of the desired rich pickings appeared; apricot, strawberries, aubergines — items usually commanding black-market prices up north too high for ordinary Intourist catering. But here close to their source, the warm, well irrigated valleys of Georgia waited just over the mountains.

When Viktor later joined us at the table, he responded to our curiosity towards this fine spread with his usual bright-eyed candour — so often directly contradicting his sentences. "Here in Pyatigorsk I've eaten two bananas, and once I saw a pineapple!"

Then all further conversation ceased. In its place came that dreaded Russian dining custom, the 'floor show.' The lights dimmed ominously, a Yamaha drum machine and keyboard sprang to life with a joyous, folky vibrato; and with it began a most extraordinary exhibition of Soviet evening entertainment.

Parading out before the diners came the standard procession of almost naked girls, but not in the standard costume. For in brazen defiance of the Las Vegas 'look-alike' styles all the rage in Moscow, came a group of dancing hammers and sickles. Perfectly proportioned female limbs in bright red leotards and hats emblazoned with Communist insignia, began to gyrate and spin before the delighted diners. Donning coy imitations of militia caps, they strutted and saluted with military precision, or shivered seductively before the front row of tables, flinging back their heads in abandon. A startlingly honest display of eroticism, and utterly faithful to the licentiousness saturating every strata of Soviet society (to the shock of every foreign visitor encountering their first hard-currency prostitute at hotel bars). The music propelling them seemed to blend traditional Russian folk ballad and Western pop. As the Yamaha belted out the hits, *Misha Misha* gave way to *You're in the Army Now*, a Status Quo hit from the early 1980s, and the Soviet girls paraded half-mockingly, half-reverently before the rows of holidaying officials, who gazed back with glassy smiles.

A glorious parody of Soviet Socialist style . . . or a stylish glorification that ended up as parody? I couldn't tell. Yet as I watched it quickly ceased to matter; the event taking on a surreal quality all of its own. The macabre death dance of the Soviet ideal being performed out in the open, only thinly disguised as its opposite. Male soldier's faces replaced by women's, their limbs responding not to the clean-living Soviet Russian melody but the decadent siren call of Western rock music; the new revolution starting to eclipse that of October 1917.

For Pyatigorsk the act was an instant hit. The Georgian and East European men saw these nymphetic symbols of Communist power — as a delicious challenge to their prowess at seduction — after the show. The good, solid Soviet patriots watching on from their all-union tables, had their egos stroked by this female re-incarnation of the May Day parade and its iconography of power. And the delighted Western Europeans . . . we just couldn't believe our eyes.

But one thing was for certain, there could be no better finale to this short stay in the Soviet Union — the following evening we would dine in Georgia.

The Massacre – April 9th

Before we left Pyatigorsk, our group was joined by a Georgian woman called Marika. She'd arrived from Tbilisi, the Georgian capital, to act as cultural guide during the journey over the Caucasus. All eyes now turned to this strikingly different, olive-skinned woman. What a dramatic physical change from those Slav cheeks and faces all around the restaurant. Intensely black eyes, the round, eagle-like nose of Persia or Arab cultures. A face accustomed to sun and a hot southern climate rather than the snow bound north; yet the skin also showing just a slightly paler tone from all those many generations living among the mountains.

Her arrival bought a chorus of questions all on the same subject. What had happened a month ago in Tbilisi, on April 9th? The British press reports spoke of demonstrations calling for independence, unleashed by the arrival of glasnost. A gradual escalation of marches, strikes and various non-co-operations with the Soviet system, all climaxing on April 9th when 16 Georgian women and four men on hunger strike on Government Building steps had been butchered by an angry Soviet Army militia.

The strike had focused on the recent Abkhazian call to secede from Georgia — the Abkhazians are one of the many nationalities living within Georgia's boundaries, in their case within a small Autonomous Republic on the Black Sea coast. While the Georgians called to secede from the Soviet Union, the Abkhazians demanded to secede from Georgia. Georgians believed the Abkhazians had been put up to it by Moscow. When the Soviet Army's 'Special Forces,' arrived on the Tbilisi streets to restrain this protest, it became another cause for protest.

Marika decided to try and answer our questions all in one go, by giving us an authentic Georgian account of the horrible event. Her words came at us in one continuous river of emotion. Nobody dared interrupt. "On the 8th of April, the Soviet Special Forces troops were sent into our city, and we had the horror of seeing Soviet tanks and soldiers on our streets like an occupying army."

1989 — Free Georgia demonstrators, racing down the 'government lane' (reserved for official Soviet cars only), waving the single cross of Georgia. Some claim this to be Georgia's original flag.

Immediately I was struck by the completely different tone to her voice. The sharp, strident sounds of Russia had been replaced by a far softer, more mellifluous, accent. She chose her words slowly, carefully matching sound with meaning as if both carried equal importance.

Her hands continued the discussion, moving like conductor's batons. Sometimes, as they struggled to find unknown English phrases, they attempted to mould them in the air before us like tiny sculptures. Hers was such a different personality to that of the Russians, with their swift, nervous gestures, sudden dark silences.

"Our people demonstrated, threw themselves in front of the tanks until eventually they withdrew. There followed a strange calm; the city came to a standstill and many people celebrated the disappearance of the Army on Rustaveli Avenue, yet at the same time we all sensed something awful was being planned." She paused; we could all sense a rising emotion. "Then our General Secretary came on TV telling us we were on the edge of a great catastrophe. We all thought he was just saying this to frighten us. But suddenly the tanks appeared again, this time heading up Rustaveli Avenue toward the Government Building. Nobody attacked them or resisted. Everyone just said 'let them go', and stepped out the way and began to sing songs. But the Special Forces troops were right behind, this time carrying shields and batons. They advanced in through the crowd and surrounded the hunger strikers on the Government Building steps with a cordon. Then all of a sudden they threw gas in the air, and began attacking the protestors — most of whom were young women — and beating them with spades.

"The troops took out aerosols sprayed them in their faces, broke ampoules full of poison under their noses. Many died right there and then in violent spasms, but without showing any visible wounds. When they tried to run away they found they were trapped inside the cordon and the soldiers chased them.

Meanwhile the men protestors and the Georgian police tried to prevent this and break the cordon; but without weapons — the police had been disarmed two days before. They were attacked too, and many of our Georgian police ended up in hospital. These soldiers behaved like savages, almost as if they were mad. One 17-year-old girl was chased half a kilometre and killed with a spade outside the Iveria Hotel."

As the feeling rose her hands cupped the air before her, as if holding out the weight of the atrocity for us to see. "Afterwards our government came on the TV and said it was very sorry for what had happened, that 16 people had unfortunately died accidentally within the crush of the rioting, that they weren't killed and it was an unfortunate accident. But can you believe it!" she looked at us beseechingly. "It was so absurd, half of the city was there that night and saw it all with their own eyes. Nobody believed them."

She sighed deeply and one sensed in her the voice of the long standing hurt of this small nation; its ages of helplessness before mighty neighbours. What could any of them do beside the might of the Red Army? As to the event itself, it smacked of a carefully planned military operation, as if the Old Guard army leaders still seriously believed they could continue to rewrite history; that glasnost never existed. By not killing with bullets they might get away with a statement that the rioters were killed in the struggle to escape. I remembered those grinning Party officials at the front row of the 'floor show' half an hour earlier. It seemed one should never underestimate such a mentality in the old Soviet hierarchy — as evidenced later in 1991, by the putsch attempt in Moscow.

"After this," Marika announced, "the commander of the Caucasian Army appeared on TV to announce martial law. For several days our streets were full of soldiers stopping everyone, at times threatening to kill us — and everybody believed they would kill."

Then her strained expression lightened slightly. "But when we all felt most helpless about 20 cars with our boys and girls leaning out of their windows, began driving at great speed through the streets of Tbilisi their horns blaring, our old Georgian flags hanging out the window. When they found the soldiers they drove up and down in front of them as a challenge. They said: 'You are cruel but we're not afraid of you. You can kill us but that's all, you cannot break us!' You know when I saw this I suddenly felt a feeling of joy. I suddenly sensed the spirit of our nation, a spirit that would stand up to even them."

Looking round the small audience of rapt faces, I realised we'd all just taken several solid steps into that precious feeling Georgians hold for their country. The moment she stopped talking a chorus of questions rose up from the audience. She then explained that shortly afterwards Eduard Shevardnadze, then Mr Gorbachev's righthand man, had arrived in Tbilisi to take control of the army. That the turbulence gradually subsided.

Someone asked her what had been the most memorable moment for her during the whole the event. She thought for a moment. "I don't really know, but I remember how at the darkest time when there seemed to be nobody willing to support us, when everyone seemed to have given up, a group of Georgian soldiers who had fought in the Soviet army in Afghanistan suddenly came to the TV station and said on air that next time they would put themselves between the protestors and the Special Forces. They said they would be prepared to die first. They gave out a telephone number that people could ring if there was trouble. And you know they really defended us."

She emphasised the word "really" — as if to imply nobody could ever properly describe the event. She continued: "They drove about the city at any time during the day or night and without weapons they fought these Special Forces, pushing them away from people. You know when I saw this happening, all these young people standing up and prepared to die, for the first time in the whole event I cried."

Mt Elbruz, from Pyatigorsk in the Russian Federation. The summit is in the Kabardino-Balkar Republic, its southern slopes in Georgia.

3

The mountains of poetry

On that final morning at Pyatigorsk my alarm rang at 7am. I'd decided on one last reckless bid for the "silver-capped Caucasus" of Pushkin. The hotel lift took me to the 17th floor, then I strode down the corridor toward the south-facing balcony door, imagining myself a bleary-eyed Lermontov with cameras, tripod and lenses clanking under my arm.

By halfway along the threadbare carpet, I started to squint at light pouring in through the far door — as if a brilliant neon strip had been lit at the point where the earth and sky collided. With every step it grew brighter and fiercer, until finally, pushing open the door — unleashing a blast of freezing mountain air — came the reason. There they stood! The stunning white ridges of Asia set into a dazzlingly blue sky, striding across the horizon, to disappear over the curve of the earth for 400km in either direction. The silver, glittering peaks of the Greater Caucasus, exactly as Pushkin and Tolstoy saw them 150 years ago.

I leaned against the balcony railing transfixed — quite oblivious to the bitter wind. The sun had already crept up over the Daghestan Caucasus to the east, converting the far western mountain-tops to pink-tipped fingers. Such a deceitful flirtation of light, overcoming every first-time viewer with its natural painterly beauty. I remembered once before another first glimpse, this time the Himalayas in Nepal. How almost hypnotically they drew me up into their glaciers, only to turn all ideas of beauty upside down by leading me straight into the arms of disaster. I found myself having to help two Sherpas carry the tombstone of their friend, an English climber, up to the base of Anapurna One. I'll never forget cementing it into place at the foot of that deadly lily-white mountain after a journey nearly taking our own lives.

But now all tragedies were ignored, for lording over the entire range stood the twin volcanic peaks of Mt Elbruz. At a full 5,642 metres, they pressed their two 'white breasts' (as I was told 'Elbruz' translates) into the icy air. Through my 300mm lens I could just see their nipples — small dark areas of rock around the summit.

With fingers now shrinking from cold I fumbled to change camera settings, reflecting all the while how these mountains had taunted poets, politicians and armies, again and again. When the Nazis first saw Mt Elbruz during their 1941 invasion of the North Caucasus while heading for the Baku oil-fields, they'd vowed to climb it and ritually reconsecrate it as mother of their Aryan ancestry (they believed the ancient tribe of Caucasian Alans played a crucial role in fathering the Teutonic master race).

Such a provocative domination of the skyline had led to numerous switches of ownership, and today Elbruz belongs not to Georgia but the Kabardino-Balkar Republic — a part of the Russian Federation containing most of the highest Caucasian peaks. But the mountain was not without its own human catastrophes. In 1941 its nearby inhabitants, the highland Balkars, chose to side with the Germans in the hope Hitler might free them from Soviet domination. An act that earned the entire tribe relocation to Kazakhstan by Stalin.

The other major bump in the panorama, Mt Kazbek, belonged to Georgia and represented our journey's next destination.

With hands almost too cold to move, I just managed to press the shutter. Elbruz was mine too.

The ends of all the earth

The main road into this formidable rockscape is the Georgian Military Highway. A Russian road built to supply the colonising army during its steady push southward in the 19th century. It begins outside Georgia, in Northern Ossetia and ends, effectively, beyond it (although technically Tbilisi marks the finale). Our bus quickly picked up the road's scent in the Pyatigorsk suburbs, with a cantering, swerving motion. The driving-style prompted a sharp glance towards the driver — and yes, we were now in the hands of a Georgian. Like most Georgians a hugely friendly, spirited man, with a tree-trunk of a neck and many grins for his guests as well as those he attempted to drive off the road. And our first stop?

"Tbilisi," he shouted back.

I rephrased the question. Not the ultimate destination, our first one.

"Tbilisi!" came the reply again.

According to our schedule, arrival there wasn't due for four more days. To begin with nobody commented on his desire to drive a forty four-seater bus like a coupe Ferrari. This gusto was the Georgian way, and we'd elected to be its guests. But eventually our anxiety transmitted itself to Marika who passed it on, and he slowed just enough so we could relax our grip on the seat ahead and begin a hesitant observation of the scenery. Thankfully he decided Tbilisi could wait.

The opening miles took us along the rippling southern steppe towards the town of Vladikavkaz, at the time still called Orjonikidze, in honour of Stalin's hatchet-man of the same name — another zealous Soviet monster who in the 1920s inflicted such a vicious campaign against 'counter-revolutionaries' in his native Georgia that the cruelty even horrified Dzerzhinsky — head of the Cheka, the Soviet secret police. Lenin too had been appalled, and Sergo

Orjonikidze's brand of Bolshevism played an important role in his break with Stalin in 1923. Unfortunately due to Lenin's illness this pronouncement never saw the light of day until 1956 — one of those great mistimings of history. By then the Communists had promoted Orjonikidze's name across the Soviet Union as a People's Hero; most of Georgia's major towns collecting their own Orjonikidze Streets, statues or plazas.

Needless to say his name had started to suffer its own purge. Statues were being felled — the one in Tbilisi was paint-bombed until it had to be at first covered, then removed as an eyesore — the 'Orjonikidze Avenues' renamed, and praise-giving records rewritten. The town Orjonikidze regained the name of the former Russian fortress there, Vladikavkaz translating as 'Rule the Caucasus.' But when this was safely achieved the local Ingush people stood up and called for yet another change — back to its pre-Russian name (yet to happen).

Outside the window the land grew steadily greener and wetter; the white-caps of the Greater Caucasus darted in and out of the roadside trees; poplar, ash, chestnut, sycamore. Every so often an open field of deep brown earth put a space between them, with a small green burial mound sprouting from the furrows, topped by primitive crosses or heaps of stones. Clearly we'd entered the territory of a proudly ancient people: a population whose history refused to be ploughed under or rewritten by the universal imposition of the collective farm. This earth carried the names of tribes whose ancestors still haunted the pedigrees of many modern Europeans. The bones of the Scythians, Parthians, Alans, Hunsa and Khazars all nourished this soil, as do their tribal offspring of today — the first of whom we were about to meet.

An Ossete.

An Ossete wearing a 'nabadi' — the Georgian word for 'burka,' as recorded in the 19th century by the British climber, Douglas Freshfield (who first climbed Mt Kazbek in 1868)

Marika had clicked on the intercom.

"We're now entering the territory of Ossetes or North Ossetia," she said. "The Ossetians are both Christian and Muslim, with many pagan elements to their religion. Their language is the only one in the Caucasus of Indo-Iranian origins. We don't know why."

At the time the dispute between the Ossetians and Georgians had yet to flare up into the war of 1991. Marika spoke of this Caucasian people with a trace of pride. Their roots sank deep into this area and earned them a noble lineage. She continued: "The Ossetians are said to come from the tribe of ancient Alans, who came here around the sixth century before Christ. Later this tribe migrated to North Africa, France and Spain, and lost its originality. But the Ossetes here still have a very pure blood."

"Purity of blood" — I would hear this phrase again and again in Georgia. It referred to strong cultural resilience and determination, qualities much admired by the intermixed Georgians. Yet this determination also led the Ossetians to dispute ownership of their recently colonised area of Georgian territory, known as South Ossetia. As just one more element of the raging nationalistic whirlwind ripping across the Soviet Union, they wished to be joined to Northern Ossetia, thus recreating their own pure blooded nation of Ossetia. In spite of this Marika's voice couldn't conceal an enthusiasm for this ancient race.

"Ossetian mythology is very interesting and has influenced many Caucasian tribes, especially the Ingush and Chechens. The Ossetians believe they are descended from the Narts; a legendary tribe half giant, half human. We think Nart comes from the Indo-Iranian word *nar*, which means 'strong man.' Today Ossetians will even show you ruins of Nart villages."

I wondered about these former 'strong men,' now steaming ahead into visions of independence similar to that of the Georgians. 'Autonomous Socialist Republic' no longer sufficed for the Ossetians, just as 'Socialist Republic' no longer suited the Georgians' new image of themselves. During the years of brutal central planning these small nationalities had lost not only much of their self esteem, but that crucial everyday initiative to direct their own trades and professions. They'd watched the stupidities of Gosplan (the Soviet state planning organisation) blunder through their local industries and agriculture again and again. Now those years of frustration finally rose to the surface in a single, all-encompassing cry for 'independence.' After 70 years of silence, it cut the mountain air with a hysteria that saw little beyond its own volume. As a result the Ossetians and Abkhazians now glared at the Georgians with the same hatred and lust for independence that the Georgians glared at the Russians.

When Marika shut off the microphone, I asked her about these Ossetian grumblings.

"It's so silly," she said. "We get glasnost and suddenly everybody, down to the smallest little tribe, wants independence!"

I wondered what gave the Georgian claim on independence more tenure than the others, but decided to hold an open mind. Meanwhile the bus thundered into this tribal melting-pot that never melted — these mountains of peoples that even Stalin's mighty stick couldn't mix together. The road deteriorated, dramatically increasing its number of pot-holes, due to a winter thaw that plainly found little to forgive here, under the foothills. We passed several bolder-strewn, shaley rivers, their unconvincing bridges showing all the evidence of violent flash-floods. My confidence wavered at the sight of one brand-new metal girder bridge washed away, obviously just a few weeks earlier. But our driver shot fearlessly across its wooden replacement, still in his Ferrari.

With these scenes of destruction the road offered up reminders of just how thoroughly humankind had followed its example. First came a tall minaret (the Minaret of Tartartub) marking the place where in 1395 Tamerlane the Great won a great battle over Tokhtamysh, leader of the Mongol White Horde. Then another monument proudly proclaiming the limits of the German advance in 1942 during the Great Patriotic War. Markers that just as easily could have stood for the numerous battles fought along the famous Cossack Terek Line, which until the 19th century represented the high water-mark of the Russian Empire. In these fields the Russians had repeatedly fought Persians, Turks and the various Muslim warrior tribes — like the Circassians from the Northern Caucasus. Today the Circassians still survive to the West, just as the remnants of Cossack tribes still mingle among the local foothill populations. Tolstoy had visited the Cossack villages in his youth, observed the deep codes of honour, the strength of character forming the backbone of their communities. If the Northern Caucasus had ever been a melting-pot, these fields and washed-out flood plains on either side of the bus were the crucible.

The town of Vladikavkaz quickly came and went — as a row of spiritless tower-blocks encircling the former Russian fortress; the goal and haven for those like Lermontov, who travelled from Tbilisi through these mountains in the 19th century. For me the town remained memorable for one giant spotted pig indolently strolling beneath military microwave towers. But more importantly, here began the Georgian Military Highway, a route unchanged since Pushkin's day — when it served as the Russian Army's life-line to the front. And here we picked up a faithful companion and chaperon for the High Caucasus to come, the much praised, richly poeticised river Terek.

This 'laughing,' 'smoky,' 'agonized' torrent had drawn adjectives from all the 19th and 20th century century poets passing through the Caucasus. Its origins, high up in the rugged Caucasian glaciers, were much gazed upon by Pushkin, Lermontov, Tolstoy, Mayakovsky and many others, before they too poured forth their lines of devotion. The Terek would remain our companion along the Military Highway all the way to the Jvari Pass, the highest moment on the road.

Then came a shout from the back of the bus. "Turn right!" It emanated from one of our group — who had carried out some earnest research before leaving England.

"Turning right somewhere round here will lead us to the Fiagdon Valley and the Ossetian City of the Dead," he announced confidently.

Did the driver know anything about these places, or indeed the turn-off?

"*Kho!*" came the cheerful reply (the Georgian for 'yes').

But would he or our representative from Intourist permit such a major deviation from the Moscow-approved route? To my surprise, a few minutes later the driver simply swung the wheel to the right, away from the Georgian Military Highway. Suddenly we careered up a narrow, car-free mountain road, heading straight into the Greater Caucasus.

Densely wooded foot-hills quickly closed in on either side. Then came high cliffs, a narrow gorge and thick vegetation, as the road converted into a violently winding band of tarmac, pitching left and right following the course of the gushing Fiagdon river.

Watching a shaggy, Chinese-like hillock passing by I suddenly experienced the distinct feeling of entering Asia. To greet it the engine roared, the gears crashed and the bus leaned horribly round corners, until suddenly another shout came from the back and we skidded to a halt. Someone had spotted a mural high up on the cliff-face beside the road.

Following the direction of the pointing fingers I saw the image of a man's face painted in a seemingly inaccessible position high on the rock — at least ten metres from any solid ground. The cleanness of colours indicated a recent creation, yet its position directly above the raging torrent gave it the air more of an act of inspired bravery than a work of art. Clearly the face carried a deep significance for those who lived up here in the middle of nowhere. But who could it be — an Ossetian saint? Directing this question at the driver we received a stark reply.

"Stalin."

He then lurched us forward again up into the gorge and toward the City of the Dead. I was still mulling over his casual tone of voice when the bus shot round a corner and out into a vast and treeless valley. With it came the signs of former human habitation; ruined houses, hamlets, and the remains of the famous Caucasian look-out towers. Gaunt stone pillars of great antiquity, standing beside their decaying homesteads, in various states of collapse. Here in the Fiagdon Valley came the first clues of the dramatic shifts in the Caucasian populations; begun after the Revolution and the relocations, continuing on to this day, as these remote valleys continue to depopulate. At the end of the last century 50 per cent of the entire Caucasian population lived in mountain valleys like this. Today the figure barely touches ten per cent.

As if to confirm the statistic came more pointing fingers, levelled this time at a dramatic ruined village clinging to a mountain-side high up above the valley. With ghostly walls and crumbling towers it silhouetted against an awesome backdrop of snow-streaked summits and steaming black cliffs. It looked more like an abandoned earth-base for aliens than any human settlement, and for the first time I felt that creeping sense of otherness — that would return again and again in the Caucasus. As if we'd just glided up a valley on a whim and discovered a lost civilisation.

"Is this the City of the Dead?" someone asked.

Marika consulted the driver. "No," she then answered. "The city is further on and is too far for us to visit today. This term refers to the Ossetian burial towers. From the Middle Ages they buried people in towers. But I can't tell you more than that."

The driver revealed the name of the hilltop town as Tsimitar, and explained the so-called City of the Dead was a large Ossetian cemetery comprising many large burial towers.

Yet Tsimitar's ragged outline, with its fan of drastic snowy peaks beyond, gave us an undisputable taste of why all those 19th century poets found themselves compelled to return to the Caucasus. In those days these towers and villages thrived as communities — before the five year plans and intense Soviet industrialisation in the plains below, with its demand for workers.

Tsimitar village in the Fiagdon Valley, North Ossetia

Then, as if to remind us the process still continued, a two metre high display board appeared at the roadside. It stood out in the empty landscape like a forlorn iron tree, its flaking surface portraying a young Soviet woman holding her fist in the air in a gesture of defiant worker's solidarity. Yet the rust now spoke more of the decaying system that designed it. Socialism had come and gone from this far-away region. It left a few relics in the hillsides, soon to be uprooted and forgotten.

The driver wanted to know how much further to go? "We go to Stalin?" he asked. Marika translated his words, then looked at me inquiringly. I just nodded. About a kilometre further on the bus slowed to a halt beside a small statue on a hillock; and yes, contrary to all my reading on the Caucasus — there, right in the centre of this enormous barren valley, stood a bust of Stalin, the eyes of his mustachioed face gazing solemnly up into the snowfields above.

What on earth did he still see up there? What kind of inspiration did he tap down from heaven for these local villagers — illegally? Officially only one statue of Stalin had been permitted to remain in the Soviet Union — at his birthplace in Gori, a hundred kilometres to the south. Even this had been hotly disputed, yet up here, just below the snowline, the personality cult flourished. At the base of the statue a number of fresh-cut flowers had lovingly been placed, an ongoing and spontaneous tribute to the tyrant. I hadn't seen any Lenin in the USSR so cherishingly adorned. It seemed this great monster continued to blossom long after Khrushchev's famous reversal of the cult in 1956. Stalin, the greatest Caucasian of all time, responsible for seven to 10,000 Georgian deaths during the Georgian uprising of 1924; for sending a further 20,000 to Siberia; who wiped out the Georgian intelligentsia and many of his supporters in the insane purges of 1937, then deported whole tribes from their homelands, including the nearby Chechens, Balkars and Ingush after the war — still gathered the accolades of a God.

I turned to Marika for help.

"The people in valleys like this are quite simple," she said hesitantly. "They feel their world to be small, and Joseph Stalin was very big. He won the Second World War and saved the world. He was internationally famous. He was also half Ossetian, on his father's side. It sounds silly, but they're probably proud of him."

"Also a little sinister? I suggested.

"No, not at all," her voice broke into an affectionate laugh, as if talking about children. "These are just country people; they don't support his ideas, they just like him. The big man."

But one could tell, to this educated, liberal woman from the capital, the ongoing presence of the Stalin cult caused some embarrassment.

"What about the purges and the local deportations?" I asked.

"They think, well he made a few mistakes, but so does everybody." Her voice sounded conciliatory, as if playing it down as but a minor blemish on what was at heart a liberal nation.

On our way back down the valley, still not entirely convinced, I found myself concocting exotic explanations of my own, connecting the Ossetian myths of the 'strong men' Narts to the big man Stalin. Had this early race been given human form, after religious worship had been suppressed by the atheist Soviets? Did the modern personality cult in any way resurrect the ghosts of the Zoroastrian gods of light and darkness, the Truth and the Lie, dominating these mountains before Christianity?

My thoughts were drowned out by more shouts from the back of the bus.

"Stop!"

"City of the Dead!"

"Nart houses!"

Everybody looked at a fortified Ossetian farm under a cliff, with strange, stupa-like outbuildings. We piled out of the bus — hungry for anything approaching the sepulchral city so far denied us. For here, clearly were a few of the Ossetian burial houses.

They stood behind the farm, looking more like tiny stone barns than towers, the blocks of their roofs stepped into each other in jagged, oriental shapes. Clearly smaller versions of the 'City of the Dead' towers up the valley, but hardly less macabre. I imagined an innocent visitor to this 'City,' wandering around knocking on the doors (from photographs I saw later, the towers did appear similar to buildings) — then peering inside a window to find the village peopled not by living families but thousands of corpses, layered one on top of the other.

I approached the nearest burial house with caution, but found my way barred by a viciously barking dog, leaping at me from the end of a thin rope. I retreated smartly, but as I did so felt the Asian world take several steps towards us. These towers bore strong resemblances to the 12th-17th century *turbes*, or tomb-towers of Iran and Anatolia. Furthermore the jagged stupa-esque shape of the roofs offered a clear architectural connection with those I'd seen in Ladakh and Nepal.

Georgia once held a key position on the old Silk Route and mountains served as crucial repositories for religious texts and ideas flowing East to West. Caucasian monasteries preserved several critical religious and philosophical texts at a time Europeans persecuted them out of existence. One of the first accounts of the Buddha arriving in the West came via Georgia in the tenth century — translated into Greek by St Euthymius at the Georgian monastery at Mt Athos. The story survives today as the Balavariani folk-tale (also called *Barlaam and Josaphat*) and, according to Tolstoy's autobiographical piece *A Confession*, exercised a strong influence on the great writer. The text was inevitably Christianised (Iosaphat is converted to Christianity) and Barlaam and Iosaphat venerated as saints of the principal Catholic and Orthodox Churches. Among other writings otherwise lost to history were *On Nature* by Zeno, the founder of the Stoic school and the neo-Platonic writings of Porphyry (saved by Armenian and Georgian scholars, then transmitted to the West). The people who today tended these strange single windowed chambers almost certainly knew nothing of this, yet the designs hinted at a time when their ancestors did.

Back at the bottom of the valley, lying on the rich green grass, engaging in that fine Caucasian tradition of the picnic, I began to feel the centuries-old fingers of legend slowly wrapping around our journey. The ghosts of these ancient Caucasian cultures still haunted the hillsides, moved between the trees. In the grass around us daisies, wild garlic, numerous herbs and wild flowers sprouted from the same soil; above I noticed a white-winged eagle circling lazily among the crags. I felt we'd just glided up into a majestic, disappearing world of a former mankind, then back again to the modern Soviet world. It had all taken place in an instant and now seemed too much like a scene in a dream. I wondered how much I indulged in our popular condition of modern

A 19th century engraving of the Daryal Gorge, at the time Lermontov and Pushkin saw it

nostalgia, that self-manufactured state of yearning toward delight and terror — the same feeling motivating the European Romantic movement and all 19th century poets who visited the Caucasus — the phenomenon Marxists described as a "drowning in honey" and "rural idiocy." But the Marxists were being drummed out of the Caucasus. The space they left behind would be filled by new winds rushing into the vacuum. Might not one of these be the modern European nostalgia industry? Would our unquenchable cultural thirst inflict any less damage on these valleys than Leninism? Only the silent barometer of eagles and wild herbs would ever let us know.

The Daryal Gorge

The entrance into the Greater Caucasus true, begins when the Georgian Military Highway delves into its first gorge in the company of the rushing Terek. From here the assault on Georgia begins in earnest with the endless climb to Kazbegi (or 'Qazbegi' in Georgian) — the first major town after Vladikavkaz. I'd been told the Georgian Military Highway ranked among the world's most dramatic — when not socked in with mist, rain or snow. That it had a habit of dropping down all three at once on its most eager visitors. However for us the vapours held back at the entrance of the Terek valley, allowing the sun to dab down patches of burning mountain light onto the valley-floor stones.

As the haggard mountain-sides closed in, so the promise of drama fulfilled itself. Our tiny red Intourist speck crept slowly upward among the rock ramparts and cliffs, a landscape far more suited to Narts than mechanical conveyance. As the first glimpse from Pyatigorsk suggested, these mountains shoot up with great determination at the end of the former Russian empire. At every gear change and battered road sign, I sensed this angry Asian curtain stiffen at our advance. These formidable ridges quietly loathed all intrusions, but as always the Terek obliged us Europeans with its persistent, rapidly narrowing slice up into the massif.

We now followed the route that for many centuries served as the main artery into the Kingdom of Georgia. Until the arrival of the Russians the river provided the most reliable guide south, in the form of a bridle-path. By the end of the 18th century this had evolved into a rough-shod, frequently avalanched, often subsiding carriage path. In the Soviet era, the military road was built up, widened and given today's decaying, pot-bellied tarmac surface, while a separate rail link had been established via Baku and Sukhumi. Yet for all its modernity this road amounted to no better than a narrow two-lane thoroughfare that most Americans would declare a single. This fact only seemed to spur on our driver, who recommenced his imaginary death race, wrenching the bus up the winding, clinging highway as if views never existed.

Leaning back in my seat, trying to enjoy the cavernous drops and fleeting panoramas, I took a philosophical stance. His return to the death-track simply replaced the former bandit-threat of this road with a modern equivalent. Our senses now attuned themselves not to sword waving Chechen warriors, but the next 16-wheeler, Soviet-built truck careering round a corner, under the control of a driver just like ours. An easy match for any disaster inflicted by the 19th century Muslim rebels.

But the miraculous absence of traffic preserved us and we rocked and swerved our way ever upward toward the descending snow-line. The gorge below us sunk deeper, the mountains stretched ever higher as the road increased its supply of heart-stopping blind corners — with only the occasional tyre-marked bollard between us and the smoky Terek. Marika then added to everyone's paranoia by including a purely historical fact.

"They say in the 1830s a great avalanche bought down a boulder of two thousand tons, dropped it across the highway and closed the road for two years."

Neither the road nor the driving perturbed her in the least. But from my own front seat I missed nothing; and after one last-minute wrench at the wheel only just saving us all from a visit to the Terek, I couldn't restrain a comment. But she just smiled.

"This is nothing. If you ever go to Svaneti, then you'll find out about Georgian driving!"

I vowed never in my life to visit Svaneti. (I would of course.)

Meanwhile she switched on the microphone again. "We are now approaching the Iberian gates — the point at which the Roman general Pompey ceased his advance into Asia. Classic historians have described this place as the 'Ends of All the Earth' but we call it the Daryal Gorge — or *Dary Alan* which translates as the 'Gates of Alan.' It was traditionally the doorway to Ossetia, the land of the Alans. For you it's the doorway into Georgia. It is one of the narrowest parts of the Military Highway and was much attacked."

As the 12 kilometre long gorge clamped itself around us, one could easily see why. Its cliffs rose up a good kilometre on either side of the road, and at times plunging down the same below. When Pushkin travelled through this deep crevasse of rock he described the sky as "a narrow blue ribbon far above." Today the mountains disappeared into swirling mists and cloud, never able to decide whether to drop rain, fog or burning sunshine. How easy for a bandit to drop something else — which they frequently did. In 1804 local tribes almost brought the Russian Army to its knees by severing its supply-line in this gorge.

As if still afraid of attack the bus never slowed, until the moment we flew round a corner and found ourselves face to face with a Crusader-like castle, perched on a bank beside the Terek.

"This is the Daryal Fortress," announced Marika. "It dates from medieval times and is one of the last in the ancient string of fortress-castles and watch-towers running across the Caucasus from early Christian times. They would light fires on the flat roofs when an army approached in order to warn the kings of Georgia on the other side of the mountains."

Her words conjured up the image of numinous dark watch-towers, of the kind in the Fiagdon valley — igniting one after the other across the Greater Caucasus, creating a long orange necklace of light all the way to Tbilisi.

This particular fortress, restored and then used by the Russians in the 18th century, had now been left to rot. Yet its turrets held up sturdily in spite of numerous years of neglect, leaning crisply over the left bank of the Terek in readiness for the next supply caravan from Vladikavkaz. Above it rose the shadowy gorge of "depths obscure and dismal," into which Lermontov landed the tormented Demon in his narrative poem of the same name.

I found myself remembering the young poet again, his self-portrait at the beginning of *A Hero of Our Time*, perched on a bullock cart, his face battered by the wind, his "portmanteau half-filled with travel notes on Georgia." A young man possessed by what he described as a "mania for romantic places," and also that terrible new malaise afflicting the officer classes of Tsarist Russia — boredom. In an unnervingly modern and almost certainly autobiographical passage from the book, he describes the feelings of a 25 year old in the 1830s:

As a young man, as soon as I gained my freedom I threw myself wildly into all the pleasures that money can buy, and needless to say, soon tired of them. Then I went in for society high-life and before long tired of that too. I fell in love with fashionable women and was loved in return. But their love merely stimulated my imagination and vanity, my heart remained empty. I took to reading and study but even wearied of that. I began to realise I had no need of learning to win fame or happiness, for the happiest of people are the stupid, and fame is a matter of luck and you only need a little cleverness to achieve it. After that I just got bored.

Later in the same monologue he admits:

My soul's been corrupted by my society. My imagination is eternally restless, my heart insatiable . . . All that's left for me is to travel.

In these passages come the first germs of that universal despair which eventually led to the popularisation of nihilism by Turgenev and other great 19th century writers. It also laid out the opening moves for the idealistic 'Cult of the Young Man,' a phenomenon much more 'of our time' than Lermontov's.

Lermontov had also travelled to Georgia searching for that experience of 'otherness' to lift him above the deadening sophistications of his own society — the same motive that took me to India in the early 1980s. In these mountains he clearly found something — although not enough to make him forego his passion for duelling, which ended his life (like Pushkin before him) at the age of 26.

A century later, the Russian Constructivist and poet Vladimir Mayakovsky travelled through these mountains believing he carried the torch his predecessors lacked — Bolshevik Socialism. He passed through this very gorge in 1924 composing his own irreverent sequel to Lermontov's epic poem *The Demon*. As in previous poems, like *Ode to Revolution*, Mayakovsky proselytised on behalf of the new Communist regime with unruly zeal, fusing his Bolshevik fury with Nature mysticism. This zeal also earned him an untimely end — he committed suicide in 1930, a bitterly disappointed man, having turned on the system he'd once so wholeheartedly promoted.

With my head lolling against the velvety headrest, I looked up at the twisting rock formations, the fog funnelling between cracks in the cliffs. These mountains seemed to hold their breaths, awaiting the next set of idealists and poets, the newest, furiously improved system of human government.

Minutes later the bus shot out of the gorge and into the luxurious, wide open valley around Kazbegi. Finally, we'd arrived in the generous heartland of Georgia.

Kazbegi village

4

Kazbegi

To arrive into the spacious Kazbegi valley straight out of the Daryal Gorge — is to transfer from one absolute of landscape into another. From the shadowy claustrophobic cliffs of the canyon we sped out into a brilliant white arena of peaks and luscious Alpine meadows. Before us a transparent green grass rolled out like a welcome mat across the valley floor, climbing up the steep hillsides toward the white line of snow, then finally ebbing away into the frosty blue firmament.

Through the bus windscreen I saw the next watchtower in the line leading straight into the heart of Georgia's old kingdom, Mtskheta, beyond the Greater Caucasus. But unlike in the Ossetian Fiagdon Valley it stood in perfect repair. Beside the road the Terek had also changed. From a violent, steaming attack on rocks hundreds of feet below, to an obedient river burbling along quietly beside the road. To celebrate the change in mood the highway gaily crossed and recrossed the water, making up for all those embittered kilometres clinging desperately to the western valley wall.

"From here the river's name is Tergi," said Marika. "Its Georgian name."

Then buildings appeared beside the road, and without warning the bus suddenly swung off the Highway, climbed the valley side past a few blocks of well spaced tin-roofed houses, and pulled up before a long, balconied building.

"The Kazbegi Intourist Hotel," announced Marika.

With my back to our new home I looked down on my first Georgian town. A community of perhaps 4,000, whose houses nosed down to the Terek, then on up the other side, as an untidy scattering of silver and brown roofs, smallholdings, miniature market gardens. The only real landmark showed itself as a rusty pylon rising up in the centre of the village on the opposite side (Gergeti) like a fleshless totem pole. Plainly the centre station of a cable car, but where was the cable? The base station in Kazbegi also seemed dysfunctional or broken. I was about to ask Marika what had happened, when a casual glance up into what I thought was the sky, stopped me dead. For there in place of empty space stood one utterly vast mountain. It rose up into the air like a menacing white hammerhead, poised to strike down on a submissive community below. Directly before it, as if in supplication to stay the execution, a picturesque twin-peaked church (the Gergeti Trinity church) knelt on a small mountain top.

So this was it: Mt Kazbek. The great pivot, the horn of rock and ice around which the ancient Caucasus revolved, the father of our own Prometheus legend. It lifted up another 3,250 metres (11,000 feet) above the tin roofs of the town; and most of it in a single gigantic thrust of granite to scrape the heavens at 5,047 metres. Seeing it so cleanly defined in the gin-clear air generated a rush of exhilaration, followed by a twinge of anxiety. This monster stood a shade too close for comfort. Experience had by now taught me to beware of all breath-taking beauties; mountains in particular. For in spite of all the grandeur, something afflicted this town. It had to do with that abandoned cable car, and also numerous fluttering strips of black cloth hanging off buildings and road signs. Marika offered the first clue.

"These flags are flying all over Georgia at the moment," she said gravely. "They're marking the 40 day period of mourning for the protesters killed on April 9th. Many are choosing to dress in black, to go to churches, light candles, and place these flags in public places as a respect and also a protest."

This would explain why none had been seen before, as Northern Ossetia stood within the Russian Federation, not Georgia. Yet here, just across the border, the atmosphere changed dramatically. I walked down to the town square and discovered small knots of loitering men, their burnt Asian faces glancing at me from under flat cloth caps. They seemed disgruntled, apathetic, or both. The streets oozed the same sense of unease and decay. Mountain cattle (like the local Khevsuretian cow) and chickens strolled untended among the main avenues, as the men idly watched on. Beyond the town I noticed a bulldozer left to rust in the middle of fields — as if once broken down it immediately became useless, irreparable — like the Soviet system supplying it. I watched a cow push open the gate of the Intourist hotel and amble in towards the lusher tourist grass beyond, and in the main square a pig sniff her way around the black granite platform bearing up the main statue of the town hero, the 19th century novelist Alexander Kazbegi. Nobody cared.

Walking up the hill I encountered a large vandalised building. On its walls the words 'Kazbegi Cultural Centre' were written in Russian. Next to it, sitting under its Lenin statue (since disappeared), three local teenage girls chatted among themselves, all wearing knee-length dresses. Could I take a quick photo?

"*Yaa danker-shern*," came a casual reply — imagining me an East German tourist.

I tried a few words of Russian.

"Why is the Cultural Centre broken?"

"We don't use it," came the offhand reply.

"But why break it?"

My question received a shrug in reply. They'd already lost interest in me — by now just another part of this lackadaisical equation of a Georgian mountain village. Yet back in England, the processed film revealed three utterly charming and alert smiles, overhung by the thickest, darkest female eyebrows I've seen.

Lenin (now removed) surveying the Trinity Church above Gergeti village, from the Kazbegi Cultural Centre

Back at the hotel the atmosphere of lethargy and staggering beauty only deepened. Standing in the lime-disinfected reception area (the hall-mark of all Intourist hotels) it took half an hour to find anybody able to supply us with room-keys. Eventually a Russian woman provided a solution. She pulled open a draw in the small table beside the front door, then simply spread out all the room keys.

"Take," she said trying to show willing.

When one of our group asked if they had room service, it produced a confused look.

"Er . . . yes," she replied, thinking the question meant 'Service Bureau,' a kind of internal tourist information centre.

Since this hotel clearly had neither I couldn't understand why she'd answered "yes," so I asked where it might be.

"Here," she replied, pointing at the humble table with its three now empty draws. I realised this wooden table stood as the solution to all tourist dilemmas, manned or unmanned. As long as a 'Service Bureau' existed Moscow would be satisfied. The staff to operate it were mere incidentals.

Then another of our group descended from her second floor room to complain of unmade beds, no sheets, toilet paper or towels.

"Where is our floor lady?" she asked hopefully.

"Here." The Russian manager pointed at herself and smiled feebly.

"Isn't there anybody here to do the rooms?" someone asked.

"Yes, but not now . . . or so often," came the awkward reply.

These words turned out to be prophetic, and for the next three days we appeared to live in a medium-sized hotel run by one person. She later explained that Intourist had great difficulty recruiting staff from the local Kazbegi population. When asked why, she shrugged just a little too casually.

"No money from Moscow," she said.

Again and again at the end of the Soviet period I experienced the same inefficiency in Georgian hotels as in those up north. Much of the reason, as Marika later explained, was to do with the fact that hotel jobs, especially the menial jobs tended to be carried out by non-Georgians. And the reason for this? Marika smiled a little sheepishly.

"Well, you know Georgians don't like to be servants. And although many Georgian women would be willing, our men don't allow us. Once it was even a shame to be a merchant here, but then the Armenians came in and started taking over everything, so we Georgians had to learn."

And then came dinner. Informing the kitchen of my vegetarian needs (a practice still not recommended to travellers in Russia — although Georgia is usually a vegetarian's paradise) I awaited my meal with anxiety while the others first received a slice of bread, then a bowl of greasy soup followed by a lump of boiled mutton. Then, when all around me were scraping their chairs to leave, my food finally arrived — a single boiled potato placed in the middle of a chipped white plate.

I stared at this piece of fluffy conceptual art with disbelief. Kazbegi knew no shortage of food or produce. We'd passed plenty of prosperous vegetable gardens and farms on the way in, some only yards away from the Hotel. No; my steaming potato had been placed before me as a message. It spelled out the words 'go away' as vividly as if they'd been emblazoned across the hotel front door. Tourists were not wanted in Kazbegi, even foreign (hard-currency bearing) tourists. And those with eccentric, unreasonable eating habits — who did they think they were?

Sitting in that deserted restaurant I ate my potato in silence, chewing over its brief significance. Since they didn't know me personally, the kitchen obviously hated what I represented. I, who arrived in Kazbegi not at their invitation, but on behalf of the Moscow regime, as one more unit of Intourist's currency-earning machinery. And what did Moscow do with this currency? It simply furthered itself, or furtively invested it in more hard currency projects, like cable car schemes, designed to turn peaceful Caucasian villages into a booming holiday resorts. In return the Intourist head office on Prospekt Marx, would pay

Georgian drainpipe on Rustaveli Street, Kazbegi

these minor, rebellious outposts a few worthless roubles.

These villagers detested what they saw as the Moscow dictatorship, long before the arrival of the Soviets. Georgia had entered the Russian empire willingly in 1801, only to then watch the Russians renege on their 1783 treaty, banishing the Georgian royal family and attempting to disestablish their Orthodox Church. Resistance had passed on from generation to generation. Georgians had no desire to please their masters in any way. If guests at this hotel carried away terrible reports, so much the better. Intourist might drop Kazbegi from its schedule.

Actor Lado Burduli, wearing Khevsur dress in Kazbegi. Today he is a rock star in Tbilisi.

5

The mountain

The following evening I sat alone on the first floor balcony watching the sun slide away to the west beneath Mt Kazbek. The town before me seemed ravaged by beauty and decay at one and the same time. Furthermore, up here in the High Caucasus there existed a quality of light I'd never seen before. A translucent, airy emerald in the grass that seemed to penetrate everything; the rock, the sky, one's thoughts. In the face of so much snowy splendour, so much infinity right before one's eyes, what did the smaller things in life (like work) matter?

As the sun settled down over the valley, I watched it spread out its delicious deep glow behind the mountain, gradually erecting an enormous golden dome over our heads, pricked with stars. Night now approached from the east, and out along the Military Highway the lights of traffic blinked on, hurrying their journeys southward on toward Tbilisi. Above us all and still kneeling before the colossus of Mt Kazbek, the mountain-top Gergeti Trinity Church ('Tsminda Sameba') now pushed itself to centre stage, its twin towers crisply silhouetted against the sky.

According to Marika the church had stood in that position since the 16th century and the bell-tower beside it, since the 15th. But in the presence of all this other-worldly radiance, what did the facts of history matter either? Its sentinel shape, set prominently beside the holy mountain, said everything needed about religion in Georgia.

Then as I gazed at it, to my utter surprise the church abruptly ignited in a brilliant bath of yellow light. I could hardly believe my eyes. The villagers must have run up a cable and floodlights from the town, a good 500 metres below. I stared at its now luminous twin towers floating up against the growing darkness like a squat celestial lord. What an extraordinary place, human indolence below and fierce religious enterprise burning above, plainly representing the only political force they trusted.

Georgia's Orthodox Church, founded in the fourth century, had been the single rock to which this small nation had clung throughout its terrible history of subjugation. After the Muslim Persians and Turks had done their utmost to destroy it, their allies, the Christian Russians attempted the same by abolishing its autocephaly in 1811 (viciously reneging on the 1783 treaty), and replacing it with their own Russian Orthodoxy. Instead of razing the churches to the ground (like former invaders) they simply abolished its power structure and painted over the fine Georgian frescoes. Yet the many centuries of similar atrocities had only hardened Georgian will to maintain its Church. By the time the Communists arrived with their own crusade — to wipe out religion all together (establishing an extraordinary organisation called the Georgian League of the Militant Godless) the Georgians were well equipped to outride this one too. In the end Stalin himself restored the autocephaly in 1943, as an attempt to woo fuller Georgian support during the Great Patriotic War (World War II).

But to the locals at Kazbegi, their religion sank down roots beyond even the Christian arrival in Georgia. While they still call Mt Kazbek the 'Mountain of Christ,' they also believe the tent of Abraham is pitched on the summit (in some versions of the myth it becomes an inaccessible citadel); that inside an infant sleeps in a cradle held up by unseen hands. Some also say a sacred tree grows on the top with treasure spread around its base, a treasure with the ability to let some see it and others not. It is said most humans are now too impure to see these wonders — including the London Alpine Club who first climbed the mountain in 1868, in defiance of claims they would be driven back from the summit by furious storms and invisible forces. In 1913 this mountain revealed more of its religious secrets when climbers discovered the ruins of a church bearing a cross at an astonishing 3,962 metres.

Next to the Gergeti church, the Kazbegi skyline carried another man-made silhouette — an ugly Soviet-built cube about 30 feet high, announcing more effectively than any plaque or statue, the attempt to force modern leisure values into this valley. Set beside the church, it too broke the skyline (I suspect deliberately) as the trademark of materialism stamped on the mountain-side. As the cable car headstation it intended to serve a thriving tourist industry by sparing visitors the two hour switchback trek up to the 'tourist attraction' Gergeti church. So where had the cable gone?

Marika could tell us nothing. Eventually our local bus driver solved the mystery.

"The cable car was finished in October 1988," he replied flatly to my question.

"But what about the cable?"

"It's there," he replied, adding quietly, "on the ground. Go to the base station, look for yourself."

He seemed very keen for us to go — which we did later to find a brand new concrete structure, recently (and deliberately) destroyed. The giant pulley wheels lay on the grass among twisted iron girders and lumps of concrete rubble. Spread between this debris lay sections of the cable, cut into pieces and left to rust.

After some determined questioning, a curious history emerged. Apparently the Soviet-designed cable car had taken no less than ten years to build. The protesting locals had been employed in its construction, earning lethargic roubles, joking and jeering at the thing they erected.

The mountain

The Trinity Church of Gergeti (15th-16th century) under Mt Kazbek, lit up at night

"It cost them one and a half million roubles," said our driver emphatically. "It was being built for Russian workers in the All-Union holiday camp above your hotel." His tone of voice clearly lumped our hotel in with the camp. "We wrote to our First Secretary, asked him not to put the head-station too close to our monument (the Gergeti church), but he didn't listen." He paused, then added matter-of-factly: "So in December 1988 we knocked down the lower station—" his voice picked up enthusiasm "—and we're going to do the upper one soon."

Responding to my surprise, he said sternly: "Nobody wanted that thing, even the tourists didn't want it." He turned round and glanced at me, not for confirmation, but to let me know.

With his look the listlessness of this town began at last to make sense. A community instructed by Moscow to participate in its grandest enterprise since building the Gergeti church; a project whose only achievement to these villagers would be to pull it right down again — which they did. Today it is gone.

Looking up at this huge mountain, now just a glowing shadow, I thought of the similar sense futility and despair experienced by the Prometheus who, according to myth, had been chained to this mountain by a jealous Zeus, then tormented by an eagle sent to pluck at his liver. These villagers had suffered their own Promethean ordeal at the hands of a covetous Moscow central planning committee.

The crime of the Greek Prometheus had been to form mankind out of clay and give him fire. Yet his story bears a curious similarity to the local Caucasian legend of Amirani — another god-like man chained to this mountain. Amirani's sin had been to challenge the almighty (and here wise) Zeus or great spirit, to a test of strength. But unlike Prometheus, Amirani's lack of psychological insight had been the cause of his imprisonment.

Looking at the now almost faded mountain, I found it easy to imagine a giant, tormented man strapped within the enormous silhouette. A few months later, driving along the Inner Kartli valley of central Georgia, I had the man in the mountain pointed out to me from the south. The knobbled shape of the old man, hunched over as if by some burden, was clearly visible.

Later that night at 12.30 I lay in the room, waiting for my roommate to return and turn off the light. From upstairs came the sound of a room-party hosted by a Georgian film crew from Tbilisi's then flourishing Gruzia Film studios. The sound of twin pipes and delighted off-key riffs, floated through the paper-thin hotel halls, past the silent doors; a sound far more oriental than European. I couldn't imagine such a wilful disturbance in any Russian hotel at this hour; the babushkas would have dealt with it swiftly. But in Georgia the rules of hospitality carried new meaning. Nobody complained. If you couldn't stand the noise, you joined in.

The volume of laughing, clapping and stamping steadily

Doorway to the Gergeti Trinity Church

increased as the revellers gathered more guests, who began to dance. Soon the floor boards creaked directly above my bed, occasionally shuddering alarmingly as dancers stamped out the rhythm. Then suddenly the music stopped and in its place came one solitary male voice singing out a single note, then another voice joined on a different note, then another. Soon our two rooms quivered under the force of an entirely new vibration — the full-blooded dissonant harmony of a male choir, the sound for which Georgia has been famous for thousands of years.

I imagined the all European and Russian tourists tossing in their sheets trying to close their ears to these proud male chords pealing one off the other. Yet for myself, I found the sound enlivening rather than annoying. These polyphonic chords — a Caucasian phenomena unique to Georgia — dated way back into pre-history. In 400 BC the Greek historian Xenophon described Georgian soldiers launching into battle singing in chorus. To me in the 20th century they resonated with a refreshing and genuine brand of 'soul,' quite unlike the relentless dull throb of 'soul music' emanating from speakers at European hotel parties.

But where was my room-mate? Then suddenly I was putting on my trousers and jacket, and hurrying off down the hall. There could only be one place . . . Following the choir back to its source I knocked loudly on a door which immediately swung open. A grinning dark face invited me in, not even remotely curious who I might be. And there sat my room-mate, a glass of red wine in hand, an embarrassed smile on his face, watching the Georgians gather up steam. A glass was thrust into my hand, a slap deposited on my back and suddenly we'd all been friends for life.

A minute or two later the singing stopped and a dark mustachioed face stood up and proposed a toast: "I give a toast to our faith, our Georgian faith. To Saint Nino who bought it to us; to the glory of her work in Georgia, may it continue, may the Georgian Church flourish, may all who visit it grow bold . . ."

The glasses were all raised and, to my surprise, downed in one gulp then immediately refilled. I looked around the hotel room filled with Georgians and a couple of our group; a small silver pipe lay on the bed. But the ritual had not yet finished.

"To our guests from England." shouted the *tamada* or Georgian toast-master. "To their noble country!" Then he lowered his voice to an earnest whisper. "May the Russians give up their empire as graciously as the British gave up theirs!"

A cheer erupted from the Georgians, most of whom understood English. All glasses were then raised again, and in a sudden silence, downed to the dregs.

During that hushed, religious moment as the liquor flowed down the throat, I reflected on this Georgian style of hospitality; it gave the process of getting drunk a pleasant, ceremonial air. Later, when I explained that in England anything declared with a glass in the hand, toast or not, is usually taken with a pinch of salt, the Georgians laughed heartily.

"To us Georgians, this means it is to be trusted!" they replied.

Not entirely convinced, I asked one of the toasting crew what they were up to in Kazbegi.

"We're making a film," he said vaguely.

"What's the film?" I persisted.

"I think in English you'd call it *The Sons of Sin*. It's about the conflict between Christians and Muslims up here in the mountains. About a Christian who kills a Muslim then realises he was a noble man, and so he prays for his enemy. It's a story of honour, because honour is really the only possession the people have up here. It's the same for both religions. Have another vodka.

Now we will toast the Queen of England. May she live long. May she vanquish her enemies. God save her!"

Another profound silence gripped the room as we all solemnly raised our glasses and knocked back what in an English pub would amount to about five shots of neat vodka.

I asked him why he toasted our Queen — didn't he realise she no longer wielded any power or vanquished enemies.

"Yes I realise," he said, then added emphatically: "But she's your Queen. In Georgia we still like kings and queens. We once had our own Queen—" he took a deep draught of his vodka "—Queen Tamar!" I could see him winding up for another toast and interceded quickly.

"In England our government takes the role of King now—"

"Yes I know," he interrupted then grinned, "Margaret Thatcher, Queen Tamar!" Then he looked at me boldly. "Now you, you make a toast! I saw you sitting on the balcony, alone, looking up at the church, writing. I thought then 'He's one of us!' — a poet. So propose a toast!"

I faltered. Noticing my embarrassment he stepped in to help with a question: "What do you think of Stalin?"

Reaching for my glass in desperation, I remembered Marika's words earlier back on the bus, while responding to a similar question in reference to the Ossetian villagers. In a voice louder than I intended I replied: "He was a big man."

"Yes, a big man, yes!" he agreed heartily then raised his glass. "To Stalin!"

6

Kazbegi to Tbilisi

We left Kazbegi chewing on this blend of contradictory impressions. Georgia, regaled as one of the world's most hospitable nations, had supplied one of its most unaccommodating hotels. Georgia, the seething single voice of nationalistic rebellion against the Russians, seemed split within itself. Its Ossetian and Abkhazian populations sought separation, not from the USSR but from their old Georgian alliance.

Others in our group had encountered their own paradoxical experiences of Kazbegi. The novelist Fay Weldon — accompanying us both with her husband and mother — told the story of attending a Kazbegi wedding party. Joyfully accosted on the street, they willingly accepted this first invitation of genuine 'Georgian hospitality,' only to find themselves quickly elevated to the guests of honour at the dinner as 'the foreigners.' They then watched in stupification as the *tamada* proposed toasts not only to Stalin but Hitler as well.

Almost certainly not Georgian Fascists, these unsophisticated mountain people simply loved Stalin as the Big Man — and Hitler, one supposed, as the attempted liberator of the cruel Soviet regime. Somehow the deeds of Stalin had separated from the man.

As the bus steered a southern course along the Khevi valley or 'gorge,' and across the wide flood plains of the Terek, I wondered about these enormous gaps in memory. Some purpose far more compelling than history had opened the gulf. The 'bigness' of the man remained crucial to these remote villagers.

Then I remembered Marika's description of the local pre-Christian legend of Amirani. She insisted it stood as the "central and formative myth underlying Georgian culture." Could this pre-Bronze Age myth of a stubborn superhuman still supply links with the modern character? I doubted it. But the story was interesting, especially if one took the legendary Amirani to represent the emergence of the Georgian people. This interpretory tack can produce many hours of intriguing speculation on the mysterious beginnings of this nationality — so obsessed with all links to its past.

According to the myth, Amirani was born in a dark forest, the son of Dali, the Georgian goddess of the hunt. He grew up displaying prodigious strengths and the capacity to outdrink and outeat three ordinary men. During his first quest for treasure he encountered a three-headed monster who, just before Amirani slayed him, begged the hero not to kill the three worms that would come from his mouth on his death. Amirani agreed. After he'd dispatched the monster, the worms grew and were transformed into three dragons: white, red and black. Amirani killed the first two but was swallowed by the black dragon, leaving his brothers to cut him out from its stomach.

Amirani then began his quest for a beautiful maiden called Qamari — "covered in silk as gold as sunbeams," and "so beautiful even the sun daren't look at her." He found her in a magnificent celestial castle suspended from the sky by a chain. Cutting the chain, he entered to find Qamari in the middle of her domestic chores. Begging her to run away with him, she agreed — but only when the dishes had been cleaned. Amirani started to help her but quickly lost his temper with a dish that refused to stand upright and smashed it with his heel. At this point all the other dishes cried out in alarm and rushed up into the sky to alert Qamari's father.

A terrible pursuit and battle ensued. At one point, hearing of the deaths of his two brothers, Amirani committed suicide (by cutting his little finger), only to be bought back to life by Qamari, who discovered a magic herb after listening to the advice of a mouse.

After Amirani had rid the world of nearly all its dragons, monsters and wild animals, he finally threw down the gauntlet to God himself. God warned him of its futility, that it constituted a punishable offence, but Amirani stuck doggedly to this quest for omnipotence. So answering the challenge, God plunged a stick into the ground and asked Amirani if he were man enough to pull it out. Amirani wrenched and wrenched but the stick had secretly sunk roots deep into the world and refused to budge. For punishment Amirani was chained to a pole sunk into the side of Mt Kazbek. As he struggled to free himself, each day God sent a raven to feed him a piece of bread and a glass of wine. In his fury Amirani would hurl a stone at the raven, miss and knock in his pole ever more firmly.

From this I began speculating on the emerging nation of Georgia, a chain of thought that lasted a good many kilometres up the valley. With Amirani representing the Georgian race, at first one saw their dark beginnings as Neolithic tribes hunting in the prehistoric forests, followed by their mysterious link or mating with the supernatural world (the goddess Dali). The birth of the child Amirani symbolised attaining a powerful semi-divine vision (or consciousness). This infant born with enormous strength to follow quests, slay dragons, seek out unearthly and beautiful women, symbolising this new vision of *homo sapiens*. As the tribe (Amirani) pursued this new mission they gradually lifted themselves out of the unconscious age of man, and towards civilisation.

After his various battles and successes — indicating the strength of human consciousness over the unconscious animal world — Amirani began to run out of heroic physical challenges. Throughout his many quests numerous tiny reminders kept hinting at him to stop focusing so grandly on the world of physical prowess, to notice instead the smaller details of heroic life: tiny worms that grow into dragons, taking care of dishes, his own little finger, mice . . . Such incidents pointed always toward the more subtle side to bigness. Yet amid all his successes he never noticed it was these smaller things that in the end brought his downfall. In his misguided belief in superiority he finally attempted the impossible (like all great dictators): the conquest of his own creator, God. Thus he was crushed by his own psychological blindness. Yet even God, when he threw the stick into the earth, tried again to remind his warrior hero that to mature Amirani must stop looking at the top of the stick, and to recognise instead all his increasingly empty victories, his quests for dragons, treasure, and beautiful women, as superficial victories and as nothing to the deep roots below the surface of consciousness. Now that he'd outgrown the tribe's early successes he must add a level of philosophical introspection. This, in his dogged tugging at the head of the stick, he refused to do; and thus found himself chained to the rock of futile conquest, power and rage, for all eternity.

Meanwhile we sped past the village of Kobi, its long plastic greenhouse tunnels of tomatos and cucumbers, and on toward the highest point on the Military Highway, the 2,395 metre Jvari Pass. I began to ponder the role of Prometheus in all this. Could he in any way be the reformed successor of this Caucasian hero — transformed into the God who moulded mankind out of clay then, at great personal sacrifice, investing in him the fire of intelligence? Marika told us in some versions of the Amirani legend, Amirani had also given fire to mankind and suffered at the hands of opposing heavenly forces. But perhaps more important, what about the lessons of Amirani when applied to Georgia's modern deity of masculine power — Stalin?

As we passed more black flags this message from the Bronze Age seemed

Soviet viewing-platform at the Jvari Pass — Mt Gud Gora is in the background

ever more applicable today. Amirani had not departed from Georgia. In the civil war lurking round the corner in 1991 he found another reincarnation in the shape of independent Georgia's first president, Zviad Gamsakhurdia. Again the foolish hero would receive a lesson against omnipotence and infallibility as his former supporters in the National Guard turned against him, only to become gun-slinging warior heroes in their own right.

The unusual sensation of the bus slowing down bought me back to the present and the sound of a hundred tiny tinkling bells. Looking out the window I found the bus suddenly afloat on what appeared to be a rippling, choppy sea of wool. All around us an enormous flock of sheep swarmed and bleated across the road, blocking out all sight of the ground for a hundred metres on either side. Some distance away on the mountain-side a single shepherd wearing a *burka*, leaned on a long crook, looking away unconcerned. The bus driver opened the window, shouted something rude. The shepherd did nothing. Then a few seconds later he turned and shouted something equally rude back. But instead of thrusting the bus into gear and charging down the sheep, our driver suddenly leaned back in his seat and laughed heartily, then nodded at the shepherd. A good joke in the Caucasus carried much of the distance to forgiveness. The shepherd's humour saved his sheep from our despotic driver and eventually we pulled forward respectfully.

On the final assault on the pass we flashed past snowdrifts and broken avalanche tunnels as the bus slowed. The sheet of tarmac deteriorated drastically, often doubling as a river. At times the surface disappeared altogether under stones, mud and bubbling water. Yet as we climbed the light grew brighter on either side and the mountain-sides shrunk, I recalled reading about travellers in the 19th century descending from their carriages at this point, preferring to walk over the summit. One foreign diplomat even had himself blindfolded and led through by hand.

As the light swelled, the revving bus slowed to walking pace and the mountains stretched down long fingers of snow on either side. The moment they touched the tarmac they turned into floods of wild Terek-like water. The torrent then raced along the road, before diving over the far side and collecting into the slim river beside us — the Terek's beginnings. Every so often vivid red gashes of mineral deposits coloured the river bank, like flowing wounds. These open veins belonged to the bubbling Narzan spring water, then common in many areas of the Caucasus; a tonic water popular for its high iron content — hence the colour. We stopped to try it and fill a few bottles. It tasted tingly and metallic. A few hundred metres on up the hill we discovered why. Several loud pops from the back of the bus announced the corks on the wine bottles blowing out, pouring the Narzan water all over the seats.

"The water is also naturally carbonated," remarked Marika, way too late.

Later I heard of a nearby lake of this same gaseous water where, due to the water's carbonation, the surface appeared permanently on the boil.

At the crest of the pass, Marika clicked on the microphone. "This is what we in Georgia call the Jvari Pass. *Jvari* means 'cross.' If you look on the left you should see a cross. It marks the top of the pass where the Teregi's watershed ends and the River Aragvi begins. It's a very important cross for Georgians and is called Queen Tamar's Cross. It's said to have been put there by King David the Builder during Georgia's Golden Age between the 12th and 13th centuries." Then her voice picked up enthusiasm. "Queen Tamar was the most famous and inspirational of all Georgia's monarchs. During her reign from 1184 to 1213 Georgia extended its empire through much of Armenia and into present-day Turkey. It also underwent a major cultural and spiritual renaissance. During her reign much of the great Georgian movements in religion, art and epic poetry were begun."

Still mopping up Narzan water I missed it and privately wondered why the fuss over a simple cross. For the second time I'd heard the name of this queen spoken with reverence; almost as if she still lived. At 800 years old she obviously played a pivotal role in the complicated self-image of modern Georgians. As Marika was to say on a later occasion.

"We Georgians have a strong feeling for our past centuries; much stronger than Europeans. We feel very close to our 12th century — for some of us, it's almost as if it were yesterday."

At the time I thought it a strange statement, but the longer I spent in Georgia the truer it became.

The nose of the bus then dipped downward for the first time in several days, thus beginning the everlasting descent to Tbilisi, the capital and fusion of these enigmatic 12th and 20th centuries.

To our right the giant zebra-striped summit of Gud Gora slipped past and next to it the Gudaur Abyss, a 600 metre drop offering spectacular views of the southern mountains. But the Soviet propagandists, not content with a majestic view of barren mountainscape and moraine boulders — known locally as the 'Stone Chaos' — had added a stone chaos of their own. Disguised as a viewing platform, they'd constructed a giant semi-circular piece of 'people's art' right on the edge of the Abyss: an enormous 50 metre long mosaic replacing the view with a joyful proclamation on the fruits of the Russo-Georgian Treaty of 1783; a pact marking the formal beginnings of fraternity between the two nations. A treaty callously abandoned by the Russians a few years later with the abolition of the Georgian monarchy and then the Church. These facts were well known to every Georgian; yet in blithe obedience to that old slogan 'tell a lie enough times loudly enough and it becomes a truth,' this mural portrayed in candy colours a history of the inseparable 'friendship' between the Russian and Georgian peoples (the Communists even renamed the Georgian Military Highway 'The Road of Friendship').

In the illustrative style of a child's colouring book it depicted a carnival of Georgian mythological figures, Russian and Georgian churches side by side (both persecuted by the Communists), an enormous flowing red young man to signify the Revolution, a group of cheerful, obedient women workers, then a laughing soldier holding up a Kalashnikov and a bunch of flowers representing the Great Patriotic War. At the end of this sugar-coated version of the past came the future. It appeared to belong to a teenage boy and girl portrayed in rainbow colours, running beneath a firmament filled, not with angels but flying cosmonauts, their arms outstretched towards empty space.

This enormous tableau of lies presented ever more gainfully, not the truth, but the images the Soviet authorities intended other people (and themselves) to perceive as truth. As if they too also sensed the imminent ideological collapse, and hoped the tons of concrete poured into these enormous public monuments would somehow shore it up.

As a result of this mon-strosity, none of the passing

Lower chair-lift of the main run at the 4-star Gudauri Sport Hotel

Georgian cars stopped here any more, preferring (quite naturally) an uninterrupted view of nature's achievements further up. The huge monument sat forlornly on the cliff-edge like a gaudy pimple in competition with everything un-Soviet — in this case open space itself.

I thought of those blandly smiling faces at the Pyatigorsk floor show again; did they ever consider the messages of their art? Did they not detect the futility in these statements? Already nature had begun her first moves toward renovation by attacking the outer layers of concrete. Cracks shot along large sections of the platform, and parts had already crumbled back to the reinforcing bars.

Marika also expressed a healthy dislike of such monuments. "I don't know who they think likes these things," she remarked. "They never ask us."

In the meantime the ancient village of Gudauri passed by, with its modern Austrian hotel and skiing facilities built by a solo Austrian entrepreneur. At the time this new 4-star Western hotel and mini-resort painfully lacked business — having to rely on the centralised Soviet air transport (Moscow or Leningrad first) to bring in the European, currency-bearing public.

But eight years later I revisited it during high-season and found it packed. Even the cheap, dormitory chalets were full, the slopes chock-a-block with Western aid-agency personnel and Georgians — who skied in much the same way as they drove, with delirious abandon, and in several cases, blind-drunk. It seemed that investment in Georgia had at long last paid off — although the Austrian owner had since sold it on.

Several kilometres later, along the edge of the Aragvi precipice we arrived at the head of the infamous Mleti Descent, a terrifying series of 18 hairpin bends winding back on themselves, as the road slides down a 600 metre cliff to the river below. For our edification the driver stopped so we could survey this death trap from above, telling us he'd lost several friends here.

Glancing behind me I saw a huge metal figure of a man standing in the middle of an empty field — unremarked on by Marika. More people's art it seemed — this time of the Russian poet Mayakovsky. Although born in Georgia (of Russian parents), Mayakovsky never endeared himself to his childhood compatriots (one possible reason why this huge statue mysteriously disappeared in the early 1990s, rumoured by some "for scrap"). His point of view makes itself all too clear in poems like 'Vladikavkaz to Tiflis,' written in 1924, just two and a half years after the Bolshevik Red Army had bought the Georgian government to its knees (ignoring completely their 1920 Soviet-Georgian agreement) and then instigated a horrific purge:

> . . . *I'm from the Georgians,*
> *But not the old nation.*
> *I'm an equal comrade in one federation,*
> *The Soviet world which we forge.*

And later in the same poem, exhorting the Georgians toward a bright bold Bolshevik future:

> *Build with gusto, for all you're worth,*
> *From no demolition desist!*
> *If Kazbek's in the way*
> *Raze the hill to the earth . . .*

This terrible materialist zeal of the new Communists would be pursued true to Mayakovsky's words, for decades to come, and almost to the letter (sparing Mt Kazbek). Looking down on the lush new panorama with the fine silver thread of the Aragvi river snaking its way hundreds of metres below — suddenly I felt a sense of relief at entering a nation never falling for this manic, political ardour. In the aftermath of the Revolution, the Georgians had rejected Bolshevism in favour of the opposing Menshevik Socialist system. The Mensheviks, a non-

Roadside kiosk in the valley below Gudauri, selling traditional 'papakhi' hats and traditional Georgian skiwear

Leninist wing of the Social Democratic Workers' Party, disagreed with the Bolshevik insistence on a highly centralised, dictatorial party, even declaring themselves willing to create a liberal capitalist regime as the precursor to full Socialism. They were to achieve three halcyon years of office, 1918-1921, the period now lovingly referred to by Georgians as "independent Georgia" and by others as "the world's first example of genuine democratic Socialism." Ramsay MacDonald — Britain's first Labour prime minister to be — visited this Socialist government in operation and hailed it as "a great and bloodless social revolution." But this brand of Socialism, however, was swiftly snuffed out by the Bolshevik Red Army in February 1921.

Standing on that cliff edge I also looked down on a climate and geography equally as separate. A landscape responsible not only for the fruit and vegetable laden central valleys of Georgia but Marika's olive skin. With this change the colour green bombarded us again, this time warming a few degrees, keeping pace with our steady progress southward toward the arid Anatolian plateau, Turkey and Iraq.

The bus bagatelled its way down the cliff to meet this luxurious new land. Softly wooded hillsides, wild fruit trees, ivy-clad cliffs, villages of silver and rust coloured roofs sprinkled across the valley floor like plates. At the bottom we accelerated down the Aragvi Gorge, as the river steadily fattened, care of the numerous streams and rivers cascading down from the High Caucasus. The hillsides rose up covered in a green tree-fur, with watchtowers poking out curiously above the leaves at every prominent crook in the valley.

Seventeen kilometres beyond the Mleti cliff we arrived at the village of Pasanauri. At this point the White Aragvi met with its twin sister the Black Aragvi, bounding down from another quite distinct region of Georgia, Khevsureti. As if to acknowledge this, the waters refused to merge immediately, the light and dark coloured currents running side by side — like the independent tribes at their source.

I'd read about these tribes, peoples such as the Khevsurs and Pshavs, thought at one time to be descendants of the Crusaders. In the 1930s travellers to Tbilisi told of Khevsur families walking round the capital wearing chain-mail shirts and large red on white crosses front and back. Another example of time standing still in Georgia. Until the 1980s they could be seen at festivals riding their stocky mountain horses carrying shields and broadswords, but more for the pageant than any ongoing culture.

As we raced on towards the modern capital of Tbilisi, now less than 50km to the south, I felt myself hanging somewhere between the Middle Ages and about 1960, unable to unhook my mind from the misty images of St George, dragons, and all the unreal Tolkeinesque pictures and prancings that seemed inseparably tethered to this landscape.

Yet amid all this came the technological contradiction of the Soviet Space Age within which tribes like the Khevsurs still existed. I wondered just how the Georgians, a people adoring its past with an almost disease-like passion, handled the 20th century in its humming capital now just down the road.

Then, as if in conspiracy with these thoughts, an immaculately preserved church-fortress suddenly presented itself. Situated, according to the Intourist guidebook at the 140th kilometre of the highway, again the Middle Ages pressed themselves right up to our faces — this time as a beautiful 17th century Ananuri church surrounded by a tall walled keep.

Stepping out of the bus I found the atmosphere completely changed. The temperature had risen and the air was filled with new scents and sounds — walnut-groves, vineyards and buzzing insects. The church also seemed to have shifted hemispheres. Adorned with many carvings and geometric patterns, not quite Christian, not quite Oriental and not

The huge Mayakovsky statue at the head of the Mleti Descent. It mysteriously disappeared after independence in the early 1990s.

quite Celtic. They climbed the west facing wall of the transept around the windows, flanked by a giant cross rising on the backs of two dragons. Beside this floated two lions, two very strange angels wearing both dresses and moustaches, and two trees with grapes and domestic animals in their branches. Pagan symbols but also hinting strongly at Persian influence. Marika spent quite some time going over these symbols and their historical significance, without once mentioning the large silting-up lake, close to the fortress base — the result of the ill-placed Zhinvali -station nearby.

I felt we were stepping into a strange, museum-piece country, preserved accidentally by the Communists who bypassed the kind of commercial exploitation that defaces so many Western monuments. It seemed ironic that the engine of fiercest cultural change, State materialism, in a way only helped preserve Georgia's cultural identity. Communism maintained itself by its great simplicity, forbidding all major change within the lumbering, initiative-stripping bureaucracy. But now all this was crumbling, I began to ask myself, and not for the last time, how would Georgia deal with the other 20th century scratching at its borders every day? In which century did the Georgians truly wish to live? Tbilisi was now just 60 minutes away.

Ananuri Fortress and church (17th century)

7

Tbilisi

Tbilisi has been the capital of Georgia for the last 1,400 years and, due to its unique positioning between the Greater and Lesser Caucasus, also the unofficial sovereign of these 'Mountains of Languages.' Ever since the fifth century when it took control of the Kingdom of Kartli (then East Georgia) Tbilisi has had to disguise its trade within whatever system the current invading army decided to inflict. As a result, its amiable riverside streets, numerous parks and tree-lined avenues have jostled with every brand of hot blooded mountain man, trader, traveller and soldier, all presenting an honourable front — the more to conceal a vigorous, less honourable free-for-all of human instinct.

When I first arrived in Tbilisi I, like all visitors down through the centuries, found myself welcomed with wide open, hospitable arms, then sweetly charmed towards its thriving black market. As if to acknowledge this, the Soviets had built a giant 20-storey Tower of Babel right in the centre of the metropolis then filled it with the bearers of the most desired commodity of all — *valuta* (foreign currency). Until the 1992 war with Abkhazia the Iveria Hotel was where most foreign tourists usually found themselves housed. Named after the ancient Greek word for Eastern Georgia, 'Iberia,' it started life as Tbilisi's premier Intourist hotel and for a number of years remained the focal point for anything 'valutable.' When the civil war began, and tourism abruptly ceased in the former Soviet Union's favourite holiday resort, the Iveria transformed into a public totem pole for disaster — a refugee camp for a thousand or so displaced peoples from Abkhazia and Ossetia. Only in 1996 did it begin, very nervously, to return to hostelry — opening a single floor for those wishing to live among refugees at $15 a night.

Perching precariously above a cliff-face at the head of the city's main street, the furious Rustaveli Avenue, the Iveria dominates the city like a beacon — visible from just about every corner. In return it offers occupants stupendous panoramas.

Back on that first visit, with fingers gripping the railing on the 14th floor, I looked out over the city of one and a quarter million. A metropolis razed to the ground, its identity plundered so often, its survival seemed miraculous. Bar its rebuilt churches, old town fortress and wall, almost no building prior to 1795 stands in Tbilisi due to the ferocity of the final Persian invasion. Yet there it lay, spreading leafily away across its many hillsides and still expanding.

Metechi Church and domes of hot-spring baths, Tbilisi

Over to the north and east the skyline sprouted thickets of tall, white tower-blocks — the proud spires of Socialism. Running through the centre, like a boiling brown life-line, flowed the powerful Mtkvari river (called Kura by the Russians). Along its banks the houses and roads swept north and south in diversifying waves of architecture.

Like all Soviet municipalities the city's layout had suffered at the hands of centralised planning — but less than most. In spite of its tower-block fever, and unlike many other Russified cities of the Republics, Tbilisi also attracted a substantial amount of 19th century Russian architecture — of the Moscow/Leningrad ilk. These graceful pastel-painted buildings and avenues date back to 1801 when Georgia officially joined the Russian Empire —

having invited in the Tsarist army after the Persians' demolition. On top of this, a good section of Tbilisi's Old Town has miraculously survived Soviet recon-struction; its maze of higgledy-piggaldy homes, wooden back alleys and charming Persian balconies, crashing into each other beneath a fourth century cliff-top forti-fication — the Narikala fortress.

Soviet era photo-booth (since removed), with the three tourist languages of Soviet Georgia. In 1989 Georgia had 1.8 million visitors — 280,000 from outside the Soviet Union. In 1998 it expected 3,000 foreign visitors.

Up onto that balcony back in those clean Communist days, floated another all-important impression of any modern city — its smell. In contrast to Moscow's odour of cheap sickly gasoline freezing against your cheek, Tbilisi gave off a faintly sweet, nutty, petroly, fragrance. A hint of mountain air, a sniff of expensive black market perfume and tobacco from the floors below; a feeling that life had suddenly returned to something closer to normal, after all those unsettling hours, or days, in the cities of the north.

I'll never forget one visit to Tbilisi, standing transfixed on a Hotel Iveria balcony for a good half an hour as a thunderstorm swept its way across the city, stabbing sparkling blue fingers down on the ground. It left a trail of freshly washed cobbled streets, oriental wooden balconies, colonial Russian avenues, and a glistening forest of green, healthy trees rising between the roofs.

Yet on that first visit I couldn't help but feel a slight disappointment. Looking down on the squat, hell-for-leather Ladas, the figures earnestly squeezing between them, the cable-car slowly climbing Tbilisi mountain, it seemed like any other fully modern, industrialised city. How could those anonymous scurrying figures represent a Christian belief blending with the emotions of Islam, or a 12th century psychology living in the 20th century? Had not the forces of modernity, so evident in those manic Ladas, now wiped out all these much longed for Georgian qualities of the past?

Today those first impressions seem so innocent having witnessed the economic disaster following Georgia's civil war. But, interestingly, even now in its new state of poverty the city struggles to recapture that former self of perfume and riches. Almost from the first day of civil war the word 'Casino' emblazoned itself across the Iveria restaurant door — while the hotel above decked itself out with refugee washing.

Back in the 1980s, my first steps into the city took me across the Iveria's gusty plaza and straight into a shower of water flung from its large fountain of short, evenly jetted water — nicknamed 'Shevardnadze's Hair' — after Georgia's former First Secretary, then later Gorbachev's Soviet foreign minister. Nobody then expected him, even in their wildest dreams, to become their second capitalist head of state.

Iveria Hotel, as a hotel in the 1980s

Behind this stands Republican Square where, in perfect counterpoint to the fountain, a series of enormous triumphal arches rise above a small podium; Georgia's answer to Red Square's parade platform. Georgians nicknamed these arches 'Andropov's Ears' — after the former KGB chief and General Secretary, as the concrete loops fit one inside the other like ears within ears.

Well-positioned directly opposite stands Tbilisi's telecommunications centre — its large marble ground-floor serving as an eternal waiting room for scores of Georgians passing hours, sometimes days, waiting to call distant relatives. The calls are connected somewhere within the five neon-lit floors above and, in Soviet times, occasionally listened to. I remember in 1987 once finding a message on the information sheet at the Intourist Hotel, Novgorod: *When leaving the room, please be sure to turn off your TV set, air conditioning, lights and the mike.*

Almost certainly a printing error for 'the like,' it gave the Freudian slip a new Communist dimension.

Most people's route away from the Iveria, both then and now, is down Rustaveli Avenue, Tbilisi's elegant main street built St Petersburg style in the late 19th and early 20th centuries, but with the additional lining of grand maple trees.

On that first visit I hurried away from its bustling beginnings, full of polite Georgians asking if I wanted to "change money" or "sell anything," and on down the Avenue, past a gaunt Institute of Leninism and Marxism (which nobody visited), then the ebullient Zakaria Paliashvili Opera House. All around me faces skimmed past in a steady dark stream; olive-skinned southerners, their eyes glancing at me, registering 'foreigner,' and glancing away. In Georgia, blond hair lit you up like a beacon, unlike in Moscow or Leningrad where I enjoyed certain levels of covert operation.

Iveria Hotel, as a refugee camp in the 1990s, with refugees from Ossetia playing football

Something about their manner set them apart from the northerners. Here men walked with far more self-importance, confronting the world from under dark eyebrows and moustaches, almost regal in their composure. It is said that until the abolition of the Georgian monarchy, one in every five Georgian men claimed noble blood.

The women, in their turn, appeared correspondingly more demure; wearing knee-length dresses, late 1960s hairstyles, deep layers of make-up and not a single set of Levis among them. For a main drag Rustaveli Avenue remained remarkably absent of European youth culture — those fully jeaned, ghetto-blasting teenagers then associated with the Nevsky Prospekt or Moscow's Arbat. Beneath the elegant 19th century facades the street exuded a presence of refined watchfulness.

I walked on imagining the time when this street of furious Ladas was an elegant Russian boulevard, Golovinsky Street, named after a prominent Russian in Georgia, and filled only with trams and carriages heading for the Old Town and Yerevan Square at its far end. An impulse made me turn up a side street. I'd proceeded not 200 metres up the hill when a Lada suddenly screeched to a halt next to me. The window wound down frantically and a huge hairy arm presented itself, leading back to a bristly Georgian face.

"Hello my friend!" said the face.

"Sorry, I have nothing to sell," I replied automatically.

But his grin only widened — and I noticed the back seat of the car full of his family, also beaming.

"No, no, no!" said the bristles. "What's the time?"

Shavteli Street, in Tbilisi Old Town

Relieved, I pulled back my sleeve to look at my watch; "It's . . ."

"Forty roubles," he interrupted, "no fifty!" and the whole car erupted into raucous laughter.

As I recovered from my confusion, he gave me a bone-crushing handshake. "No, my friend, don't worry, enjoy Georgia, happy holiday, goodbye!" He engaged the gears and the car roared off out of sight disobeying every road sign and, as it turned out, almost directly under the KGB headquarters. How different to those secretive, suspicious approaches of Moscow!

Back on the Avenue, approaching the pre-revolutionary Hotel Tbilisi — formerly the Majestic — I spotted an unusual couple walking towards me. A dark-skinned boy and blonde girl, of no more than twenty. The boy wore a flashy sports jacket of the thick, grey-flecked brand, then the rage at London's Camden Market, with a single 'identity' badge pinned to its lapel. The girl also wore snappy Western clothing.

As they drew up level I managed to read the words on the boy's badge. *Fuck off and die!* it announced flatly. As our eyes met the boy suddenly asked me: "Do you speak English?"

This time I nodded. I had to know why this boy adopted a punk slogan, so far away in time and distance from anything punk.

"Do you?" I replied.

"No I don't," he replied grinning, then added: "Not well."

"What part of America are you from?" the girl then asked in a heavy Russian accent.

I explained my London origins and we continued on down the avenue together like old friends, with no mention of buying or selling.

First they wanted to know if I'd arrived for business or holiday, how long would I stay, what hotel, and then came the important questions . . .

"What is the name of Phil Collins' newest album?" "How much does a blank 180-minute video cassette cost in London?" "What was the concert at the Hammersmith Odeon when you left?"

I asked about the badge.

"It's not punk. Here we don't have punks. It's just what we feel about those who are ordering us." He glanced towards the Communist Party headquarters.

As we talked so the boy developed an unnatural interest in my trainers.

"Where did you buy them . . . ?" he began, which soon led to: "How much do you want for them?"

I told him they weren't for sale, but fearing the end of our meeting, suggested we change some money.

"You have a few minutes?" the girl then asked, adding: "We'll go somewhere. Don't worry, it's all right."

But I already knew this — and such street-level encounters usually unearthed the swiftest, sharpest, and most propaganda-free opinions on any country. Theirs was the instinctive response to laws that disobeyed human nature. In Georgia, they and their older cousins had illegally operated a black market that some estimated to be 50 per cent of the entire economy. These streetwise black-marketeers simply lived the double lives of ordinary citizens, more openly.

The boy introduced himself as Shota, then the three of us flagged down a car and launched off to somewhere in Tbilisi.

"Do you meet many foreigners?" I asked as the car swerved alarmingly through the traffic.

"No, not so many, but we like it," she said.

I could sense her trying to work out what kind of a London representative they'd landed, the city of unlimited rock stars and black-market goods.

"What do you think of Madonna?" she asked suddenly, clearly curious about the new messages of female sexuality emanating from the West. "Do you think she's too . . . ," she paused looking for the right word to describe Madonna's wanton sensuality, ". . . loud?"

"I don't like her," interrupted the badge wearer, "she's like a . . . ,"

The musician's shop on Wine Street — renting musicians rather than instruments

he made a circular motion with his hand.

"Balloon," said the girl.

"Yes, balloon, all empty on the inside," he said.

The Russian girl looked at him doubtfully.

"I thought you liked her," she said cautiously. It was no secret that Georgian men liked Russian and foreign girls for their more liberal sexuality.

"And the Pink Floyd?" I changed the subject.

"Yes, I like it." said the girl, and her boyfriend agreed, adding. "I've got the disk *Dark Side of the Moon.*"

Something to be proud of. Original Western records in the USSR were gold dust. Normally they duplicated tape-to-tape copies then distributed them one side of the Union to the other, a kind of pirating that continues today as joyfully as then. In Tbilisi you can buy first-run Hollywood movies for seven lari (five US dollars) — before they've opened in London.

Meanwhile the streets of Tbilisi flicked by at terrible speed. Peering through the front windscreen I witnessed a type of driving quite alien to Moscow or Europe. Traffic lights blinked from red to green almost without meaning. Rogue cars careered up the wrong side of the street, daring the oncoming traffic. Occasionally drivers would stop in the middle of the road, swing open their doors and gesticulate angrily about each other's driving, swing their doors shut and continue on just as terribly themselves.

Half an hour later we stepped out of a creaking lift on the ninth floor of concrete tower-block to be led into a spacious, undecorated flat by a boy described as the "Armenian." Inside we met another Georgian boy and a breathtaking, white-skinned Russian girl. She sat the whole time on a mattress, smoking cigarettes and it seemed, staring at me.

After a few words with Shota a bottle of Georgian brandy and an enormous portable cassette player were produced. The Armenian reached into the wall — no sockets or switches had yet been installed — pulled out two live electrical cables and twisted them with his fingers into the cassette player's lead. It immediately came to life.

"Pink Floyd," he said casually.

The door opened and a nervous looking, 50-year-old East German entered. They also handed him a glass of brandy, then took him into a back room. There followed some terse private discussions, some raised voices, then the German was shown smartly to the door. The Armenian returned to the living-room and said distastefully,

"They met him in a foreign currency bar. He is a homosexual. He wants a boy and we don't have any." He spoke unemotionally, like a shopkeeper explaining an item was out of stock.

I realised I'd just arrived at a local small-time mafia headquarters, that I, like the German, represented just more business.

"How much do you want for your runners?" Shota asked again. I tried to explain these were my only shoes — which they were — and not for sale. But he only interpreted this as a ploy to raise the price. "OK, 70 roubles," he said, quite unable to understand my refusal. Meanwhile one of his Georgian friends started talking to me in an odd English accent.

"You talk the wrong English," he said challengingly. "You should talk American English."

"Why?" I asked.

He put on a strong Chicago/Georgian accent. "Because then you can talk like Al Capone."

Everybody laughed. I began to realise this boy genuinely saw himself as a gangster — a fact that with the 1991 arming of the population took ugly steps toward reality right across Georgia.

I asked him if he could pick up the BBC World Service.

"Oh yes we pick it up." He gave me a sideways glance. "But I listen to Voice of America, to modern English."

I found this attitude toward English — a language fast becoming as important as Russian — by no means the norm. Those living a life dedicated to the electronic, expensive and illegal preferred American. The aesthetes, of whom I would meet many, preferred European culture and languages.

As the others talked among themselves I turned to the white-skinned girl and tried some English on her — asking if she preferred life here in Georgia than in Russia up north.

"I don't know," she shrugged. "We do what we can." She showed little interest in my questions, but her eyes continued to bore into mine.

I guessed her to be one of the hard-currency prostitutes, usually working out of hotels. I knew the bleak lack of opportunities in the USSR and restrictions on travel drew remarkably well-educated, beautiful girls into the profession. In a 1990 survey of teenagers in a provincial Russian city, 50 per cent of boys said they wanted to join the mafia and 50 per cent of the girls wanted to become currency prostitutes.

The Russians who came to Georgia, attracted by this more plentiful, hotter, rebellious republic, very often bore the same disenchantment for their system as the Georgians. While Georgia politely tolerated the small population of Russians living in Tbilisi (unlike some of their Baltic counterparts), they never went out of their way to make them feel at home, and Russian women constantly reported harassment from Georgian men.

"Have you got what you wanted yet?" the Russian girl asked suddenly. Her eyes genuinely curious. I glanced around the room at this dissatisfied, disobeying, spirited group of teenagers. People possessed by an energy I'd never found in similar circles in Moscow. Here at the apex of the blissful black market it showed itself in a gusto for adventure and rebellion, haloed, as we found out later, by the goals of nationalism. Unlike the nihilistic northerners, these youngsters and their parents too, had never abandoned that crucial, life-sustaining sense of hope.

I tried to reconcile this strange optimism. On one side of me sat a prostitute, on the other a boy offering nearly half the national month's wages just for my shoes. I knew there were drugs and needles available too. But these nefarious Georgians still saw an inherent goodness somewhere in the future: their days were strung together by this faith. The Soviet system had been imposed on them from outside — all along they'd known it would fail.

I made my excuses to leave, but Shota insisted on accompanying me back to the hotel. He still had not achieved his shoes: the price had now reached one hundred roubles. He seemed to gain a perverse delight in attempting the unattainable.

For a moment of peace in the taxi home I pulled out my Walkman and slipped on the headphones. Pressing PLAY I found it halfway through the song *Of Course I'm Lying*, by the Swiss group Yello. As the tall concrete Brezhnev-era tower-blocks floated by outside the car, so the lyrics of a sophisticated Western future, the one waiting in store for these young Georgians, filled my head. I listened again as the singer declared with a heavy irony (that many people miss) how he loved it when his partner lied. To me it always seemed an anthem for the new, eerie savoir-faire taking root among European youth — of genuine Lermontovian proportions.

"Have you heard this?" I asked the girl and handed her the headphones. A minute later she handed them back.

"It's OK," she said without enthusiasm. Her boyfriend listened for a few seconds then handed them back without a comment. The meaning never engaged them. I slipped the headphones back on and listened again to those silky female whispers as the 17-storey high stacks of Soviet living-rooms slid by. Nothing surely, could be more appropriate than these aching sounds of the new European sophistication set against this architecture of the old Soviet alternative. These buildings, their architecture, their everyday appliances all spawned within a system whose political lies had steadily grown upon themselves into a massive fungus-like social institution. A bureaucratic system so cumbersome, in the end only terror itself would hold it together. Now the fungus finally collapsed in on itself. Everyone here looked eagerly forward to the sparklingly clean, remote-control hi-fi of the West. Yet what slick messages lay at the heart of this brave new alternative?

The song's chorus sung out its warning again and again: "You're lying, I love it . . ."

The steps of independence

While in Moscow I'd been given the Tbilisi phone number of a Georgian poet called Giorgi. I was told he wrote Georgian and English songs, and held his ear close to the ground as Georgian literature sank its feet into the soil of perestroika. We'd spoken briefly on the phone. He sounded a little surprised at the label 'poet.'

"I used to write a few songs . . . ," he'd said. "But anyway, let's meet at a 'poetic' place."

His directions left me standing outside the elegant Kashveti Church on Rustaveli Avenue, right across the road from the State Government Building. With my back to this pre-revolutionary centre of Georgian power — the Orthodox Church — I looked across at its atheist replacement, the gargantuan arched facade of the Communist State headquarters.

Giorgi had been right about poetics: the atmosphere was charged. A continuous flow of people streamed in and out of the candle-lit church, their faces uncomfortably intense. A month earlier the 20 Georgian hunger-strikers had been butchered only a few metres away on the Government Building steps. A long blue fence now sealed off the entrance from the public. Shortly afterwards many had reported symptoms of gas poisoning due, they believed, to traces of chemicals still embedded in the slabs. No amount of scrubbing could rid them of this deadly residue; just as no manipulating the media or re-writing history would remove the event's indelible imprint on Georgian consciousness. To reinforce this the fence had been adorned with numerous strips of black cloth, and below it wreathes lay on the pavement.

With no sign of anyone resembling Georgi's description, I gazed out into the traffic: the usual vortex of whirling Ladas, Volgas and the occasional black Zil trying to assert a forlorn claim on the centre 'government' lane. Every so often a high speed Lada, horn blaring, lights blazing, roared hysterically past. Out of the windows teenagers thrust streaming nationalist flags, sometimes even themselves — perched up on the window-ledge — to add a death-defying quality to their proclamation. In their ecstatic faces I saw Marika's description of the young car-drivers flaunting themselves before the Special Forces during the curfew a month earlier — the single act of heroism that restored the Georgian spirit of resistance. As backdrop to these dramatic declarations, the severe arches of Government Building looked sternly down, the Red Flag of Communism waving from its top, like the rag to a bull.

For all Georgians this imposing structure, completed in the same year Stalin died (1953), represented the accumulation of many years of paranoid, paper-pushing, mafia-enabling bureaucracies. Yet now, for the first time since Stalin took control of the Soviet state, another flag flew on many of the buildings of Rustaveli Avenue — the black, magenta and white tricolour of Independent Georgia. An event unthought of even six months earlier. But time had now restarted again for this small nation. I wondered how long before the dream of the Georgians came true and their flag flew on this building too (it took less than a year and a half).

My reverie was broken by an unexpected change in the atmosphere — silence. The traffic on Rustaveli Avenue began mysteriously drying up. The normally furious six lanes — impossible to cross on foot — slowly emptied of cars. A quick glance up the Avenue revealed why Giorgi had chosen this time and place to meet. For suddenly the street was filled again, this time not by cars but thousands upon thousands of Georgian faces. Approaching us from the north they poured forward like a slow, inexorable rising tide, filling from the side streets, and stretching away out of sight beyond the Iveria Hotel. Then I remembered the date: today the period of mourning for April 9th ended. To mark the occasion a sea of olive-skinned humanity had risen up from all corners of Georgia, to converge on Tbilisi and this Soviet building right before me — built, like many government buildings in Georgia, on the site of a former cathederal. As had happened so often before in Georgian history, the emotions of massacre returned people to the candle-lit sanctuaries of its Orthodox Church. Prayers, mysteries, communion with Georgia's martyrs and saints had healed the affront to self dignity; now the emotions returned to the streets, stronger than ever.

As this army of the new Georgia closed in, I noticed the front marchers carried large black and white photographs of next of kin, murdered by the Special Forces. But most remarkable of all, the first half kilometre of this great coiling snake of humanity made almost no sound at all. It piled ominously forward, its thousands of eyes training themselves on the Government Building, propelled by the weight of perhaps quarter of a million bodies behind. An almost supernatural sight; as if the dead and not the living controlled this enormous stealthy force.

As the crowd drew level with the blue fence, handkerchiefs appeared and individuals broke away, hurried over and pinned red carnations or independence flags onto the wooden slats. Within minutes the surface of the fence had completely changed, brimming and weeping in festoons of many red-petalled tears. Then suddenly the march stopped dead — and I felt a tap on my shoulder.

"Are you Peter?" said a voice.

Swinging round I found myself looking at a tall Georgian in his mid-twenties; his nose large and hooked, and above it deep set, sad eyes. Beside him stood a woman with jet black hair and palish skin. Giorgi had arrived, along with his friend Tamuna.

It hardly seemed the moment for elaborate introductions. After a few words we turned back to observe the spectacle. Right ahead the avenue was now chock-a-block with solemn southern faces, the marchers confronted the first of their goals, the Government Building.

Then without any instruction or orchestration, the front several thousand demonstrators suddenly sank down onto their heels and raised their fists defiantly in the air toward the building. A gesture carried out in almost complete silence. It must have sent shudders down the spines of the Soviet officialdom watching. For not only had most of the population risen up against it, it also displayed that other much feared quality of rebellion — discipline.

I noticed several rows of blue-uniformed police had now appeared on the top of the Government Building steps, their arms folded, facing the crowd.

Above them the enormous five-storey portico rose up like raised eagle wings. I watched Giorgi lift his fist too, looking not at the police, but the flag. He turned to me.

"I don't criticise our police — some of them were wounded trying to defend the women on April 9th. It's the ones who aren't here . . ."

I asked him if he'd been at the steps on April 9th.

"Yes I was here," he said quietly, "and it was the worst day of my life." He lowered his fist and turned to me. "I'll never forget when I walked up to that Special Forces soldier and asked him what he was doing; why they attacked peaceful demonstrators. He just shoved his Kalashnikov into my ribs, hard

The Government Building and demonstration against Soviet rule, 40 days after the April 9th Massacre, 1989

and told me go away. You know I looked at his face and . . . ," he paused and swallowed, glancing up at the blue fence, now ablaze with carnations, ". . . you know, I experienced a terrible feeling. Not of his gun, but of that blank, empty look in his eyes. This was not a man, this was a dead machine sent to exterminate Georgia. I saw the end of our nation in that face — I'll never forget it."

As he spoke, I thought I detected a tear creeping into the corner of his eye. Then suddenly he added in a new, harder voice. "At 3.30 today our Communist government has announced a ten minute silence all over the city. I think they want to join in." His eyes held mine for a second to see if I caught the irony.

The spooky silence abruptly ended. A single defiant voice rose up out of

Demonstrators from the Aragvi region declaring their support at the 1989 demonstration, wearing their traditional Khevsur dress

the rows of crouching faces, shouting the word *"Ga-u-mar-jos!"* toward the Government Building. Then suddenly everybody joined in and the sounds of protest — the centuries-old rebellion against Russia — recommenced. The crowd stood up and moved on. We stepped in among the surge forward of bodies, and in the momentum, somehow became separated. Surrounded by this swelling tide of dark strangers, their hands gripping banners, their lungs shouting the slogans of 'Free Georgia,' I searched in vain for Giorgi or Tamuna. Instead I found myself pressed forward with the thousands, caught up by this inexorible momentum towards independence.

Right up next to me rough male faces and women's voices shouted out resolutely. A people disowned of their own country for several centuries but not afraid to demonstrate if sufficiently moved. In 1956, still at the height of the Stalinist deep freeze, thousands had taken to the streets to protest — of all things — the denunciation of Stalin by Khrushchev. It led to a horrific reaction from the Soviet authorities — over a hundred shot dead, with many more wounded or exiled to labour camps in Siberia. But this didn't prevent demonstrations again in 1978 when the Communist government tried to lower the status of the Georgian language in a new draft constitution. On that occasion Eduard Shevardnadze, the then First Secretary of the Georgian Communist Party, had immediately given in to the demonstrators' demands.

As the chants filled my ears, I realised these people emptied their lungs with that crucial declaration of separation from the culture they despised. They shouted to restore self-respect. Within these cries also stirred the determination to believe in what they euphemistically called a "free" future (free from Russia); and to rekindle the enormous anger held down for so many years. Such demonstrations amounted to a kind of medicine against the last 70 years, and took place right across the USSR and Eastern Europe — to very often devastating effect.

As one Georgian friend said later of that time, "even if we didn't quite know the meaning of the word 'free', we were calling for the freedom to make our own mistakes, not theirs."

Then, to my great relief, I spotted Marika standing by the road and hurried over to my only ally in this ocean of grievance. She greeted me as a friend and we stood together at the roadside watching the faces surge past, each block of several thousand strong, stopping silently before the Government Building and raising their fists (a gesture ironically similarity to the original Red Front Fascist salute).

A huge cheer then rose up as a group of men and women in overalls joined the demonstration.

"Those are factory workers," explained Marika. "They've joined mid-shift."

I asked her to translate some of the banners. She pointed to a dense thicket of posters approaching the Government Building.

"These say they're from Kutaisi. It's a large town in Imereti, in West Georgia. I heard they had walked all the way here — it's about 250 kilometres."

As they dropped on their heels for the salute, so they exposed a remarkable group of demonstrators standing right behind. Men and women in a splendid, multicolored tribal dress, their leader standing before them carrying a six-foot silver mace like a chief. Beside him stood a score of similarly dressed companions. The men in knee-length, richly patterned tunics with two-foot silver daggers strapped to their waists. The women wore dresses covered in beautiful embroideries of stars and crosses. Across their foreheads they wore strange headpieces or mantles, also bearing the same crosses.

"These people are from Khevsureti," explained Marika, "one of the remote mountain tribes of Georgia." Then she looked wistful. "It's a great shame, because their culture is disappearing. Not many now can make these traditional clothes."

Looking at the unique costumes, it did seem a huge pity they and their way of life would soon vanish for ever. I asked if these weren't the people European writers had described wearing chain mail and Crusader crosses, earlier this century.

"Yes, but they don't wear them any more," Marika replied, then added, "although many still have these costumes in their families, and the older women still know how to make chain mail."

I stepped out into the street to take a photograph. Several of the faces turned anxiously toward me. To these remote valley eyes I, with my blond, Russian-looking hair, probably represented police or KGB. I found myself remembering the faces of Jewish refuseniks at a 1987 rally in Leningrad; an occasion drawing more KGB than demonstrators. Each agent, true to the Boy's Own Guide to the KGB, wore his trenchcoat collar turned up and trained a long lens on everyone coming within a hundred metres.

I took my snap and then we stepped into the crowd, following perhaps half a kilometre from the front. For me the rally had turned from a demonstration into a pageant of all the peoples of modern Georgia. A river of dark and occasionally pale mountain faces, shouting their way forward towards Tbilisi's rebuilt sixth century Sioni Cathedral, and a shrine constructed to April 9th, like a totem to this people's long history of massacre. These faces encompassed all stages of civilisation, from those Khevsur tribesmen to the spy satellite operators in the Government Building. I found myself wanting to try and grasp some place or pivot in history from where they emerged. As always I turned to Marika for the solution. She smiled at my question, but answered politely.

"Nobody knows exactly where the Georgians come from. They emerged out of several Neolithic and Bronze Age cultures in this area, growing up beside the world's great early civilizations: the Sumerians, Hittites, Babylonians, and the peoples of Urartu . . ."

But her voice became increasingly difficult to hear between the shouts and music now booming from the public-address system. I tried to question her about the early Caucasian tribes; how they may have influenced or served as a basis for many of our own in Europe. Did she think that the Etruscans (and hence the Romans) may have originated from one of these early tribes; or the Pelasgi, the forerunners of the early Greeks descended from the Iberians (the people of the East Caucasus)? What was her opinion on those who linked the Basques and Celts with the Caucasians, perhaps explaining why the term 'white Caucasian,' connects people of European extraction to these Asiatic mountains?

"Yes, these are interesting theories," she said above the noise, but I could tell she saw them as no more than theories. "The modern Georgian tribes are the descendants of these people," she said more practically.

I pressed her for more details. Then giving me a 'well you asked for it' look she said. "The people you see today are a blend of Mingrelians, Svans, Kartlians, Gurians, Ajarans, Kakhetians, Imeretians, Khevsurs, Pshavs, Mokhevians, Meskhians, Rachans . . ." She smiled at my befuddled look. "This is why the Arabs called the Caucasus the 'Mountain of Languages.' We are a mixture of all these tribes like those Khevsurs here. But many years ago the largest of our tribes, the Karts, began to rule the others, and their language is what we now call Georgian; hence today's Georgian word for Georgia, Sa*kart*velo."

Meanwhile the march had turned a corner and arrived into what was then still Lenin Square (today Freedom Square). A huge domineering statue of the Bolshevik leader stood with its fingers pointing ambiguously up into the sky.

The moment the crowd saw it their cries of *"Ga-u-mar-jos! Ga-u-mar-jos!"* doubled in volume, directed straight at Lenin's metal brow.

"Gaumarjos is a Georgian toast," Marika explained. "It also means 'to victory!' "

As she said it I glanced at my watch and noticed the hands approaching 3.30 — the hour set by the Government for its ten minutes of sanctimonious silence — an idea with eerie similarity to George Orwell's 'two minutes hate' in *1984*. I watched the minute hand clip past the half-hour and as it did, almost to the second, there came the sound of a single car horn, followed by another, then another. Within 15 seconds just about every car, bus, and motorcycle klaxon in the city rattled furiously on its mountings. As the

The huge shrine of flowers outside Sioni Cathedral, for the 20 murdered demonstrators on April 9th, 1989. It lasted for 40 days.

perfidious, ear-splitting din drilled into my head I reflected on the thoughtlessness of the Communist authorities' decree. By attempting to hijack the demonstrators' cause in calling for this silence, they'd demanded of the people the same speechless compliance of the past 70 years. No wonder the cacophony.

From Freedom Square we preceded down Baratashvili Street with its Old Town wall and elegant wooden balconies bulging out from the 19th century town inside; then on to the Mtkvari river and along its bank.

The Sioni Cathedral stood afloat in a huge milling lake of demonstrators. Above the faces, the flags still waved, but the shouting had ceased. We'd arrived at the nerve centre of the tragedy — the memorial created to honour the death of these young men and women. Its presence had doused the anger.

Marika and I moved through the thousands of faces, some wearing black sashes tied round their foreheads, others clutching handkerchiefs. Their expressions had taken on an uncertain air, as if encountering something bigger than their rebellion. On the brick wall surrounding the cathedral numerous letter-sized pieces of paper fluttered in the wind: the messages and poems of the mothers, brothers, sisters and friends of the dead. We stopped before a large sheet of paper with its curling Georgian script composed around a detailed, pencil drawing of a teenage girl's face. Underneath it three of her small shoeprints had been dipped in red paint and walked across the paper; handwritten words meticulously encircled each of the footsteps.

I asked Marika to translate, but she just stared at the paper without responding. Suddenly I felt ashamed of my curiosity. Did I really need words for this? These private messages of grief, many written in large, childish script, spoke more eloquently than any translation.

Pushing our way inside the cathedral precinct, we came up to a huge shrine of flowers spreading chaotically across the paving stones. Scores of wreathes, made up of pink, red and white carnations and roses, had been worked into elaborate shapes. Some spelt out names of the dead, some the date 'April 9th,' others had turned into crosses, or even the flag of free Georgia. Before these several piles of literally thousands of individual red carnations had been dropped by the citizens of Tbilisi: Georgian, Armenian, Azerbaijani, Russian (the local Russian population deplored the massacre no less than the Georgians). Above the flowers a row of 20 black and white photographs were pinned to the ivy of the old city wall.

As we arrived a slow procession of mourners made their way along the small path forged between the mounds of wreathes. They walked slowly stopping every so often, placing a flower or a keepsake next to a photograph then moving on. I watched a girl with deathly pale face escorted away sobbing from the photograph of a young man.

I asked Marika if it would be all right for me to join this queue.

"Of course," she said, surprised at my question.

A few minutes later I found myself just inches away from the faces of the dead, most of them young women, no more than teenagers. Their eyes looked back filled with the same bright hope for Georgia as I'd seen just a few minutes earlier in the demonstration. It seemed impossible to understand how any human being could deliberately kill these children — the youngest was just 16.

Later; making my way back to the hotel alone, I bumped into Giorgi and Tamuna by pure chance, not far from the Sioni shrine. They looked very relieved to see me.

"We looked for you everywhere," Tamuna spoke up for the first time; again in good English. "We're on our way to Sioni now to pay our respects. Come with us."

I joined them and returned to the cathedral. As we descended the steps

Giorgi pointed up at the elegant pepper-pot dome of the cathedral looming above the Old Town.

"This is the cathedral of the Patriarch of all Georgia," he said solemnly. "It's our most holy church."

The interior of the cathedral thronged with people holding candles. The hundreds of tiny lights reflected on the gold patterns climbing the walls towards the dome, where a giant haloed figure of the Almighty looked down as if from heaven. He gazed at us sadly, his face slightly obscured by numerous shafts of smoky blue light. He too seemed to deplore this action of the Soviet authorities.

We joined the hundreds of mourners walking from icon to icon, lighting candles, whispering prayers. With the faces of those 20 dead so fresh in my memory, I found myself also wishing to light a candle, but Tamuna had already bought a large bunch and handed me a couple. I looked around for a suitable icon. The walls and pillars were clustered with the sombre, glowing faces of Georgian Orthodoxy whose saints date back to AD 337.

Noticing a press of people adding to a forest of candles surrounding a free-standing icon on the floor, I walked over to find a strange modern painting of a smart, 19th century man, wearing an ordinary jacket and collar, but with the peculiar addition of a halo round his head. Who could this secular looking man be?

"This is our new saint, Ilia Chavchavadze," she whispered. "He was a great poet and writer of the last century."

Then Giorgi added: "He was a great Georgian nationalist."

I sensed in Georgi's voice just a hint of the anger lurking in the nationalist call filling the streets. I asked if the phenomena of nationalism might not be dangerous when held in the light of history's other great nationalist movements?

"You mustn't criticise our nationalism out of what you in the West have seen before," he replied firmly. "You must think about us, what we've been through. The Soviet system has tried to take away not only our nationality, they've tried to take away 'us' from us. Our own individuality. It's not surprising now we have a little freedom we want back the first thing they tried to take away, our country."

I looked at Tamuna for her response, but she said nothing. I detected a sense of unease. Could this be a note of hesitation toward the great common cry? I made a mental note to ask her about this later. Instead I asked why they chose Sioni Cathedral for the shrine, and not the Kashveti church right across the road from the Government Building steps.

"Because this place is more important to us. It's the heart of Tbilisi," Tamuna said. "We have here Georgia's most sacred icon, St Nino's Cross."

She pointed to a recess in one of the church's pillars. Behind a sheet of glass I saw a strange wooden cross, its horizontal arms sloping downwards, made up of interwoven vine branches.

"This is a replica," she said. "We'll light our candles here." She added our flames to the others flickering before the icon then crossed herself. We stood silently for a moment. I began to feel the presence of the brimming emotion permitted by this building. No wonder Georgians always stuck by their church; where else could they go with such deep feeling? What a different atmosphere to the steely clamp of the chilling Communist world outside. As people busied themselves between the icons, so more hurried in, and the building did indeed take on the quality of a huge heart. The inner muscle of Georgia, with all these faces flowing in and out of the arches like corpuscles of blood through ventricles.

"The real cross is here too, behind there," Tamuna said eventually, gesturing toward the iconostasis.

I asked her why St Nino had been so important to Georgians.

"Because she bought the Christian faith to Georgia," she said matter-of-factly, then explained that Nino had journeyed all the way from her Jerusalem home guided by a vision of the Virgin Mary that told her she would find Christ's crucifixion coat in the pagan land of Iberia (Georgia). According to legend she arrived among the local Karts — by then the largest Georgian tribe — armed only with a cross made out of vine-rods bound by her own hair. Described in ancient texts as a 'captive girl' she then performed a number of miracles, eventually converting the Kart King Mirian to Christianity.

"We feel the original spirit of the faith is still living inside this cross," she said quietly.

Trying to understand the difference between Tamuna's relationship with this building and Georgi's firmer, more nationalist feeling, I asked him about the importance of the church in resurrecting the spirit of independent Georgia.

"It's very important," he replied then gestured to the icon of Saint Ilia Chavchavadze. "We now have a new political party named the 'Society of Saint Ilia the Righteous' (led by Zviad Gamsakhurdia, who in 1991 became Georgia's first non-Communist President). Religion is stronger than ever in Georgia now. Young people are going to the churches again; the church wants independence as much as we do. You see the frescoes in this church?" He pointed up at the ceiling. "They're Russian. The Russian Church painted over our old Georgian frescoes last century. Then afterwards the Russians brought the Soviets here who tried to take God away from us completely."

He looked at me incredulously. "It was like trying to separate our bodies from our heads. They told us we could only be married by their bureaucrats; that we had to go to their office, or that horrible building they built near here and sign the book. Then afterwards we would go in secret to the church to be blessed."

Then his voice hardened. "Many things have changed and will change in Georgia, but our God never will."

Tamuna nodded silently.

*

Tbilisi

A few days later I came across a poster in Tbilisi's Ajara Hotel advertising Georgi's 'horrible building.' It caught my eye as it seemed to resemble a cathedral doubling as a rocket-launcher. Underneath it were written the English words:

Curious how the Soviets might implant their theology of materialism into 'new ceremonies,' I decided to do just that. Never before had I come across any attempt to replace the rituals of religion in the USSR. To then supply a purpose-built cathedral for the job . . . this had to be seen.

The palace stood on a hillside a kilometre down the Mtkvari from the Sioni church. In fact, it was a highly glorified registry office that the BBC had dubbed the "Cathedral of Atheism" during Margaret Thatcher's 1987 visit to Tbilisi. Arriving at its strange, semi-organic towers of tubular concrete, the architectural message seemed to defy all analysis. Reaching for my notebook I scrawled the first words entering my head. I ended up with only two: "blatantly phallic." The central tower rose up out of two rounded concrete swirls on either side — mimicking, one supposed, the central column of a church. Yet this tower also carried suspicious chimneyish, or factory-like overtones.

Climbing the steps into its impressive, airy antechamber, I realised to what

The Palace of Rituals, the Soviet alternative to a church — still used as a registry office

lengths the designers had gone, hoping to seduce Georgians away from their 'primitive' religious habits. The abundance of light, pastel-stained glass and marble flooring did everything in its power to convey the theme of a 'Palace of Happiness.' It may even have succeeded but for the building's thinly disguised duplicitous intent — and the enormous failure of Soviet Communism to understand (or even accept) a religious instinct.

Threading my way among two separate wedding parties, I sensed the awkwardness among the smartly dressed families. Everyone seemed twitchy, awaiting the moment when the gleaming black Moskvich limousine, waiting outside, would hustle the couple back to their Orthodox church and the real ceremony.

I walked up into the wedding chamber and slunk around the pillars while an Armenian couple prepared to be married. Above them the ceiling lifted up a good 30 metres, with its light focusing down onto a small marble desk draped in velvet cloth. Behind this altar substitute stood the substitute priest — the local registrar. I watched her lift the ceremonial pen from its stand and scratch her mark in the official ledger. The couple had now become man and wife.

But did they feel it? To me the building seemed more a Palace of Bureaucracy than Happiness. The only happiness I saw belonged in the self-important expression of the registrar.

To help sanctify the event, a giant candy-coloured mural reached up above the desk some twenty five metres or so into the concrete heaven. A sickly medieval landscape depicting an idealised marriage ceremony between a naked man and woman, held beneath a colossal 'Mother Georgia' figure, who dropped flowers of good fortune on their heads. But to my mind this Mother Georgia with peasant-scarfed, blonde features smacked suspiciously of her rival, Mother Russia.

I watched another couple and their families approach in the background. The taped music was rewound and began to twinkle down anew from the public-address as the next 'new ceremony' was prepared. The Armenian couple were quickly hustled away into another smaller chamber to the side, and the next wedding party then stepped forward.

Standing discreetly to the side with my camera, I was suddenly spotted by a palace official. With nothing but the best intentions in the world, he beckoned eagerly for me to step up and join the wedding party, wishing me a better view for my camera — much to my embarrassment.

Taking my place right next to the relations I stood there feeling nobody quite understood what might be appropriate and what not, in this building. I imagined a christening taking place in a bingo hall and waited for this humiliation to be over.

As I tried to look enthusiastic I remembered the film *Repentance*, made by the Georgian director Tengiz Abuladze. Its final line was spoken by an old Georgian woman, of the generation before Stalin. Approaching a younger woman on a modern Tbilisi street she asked for directions to the street's church. The younger woman replied that the street no longer contained its church and had now been renamed Varlaam Street (after the Stalinist mayor). To this the old woman replied: "What use is a street if it doesn't lead to a church?"

Suddenly this statement seemed to answer one of my enormous question marks placed over Georgian society. As history prepared to turn everything on its head yet again, Georgians still, even in the 1990s, had a ceremony to return to. The confusing version of modernity supplied by the Soviets had only annoyed everyone. The new variant from the West just around the corner, remained just as baffling. It would need some help in the transition; a genuine 'age-old ceremony.' No wonder Georgians, even young Georgians flocked to the churches. This at least they understood.

Hurrying for the door along with the bride's relations, my pictures taken, it struck me as not a little ironic that the days when the hypocrisy of the Church had shocked a whole class into the Russian Revolution had now turned full circle. Now the even grander hypocrisy of the revolutionary zealots had shocked a population back to the Church.

Café society

I sat at a café table at the Caravanserai on Sioni Street, waiting for Tamuna. She'd promised to show me the Old Town of Tbilisi. All around, the former hotel's three floors of balconies rose toward a giant arched ceiling; to my right a small fountain lifted a fine spray of water into the air, giving out more than a whisper of the time when camel trains and not Ladas dominated the Tbilisi streets. Today this 17th century hostel for travellers and their animals, remains more or less as it had since its reconstruction after the Great Khan's demolition of Tbilisi in 1795. The only changes were its central drinking pool, now replaced by a fountain, and its 33 rooms — recently remodelled into shops, an art gallery, and an excellent History Museum of Tbilisi.

I'd arrived half an hour early, bringing with me an example of that rare commodity, English translations of Georgian poetry. I wanted to try and climb inside that strange quasi-medieval self-image of the modern Georgians; that combination of Byronic chivalry with materialist Soviet zeal. When I'd asked Giorgi where to hunt out these origins, at first he said: "Try the Byron Society in Tbilisi, they've just re-inaugurated it," then changed his mind. "But actually it would be better just to read Shota Rustaveli's *The Knight in the Panther Skin*. It's probably even more relevant for us today."

As the delicious aroma of Turkish coffee heated in hot sand swam into my nostrils, I reflected on those many others who, down through the centuries, must also have reached for this 12th century text as a handhold on the Georgian character — and more often than not in places just like this. Men like Gurdjief,

Chekhov, Lermontov, Tolstoy, Pushkin, Tchaikovsky, Dumas, and even Dostoyevsky (I've been assured) had all sat by fountains like this one in Tbilisi, deep in the shade of an ancient courtyard. I pictured them in their turn, savouring the atmosphere of other bygone Georgian centuries, when the likes of Marco Polo had done exactly the same.

I reached toward the volume of Rustaveli, but an impulse made me pick up the other book first — the anthology of Georgian poetry given to me by Marika. This book contained the more recent followers of Byron, and inside it I found names like Alexander Chavchavadze, Niko Baratashvili, Raphael Eristavi, Akaki Tsereteli, Vazha Pshavela, Galaktion Tabidze, with elaborate praises attached to their work. Their poems were saturated with those ineffable, soul

Tbilisi style in the 19th century — Shardin Street by the Caravanserai

searching perceptions typical of the 19th century romantic movement, as well as violent, over-the-top phrases dedicated to the heroes of remote Georgian tribes like the Khevsurs and Svans.

But try as I might, the grandiloquence washed right over me. I turned to the later, 20th century poets like Paolo Iashvili and Titsian Tabidze — much praised by Boris Pasternak who translated their work into Russian — but experienced more of the same lacklustre English. Then I noticed the date of the book's publication — 1958, only five years after Stalin's death, and by the Soviet Publishing House, Tbilisi. Could my disinterest have anything to do with the translation?

Flipping back to the book's introduction, I encountered a thought-provoking line to sum up a collection of any nation's poetry: "Their voices rise in a mighty choir to glorify friendship among nations, the cause of peace throughout the world and the building up of Communist society."

Smelling a rat, I turned to the biography section at the end, and sought out the reference under Titsian Tabidze (Pasternak's close friend). It blithely stated that before the Socialist Revolution Tabidze was influenced by the 'decadent symbolism' of Tbilisi's Blue Horn group, the movement that "attempted to introduce into Georgian literature traits characteristic of putrescent West

European art." But after the Revolution, "the pessimistic, depressive strains of his poetry gradually gave place to enthusiastic songs that rose in beautiful melodies of happiness and joy." This, I assumed would have been around the time the Socialist regime had him shot for subversion — 1937.

I found myself stunned by the brazenness of these printed lies and wondered if any of us, growing up in the Western 1960s and 1970s, could ever understand the extent of terror and helplessness inflicted on writers by this regime. Later, the British writer Victoria Field visited Tabidze's House Museum in the company of his now elderly daughter Nita. She wrote of it:

I was shown scenes of her father, who on falling in love with her mother had nothing to give but a carnation. Also the large extending table where all 13 friends and members of the Blue Horns would gather to entertain poets visiting from Moscow and Leningrad, and where a four-year-old Nita was dandled on the knees of Yesenin, Mayakovsky and Mandelstam. The cabinets were full of letters of thanks for the wonderful Georgian hospitality and unfulfilled promises of return. Love and kisses were sent to the poet's charming little daughter. A corner was filled with books, photographs and documents displaying the close friendship of Tabidze's wife with the Pasternak family, and how she nursed Boris on his deathbed.

Vases of carnations were everywhere and Nita focused on them as she described, trembling, how in 1937 Beria accused Paolo Iashvili of being an American spy and asked his friend Tabidze to join in denouncing him for the sake of his wife and daughter. Nita described her father's agony as for days he prayed for the right course. On the night he decided he could not, would not betray his friend, nor live unable to look others in the eye, he slept soundly. By not signing he effectively signed his own death warrant. Nita recalled the 3am knock on the door and her father being taken away down to the waiting car and her mother's white face. She pointed to the clock on the desk, stopped at the precise moment he left, as if she

Caravanserai interior — the animals would live on the lower level by the fountain. Today it is a Caucasian shopping mall, and nightclub at the back.

79

could never forget that night 60 years ago . . . Although Tabidze's family hoped for decades their brave husband and father was in exile, simply not permitted to write letters, the truth is he was shot days after his arrest and buried in a mass grave in nearby Rustavi. Pasternak wrote that art is always meditating on death and thereby creating life. As I stood in this apartment holding the cold hand of a woman who has lived first hand both the glory of art and the terror of the 20th century, it seemed here the reverse was true.

I thought of Pasternak himself, a man excessively sensitive to all this, as his letters reveal, and who, it is argued, only escaped execution himself due to his affection for Georgia and its poetry (along with Stalin). This was the novelist who in 1956 submitted his *Dr Zhivago* to a leading Moscow monthly, only to receive its rejection as a "libel of the October Revolution," and then within a year and a half watched it published in 18 Western languages.

These poets whose mistranslated idylls I now read had been published into English here in Tbilisi, the same year (1958) their Russian translator Pasternak was awarded the Nobel Prize for Literature — which he was forced to decline. At times like this I began to feel my carefully maintained ironic distance shrinking to zero.

Surely this anthology stood guilty of the same promotion. I put it down and turned to Rustaveli. The first translation into English of his *The Knight in the Panther Skin* had been, blessedly, pre-

Shota Rustaveli — as depicted by the 19th century Russian artist Teodor Burov

Soviet, by the Englishwoman Marjory Wardrop, sister of Oliver Wardrop, the 1919 Chief British Commissioner of Transcaucasia. Hers was the fruit of a great love of Georgia imbibed first from her brother. After a memorable personal visit in 1894, the Wardrops were to become great scholars of Georgian literature, producing many translations between them — for which they too are much loved in Georgia to this day.

Reading the first few pages of Rustaveli's poem, raised quite different emotions. The prologue of this enormous text, amounted to the poet's unashamed declaration of spiritual and it seemed almost erotic love for his country's Queen Tamar. The wholehearted surrender by the poet immediately sank in the hook, and gave a reminder of the French and English tradition of chivalric poetry of the same period. He proceeded to say of his political leader:

Illustration from a 17th century manuscript of the 'Vepkhistqaosani' — 'Knight in the Panther's Skin' — part of the Wardrop Collection at the Bodleian Library, Oxford

Georgia: in the mountains of poetry

She bade me indite sweet verses in her praise, laud her eyebrows and lashes, her hair, her lips and teeth, cut crystal and ruby arrayed in ranks. An anvil of soft lead breaks even hard stone.

I found myself wanting to read on. The plot then cleverly traps the reader with an emotional description of a mysterious heart-broken knight, Tariel, sitting beside a stream, his armour studded with pearls, his shoulders wrapped by a panther skin, tears and blood streaming from his eyes. Yet also a man of immense will and strength who slaughters all his challengers then disappears. The next 1,500 verses of the poem tell the tale of a hero-prince called Avtandil who sets out to find this superhumanly tragic knight. Finally the two meet, become lasting friends and together set out to right the wrong that caused the knight his enormous sorrow, by saving his beloved Nestan.

Written a hundred years before Chaucer, the verses showed themselves fully familiar with Platonist ideas, referring to God as a universal force rather than a Christian one (to the extent the Georgian Orthodox Church has in the past destroyed copies of the poem, declaring Rustaveli a Muslim). Certainly he espoused the doctrine of perfect love or the cult of friendship, still prominent in modern Georgian culture — and indisputably linked with the convention of hospitality. But one also feels a curious link with the Sufi doctrine of divine love, at the time of Rustaveli reaching its zenith in the cities of neighbouring Western Persia. This is the path in which a devotee attempts to annihilate the self by surrendering his (or her) mind, body and soul to the image of a divine lover. The device of an earthly figure is often employed along with deeply allegorical romantic, even erotic language to nurse the devotee up to the spiritual plane. Some argue Rustaveli's prologue (one verse quoted above), with its lengthy discussions on his love for his Queen, is a fine example of this.

But whatever Rustaveli's origins, most Georgians love the poem and when asked to explain that difficult phenomenon of the 'true spirit of Georgia,' often refer to it. Disguised within the depths of the text lies a purposeful code of chivalry espoused during Georgia's Golden Age, a period of enlightenment in full bloom at the same time most European nations hurled themselves into the dubiously motivated Crusades. As Christian sword sought Muslim throat in the Holy Land, in Tbilisi Georgians, Armenians, Jews and Muslims lived side by side in relative harmony. One of Georgia's traditions had always been that brides at every level of society would be expected to learn much of this poem, and even today their trousseaus usually contain a copy.

The appearance of a shadow over the book made me look up. Tamuna had arrived. We exchanged greetings and she immediately suggested we leave for the old town. As we stepped out onto Sioni Street she glanced down at my books.

"Do you like Rustaveli?" she asked.

I told her I did so far.

"It's a great pity you can't read it in the Georgian," she said seriously. "Then it's something else entirely. Really about a noble way to live, to treat other people."

She led me down to the Mtkvari river and towards the dramatic Metekhi Church perched on top of a cliff above the boiling current. I'd seen pictures of it with the Tsarist prison buildings wrapped around the edge of the cliff — since removed.

"This used to be a prison, then a theatre," she said, "but now it's about to become a church again."

She spoke in a quiet, unassuming voice and I wondered if I'd been right in thinking — after her brief remark beside the icon of Ilia Chavchavadze — that here walked a Georgian who loved Georgia without the nationalism.

We crossed the road into the low-lying Gorgasali Square, where she explained some of the local history.

"This used to be Tbilisi's main market. The camel trains and traders would come up the Mtkvari and stop in Tbilisi for the hot baths, then they would trade in this square."

I tried to imagine the furious business taking place here. The bartering voices in Georgian, Armenian, Azerbaijani, Persian, Turkish and Yiddish, as the bales of brocades, spices and silk were unloaded and traded for rugs, guns and Georgian wines, sold in their large wine-skins.

Children playing on the roofs of Tbilisi's hot springs. The mosque tower is in the background.

Today, tarmacked-over and market-less, it offered only a further opportunity for Georgian drivers to scare each other. We walked on and she pointed out the names of the surrounding streets: Silversmith, Blacksmith, Bathhouse, Dyer, Wine Rise — all indications of the professions formerly thriving there. Then suddenly she stopped walking and asked: "This information is interesting for you?"

I think she sensed we hadn't just met to play the 'city tour.' I confessed my interest in her background and opinions on modern Georgia. She told me she had studied English literature and language at university, and now vaguely pursued an urge to write. So what had she written?

"Some poems and short stories," but added dismissively: "They're only fairy tales. I would never get my stories published here. Anyway, they're no good. I think they're wrong."

I asked what did she mean by "wrong."

"I don't know. I'm not saying what I should be saying." She looked at me earnestly. "There's something very important here to be said now. It's about Georgia, some central, crucial part that is being lost, that nobody is talking about. And I don't mean a physical part. It's in our soul, and I really mean 'our,' because I fear it's also a part of myself. I feel Georgia is dying — is losing itself for ever." Then she said more quietly. "The louder those nationalists shout, the harder they wave their flags, the further away they push from this place that 70 years has made them forget. I think this is why my stories are not correct. I'm already forgetting this place."

She lowered her eyes to the road and I realised this troubled her deeply. "It's like a great craziness what's happening now," she added gazing at her feet.

I looked at her walking beside me, ashamed at not being able to say what she felt. An intelligent woman, a couple of years out of university, yet filled with a childish shyness and lack of confidence. One too sensitive, too contained within herself for the new society she saw forming around her, feeling herself cut off, unable to integrate with the noise and histrionics of Georgia's new politics.

I wondered if she, and the others like her, now experienced the sense of alienation for the first time; the phenomena we in the West accept as normal. Georgian culture had until recently been fused together by the single focused quest for 'freedom,' with any likelihood of it arriving safely prevented by the almighty Soviet obstruction. Now everything had changed; the barrier had simply rolled

The former Mother Georgia, constructed in 1958 during the Soviet heyday

away and there it stood, or something stood, right ahead, a kind of blinding blur. The nation now faced something it couldn't define.

I felt for these Soviet-educated women like Tamuna. Statistically the Soviet population was always more widely educated than the British. Practically their application of knowledge was far more restricted. Well into glasnost, students could still face chiefs and professors of the old regime all clinging jealously to their positions. Graduates faced that same terrible self-debilitating dilemma — educated for what?

We walked on up the hill in silence. The streets on either side began chopping, swerving and changing direction, narrowing and widening according to the houses they encountered. Here homes came before roads, and no two were alike. We walked past fine old Persian-style galleried balconies, their paint peeling, their supports sagging to hold them up, daring only the foolhardy to walk; yet washing had been strung gaily across the arches. There were houses with courtyards, their front walls built entirely from uneven panes of glass; filling the rooms beyond with light; above them the first floor balconies opened out with their intricately carved railings, ready for those cool Caucasian summer evenings. Here Georgians, Tatars, Azerbaijanis, Jews, Kurds, and Armenians lived next door to each other. The place felt friendly, intimate; the higgledy-piggledy houses although seeming on the verge of collapse, looked clean and lovingly maintained.

I began to sense the Georgia Tamuna feared might disappear. Not so much these houses, as the spirit within them. The indefinable quality of life that most Georgians found impossible to articulate.

The new independent Mother Georgia, replacing it in the mid 1990s

A couple of young children, three and four at most, walked towards us, unaccompanied. They stopped still and stared. Then just as we passed, the older one turned to me and shouted out shrilly *"gamarjobat!"* — the Georgian for 'hello.' He almost seemed to be welcoming us into his home.

Unlike in so many other shanty-type towns around the world, the greeting was not followed by some request or demand. Here they just received the stranger automatically — as no doubt, so did their parents.

I suggested to Tamuna they wandered the streets because their house threatened to fall down. She laughed.

"These houses are strong, and always repaired. People like living here very much. Living in the Old Town means something to Georgians. This is real, *this* is Georgia."

The higher we climbed toward the Narikala fortress so the streets became more cobbled and crooked, sinking ever further back into time. Then as if to deliberately sabotage the illusion, I noticed the giant silvery figure of a woman, flashing between the roof tops, high on the Sololaki ridge. This 20 metre high representation of Mother Georgia, constructed by the Soviets in 1958, stood above the old homes like a severe Space Age matron. She carried a cup of wine in one hand and a sword in the other, half threatening, half welcoming the city. To me it seemed another example of that Soviet addiction to sword-bearing women statues. I asked Tamuna if she didn't resent this attempt to woo Georgians into the steely orbit of the Communist future, by appropriating this much loved symbol.

"I don't know," she said politely, "but I don't mind this statue."

Obviously I'd been mistaken thinking all Georgians believed all things Soviet were 'wrong.' This symbol — not a Lenin, Orjonikidze, or some other dictator — was Georgian, and for this she tolerated it, just as Georgians, in spite of all their clamouring against imperialists, learnt also to tolerate them to some degree. Georgia espoused, at least in principle, the maxim 'the best way to master your enemy is make him your friend.' After all, the Russians, then the Soviets after them, had also bought very real benefits to the nation. Without the Russian army Georgia might still be a part of the Persian or Ottoman Empire. Without the Soviets' hydro-electric power, air and rail links, hospital facilities and subsidised oil, they'd almost certainly be less economically developed (as independence would painfully bear out). On top of this came the extensive educational facilities, the scholarships in Moscow, and that most beloved of all institutions, the Dynamo Tbilisi football stadium.

Interestingly, when Georgia did finally achieve its independence from Russia, one of the earlier civic events was to replace this Mother Georgia statue with one almost totally identical. Many seasoned Georgia visitors still don't believe me when I tell them the current one is new. As for the reason, except for a slight resemblance to the Statue of Liberty, I've yet to find an explanation.

Finally reaching a dead end we descended back down the hill, passing the mosque, then the Chreli bathhouse — whose mosaic-tiled front and twin minarets made it more mosque-like than the mosque. Below it lay Tbilisi's popular sulphur baths, their sealed domed heads poking above the ground like buried old men.

"This is where the tourists go now," said Tamuna flatly.

These baths had served as the city's mainstay attraction for over a thousand years. In the 12th century Tbilisi possessed 65 bathhouses and since that day had found many people, including Pushkin and Tolstoy, who liked lounging in their elegant marble pools — as Tolstoy put it, "imagining oneself a Pompey or Lucullus."

Curious about this poet's haunt, I stepped into the entrance and begged Tamuna to ask the burly attendant if I could take a photo.

"*Ara*," he said flatly (Georgian for 'no'). Then I placed a packet of Marlboro on the countertop; he held up two fingers. I put down another. He then said in exactly the same voice, only in English this time: "Pushkin cubical three."

I pushed open the door to be bowled over by the blast of sticky air, and a barrage of German voices — the foreign tourists. The room appeared just as Tolstoy had suggested: white marble, with jet black statues beside a murky, odorous water. But the sight of noisy, naked Germans, drinking Georgian champagne and singing loudly drove me quickly back to the street. I told

Tamuna about the baths' occupants.

"Yes I saw them yesterday," she said. "They were wearing shorts — everybody was laughing about them."

"Why?" I asked.

"Only foreign men wear short trousers in Georgia," she said with a trace of amusement.

We walked away up the refurbished Leselidze Street toward (then) Lenin Square (formerly called Yerevan Square for the huge quantity of Armenians living in Tbilisi), past Georgian Orthodox and then Armenian churches, with the synagogue and the mosque only a stone's throw away from each other, and a slick-looking new building with the words *'Advertizing Agency'* printed across it in English. I stopped to take a photograph and began explaining how this might be just the tip of the looming Western invasion of Georgia; but Tamuna only nodded politely as if she already knew.

"Would you like a drink of coffee now?" she suggested.

A couple minutes later we sat opposite each other in a dungeonous, brand new designer café called The Argo (after the ship carrying Jason and his Argonauts to Colchis), only a couple hundred metres from the Sioni Street Caravanserai. Sitting in this then fashionable new meeting place for the re-emerging Tbilisi café society, I realised we'd come full circle. From the 17th century courtyard to these dimly lit cubicals cleverly constructed over a real fishpond.

Concealed within the shadows and candlelight Tamuna relaxed. I began by trying to encourage her writing. She received my words with a tiny smile, as if touched, but I couldn't decide if she really believed me or not. Finally she interrupted.

"It's not just my writing that's the problem," she said. "It's how rapidly everything is changing here in Georgia. I don't think we can understand it. I think we've given up, just surrendered ourselves to the instincts of the moment. We're out of control, our culture is approaching . . ." she paused, ". . . yours, I think. Not that yours is wrong — it's just too big for us to see."

I asked her for an example.

"Look at us, the Georgian women. We've been told one thing for centuries: about chivalry, modesty, purity. Now we're being told we're liberated, we're free. So who are we?" She looked at me, almost expecting the answer. "If you look at some young Georgian girls now, they're more confused than ever. They listen to Western rock music, it tells them to do what they feel. They now have many men, not even boyfriends. For them it's the great release from the centuries of tradition. But afterwards does it help them? Do they know who they are? I don't know. Sometimes I fear they are just losing everything, and are taking us with them."

I asked if she could see an alternative.

She lowered her eyes. "No I can't see an alternative," she said. "But there is one. I feel it. We still have something but we're missing it."

I asked about Georgian men. She looked back painfully.

"For Georgian men, it's different. They don't have to behave. For them all this revolution is a great pleasure. And they've always got the Russian girls. Nobody's telling them to be pure any more. Then they turn to us to be good wives."

I told her I couldn't believe all Georgian women still fell for this one.

"No," she admitted, "things are changing. A few wives aren't so pure any more, and some, in fact a lot of women now, aren't getting married. We're waiting for men to catch up . . ." In the dimness I caught the trace of a despairing look. I asked if a huge world of secret sensuality didn't exist here, as it did everywhere else.

"Yes," she said matter-of-factly.

I asked how this could be when most single women and men still lived with their families.

"It's possible. There are places to go. Most Georgian families have two houses, one closed up in the country. We Georgians are 'craft.'"

I looked puzzled. She took a piece of paper wrote down the letters '*craft*'. When I added the '*y*' her eyes lit up.

"Yes," she said. "That's what we are!"

"And you too?" I asked,

"No," she replied. "I'm not crafty."

Then she looked sad again. "I shouldn't tell you," she said, "but I'm 25 now and I've not yet kissed a boy."

The bright white touchpaper

Tamuna's urgent but forlorn reaction to her country stuck in my mind. Unlike any other Georgian I'd met she seemed to detect something dark looming beyond the radiant ambitions of the nationalists, but felt her voice drowned by the political hysteria sweeping the streets. Until then I had only sensed an unnatural charge to the electricity in the passing faces, hoping, like most, the imminent non-Communist government would harness it to good effect. But Tamuna's profound despondency had awakened a curiosity. Perhaps such pessimism also found an airing amid the Georgian arts? Then the phone rang.

"There's a performance at the Rustaveli Theatre tonight. It's quite unique, you must see it." These words came at me in a clipped Oxbridge accent in-between the crackles on Tbilisi's dying and resurrecting telephone system. I'd met their speaker, Zura, a few evenings earlier in one of the city's hotel bars. At the time, I had watched him speaking, wondering why this educated Englishman had made such an in-depth study of Georgian history and culture. Finally I'd put it down to his eccentric personality; the sudden, un-British bursts of enthusiasm, the proximity of deep emotion lurking beneath his words.

Tbilisi

Discovering him a Georgian came as a profound shock. I'd retreated to the bar for a stiff drink and some soul-searching on my ability to discern character. Zura's profession as an English teacher had provided him with the correct English but not the accent. His second job, as translator for Tbilisi's Rustaveli Theatre Company — one of the few companies in the world to impress the English with Shakespeare — may have explained it. I accepted his invitation and he told me to wait outside the entrance on Rustaveli Avenue.

Peering in through the glass, I saw a spacious pre-Revolutionary vestibule: elaborate gilded arches, marble staircases, Greco-Roman statues — an example of Russian classicism at its most opulent. The theatre had been purpose-built as a theatre/opera house in 1899. Beyond the vestibule a 850-seat galleried theatre awaited the appreciative Tbilisi audiences — who regularly packed the house.

It has been said that nations of dramatic temperament (like the Georgians) are less inclined to life's falsified, second-hand versions on the stage, that because they themselves indulge feverishly in everyday drama, they lack the kind of fascination that so drives us English to the theatre. But the Georgians are the exception to this rule — adoring drama so exorbitantly, it makes no difference, on or off the stage. Around me on the street came further proof. A large crowd of other invitees steadily collected beside the door. I watched a couple of girls in their early twenties walk down the street together, their fingers entwined like children, then stop and stand a few feet away. Guessing they might speak English I leaned over and asked the subject of tonight's performance. They gave me a dark look. It seemed to say "this is no performance for a tourist." Then after a long pause one said quietly *"Dyevyatoye Aprelia"* ('the ninth of April' in Russian) and turned away, continuing her conversation in Georgian. I began to feel the weight behind Zura's words.

A few minutes later he arrived. We shook hands swiftly and after some earnest discussion with the babushka behind the stage-door desk — who looked me over as she would a serial killer — I slipped through and into the gilded inner sanctum.

"Tonight it's the unofficial performance—" Zura explained, "—or, as they say, the official rehearsal of tomorrow's performance. It's a theatrical requiem to the 9th of April. A one-off event, designed for Georgian people, not the international audience. It's something very personal to us."

Under the theatre's splendid walls, gold cornices and sparkling chandeliers, the grim tone to his words didn't fit. He led me into the main auditorium where, under an even more fabulously ornate ceiling — with cherubs dancing around a massive mandala-like light cluster — stood a single, lifeless tree centre-stage, its branches hanging limply down. From its sticks hung two red bandages, of the kind attached to the fence now surrounding the Government Building steps. I asked him to explain.

"In the Georgian countryside we have many sacred trees," he said unable to disguise a rising emotion. "Some call them wishing trees. The local people tie small prayers onto their branches so they blow in the wind, in the hope they'll come true. This tree is like one of those; a kind of tree of life, but as you see all its branches are dead, and the wishes have turned into blood. The tree also symbolises the Georgian people. Our culture is one so full of growth, fecundity, yet so often in its history has had all its new growth stripped away."

I asked who had written this theatrical 'requiem.'

"It has no words," he replied. "It's a series of enactments to a piece of music by the Georgian composer Gia Kancheli. Our theatre's director, Robert Sturua, created stage drama to go with it."

Then he looked at me seriously. "It will be a strong performance."

The Rustaveli Theatre; contains two theatres. Its most famous modern production, 'Richard III,' played at London's Roundhouse to critical acclaim. It was also the choice of demonstrators protesting the Soviet invasion of Afghanistan (ironically, the production itself presented a subtle Georgian critique of Soviet power).

I already knew of Robert Sturua's work. His burlesque-style production of *Richard III* had deeply impressed Peter Brook, Vanessa Redgrave and most of England's critics when it toured Europe. Since then his productions have often appeared in London's West End. The Novosti Press Agency, in its 1987 official guide to Georgia, credited him with an entire chapter — entitled 'Robert Sturua's Phenomenon' — citing his theatre's worldwide success with Shakespeare as a fine example of how 'Soviet' artists can make deep impressions into the domains Westerners believe exclusively theirs.

Zura then led me down a rabbit warren of rooms and corridors, away to the back-stage area, where he left me amid a feverish community of actors squeezing themselves into costumes, to hunt the director. Standing alone among priests, nuns, noblemen and commonfolk of the Georgian 19th century, I experienced a moment of eerie disassociation; as if just stepping into a living corner of the old town I'd visited earlier on with Tamuna. Now trader and customer pulled on boots, straightened their jackets and talked earnestly in Georgian. These modern men and women had now metamorphosed into their proud, pre-Soviet selves, donning the clothing of their great-great-grandfathers and grandmothers.

Then, walking through the 19th century bustle came a distinctly 20th century man, with casual open sweater, middle-age paunch and immensely round, hamster-like face. Robert Sturua had arrived. Shaking hands I apologised for the bad timing of my arrival — only 20 minutes before curtain — and asked him to suggest a time when we could chat.

"What about right now if it suits you?" he replied politely.

To my amazement he then found us a bench just inside a buzzing wing of the stage, where we sat talking right up until the moment the lights dimmed.

"This play is about the history of Georgia from the start of the 19th century to the present day," he said in a deep and slowly pronounced English. "It's about our partnership with the Russians. On April 9th our nation received a slap in the face which woke us up from a sleep that had been going on since 1956. This is the touchpaper to a flame that now is catching on in republics all over Russia."

He spoke with all the composure of someone sitting in their own living-room. I constantly expected to be interrupted by nervous actors, stage managers, technicians in the final crucial countdown to curtain. But nobody disturbed us once. His voice seemed fully in tune with his private thoughts.

"Until now the feeling in Georgia has been a confused type of dissatisfaction. This event has purified our emotion. It makes us feel more noble, more chivalrous. Georgians prefer this and would rather fall in love with tragedy, than worry about every little consequence of their actions." Then he looked at me. "This is like a Mediterranean zone here. All the emotions of life and death are taken more dramatically than elsewhere."

But surely such carelessness for the future might be dangerous, I suggested.

"It's true," he said more gravely. "Some people are very caught up in this emotion, but not everybody. The question we all wait to see answered is, who will dominate?" He took a deep breath, and glanced at the actors bustling around us.

I asked how Georgians related to his "elsewhere" — which they would soon have to deal with as an independent nation. What had he, as a Georgian, detected in us when he toured the capitals of Europe?

He thought for a second. "I detected many things; but one thing I feel is, in developed Western countries people are struggling towards something that we, in a way, have born into us here in Georgia. Qualities of direct emotion, an instinct for genuine chivalry: qualities we've deliberately held onto from our history."

I felt the blossom of a fine conversation just beginning to open when suddenly the lights faded. Before his face completely disappeared into the blackout I quickly asked if this Georgian idea of self might not be slightly inflated?

"Oh yes, it's inflated!" came a cheerful reply out of the gloom. For the first time I wondered if this enormous, swashbuckling ego of the Georgians might also be capable of great practicality and vision — when blended with an appropriate discipline. I wanted desperately to ask Robert Sturua for his opinion on this, but a hush had already descended on the auditorium, the air around us filling with a ponderous silence.

It may have been only symbolic, but that night I watched the performance from back-stage. The following night I took a place with the public in the stalls among a dignified Georgian audience including many senior public figures. Looking at those silvery, bushy moustaches and heavy-eyebrowed faces of the not-so-forgotten Georgian nobility — many with prominent positions in the then Communist regime — I saw how, to this proud gentry, the Rustaveli Theatre had always worn the mantle of liberal respectability. I could also sense the 2,000 kilometres between this theatre and Moscow; a distance aiding Georgian theatre and film productions past the censor's nose. Several times in Moscow I'd heard jealous film-makers claim the celebrated films from Tbilisi's Gruzia Film Studios had been shown only "because the censor couldn't understand Georgian."

But this performance never saw the shadow of a censor. To a surging orchestral sound-track the lights dimmed and a sinister white gas (dry ice) crept ominously across the stage toward the audience. A quite unambiguous reference to the gas used by the Special Forces on April 9th. Then a man stepped forward through the stage mists holding an infant in his arms — I assumed the symbol of the emerging nation of Georgia. The music then crashed, the lights flipped to red and he collapsed — the Russians had arrived. The stage then flooded with women covered in black, Arab-like head-dresses who stood in the background, hands stuffed into their mouths in the gesture of enforced silence: a reference to the period after 1801 when the Georgian royal family were sent packing and Russian law superseded the code of the Georgian kings.

I heard someone sniffing a couple rows ahead. For this audience these ghostly mementoes of the past wedded perfectly with the symbols of the present. A symbolism everyone instinctively understood. The history of Russian calumny in Georgia is drilled into every Georgian child at home (making up for school where Georgian history was then hardly taught at all).

After some dramatic struggles, symbolising the Red Army's conquest of Georgia in 1922, a man in a black vinyl jacket — representing the KGB, and Beria's former dreaded Cheka (secret police) — rose up through a trap in the floor to announce the arrival of the first Stalinist purge of 1922-24. This event forced many Mensheviks to flee to France. Crowds of women were rounded up, bundled away, and a priest was handcuffed (the suppression of the Orthodox Church). During the second purge of 1936-37, the priest was shot and not only intellectuals but many prominent Bolsheviks and former allies of Stalin were led away. During this terrible period one quarter of Georgia's Writer's Union was either exiled or liquidated. In 1936 Boris Pasternak had written to Titsian Tabidze praising his recent book of poetry as "a reminder of the time when people such as poets survived in the Soviet Union." It is said that Tabidze's death at the hands of Beria's thugs, along with that of the poet Paolo Iashvili, profoundly influenced Pasternak's *Dr Zhivago*.

Then came sincerely gesturing bureaucrats (the Communist Party) strutting across the stage. A giant black jackboot was placed centre-stage (symbolising the Red Army's presence). Then as a trembling crescendo of strings scaled the heights of what seemed like saccharine sentimentality, a woman dressed in white held out her baby before an evil bureaucrat. The lights snapped again into deep red and she fell to the ground, dead.

For me the drama had entered the sublimer realms of cliché, swinging far too heavily to one side of Georgian history. But for the audience, a suppressed truth was at last being told in public — the rewritten history books from their schooldays corrected. They hadn't come for intellectual stimulation, the spectacle intended to recreate the sense of collective emotion, the re-awakening Robert Sturua had mentioned in our talk.

At the final, climatic moment of the drama, amidst a great din from the orchestra, the entire lighting rig descended low over the stage, every one of its filaments burning brilliantly, to announce the brash April 7th arrival of the tanks in Tbilisi. Then suddenly every one of the lights swivelled onto the audience, glaring painfully in our eyes — an indication not only of the April 9th Massacre but of the threat still remaining. Everyone knew the tanks had simply retreated to their bases just outside Tbilisi, or on the Turkish border. They could return at any time.

Thus the performance ended, none too soon for me. I wondered vaguely why I'd never heard a Georgian mention the benefits of the Russian Caucasian army in the 19th century — saving Tbilisi from further ruin from the Turks and Persians. But the many sniffles told me now was not the time to acknowledge any benefits from the Russian Army. The performance, with all the tricks and devices of theatre had presented a dream of Georgia for the last 200 years, the "universally forgotten land" as their much praised poet Ilia Chavchavadze described it. The play told the endless tale of an inferiority complex, drilled into this proud people again and again. Georgia it said, had been the vassal state of a cruel and sinister overlord for too long and, in that final climactic blast of light, it seemed to me the onlooker received the glare of a clear challenge to respond.

I rose from my seat with the audience: had the touchpaper been lit? All around the faces streamed out onto the street, the elegantly dressed women in their black dresses and gold jewelry, next to their well-established husbands:

Free Georgia demonstration outside Tbilisi University in 1989

the senior Georgians, the grander intellectuals and politicians. No. Here one felt the political message more or less safely contained. The long-tied knot of power between the Georgian government, KGB and mafia would continue to hold together for some time yet.

But as the cold air of Rustaveli Avenue touched my face, so a hysterical, horn blasting, flag-waving Lada screamed past the theatre entrance, its cargo of wild-eyed nationalists revelling in the new identity of 'independence.' I began to feel again this huge head of youthful steam aiming itself towards adventure and 'freedom.' I changed my mind; the touchpaper was already fizzing. The question was simply — which way would the rocket now shoot?

The symbol of a nation

I'd already visited Tbilisi's Art Museum once but Tamuna insisted on taking me again. "I want to show you the museum's treasury," she said. "It's important. You should look at it not like a tourist."

I asked her what she meant, but she didn't reply. However having already seen its sumptuous collection of icons from all periods and areas of Georgia, and the quantity of guards around its entrance, I guessed this exhibition served more as a church than a museum: a kind of super-reliquary or Holy of Holies — open to the public.

The building stood on the diminutive Pushkin Square, next to Tbilisi's Freedom Square, its grand Ionic portico grinning back at the bustling traffic.

A fully appropriate setting for art, yet until 1905 the building served quite a different purpose, housing Tbilisi's seething Theological Seminary. This establishment can claim direct responsibility for Georgia's two greatest revolutionaries. It educated the democratic socialist politician Noe Zhordania — who led the heroic but brief government of Independent Georgia between 1918-21, and the not so democratic Joseph Stalin. Besides these two, the school fomented numerous Bolsheviks, socialists and Georgian nationalists who never became priests due, at least partly, to their expulsion. One of these, Lado Ketskhoveli, a militant Marxist revolutionary, met and then took under his wing the 19-year-old Joseph Jughashvili (who later renamed himself Stalin), then installed him as a leader among the secret ring of worker's discussion groups in Tbilisi. From this point Stalin quickly rose to become a leader among the radicals. A small plaque on its outside wall couldn't resist announcing Stalin's presence in this building between 1894 and 1898 (since removed).

Looking up at this writing on the wall I asked Tamuna for her opinion on the great Joseph.

"We have a saying in Georgia," she said. "'Don't expect heaven from the parish priest.' Stalin set out to be that priest, but along the way he forgot this because he thought he could supply heaven. A great and foolish man and still a large shadow inside the Georgian character." She glanced at me. "He's still hard for many to look at properly."

We entered the building and deposited every conceivable item that might be used to steal an icon at the museum's cloakroom, then submitted ourselves to the armed police guard at the Treasury entrance.

Safely vetted we stepped into an intimately carpeted chamber, with numerous well lit exhibits set inside sturdy glass cabinets. The atmosphere was hushed, more akin to a church than a museum as the Treasury functioned as a much needed bank vault for Georgia's most valuable relics. Most had been

Painting of a Persian courtesan, 18th century — Tbilisi Art Museum

rescued from churches throughout the Caucasus, as well as Western Europe. When the Bolsheviks ousted the Georgian Menshevik government in 1921, Zhordania and his ministers fled with a portion of Georgia's transportable heritage, fearing for its safety. Possibly a wise decision, bearing in mind the subsequent purges up north, where icons were chopped up to make potato crates, burnt as firewood or painted over with Stalin's face. But now, with the circular irony of history, Georgian icons are in danger of disappearing once again, this time via the West's voracious underground art market.

Tamuna beckoned from a small, heavily built cabinet.

"This for me is Georgia's finest icon," she said earnestly.

I looked into the cabinet and recognised Queen Tamar's small pectoral cross.

"This is her only known relic," she explained, then stood silently before it in deep admiration.

Following her gaze I saw a simple cross, a couple inches long at most, composed of six pearls, four emeralds and five rubies, set within a thin gold frame. The emeralds, roughly cut into oblongs, formed the arms of the cross, with a ruby at each tip and one in the middle. The smallness of the relic seemed appropriate for this modest-sized nation; a country that, under its Muslim rulers, had worn crosses hidden beneath its clothing. But what else? Tamuna's motionless face told me I'd missed something far more significant.

Then I remembered on my first visit to this museum, watching a middle-aged Georgian woman burst into tears the moment she saw this cross. What did Georgians see here? I tried to imagine this

Queen Tamar's Cross, at the heavily guarded Art Museum in Tbilisi

pendant hanging over the bare shoulders of a young 12th century woman: tall, slim and large-eyed, of the kind endlessly portrayed in Georgian art. Standing here, did they feel the presence of the noble Queen, a nearness to that bygone Golden Age?

Tamuna stood before it for a long time then touched my arm in an uncharacteristically confident gesture.

"I wanted you to come here so I could tell you about this cross," she said quietly. "If you really look at it you can feel what it's like to live in our country. You know this spot here for me is the very heart of our nation."

She fell silent; and I had to ask what she meant.

"When I look at this cross," she said staring right at it, "I think how wonderful it is that right here in the middle of Tbilisi we have a museum of our history, and right in the centre of this museum is this cross, and in the heart of the cross is a single red ruby stone! This ruby is like a drop of the blood that used to run in the Georgian people."

She glanced at me then gazed back at the cross. "For me this is the most beautiful cross in the world."

Her voice betrayed her emotion. I could see now how Tamuna wanted to tell me something about herself through this icon. As if it and this museum contained an example of all the ideas of art, beauty and courage she admired in her idealised Georgia. That this museum might be an attempt to show me an alternative, more reflective nationalism.

I thought of the power of the cross as a symbol among the other rebellious Soviet republics. Who could ever forget that extraordinary Hill of Crosses in Lithuania — the small hillock bristling with over a million wooden hand-carved crosses. The way it reached up out of the earth like a huge crop of human hands seeking God and independence. The Communists had bulldozed the hill twice, but each time it grew back more vigorously than before, as if from an indestructible seed inside the soil.

The same held true in Georgia. The red cross of St George (also the English part of the Union Jack) had been re-adopted by some of the nationalist groups and printed onto flags. These red on white designs had become a favourite with the Monarchist Party, a highly vocal section of Georgia's independence movement since the 1830s, calling for a constitutional monarch and the restoration of that intermediary between heaven and politics — the King (abolished by the Russians in 1801).

"The cross in Georgia," said Tamuna, "is the most important sign for us. It means unity and nearly all Caucasian cultures have it at their centre. Even in the different languages it is the same. In Georgian *jvari* means cross, in the Khevsur dialect it is *jurri*, and in Ossetian, which is from another language group entirely, *juar* means cross. The symbols are everywhere around us."

I looked up at the museum chamber; and noticed for the first time just how many crosses it contained. They stood everywhere in cabinets or embedded in icons like marker-buoys in the long embattled history of this nation, from the tiniest eighth century bronze medallions and tenth, 11th and 12th century processional crosses, to the splendid six foot ante-altar cross from Gorijvari in the 15th century.

As we walked towards it Tamuna stopped me beside some tiny 11th century cloisonne enamel encolpoins (breast pendants).

"Look at the dragon," she said pointed to an exquisite plaque of St. George the Victorious spearing his dragon with great ardour. Every scale on its back had been separately created with an extraordinary attention to detail.

"You can see how this artist loved this icon," she said, adding: "It's as if he wanted to draw attention to the dragon."

At the Gorijvari Cross, we found the dragon again, but this time as one of many scenes from St George's life. This enormous wooden cross, encased in a skin of 16 silver plaques, carries some of the most intricate reliefs in Georgia. Each plaque depicts either a miracle or one of the tortures he endured during his trials of faith.

As we looked I could sense Tamuna debating whether to say something. Finally I asked her what it was.

"These illustrated crosses are not only icons to be worshipped as the church would like you to," she said more quietly. "You know they're like secret messages, if you can understand them. If you take them seriously they're like guides, because they show the step-by-step development of the psychology of holy men and saints." Then her face showed a momentary glimmer of uncertainty. "But our church doesn't like this kind of analysis. It doesn't understand it."

I studied the silver plaques of the cross. They showed St. George undergoing a horrific series of tortures, boiled in a cauldron, flayed with bull-whips, tied and stretched around a wheel. It also presented him carrying out miracles, bringing a farmer's bull back to life, slaying the dragon. I asked Tamuna if she could explain.

"I can't really," she said apologetically. "But anyone who thinks must realise the St George story is purely an allegory. Every icon tells us this because of course, dragons don't exist." She smiled faintly.

I knew even the Roman Catholic Church had guessed as much when they decanonised St George in 1961, for lack of any solid evidence proving his existence.

She continued: "To me it's the story of a saint's struggle against different parts of his personality. You can see two opposite sides of St George's character in this icon: St George as the Martyr and St George the Victorious." Suddenly she looked crestfallen. "But I know so little about this, I can't really talk about it."

I suggested it might have something to do with the actual tale of St George's slaying of the dragon, and went through the tale in my mind. The terrible fanged monster devouring beautiful maiden after beautiful maiden, until finally the king's daughter is led out to the beast. Then out of nowhere rides a youth on a white horse, his cloak billowing in the wind. The youth stabs the dragon through the eye and blinds it. The king's daughter then binds the dragon with her girdle and the beast is mysteriously tamed. Together they lead it to the market where St George then kills it before a crowd of pagan townfolk, and so doing immediately converts them to Christianity.

"Yes, it's also an allegory," she said. "But to me it's like a dream, I can't fit it with myself."

I knew the feeling having once scoured a Buddhist Wheel of Life in Dharmasala, north India, for similar clues. How earnestly I wanted to believe that these bright images carried a crucial message for me personally. It was followed by dogged attempts at 'understanding' them — without success.

Standing with Tamuna before that cross I wondered suddenly if I hadn't given up the quest too quickly? For after Dharmasala came that flight back from Delhi to Europe (via Moscow), and its realisation I could no longer 'think' my way out such dilemmas; indeed, thinking itself might be a dilemma all of its own. There at 10,000 metres I'd decided the only solution had been to attack those huge chunks of trapped consciousness with raw experience, and thus resumed travel.

Looking at Tamuna's puzzled face I realised she approached that icon of our own English St George, 'Protector of the Realm,' with a good deal more hope than I'd ever been able to muster before him in England.

She spoke again, with just a trace of guilt. "You know I think I love St George. I know I shouldn't because it's really worship." Then she said more shyly: "But you know I also feel for that poor king's daughter."

After the treasury Tamuna had one more room to show me.

"You must see Pirosmani," she said more brightly.

(Left) Niko Pirosmani's painting 'A Tatar Cameleer.'
(Right) Section of his 'Feast with Organ Grinder, Datiko Zemel' (1906).

We skirted the museum's Iranian rooms with their fine paintings of 19th century Persian courtesans and dancers — costumes strikingly similar to those of the dancers I would see later at the Pioneer Palace — then up the stairs to two low-ceilinged rooms filled by bright, childlike paintings — the largest space given over to any one painter in Georgia.

"This is Niko Pirosmani," she said. "He's a Primitivist or Naive-Style artist."

Across the walls stood strange, bold animals and scenes of 19th century Georgia, with men in national dress drinking horns raised, picnicking amid wineskins and great spreads of food. Every part of his pictures, the food, the animals the human beings, were presented in the same stark lack of detail.

"I love these pictures," Tamuna said in one of her mysterious fits of enthusiasm.

I began to realise, that for all the gloom and sadness in her life, she found genuine companionship, even a kind of friendship, among these icons and works of art. No wonder she wanted to take me to this museum.

She led me straight across the room to a painting simply called *Janitor*. It presented a bearded old man holding a staff. He wore an apron round his waist and a cap jammed on his head as he stared blankly out of the canvas, like a tramp kitted out in a uniform he didn't understand. The writing on the Georgian old-timer's cap was in Russian, but his face was anything but.

"We know very little about Pirosmani's life," Tamuna said gazing at the painting. "He seems to have left almost no mark at all. Nobody knows where he was born, where he travelled. He is said to have lived in woodsheds, under stairs, and made all his own paints. I think of him as a silent man, a kind of holy man who just painted and nothing else. A real poet. You know when they found him dead, nobody even knew he was a painter."

I could see how Pirosmani played a role in her life almost equivalent to Queen Tamar. Yet I found her enthusiasms echoed in most Georgians I met. Pirosmani drew almost universal praise not so much as Georgia's only significant modern painter, but more due to the qualities of bold childishness and innocence in his work and life.

Tamuna produced a book of his work — borrowed from the gallery guard — and held open a page showing a very strange picture: a giraffe, painted completely wrong, its neck far too short and thick, its head disproportionately large and coloured in black and white.

"This is my favourite picture," she said. "It's a great pity it's not here in this museum. Pirosmani painted many animals without ever seeing them; he just loved the idea of the giraffe. He was like those icon painters of the 14th century: he saw with big eyes, he felt everything and tried to paint the myths inside them."

In her words I could sense the artist, now 70 years after his death, slowly transforming into legend. The Georgian film director Eldar Shengelaya had already begun the process in his excellent film *Pirosmani*, a depiction of his life in the same style of colourful unsophistication as his paintings.

Standing surrounded by the artist's work I too found myself taken by his bright, guileless pictures. Like odd remarks by a child they seemed to cast an immensely simple but clear light on what they touched. Tamuna pointed to another of her favourites, a huge, hairy camel with a Mona Lisa-like smile, standing solemnly above his owner, a Tatar trader. The two were thinly connected by a string. The picture seemed to beg the question, who controlled who? Did the big animal emotions rule the nation of Georgia or the smaller guiding force of the man?

I asked Tamuna what kinds of subjects she thought Pirosmani might want to paint today.

"I don't think Pirosmani could exist today," she said plainly.

*

The gift from God

I was staying at the house of my Georgian friend Ilia and his family. Their set-up was typically Caucasian, with grandparents, parents, parent's sister and children all living together in one large, antique-crammed flat. Ilia invited me to stay at the drop of a hat and, at a second drop of the hat, re-arranged the whole household on my behalf. The sister moved out of her room, which became mine, and the kitchen geared itself up to handle the 'guest.' But, unlike most household kitchens around the world, my vegetarianism was greeted with a casual nod — instead of the usual protestation and panic. Georgia's 3,000 year history had not limited itself just to rebellion and Rustaveli.

On my second evening, a dinner was prepared that matched any I've eaten. In a nation that six months later would initiate rationing for certain foods, and a year later have the West handing it food aid as it would a Third World state, Georgia stood mysteriously well-stocked.

No sooner had I finished one delicious and unknown item, than another just as delicious and unknown appeared. After that ominous beginning with the 'Kazbegi potato,' the nation now unlocked another of its secrets.

In between mouthfuls I attempted to note down the dishes before they disappeared. The first and most common was *khachapuri*, an item of specialty in every Georgian household.

The Georgian table — 'khachapuri' (front right), 'pkhali' (front left and centre), 'satsivi' (left centre), 'khinkali' (top right) & drinking horn (held in hand)

A distinctive bread of unleavened dough wrapped around cheese and baked into round flat tablets or shallow pies. A staple in Georgia for centuries, and a truly portable meal.

"A toast," Ilia then pronounced solemnly, and the whole table waited in silence as he filled everyone's glass to the brim. "To our friendship," he said rising to his feet and gesturing at me to also stand. "I hope with all my heart yours is a deeply enriching stay with us in Tbilisi. That our personal friendship will grow and that you will come to love Georgia. That you will find everything you want while you're here and you will return to England to bring the friendship between our two countries closer."

He then downed his glass in one gulp. Covering my embarrassment I did the same — the correct response. The tradition of 'friendship,' as expounded by Rustaveli, still held its central course in Georgian daily life. The guest was, in the chivalric sense, 'a gift from God,' even to my liberal doctor friend Ilia, lover of Japanese electronic goods, Pink Floyd and the Grateful Dead.

Like most foreigners, at first I found this tradition awkward. But by the end of a fifth visit to Georgia I

Pigs' heads on sale in the Tbilisi main market. The pig's head is a symbol for the 'tamada' or toastmaster at the Georgian table.

came to enjoy this formalised opportunity to express affection or deep, underriding emotion. As one Georgian friend asked me after returning from London, "where in your culture are the moments every day to speak about your important friendship, your serious thoughts, your deep hopes?"

I couldn't think of any.

"Be careful," he warned cheerfully, "you'll become too sophisticated!"

He then went on to admit this old Georgian tradition of speech-making via a 'tamada' or toastmaker, could sometimes overwhelm the meal; that their glowingly emotional speeches occasionally drowned out most normal social behaviour. I told him the tale of a West German friend who once arrived at a Georgian's house for a sumptuous feast, only to find every time he reached out to put something on his plate somebody proposed a toast. He said he spent so much of the meal standing up and sitting down, he arrived back at his hotel starving and had to beg the kitchen for food.

But at Ilia's this was never a problem. In fact the reverse. My neighbours at the table kept slipping new items of food onto my plate. I speared a piece of what looked like white meat with my fork, held it up inquiringly.

"*Sulguni* — roasted cheese from the mountains. Eat it!" I was told.

I did so and found it delicious. I was then told Georgia produced numerous cheeses in its mountain regions — at least as many varieties as there were tribes (*katazeli* is one I recommend). But my stomach had already reached overload. I asked my hosts to teach me the word I was to find the most useful on all subsequent trips — *kmara!* the Georgian for 'enough!' On this occasion it only produced hoots of laughter and more exotic vegetable pates thrust my way. Excellent combinations of aubergines, carrots, beetroots, fennel, ground walnuts and peppers. On another occasion I managed to pin down the generic name for these patés — *pkhali* — my favourite being a mixture of finely chopped spinach or beetroot leaves, blended with walnut paste, pomegranate seeds and aromatic herbs.

Then finally there came *khinkali*, pasta envelopes stuffed with meat, shaped like little money bags. These received much praise from my neighbours, and kept mysteriously appearing on my plate, along with exhortations that I'd reached the appropriate moment to abandon years of vegetarianism.

In the meantime Ilia, proposed another toast, announcing with all the gravity of a priest, "to the cook . . ." As a male I rose to my feet and downed in one gulp another full glass of delicious Kvanchkara red wine. Sitting down again I complained that such a fine wine should be sipped, not instantly drained.

But Ilia simply replied: "Don't worry, we have more . . ." — and immediately another bottle was produced, opened and my glass refilled to the brim.

As the bottles came and went it almost seemed that the meal in Georgia became an excuse simply to open as many bottles as possible. I asked about the wine's point of origin.

"Stalin's favourite," Ilia replied, not answering my question. I asked again.

"It's from Kvanchkara!" He looked at me amazed, then explained nearly all Georgian wines bore the name of their village of origin — this one in West Georgia.

On another occasion Ilia and his wife took me out to the Aragvi Restaurant beside the Mtkvari, for yet more gastronomic experience. But nothing I tasted in any Tbilisi restaurant compared with the cooking of his family. Eight years later the restaurants of New Georgia set about rectifying this fact and a few are now quite superb. I also like to experiment in some of the new 'ethnic' Georgian restaurants that give the dishes of other nations (like China) a curious but delicious Georgified slant.

At the Aragvi, the table beside ours had been laid for another party. At the head of the table sat another remarkable dish, right out of an Arthurian banquet — a grinning piglet's head on a silver platter. I asked Ilia to explain this delicacy.

"It's not for eating," he said emphatically.

"What's it for then?" I asked.

"The pig is for the *tamada*," he said, then reached over to top up my sixth glass of Georgian champagne.

"Hey Pete, why you're not drinking?" he asked.

The future belongs to us

Over successive visits to Georgia I began to detect the presence of a new brand of young Georgian growing up within the society. One enormously different to anything before and yet fully familiar to us in the West. It had something to do with a alliance between personalised ambition and a liberalisation of traditional ideas of nationalism, chivalry and manners. The secret of its success — if one could call it that — grew out of Georgia's well maintained school of rebellion.

My first meeting with Manana took place in London, a sure sign of her membership into this new clan of the independent citizen. For, at the age of 24 she'd managed to engineer this trip entirely by herself.

"Tell me how can I help your visit to Tbilisi," were her first words to me in Tbilisi — she spoke excellent English which always homed in straight to the point.

I mentioned a desire to meet people of her age and see more of the renowned Georgian dance. I'd recently heard Georgian traditionalists criticise the work of the Georgian State Dance Company — one of the country's chief cultural exports — as a sensationalised version of former indigenous dances, yet I knew these dances still touched on many qualities of the old unified culture.

Young Georgian dancer at the Pioneer Palace, Rustaveli Avenue

"OK, I'll arrange it," she said almost before I'd stopped speaking. "I'll pick you up tomorrow lunchtime."

Although more or less the same age as Tamuna, the similarity between the two girls ended here. While Tamuna watched and listened helplessly to the events taking place all around her, Manana effected them; in her case bombarding Tbilisi with a sparkling, green-eyed energy and ambition. She arrived at Ilia's house driving her mother's car, its back seat ready-crammed with girlfriends of her age. "We're going to a restaurant now," she announced and followed it, as always, by a disarming smile. "It's a place where we go," she gestured to her friends in the back seat and promptly raced the Lada across the city as lawlessly as any Georgian man.

The London Hotel at the turn of the century — where Knut Hamsun stayed. Now it is flats. Behind is Alexander Park, and behind that the dome of the Caucasian Army Church, destroyed to make room for the Soviet State Government Building.

As we walked down the steps into a smart pre-Revolutionary building I asked what class of people frequented this café.

"It's a café for lonely people," she smiled enigmatically.

As I rightly guessed, Manana herself didn't suffer this affliction.

"I'll be meeting my boyfriend later," she said at the table. Then leaning forward added in a conspiratorial voice: "But you mustn't tell anyone. Not even your hosts. You see my parents don't know; they won't allow me to have a boyfriend, especially not this one and we have to meet secretly. My parents think I'll be with you all morning."

I promised not to tell, and glancing around the room saw groups of girls and boys gathered at separate tables, huddled over tea or coffee, dark secret looks flashing round the room. Many of the girls had plastered themselves with make-up in a fashion that preferred warlike dashes of cherry blusher across the cheeks. Their ages varied between 17 and perhaps 25, yet all wore the clothing of women twice their age in Europe — interlinking gold chain belts and below-the-knee dresses. The boys also presented themselves smartly in new black-market jeans and clean-cut jackets. The familiar sound of Madonna, the Pet Shop Boys, throbbed from the expensive Sony sound system amidst the intense, fizzing electricity of teenage sexuality.

A full plate of cheese *khinkali* then landed before me unordered. I protested to Manana I'd only just eaten, or rather fended off as gallantly as I could, another huge and delicious lunch at Ilia's.

"Don't worry, they're very good here," she replied, refusing to hear the word 'no.' She then focused her eyes on me ready for another revelation in the romantic conspiracy, but her voice only increased in volume. Suddenly I had the distinct impression Manana knew foreigners found this type of story particularly fascinating, and also several of her middle-class friends found it correspondingly shocking.

"You mustn't tell anyone this, but I'm going to run away from home with my boyfriend. In two months we're getting married. You know I'm fed up with this secret life. Now some people are spreading rumours I'm pregnant. It's not fair because I'm a virgin."

The last word, spoken so brazenly several of her girlfriends around the table blushed visibly.

"What will you do then?" I asked.

"When everyone and my parents have quietened down, I'll come home again," she said calmly.

It struck me that Manana, at the age of 24 went through the same rebellion most European girls undergo at 16 or 17. It also struck me several of these faces

Teenage girls practising the 'samaya' dance

around our table would probably never go through this troubled stage; slipping easily into the well worn tradition of Georgian courtship and marriage. But Manana's future proceeded apace, her green eyes shining with all the determination of new youth. She'd entered the glorious fray against dogged traditionalism, Soviet or Georgian. Like a female St George she would slay the old dictatorship of her family who still tried — heaven knows why — to find her the right man.

I glanced at those other young faces in the café, all fully conversant with the rhythms of British rock music, the new siren call of pan-culturalism. Had not the rebellion of these Mananas, like that of the Georgian nation as a whole, finally entered its adolescence? The brimming qualities of rock narcissism and 'independence' was dropping onto the Tbilisi streets like manna from heaven. By the late 1990s I would even see mini-skirts on Rustaveli Avenue.

"What will happen after you're home?" I asked her.

"Oh it will be alright. I'm getting a job in television," she said casually. "Excuse me a second, I've just seen a friend."

As she hurried over to another table, I glanced at the expressions on her friends' faces. Throughout Manana's confessions I'd watched them vacillate between outrage, jealousy, and pride. When she stepped away from the table one of the more smartly dressed girls turned to me and said — as if to reassure me. "Not all of us believe in what Manana does."

But the moral disapproval in her voice was belied by the envy in her eyes.

That afternoon Manana fulfilled the second part of my request by taking me to view Georgian dance in the making — this time by the generation rising up beneath hers.

"I'm taking you to the Pioneer Palace on Rustaveli Avenue," she explained. "It's where we go to learn our hobbies."

The Pioneers were then the Soviet equivalent to a large and compulsory brigade of Boy and Girl Scouts, and one of the rare Soviet institutions then with wide popularity. After the 1917 Revolution, with the Tsar and the Governor of the Caucasus sent packing, the Governor's elegant Renaissance style Palace (built in 1807) on Rustaveli Avenue (then called Golovinsky Avenue), had been turned over to those who would build the bright new future of Georgia, its Pioneers. To me it always represented that richly artistic period between 1890 and 1922 when Russia poured its money and culture into Tbilisi. When hotels like the Majestic (later the Tbilisi), and the London (by the Dry Bridge, now an apartment block) housed artists from all over Europe. Knut Hamsun stayed in the London during his incognito visit to Tbilisi in 1899. The experiences he gained served as the basis of his book *In a Fairy Land*, and a play *The Queen Tamar*. Apparently he never found happiness in Tbilisi, but judging from his room (which I later visited), a pokey narrow cell on the top floor, his opportunities had been limited.

Commanding a central position on the avenue the Lada now zeroed in on the Pioneer Palace's grand entrance like a guided missile. We arrived in time to see dozens of blue uniformed boys and girls streaming in and out of the former palace. Inside I found it pleasantly converted into a school with its central courtyard dominated by a real Soviet sputnik suspended from a steel arm, to inspire the Yuri Gagarins of tomorrow.

I asked Manana which of all the 'hobbies' taught here carried the most popularity.

"I think, certainly, traditional Georgian dance," she said, and her friends backed her up.

In confirmation we found ourselves surrounded by dozens of excited 15 and 16 year olds, freshly transformed into princes and princesses of Georgia's beloved bygone years. With squeals, giggles and shouts the boys adjusted their silver cartridge belts, the girls straightened their jewelled head-dresses, ready for the acrobatics in one of the world's most energetic dance traditions.

Following the sound of determined drumming we stepped into a long mirrored dance studio just in time to see several red-tunicked male legs fly up into the air, then land accompanied by loud war cries. I watched these boys' burning eyes as they climbed shoulder upon shoulder to create a human pyramid, then just as rapidly leap back down to the floor.

The brooding sexual energy of the café had here transformed itself into vigourous gymnastics. We stood pressing ourselves against the wall as in the next dance older boys in bright blue tunics suddenly unsheathed their daggers and began hurling them, one after the other, into the wooden floor. Several failed to bite into the wood and skidded across the floor to where the audience would normally have sat. As a result, when the Georgian State Dance company performed in London's Queen Elizabeth Hall in 1996, the management left the front row of the stalls empty.

"This is a dance designed to prepare them for the enemy," Manana said. But who could miss the connection between these wild dervishes and the kamikaze nationalist cars screeching down Rustaveli Avenue?

In the next dance the tempo of the drums picked up, the passion rose, dancers yelled, separated into pairs, then grasping long cutlasses twirled round and around, clashing the blades together on every turn until the sparks flew between their faces.

"This dance is called *mtiuluri*," Manana shouted. "It's from the mountains."

Then one of the group broke free, dropped onto his knees right before me and, spinning like a top, sank dagger after quivering dagger into the parquet a few inches from my feet.

Manana grinned at me. "Are you afraid?" she asked.

I felt it could have been her in the black tunic hurling the knives.

Then quite suddenly the atmosphere of the performance completely changed as girls entered the dance. They glided out across the parquet in a smooth motion of white floor-length dresses and slim figures. Their presence drifted into the male frenzy like swans whafting into a hurricane. They appeared not so much to dance as to float across the stage. The long pig-tails of their costumes dangling to their waists, hardly swayed. The contrast between these graceful, passive females and the coiled springs of male aggression, could hardly have been greater. I sensed something here of the idealised, well defined roles of men and women in Georgian society. Enormous activity set against queenly tranquillity; the pre-set roles that the Soviet urbanisation of Georgia only slightly ruffled, but now, as Tamuna sensed, might disappear in the course of a single generation.

In the next dance three girl-queens glided around the room wearing long headscarves and floor-length dresses covered in imitation pearls, rubies, emeralds. On each serene head perched a coloured crown also covered in gems. The girls floated across the boards like three separate incarnations of Queen Tamar, gradually spiralling into the centre to merge into a single, six-armed, rotating queen. The costumes and movements seemed entirely oriental, the head-scarves similar to those of the Persian court. I asked Manana what she could tell me of this dance;

"It's called *samaya*," she said but knew no more.

Again I sensed the profound blending of Near Eastern or Muslim motifs with this highly Christianised culture. Later, when I questioned an authority on Georgian dance he vigorously denied any 'Muslim' links with the *samaya* dance and connected these gracious spiralling dances with the circle dances of the mountain region of Svaneti, in West Georgia. But my own untrained eyes told me otherwise.

I asked Manana if she still danced.

"Yes, of course," she said. "But not like this, just ordinary dancing at the discos. This takes a lot of practice." Then she suddenly added: "But I sing." Her eyes lit up. "Would you like to hear us?"

I'd already heard several of the male Georgian choirs and their robust polyphonic harmonies, but never the women. I asked her what she meant by "sing."

She smiled. "I will arrange a party; then you will see."

As I suspected, this new opportunity to organise a dinner also provided a chance for another evening with her boyfriend. But this time I would meet him too.

When Manana's boyfriend arrived to pick me up the car's bonnet shimmered with heat. He grasped my hand firmly but looked away as we shook. A lean, handsome man, with dangerous eyes and a hoarse, mafioso voice that knew no English. His eyes didn't so much look at the world as flash at it. His movements and actions were swift, succinct and restless, abrim with the emotion of Georgia's semi-legitimate underworld.

The party would take place in one of the new housing tracts on the outskirts of Tbilisi, and we immediately shot off across the city towards it. He drove with one arm on the window-ledge, the other holding a cigarette, every so often taking both hands off the wheel to make a point or light another cigarette. His words and actions seemed the result of sudden deep convictions. But unlike Manana, the good middle-class rebel, I sensed this boy could very easily go too far.

As the Lada greased down the avenues I noticed the central dividing line flicking past the car on either side. He drove into any empty space on the road if it speeded our passage. A traffic-light turning red meant only slow down slightly, as the way ahead may contain more traffic. 'No Entry' signs were interpreted as two-way traffic. At one roundabout, when a traffic policeman gestured us to halt and let the other traffic pass, he simply ignored him. The furious officer waved his baton aggressively instructing us to pull over, but Manana's boyfriend continued on talking casually as if nothing had happened.

It made me remember Marika's remark about Georgian driving: "My grandfather always used to say Georgians drive their cars like they used to drive their horses; but they forget that unlike the horse the car has no brain."

As for the speed limit along the Mtkvari embankment, speed limits were plainly a Soviet invention, most Georgians simply drove as fast as the road-surface would allow, and preferably faster than anyone else.

On the Mtskheta dual-carriageway he achieved such a manic velocity we missed our turning. But instead of continuing on to the next turn off, he simply U-turned and drove straight back down the fast lane toward the on-coming traffic to the missed exit. Cars came racing towards us lights blazing and horns blaring, deliberately skimming past only inches away.

"Are you afraid Peter?" Manana asked excitedly from the back seat.

"No," I lied. To admit it would only be to encourage this madness.

But for her the performance amounted to sheer delight and I began to imagine the marriage to be. She, queen of her kingdom of disobedience and ambition, joining with the prince of the underworld, living fast, dying young, suffused with mischief and honour. Manana had fallen for a hero of Georgia's warrior class, he with one of its new westernised heroines. But I decided this urban jousting between Ladas had to be a weaknesses in Georgian chivalry — road death statistics in Tbilisi were and are quite horrific.

By now the red-hot Lada clattered up a dirt-track toward a thicket of new, unfinished concrete highrises. We all had to dismount due to the terrible state of the access roads. Walking across the mud, looking up at the ghostly white towers rising out of this wasteland I began to feel the surreal quality of these young Georgians' lives. Their days and nights spent in glorious, terrible deeds one after the other. The quests for honour, independence and self-gain. Waving the flags for independence, driving their cars just like horsemen in the Georgian army hundreds of years ago, discovering an ecstasy in resisting the 'Reds' hunger-striking, refusing their compulsory Soviet military service (80 per cent at the time), disobeying every petty Soviet law they could find. In between these raids on the Soviet world they returned to these 20-storey concrete cliffsides, briefly to recharge their batteries before launching out on the next mission.

But this car ride more than any other event, gave a clear foretaste of what lay in store for Georgia in its first war-filled years of independence — perhaps also explaining why, when the mafia briefly took over Georgia in 1993-94, the main armed group called themselves the Mkhedrioni ('Horsemen'). The mountain horse of these young James Deans had become the BMW, the lance the Kalashnikov. It was no surprise that Manana's boyfriend would become one of the chief knights.

Yet inside that cliffside, order and harmony found themselves temporarily restored within the table-ritual. Carried out no less solemnly here than at any middle-class Georgian table, our *tamada* pronounced the toast proudly and with dignity; the food was spread before us and shortly afterwards, true to their promise, the girls launched into song.

I listened in amazement as they broke into a complicated three and four part harmonies, as easily as if they practised every day. At the end of the first song, a Russian ballad, I asked if they could perhaps sing me a "typical

Georgian folk song." They all laughed and proceeded to sing full-heartedly almost without stopping for the next hour and a half.

I sat before those piles of food enchanted, not eating, thinking I'd just hit it lucky with this particular group of gifted girls. Yet a few days later at another party, this time among students from Tbilisi's Foreign Languages Institute, I found myself amazed again. This other group told me none had ever received a singing lesson; that they sang purely for pleasure.

After one full-throated song, in which heads were thrown back and all shyness overcome I asked for a translation.

"Oh it's in Mingrelian, we don't know," they shouted back, whereupon they launched themselves into a Beatles hit followed by *It's a Long Way to Tipperary*, which ended in a fit of laughter as nobody knew more than the first two lines. But everyone remembered the melody and could create a three-part harmony for any tune I named.

The men just sat round the table and listened appreciatively, never joining in. One of the girls then explained that several of them sang particularly well. When I asked why they didn't join in, she said: "In traditional Georgian singing, the men and women never sing together, always separately."

A Georgian male choir singing 'Shen khar Venakhi' ('You are a Vineyard') during the Soviet period, in St Nicholas' Church, then converted to a theatre

I remember leaving that evening wondering how much longer this polarisation between the sexes would last. A single generation full of Mananas could wipe it out completely; but would they really take everything with them as Tamuna feared? The looks of enormous enjoyment on everyone's faces in that room, suddenly made me think not.

Sveti-Tskhoveli Cathedral, Mtskheta, over the Mtkvari river

8

Mtskheta

I'd come to the former Georgian capital of Mtskheta with Tamuna; it would be our last trip together. She said she had two friends in the town to visit, one from her university days, and the other . . . "You probably think I'm sentimental," she said, "but I feel its cathedral is a kind of older relation — I always learn something from it."

For the 20 minute drive up the Mtkvari river from Tbilisi, a taxi hadn't been difficult to find. The problem came in the driver's baffling refusal to accept my money.

"*Ara*," the severe Georgian face responded to every diminishing bundle of roubles held before him.

"*Ara*," to the packs of Marlboro, then the rouble's parallel currency and in Moscow an absolute necessity for taxis.

"Come on, let's leave," Tamuna repeated. "You're insulting him. The ride was his gift to you."

But my upset British rules of behaviour froze me to the seat. How could the normal financial transaction between strangers become a gift? Overcome by guilt, I asked myself what had I done to deserve this? Then why could *I* never be so generous? Deeply touched it seemed my only way out of this moral dilemma would be to give in return — but what? I carried nothing but my pen, notebook, cameras and film. Tamuna shuffled awkwardly outside.

"Let's go!" she said with unusual insistence.

Hoping a second *faux pas* would forgive the first, I reached into my breast pocket and handed him my 79p British Museum pen and opened the car door. He accepted the gift with a sharp nod, engaged the gears noisily and roared off in a cloud of dust. Tamuna gave me one of her rare smiles.

"You English don't understand generosity, do you!"

I admitted in this case I didn't.

"He liked us. He wanted to show his friendship back," she said. "In Georgia we often do it — it's far more important than money. It was his pride to refuse your money, and I think he was right."

Confused at my own reaction I confessed he may have been, and wondered why the English almost never expressed affection in this way.

But Tamuna had already turned away and was looking up at the cathedral keep's crenellated walls. I followed her gaze. Over the wall the giant 11th century basilica of the cathedral lifted into the sky, far more my idea of a 'cathedral' than the others I'd seen in Georgia. Closer up it gave the impression of the usual Byzantine-style Georgian church but placed in an enlarger, or the people streaming towards it shrunk down to Lilliput sizes.

"To me Mtskheta is still the capital of Georgia," Tamuna said enigmatically. Responding to my quizzical look she said: "I don't think you know the history of this area."

But I did have some idea. I knew Mtskheta had been the capital of Kartli from the third century BC to the fifth century AD. That this nexus of two valleys served as a major cult and religious centre for many centuries before this, with Persian, Zoroastrian, Hittite and possibly even Sumerian influences. That more pagan temples and shrines centred on this place that in any other part of Georgia.

Looking around I noticed the surrounding hills dotted with churches each one almost certainly claiming the site of a pre-Christian cult. I also noticed how this cathedral seemed to dominate the crucial triangle of land between the confluence of Georgia's two main rivers, the Mtkvari and Aragvi. The cathedral's present day name, Sveti-Tskhoveli (Cathedral of the Life-Giving Pillar), could hardly be more pagan — deriving from the legend of the seven pillars cut from a sacred Lebanese cedar growing on this site to make the first Christian church. The seventh pillar had contained magical properties, exhuding a holy liquid that cured diseases, and at one time floating up from the ground (as depicted in the main icon of the church). The myths, memories and rich religious presences of Georgia dripped off every cornice and cliffside in this valley. The mountain overlooking the town, Mt Kartli, still housed the spirit of King Kartlos, the legendary father of the Georgian people and claimed descendant of Noah's son Japheth. According to Strabo in the first century BC, the area of today's Cathedral precinct contained the palace of the former Iberian Kings, and close by a copper statue of the Zoroastrian fire god Armazi (the Georgian version of the Persian god Ormazd), flanked by numerous gold and silver idols. Other reports tell of a colossal pagan statue of Armazi (possibly the same one) dominating the summit of Mt Kartli. The statue had long gone but its Christian replacement still survived, perched high on a rock above the Aragvi river — the sixth century Jvari Church (Church of the Cross). The rounded dome of this church stood up like an erect nipple, 150 metres above Mtskheta, ready to be suckled by the re-invigorated Christian eye of independent Georgia.

As we stepped into the cathedral precinct, Tamuna crossed herself solemnly. Before us the cathedral lifted its arches from the middle of an open lawn, like a towering gothic ship moored in a green harbour. Beneath its massive stone cupola and almost windowless stone walls, a stream of tiny Georgian figures poured in and out of the entrance, like shift-workers in a factory of the emotions. For me stepping inside its cavernous, vaulted belly was like descending from the 20th century to the time of Armazi. Tiny lights flickered in the darkness against luminous icons, feet and voices bustled all around in the gloom. It took some time for my eyes to adjust. When everything came clear we stood before an elaborate white marble iconostasis, where I noticed the floor patched with irregular slabs of stone, engraved with crests.

"These mark the tombs of former Georgian kings," Tamuna explained. "The royal blood of our Bagrat family is buried under this cathedral here, and also Jesus's crucifixion robe — which is what St Nino came looking for when she bought our faith to Georgia.

"Everything is in this cathedral," she added quietly.

I began to understand why so many Georgians visited the building. They could feel the heartbeat of their homeland throbbing reassuringly just beneath this floor. The Bagrat dynasty had produced Georgia's kings from AD 888 right up until the Russians expelled the royal family in the 19th century. Above the slabs the pious faces, old and now young came to light candles and honour the memory of their last Georgian sovereign.

I remembered this place three years later during the height of the monachist movement when motions were made for the restoration of the Georgian monarchy after 200 years, I visited the first in line to the throne, Prince George Bagration at his 'Villa Georgia' in Puerto Banus, southern Spain. I found him a charming, affable man, eagerly learning Georgian — never having visited his blood nation. Although his childhood and later life had mixed itself almost exclusively between Italy, France and Spain, his mountain blood still surfaced in his career — as former Formula Three driving champion of Spain. In the end Georgia's civil war and the ambitions of several other pretenders, eclipsed any hopes of a triumphant restitution.

I remarked to Tamuna on the number of young people among the crowds — many more than in churches I'd visited in Russia.

"There's a religious revival in Georgia," she replied. "Churches and monasteries are opening up, being reconsecrated everywhere. Young people always used to come to church in Georgia to rebel against Komsomol (the Communist Party youth league, abolished in April 1990), but the religion stayed with them. Now with independence so close, they come even more."

As she spoke I found my eyes straying towards the south wall and an old fresco peeping out of the Russian whitewash (19th century Russia ordered the whitewashing of most Georgian church interiors) — almost certainly a Vision of the Apocalypse. I walked towards it.

Recognising my direction Tamuna said, "Yes, I love this fresco too. It's a 17th century Apocalypse, and I think if it were fully visible it would be one of the most important frescoes in Georgia. Look how peacefully they painted the scene."

It came across certainly as one of the more sublime versions of the great debacle, although parts of the picture had been lost. I saw human headed lions, friendly sea monsters, cherubs puffing inside clouds, dancers, lute players, kings and bugle-blowing knights. To the right a Wheel of Apostles radiated out of the central Christ figure. I asked Tamuna if she'd ever studied the psychological symbolism of this cryptic Christian event.

"No," she said. "I want to very much, but it's impossible. But I like to come to stand here because I feel everything they wanted to take away from us is still there." ('They' referred to the Communist Party.) Then she glanced at me. "Is that why you're interested in Georgia? You want to see how much can survive our politics?"

For the first time she voiced a curiosity about my motives, advancing an unusually percipient suggestion for someone who had never left the Soviet block. I remembered when the first stream of post-glasnost Westerners arrived in the USSR, many Soviets had been baffled why we wanted to visit their crippled economy, save perhaps to see Red Square, St Basils, or the Caucasus mountains. But when the tourists kept returning, and Sothebys began selling modern Soviet Art for five figure sums, some cottoned on that their culture possessed some quality unavailable in the West. I remember one Russian with almost no interest in art arriving in London and informing me: "I can organise the best art of Moscow's finest artists to be exported to London for the English to buy." I asked him to describe this art, to explain what it had that might appeal to the Western public. "We Russians have something you've lost—" he answered boldly, "—and you need it, you want to buy it." Then he added: "if you organise the venue I'll give you 10 per cent."

But Tamuna's sensibility had taken this several steps further. She already guessed that the Soviet (or Georgian) 'forbidden culture' would quickly exhaust its charm in Western eyes; that the curiosity we visitors expressed was partly a curiosity about our own culture; that we used the Soviet world as an inverted mirror to see ourselves, and in some cases as a means of boosting our self-esteem at their expense.

It seemed a great shame that people like Tamuna, whose intelligence and insight outshone these jet-setting officials so many times over, still hardly dared to present their 'fairy tales' to their friends.

As we made our way around the cathedral's icons she told me we would then visit her friend "just for a moment" — but I declined already knowing that under the protocols of Georgian hospitality, it was impossible to enter someone's house for "just for a moment." It would end up as a four hour drinking and toasting festival.

Making the excuse I needed to take some photos, I suggested instead we meet in an hour, after she'd seen her friend.

"I won't visit my friend," she said emphatically.

But I insisted, telling her I needed to be alone while photographing. Eventually she nodded, and a tiny flicker of hurt crossed her eyes.

As I turned away toward a burning blast of sunlight at the entrance, I was struck by a wave of guilt. A feeling of taking unfair advantage in my privileged position as drop-in voyeur on her life. Did I really deserve all the time and attention she gave in return?

Half an hour later, queuing up alone at the Cathedral's souvenirs kiosk hoping to replace my pen, I heard a Georgian voice addressing me in a heavy accented, but good English.

"Pentax are good cameras . . ."

I looked into the face of a clean-shaven, long-nosed man in his mid-thirties, apparently addressing my camera, not me.

". . . Could I have a quick look?" he asked.

Making a swift judgement of character I decided it could do no harm and handed him the camera. He turned it over in his hand as if appreciating an antique.

"Very, very nice camera Pentax . . . ," he looked up. "How much do you want?"

My heart sank. "It's not for sale," I said gruffly.

"OK, no problem," he said and handed the camera back with a lopsided grin. "But join us for a toast to our countries — England yes?"

The idea of a glass of wine appealed, and noticing the group of picnicking Georgians spread nearby on the grass, I realised the escape route from hospitality would be easy and accepted his offer. Within seconds that instant quality of friendship, characteristic of nearly all Georgians, had asserted itself. We drank a toast to our respective countries and quickly became embroiled in, as I realised later, a revealing conversation on the new economics about to land on Georgia.

'The Glory of Georgia' 19th century icon featuring the Life-giving Pillar and all of Georgia's saints and martyrs. Painted by Michael Sabinashvili

Guessing his profession might in some way be linked to the small or medium-time mafia (as so many people's were), I bought up the subject of 'I'll do you a favour if you do me a favour' system of Georgian business. What I later came to call 'friendship economics.'

"Yes, I know this system we have now is the Soviet corruption system," he said. "But in Georgia, as you see, we're not poor like the Russians. We know how to use their system better than they do. When we have independence then we'll start a better system, more like the West."

"Do you know what our system is?" I asked.

"Yes, it is a normal system, like our black market."

I tried to explain that the international economy was vastly more complicated; and attempted to present some of the more basic ideas, like long-term investment. He started to look puzzled, so I tried another tack.

"The main difference between our economy and yours is we've legalised your corruption. We've made the middleman into an honest broker. We've given him a straightforward percentage."

A crease suddenly appeared on his brow and I saw his mind suddenly imagined his freewheeling profits coming under regulation. He grinned nervously.

"Legal corruption, but that's what we've had in Georgia for the last 70 years! Perhaps we will do things a little different to you in the West." He smiled, put his hand on my shoulder. "Give me your glass!"

I began to feel myself in the hands of what the Georgians call a *merikipe*, or assistant to the *tamada* (toastmaster). The man who fills the glasses, stokes the conversation, but remains sober. Stalin had apparently been one of the finest, and used the spilled-out secrets to orchestrate his coups over his rivals the following day.

But I also detected a gathering incomprehensibility on the part of this *merikipe*. Like so many, he'd spent his life operating within an economy, bypassing the fundamentals of supply and demand. He would never quite understand my explanation without seeing it in operation.

One of the great problems encountered by many Western-Soviet joint-ventures at their start was that many Soviets could not trust a system not based on corruption — ironic as it sounds. It was only because they knew no other system that benefitted them personally. Long-term investment projects that took five years just to make personal profit . . . stretched the imagination too wide. All five year plans still belonged to the state not individuals or companies.

My camera, I rightly suspected, lay beneath all his argument.

"I'll give you 2,000 roubles for that Pentax," he finally said. I told him it didn't even warrant discussion. Yet I could tell that as long as it remained before him, so hope remained. Changing the subject I asked what Georgia would do when, with independence they cut themselves off completely from the Russians, and their subsidised oil, steel, power, technology, etc.

He looked wistfully up toward the Jvari Church.

"It will be hard at first, but we'll succeed—" then he looked back sharply, "—you see, we have the *will*."

I asked about the Russian Army. What would happen when Georgia abandoned this historic protection of its borders against its Muslim foe, the Turks and the Iranians?

He looked back determinedly.

"We are not weak; we will fight if we have to. Besides, the Americans will come to help us."

I told him not to bank on the Americans, but he just shrugged. I could tell this registered as only a minor detail beside the holy grail of independence.

Fortunately I then saw Tamuna approaching and explained I had to go. He looked crestfallen; the camera was about to leave.

"Another drink, another toast!" he bounded back. But I declined. He opened his mouth to make a final offer on my camera, then stopped himself.

"It doesn't matter," he said. "Georgia will soon be trading Pentaxes from Japan," he grinned and shook my hand firmly.

Tamuna found us a ride back to Tbilisi. On the way I found myself remembering a similar financial exchange had by an English friend in Moscow's first free market — Izvamailova Park. Finding a table full of *matrioshka* dolls he asked for the price.

"Fifty roubles each," replied the artist.

"How much if I buy ten?" my friend asked. The artist thought for a second.

"Six hundred roubles," he said.

"Why are they more expensive?" my friend asked baffled.

"Because if you can buy ten, it means you're rich. You can pay more," the artist said. It was a common reasoning then and took some years to change.

I glanced out the window as we passed what looked like a strange picnic area, with tables and benches apparently constructed right next to tombstones. I asked Tamuna to explain.

"It's a cemetery!" she replied, explaining the tables accorded with Georgian and Armenian customs of Easter feasts on the graves of ancestors.

I asked if she could explain this non-Christian ritual.

"It's not a ritual, it's a custom," she said. "We just leave food and wine on the table for the ancestor, that's all."

I asked if this bore any similarity to Mexico's Day of the Dead when spirits were said to return to the earth.

"My mother says she feels she can speak to them on Easter Sunday," she said. "And I suppose when I go, I do have the feeling something is watching me — that I should wear a nice dress, be on good behaviour."

We drove on in silence. Then when the car entered Tbilisi she suddenly turned and asked if I wanted to see her family's grave. "It's in the Vake district, this car is driving right past it."

We asked the driver to drop us there. He agreed and again refused to touch any of my money. This time I accepted gracefully.

Walking through the grand entrance to Vake Cemetery I instantly recognised it from Abuladze's *Repentance*. The film whose pressure for release caused uproar in the Communist Party right up to Politburo level due to its eloquent denouncement of Beria and Stalinism in Georgia. I asked Tamuna if she'd seen it.

"Of course," she replied. "I saw it in 1986, just after it was finished, when you could be put in prison for showing it, even on video." Then a serious expression crossed her face. "I think that film told some of the real truth about Georgia, the truth that's still not being told." Then she brightened. "But it did win six Oscars!" (She confused 'Oscars' with 'prizes').

Walking through that cemetery brought back the film's unforgettable imagery: the opening funeral-service scene for a high ranking Party member, the backhanders even as they paid their last respects, then the moonlit scene of a beautiful woman digging this Stalinist (bearing a remarkable resemblance to Beria) out of his grave. A painful reminder of the bitter suppression of Georgia by Georgians (Stalin, Beria and Orjonikidze were all Georgian), as well as the desperate need to unearth this terrible past, expose its continuance into the present.

Just as in the film, the cemetery immersed us in an ivy-clad atmosphere of mausoleums, tall cypresses, grand tombstones. Tamuna led me down its neat pathways, past the black marble with white plaques, proud mustachioed busts, to a modest tombstone enclosed by its own small fence. Next to it, as at many of the others, stood a small iron table and bench.

"This is my grandfather," she said.

On the gravestone a ghostly white engraving of a man's face looked out of the black slate. On the earth covering the grave lay a couple of small crimson painted eggs. I asked her how they ended up there.

"They're left over from Easter," Tamuna said. "We put them on the earth then."

Tamuna's mood had changed again, appearing calmer. I asked why she'd wanted to come here.

"I like this place, I like the feeling here. People have stopped their lying here," she said. Then she turned to me quite unexpectedly: "And I suppose after this you too will disappear for good back to England."

I didn't know what to say.

We started back for the road and the bus-stop. She began to ask me all about Europe, wanting to know what books were available. Could I possibly send her a copy of Milan Kundera (I'd created a huge obsession just describing his books)?

As we passed the cemetery gates she asked me to describe my home in London. "How far is it from Oxford Street?"

Could I tell her the names of the bookshops on Charing Cross Road? Did I still live at home with my parents (like her)? How much did the London Metro cost?

I sensed the desperation in this last rush of questions, kept bottled-up during all our previous meetings. I answered as best I could, as a trolley-bus slowly rumbled down the hill toward us.

"You will send me that book?" She asked again, and I saw a flicker fear in her eyes. Her brief brush with the West was now to vanish — possibly for ever.

I promised her I would, adding I hoped one day she might come to London and see it for herself. Immediately her eyes lit up as if I'd just handed her the plane ticket. I cursed my stupidity. To casually name the one event she dreamed about more than any other — that she wished for so violently she dared even think about it — was like opening a wound, or offering a prisoner freedom, then saying it was only a joke.

By the time the bus door opened, her face was sad again. She said "goodbye!" in a quick, nervous voice, then stepped back and the door slid shut.

As the trolley-bus drove off those last two words of parting repeated in my mind. They took on the echo of all those millions of quiet, good citizens rarely met by tourists. The dreamy, shy multitude who stayed silent not even daring to hope for a visit to the outside. What a cruel let-down I must have been for Tamuna.

I craned my neck, and through the murky bus window saw her solitary figure standing by the side of the road, not moving, watching the bus out of sight.

9

Gori

Of the many cult shrines dotted around the world, the one focusing on the town of Gori in central Georgia must count as among the more genuinely surreal. A smallish industrial town of about 60,000, 90km west of Tbilisi, Gori is a lethargic, valley community with little to lift its name out of the dust save one crumbling castle and one similarly collapsing legend. Yet to its inhabitants, this legend is all.

Gori's celebrity rests on the sole fact that Joseph Jughashvili (Stalin) uttered his first earthly demands here in 1879, being born on what is now Stalin Street, to the wife of a cobbler. While the rest of the former Soviet world now attempts to wipe his personality cult from the slate of history, so these few local inhabitants are still busily shoring it up.

As we drove through the suburbs I thought of all those senior citizens still showing up at demonstrations across Russia determinedly clutching posters of Stalin. During the huge May 1989 demonstration in Tbilisi, marking the end of the 40 days' mourning, the delegation from Gori arrived carrying large banners of Stalin's face — to be used, of all things, as a defiant symbol of Georgian independence from the Soviet Union. Apparently it took some earnest persuading for their hero to be left out.

To Georgian intellectuals their actions are a deep embarrassment; to officials an annoyance. Yet at the same time the world should never be allowed to forget how this one man from here in the Georgian mid-west completely changed the face of modern politics

Arriving in the large central plaza of Gori, I looked down the triumphal walkways and gardens, all converging on one tiny shack at the bottom, and felt an icicle running down my spine. There, constructed over the two roomed hovel stands a Doric-columned temple to lovingly protect the birthplace of one of history's most ruthless men. Until the 1920s this area of the town contained nothing but ordinary streets and rows of houses, of the kind preserved under the temple; but then came the death of Lenin. During the 30s, as Stalin set about discrediting and eliminating those who criticised his replacement as General Secretary, so the town of Gori underwent a similar redesign. A huge tract of land in the town centre was cleaned of streets, houses and all traces of its former modesty. Several hundred homes were demolished so that one could radiate out from the centre as a glorious representative of the victory of the proletariat. This brick 'hut,' as it is often described, now stands as the town's central axis point, a focus still for tourist mini buses (both local and international) turning left off the Kutaisi highway and racing down into the suburbs.

As I wandered around this monumental open space, worthy of any capital city, I tried to imagine the feelings of the locals in the 1930s who watched their homes knocked down for the sake of this dictator. But of course, in those days Stalin appeared as very much the opposite: the saviour, the great leader lifting the Soviet Union up by its boot straps and thrusting it into the industrial age. They believed in the world dominating masterplan of this visionary politician, understood he had no time for foolish voices of dissent. When the propaganda machinery declared Stalin the Great General who won the Second World War on behalf of the rest of the world, they believed it. To us in the West, now thoroughly wised up to the numbing epoch of totalitarian terror in the 1930s and 40s, the man's name still sends shudders down the spine (as it did many times to me that day). Yet those former inhabitants of Gori reacted to this redevelopment, as they do today — with pride. Indeed,

Stalin vodka — always available in Georgia

when Stalin was removed from the Red Square mausoleum in 1961, and all the USSR's Stalin statues came tumbling down, the people of this town mounted a round-the-clock guard on their Stalin. Thus he remains today, standing before the City Hall, all 17 metres of him.

Deciding I couldn't take all this in at once, I decided to relax for a moment, buy an ice-cream at a stall beside the pullman coach that Stalin used for many of his journeys. As I reached for my money I noticed a stack of cigarette-box sized photographs on the freezer top. As the vendor extracted my ice-cream, I gestured toward them. He took one off the pile and handed it to me with the words: "That's one ice and one Stalin . . ."

I studied my inadvertent purchase: an immaculately groomed, fully mustachioed, black and white photograph of the generalissimo — his chest brimming with medals. Obviously a souvenir of Gori for the town's proud visitors. Slightly taken aback I slipped this pin-up photo, complete with dates, lists of achievements and vital statistics, into my pocket. But the surrealism had only just begun. Behind the small Stalin temple rose another far grander, Stalin temple — the Stalin Museum. With a tall Italianesque bell tower at one end, the structure dominated the plaza more like a Tuscan seminary than the reliquary of a totalitarian dictator. Constructed in 1957, one year after Khrushchev's famous speech denouncing Stalin, this building has to be one of the Soviet world's most extraordinary legacies.

Wandering into the stately marbled vestibule we found a guide and climbed

The Stalin Museum, Gori. Stalin's childhood home was a shoemaker's hovel. It stands in the foreground, preserved under a miniature classical temple.

together up the grandiose, red-carpeted stairway to the first floor (the Georgian second floor). A climb that afterwards seemed as much a descent, down into the rich and terrible fantasy world of a madman.

At the head of the stairs we found ourselves suddenly bathed in a royal blue light pouring in from several church-like stain-glass windows. And there in the glow to meet us stood a life-sized statue of Stalin, carved in a spooky white marble. His gaze personally greeted every entrant from his position now somewhere in the land of the dead. I could hardly believe it. With all the unconsciousness of an act of devotion, the museum designers had moulded into stone the exact presence haunting every alley of the town, and to a lesser extent Georgia — Stalin's ghost.

In the rooms that followed the ghostliness gathered momentum in a presentation, not of the power craving human being, but a glorious God, whose cult rose to such heights during his lifetime that a metropolitan of the Russian Orthodox Church once actually invoked Stalin as 'Our Father.'

To enter the building pre-fed on a Western diet of the man's ignominy, to then find only goodness and righteousness presented, with the monster praised to the skies, is to experience a profound sense of unreality. Here, everything drilled into me as evil or demonic had been twisted around, given a smiling face. On the walls we saw Stalin the model child, the poet, the striving son of a washerwoman who sent him to the local church school hoping he would become a priest (a plan he outdid, but never to her satisfaction), followed by the ideologically pure man.

Our guide, a stern middle-aged woman wielding a metal cane, then doubled the power of messages on the walls by unleashing on us a genuine dose of Stalinist indoctrination. In her greeting she referred not to Stalin, but to our instinct to run away, gesturing to the room's floor, a magnificent parquet with a two metre wide, bright red carpet following the walls.

"Hello, I ask you first to make sure not to deviate off the red carpet," she said in a no-nonsense voice.

Under the extraordinary spell of the museum, her voice seemed to gather disconcerting authority. Suddenly nobody had any intention of straying from the red road. I guessed these instructions were meant as a kind of disciplinary warm-up message from the 'steel' man (the name Stalin, which Jughashvili chose for himself, derives from the Russian word *stal* — 'steel').

As we proceeded round the exhibition, suddenly the sound of a guttural Georgian voice speaking Russian emerged from the walls all around us. With no direct point of origin, the voice almost seemed to originate in our own heads. The museum had a hidden public address system.

"This is the voice of Stalin," announced our guide, then raised her cane toward one of the frames on the wall containing a poem.

"Stalin's early promise as a schoolboy was remarkable. He showed great sensitivity, vision and poetic qualities."

Then raising her voice above the PA she quoted from one of the poems:

> *A rosebud has just blossomed,*
> *to become entangled with the violet next door . . .*

To the background sound of the dictator's harsh voice, I wondered how she failed to notice the massive contradiction between these flowery words and the tone of his voice. By now the icicles were flowing down my back in rivers, bringing with them that horrible sense of being openly lied to by someone whose sensitivity had been so frightened and blunted, it passed on propaganda without a second thought. Her voice, more terrifying than Stalin's, spoke of that enormous submission to authoritarianism that swept the Soviet Union in the 1920s and 30s. By bombarding the population with Communist propaganda, Stalin cleverly stripped away their psychological supports, then crushed all remaining human curiosity (and independence) under the weight of the disappearances, denunciations and uncertainties about one's closest comrades.

I found myself remembering the time of

Souvenir portrait of Stalin from Gori, with lovingly retouched face

my arrest in Novgorod for taking one photograph of a town monument —
the first time the power of this lie really hit home for me. I'd been walking
alone around the city and on an impulse decided to take a snap of the local
district Soviet display. No sooner had I released the shutter than a policeman's
baton had tapped me on the shoulder. He beckoned me to follow him to the
nearby KGB headquarters, without any explanation.

Stepping inside that miniature Lubyanka in Novgorod, two years into
glasnost for doing absolutely nothing, made me realise with a jolt just how
deeply this collective paranoia had installed itself. Inside the entrance I
encountered another white marble statue at the head of a stairway. This time
the face belonged to Lenin, the goatee personality cult so extravagantly
promoted by Stalin to divert attention from the power struggle between
himself and his rivals like Zinoviev, Kamenev and Bukharin. Lenin's eyes had
bored into mine with a single word: 'guilty.' Although I had broken no known
law, I felt guilty.

Not only this, as we walked down the long marble hallway, a hidden public
address system also came to life playing, for some extraordinary reason, a
dreary Wagnerian aria. I felt I'd just entered the same surreal operatic tragedy
as so many other Soviet citizens before me; experienced a small taste of that
huge unreality known to the millions of human beings that never emerged
from such strange moments. My crime had been to walk round a city with a
camera alone. The children of Big Brother Lenin did not enjoy this open
expression of curiosity; theirs had died so long ago.

The officer escorted me to an interview room, sat me down beside an
empty table with nothing but a single red telephone with no dialler, and
locked the door. I sat there alone, chewing over my 'crime,' not knowing what
was planned for me. Half an hour passed then the door swung open and the
same officer stepped in, gestured for me to stand up. I was to be released, he
told me. He then snapped his heels together and saluted me as he would a
senior officer. Pointing at my camera, he shook his head woefully as if to tick
off a wayward child. I walked out into freedom knowing I was being followed,
realising at the same time that lone sharks like myself, wandering though their
cities were like the dark unpermitted thoughts lurking in their own minds.
Allow them a free, unbridled reign and heaven knows what might be
dislodged. (This we can see for ourselves today.)

Back in the museum I soon wearied of our guide's voice extolling Stalin's
virtues and slipped away from the group, preferring to track my own way
among the exhibits. I looked on in growing disbelief as frame after frame
recorded Stalin's departure to Tbilisi's Theological Seminary. Here was his
induction into revolutionary activities, there he conducted Marxist discussion
groups, fomenting labour strikes in major Caucasian towns. They praised him
for his numerous arrests for Bolshevik activities (seven times between 1902
and 1913); without any mention of the strange brevity of his sentences and his
easy escapes (some have speculated Stalin had operated as an agent

provocateur, paid by the Tsarist police). He appeared as a glowing, cheerful revolutionary, a man of the people and the future. It completely ignored his deteriorating ability for intimate relationships (Stalin accused his first son Jacob of being a weakling after he failed in his attempted suicide).

At the glorious 1917 Revolution no mention was made of Lenin's dire warnings about Stalin, or the brutal purges in Georgia after the Bolshevik take-over (carried out on Stalin's instructions by Orjonikidze in 1922). This had led Lenin to describe Stalin as "not merely a genuine social chauvinist, but a coarse, brutish bully acting on behalf of a great power." As for Stalin's major rival Trotsky, he didn't exist. Instead the walls proudly displayed those now infamous retouched photographs with Trotsky and other political opponents transformed into sections of furniture or whitewash. Stalin's sudden rejection of Lenin's New Economic Policy in 1928 in favour of his own state-dominated scheme of collectivisation and five year plans was praised to the skies, even though an estimated ten million peasants are said to have died during the enforced collectivisation of farms, and the terrible famine in the Ukraine. All this not to mention the mass deportations, and creation of labour and concentration camps.

I noticed it also omitted every detail of his vicious witch-hunt after the assassination of his political rival Kirov in Leningrad. This bogus excuse for his new campaign of terror was launched against the very members of the Communist Party that bought him to power (Khrushchev believed Stalin arranged Kirov's death himself). It omitted the 1936 show trials of Zinoviev and Kamenev, their forced and fabricated confessions and deaths.

Churchlike stained glass illuminating the Stalin Museum staircase

The next room devoted itself to extolling Stalin's bravery as the Victorious General defeating the Nazis in World War II. The cabinets were filled with trophies and captured Nazi memorabilia, of course making no mention of the cynical Molotov-Ribbentrop pact made with Hitler in 1939. The museum had turned into a promenade inside an imaginary Soviet Superman's head, passing from great statesmanship, to great victory, to indestructibility itself.

I began to wonder if the museum designers wouldn't attempt to display even this: Stalin as eternal, indestructable, and deathless. Stepping into the next room I realised, with another jolt, they had. For now came a room with no exhibits at all — save one. A sombre velvet-lined chamber with a single

Stalin's death mask in the Stalin Museum — formerly in Red Square, Moscow

white pillar rising up in the middle, out of a well of blackness. Placed on this plinth lay Stalin's death mask, glowing in its own light, like an eternal ambassador from the underworld. A solitary shaft of light burned down from the ceiling to illuminate the features of this old paranoiac, as if from heaven. Finally all the pretences of the museum had dropped away and the cult stood up and revealed itself in all its macabre, cloying adoration.

The bronze mask glinted in the gloom, the face of a weary, self-consumed man, the leader who at the end of his life ordered the arrest of all Kremlin doctors (the only people able to cure him) on charges of attempted murder. Also the man who almost single-handedly inspired one of the most rapid processes of industrialisations in modern history. From the world's fifth most powerful military industrial complex in 1913, the Soviet Union rose to the world's second by 1949, and this after a civil war and the calamitous German invasion. An act he achieved like any clever conjurer, by redirecting the people's attention, swiftly undermining their old beliefs then handing out the crisp new alternative of Soviet Socialism. Then, when the old adage about not fooling all the people all of the time came home to roost, he set into motion his own famous adage, declaring he didn't care to claim people's convictions any more, because convictions could change. Fear, on the other hand, never changed.

At the end of the tour I caught up with the group again in the final room. From their expressions of numbed disbelief I could tell their spirits had already started to flag. All around the room's plain glass cabinets were filled with Stalin's possessions. As the finale our guide tapped a glass cabinet to catch everyone's attention for the last point of information.

"And that," she said pointing to a small white piece of china, "is Stalin's tea-cup!" She folded up her metal pointer. The tour was finished.

"But what about the gulags?" said one of the group nervously. "What about the show trials, Lysenko, the persecution of artists, literature?"

But she had little time for these sophisticated points.

"Stalin made a few mistakes too," she said. "But who doesn't?" I realised she genuinely meant it this way.

Stepping out into the light of day bought with it a strange sense of joy. The warmth of sunshine touching my cheek, hinted that sanity might exist after all, that another wiser system of social organisation could yet be created somewhere in the world under all that blue sky. Their God was dead, and this museum (one hoped) would never bring him back.

As we walked toward the bus I remembered one of our group saying idly: "Somebody should turn that museum into the real Stalin museum, one that tells what really happened."

It took a good meal at the Intourist Hotel and several glasses of excellent local wine to shake off the feeling of having stepped into a black magic evocation of Stalin's spirit. By the time desert arrived, I gathered enough confidence to reach into my pocket for my souvenir of Gori. Looking at it again under that fierce sunlight from the window, his retouched face and all those medals, suddenly looked quite ridiculous (in reality Stalin's face was pock-marked due to a bout of smallpox as a child). Friends in London, I thought, might even find it amusing; and for the first time in my life I thanked God for kitsch.

Vardzia monastery and cave complex. In May 1998, another small section collapsed, showing the fragility of Georgia's many cave monuments.

10

Vardzia

Often Georgians would ask why I liked their country, why I kept returning — perhaps the mountains, they would say, the hospitality? Then all too frequently would come the question "Have you seen Vardzia?"

Until mid 1989 the only way to visit this cave monastery, right on Georgia's southern border, required an almost impossible to obtain permit from the Defence Ministry. Vardzia was only a few kilometres across the Iron Curtain from Turkey, and the presence of a large military base had sealed it from the public for many years. Yet the yearning tone of this question always puzzled me. From what I'd seen of the site in a book, it amounted to no more than a tall cliff-face peppered by small man-made caves, now deserted for several hundred years. The caves contained a few frescoes, but they hardly seemed to warrant the book's claim of Vardzia as a "masterpiece of world culture." Then Marika, who had obtained a permit, explained the caves carried some particularly fine 12th century frescoes, including a rare portrait of Queen Tamar painted during her lifetime. Then Tamuna, who'd never seen them, told me about a pool of crystal clear water hidden deep in the centre of the hill. "The water is called Queen Tamar's tears," she'd said. "It's like holy water to us."

I guessed that its years of Soviet military occupation had turned the monastery into a symbol of the forbidden past. Tamuna had even added: "To really understand our history I think you must visit Vardzia."

By the time the Soviets re-opened the monument (one wondered if they ever needed to close it) I'd heard its name spoken so many times and with such passion, that when my loyal friend Irakli announced permits were no longer required, I begged him to take me there. Very kindly he agreed, adding: "I'd like to see it myself too."

And so with Ilia as navigator we set out. By the time we reached the Mtskheta junction I concluded Irakli to be no ordinary Georgian, for he drove his Lada with great restraint. With the cupola of the cathedral in our sights, he swung the car's squat nose away from the Military Highway and towards Kutaisi — the nation's second city and former capital of Western Georgia. I asked Ilia why he wanted to come.

"I've been to Vardzia before," he said bleakly. "For two years I've been there, during my military service for the Kremlin!"

As he spoke he looked up at a craggy, eagle's nest of a castle perched on a hill above the road, then repeated with a trace of incredulity: "Two years!"

Before nostalgia overcame him, I asked the name of the passing castle.

"The Ksani Fortress," he replied flatly.

After this followed successive kilometres of vines and orchards of apple, cherry, pear, quince, then the road itself received a long lining of walnut trees.

"The Ksani collective farm," Ilia said, then cheering up slightly added: "Soon it will not be collective."

He was right. With the election of Georgia's non-Soviet government in 1990, the collective farms begun reverting back to privately owned small-holdings. By May 1997 nearly all Georgia's arable land had been distributed and 9,648 enterprises privatised.

Shortly afterwards we sped past Stalin's hometown, Gori, then towards the Surami mountains, the range that historically split Georgia into two halves, East and West.

"There's another fortress here—" Ilia said, "—Surami Fortress. It has a legend."

Later, back in England I saw the film *The Legend of Surami Fortress*, by the Armenian film-maker Sergo Parajanov. It told the classic Georgian tale of a young man built into the castle walls to prevent their crumbling; a myth vividly improved by Parajanov's use of painterly sets and costume. Its theme — youthful sacrifice preserving the vigour of an old collapsing tradition — has never been far from the Georgian heart.

But before we reached Surami, Irakli swung the Lada off the Kutaisi highway, south toward the Turkish border. Suddenly mountains wrapped themselves round us again, this time as the Lesser Caucasus. They lifted up furry arms on either side of the road, a more gentle mountain range with trees clinging to their rocky biceps and clouds streaking across snowless summits. Winding between them our road stuck doggedly to the course of the Mtkvari river, and soon arrived before a well-presented town.

"Borjomi," Irakli announced, "where Georgia's main mineral water comes from."

I mentioned I'd heard Chekhov had come here to take a cure for tuberculosis towards the end of his life.

"Stalin too," said Ilia, who then explained Stalin had his dacha here — which in the mid 1990s became a somewhat faded hotel complex.

Outside the car window buildings squeezed their way along the riverbank like a crinkly toothpaste, forced there by the pressure of the mountains. We passed a road sign pointing to the ski resort of Bakuriani, some 600 metres above us. Irakli slowed the car.

"Bakuriani was one of the best winter sports resorts in the Soviet Union," he said, but I noticed new emotion in his voice. "But you know what happened here . . . ? It was put forward for the Winter Olympics and the International Olympic committee came here and approved its nomination.

But then came April 9th and the Soviet authorities suddenly withdrew it and suggested Sochi instead! Can you believe it? Sochi is a summer resort on the Black Sea coast, it has no snow! The authorities said they feared more unrest, but all Georgians know they just wanted to punish us."

What a cruel disappointment it must have been for Georgia. To host the games would have put the small nation on the map and given the Georgians a pristine opportunity to charm the world with their hospitality — as is their time-honoured pleasure.

A few kilometres beyond the Borjomi water bottling plant came another of those typically Caucasian transformations. We rounded a corner and suddenly the mountains fell away, the cliffsides became hills, the trees disappeared and the grass converted from its lucid emerald into a glorious golden pelt covering a dry earth, its now mustard-coloured stalks glowing in the sun. Through the middle of this newly arid terrain ran the royal blue shaft of the Mtkvari river, a few patches of green cultivation along its banks. I began to smell the presence of the parched high-desert landscape of northern Turkey, now only a few dozen kilometres to the south, and beyond that the extensive Anatolian plateau rolling out ever eastward towards the Mediterranean.

With it came images of the numerous traders and camel-trains following this route when it served as part of the famous Silk Route; also the many huge armies that rumbled through this southern gateway into Georgia. The Ottoman conquerors who swept over in the 16th century, then the Russian generals who swept them out again during the Russo-Turkish wars. In the 1870s it served as the principal supply line as the Tsar's army pushed deep into Turkey and blockaded Erzurum in 1877. This action greatly expanded confidence in the territory of Georgia, encouraging the population of Tbilisi to double during the last 30 years of the century — a trend continuing up until the present day. Until the 1917 Revolution, Georgia extended another 200 kilometres south from this spot, but today Turkey has reclaimed most of it, although it still contains a large Georgian population, and the ruins of many Georgian churches. Georgia has constantly complained of their mistreatment by the Turks, but to no avail.

At the Red Army garrison of Akhaltsikhe, we joined the road from Batumi (Georgia's south-western port) and with it a steady traffic of thundering supply trucks heading east towards Armenia, now just 60km away. After a few minutes Irakli gave us the explanation in a single word: "Leninakan."

Every one of these enormous Soviet-built trucks carried relief for the earthquake victims. During this period many Georgians actually believed Russian atomic scientists and not God instigated the Armenian then the Georgian 1991 earthquakes. Looking around at the sleepy amber hillsides it seemed hard to imagine such a congenial landscape could produce some of the world's most vicious quakes — Vardzia itself had been reduced by half during an earthquake in the 13th century.

But these hillsides had also witnessed another of those enormous, purely human catastrophes. In 1947 Stalin had deported the entire local population of Meskhian Georgians — about 10,000 people — to Central Asia. They remain there to this day, in spite of calls to return. Before achieving power the leadership of Georgia's non-Communist government had called for their re-instatement. But once the magenta, white and black flag of Independent Georgia flew over the Government Building they suddenly changed their tune, fearing the Muslim Meskhians might re-establish links with the Turks across the border, who still claimed the Muslim, Batumi region of Georgia.

After passing yet another dramatic walled fortress overlooking the highway at Khertvisi, we left our slot in the relief convoy and returned to an empty road. About 20 minutes later I noticed caves in a cliff over to our right.

"Are these like the caves at Vardzia?" I asked Ilia.

"This *is* Vardzia," he replied simply.

So these tiny openings speckled along the rock face like a Swiss cheese, amounted to the object of all those yearning statements. Obviously what was once a substantial complex of caves had now been devastated — I assumed by the 13th century quake. As we drew closer so the scale of the cliff increased, I counted nine tiers of caves — the original apparently had 19, but I had yet to be impressed.

One of the four paintings of Queen Tamar made during her lifetime (from Vardzia)

We drove past a large concrete building to our left, sprawling across the hillside opposite the caves like a rogue shopping mall. "The Intourist hotel," Ilia murmured.

We carried on and soon arrived at a large car park, only to find it stuffed to the gills with busloads of Georgian tourists. With the restrictions lifted everybody hurried to their forbidden monument, as if fearing the gates could just as quickly shut again.

A heart-pounding, sweat-drenched climb later (Vardzia stands at 1400 metres), the three of us stood before the entrance of the old monastery, where at last, my opinion began to change. We seemed to have stepped up into an enormous stone-age highrise. All around us the open mouthed caves, stone ladders, secret passages, irrigation channels revealed a monument a good deal larger than the first glance from the road implied. Stepping into the domed Bell Tower, tour guides and photographers appeared out of nowhere and buzzed around us. Unfortunately none could speak English, so back they melted into the gaping black caves and we were left in peace. Climbing up and down between the various levels I arrived in what had been the monastery winery. A long low cave with elegantly melting window arches and well-like storage vats carved deep into the floor. The room still contained the everyday furniture of the 12th century, impeccably preserved as tufa-stone shelves, benches and cave cupboards. Could this be what Tamuna meant by understanding their history — simply imagining the everyday life of Georgia's Golden Age?

Minutes later I arrived at what looked like the 12th century wooden door of the Church of the Assumption, with its keyhole the size of a child's hand. After several energetic shoves it gave way and I stepped up into a large cave, its walls covered in delicately coloured frescoes from the same century. The church was certainly unique with its hollowed out stone interior, cut down into the Georgian landscape, instead of perching on the top. Its musty interior was filled with haloed human figures climbing floor to ceiling, or standing in obedient rows around the walls. Their partially disintegrated, scratched forms gave the frescoes the feel of primitive art, like a Christianised Lascaux. The Turkish invaders of 1578 had tried to deface these images of the infidel, and Georgians (like Marika) had tried to restore them. Amidst the flying angels, and heavenly hosts, two larger-than-life figures of a king and his daughter stood stiffly side by side on the main wall. I recognised the plump, girlish face from photographs and posters all over Georgia, as Queen Tamar. She wore a delicate black choker decorated with gems and a crown on her head. In her hand she held a model up of a church signifying herself as its founder. I looked at this almond-eyed girl with long dark eyebrows and delicate fingers, wondering if it could be a true likeness of the beloved Queen?

Then suddenly Ilia came up to me from nowhere.

"Tamar's tears," he said urgently. "Come on, quickly!"

He steered me over to what looked like a jail-cell door. There we were met by a guard who led us through a shallow arch into a long low passage heading straight into the hillside.

"You're lucky," Ilia whispered. "Most can't come here." Then he added: "I'm lucky to come with you!"

At the end of the tunnel lay Tamuna's goal: a small, simple pool of water collected under a dripping ceiling, its surface utterly clear and colourless like a sheet of rippled glass. The guard smiled at me kindly — I wondered what Ilia and Irakli had told him about me. He took my arm steered me to the pool's edge, then dipped a dirty glass under the surface and handed it to me.

"Drink," Ilia said earnestly.

Realising I had no choice I swallowed the liquid expecting some horrible, minerally, stomach-upsetting taste. But to my surprise the water tasted deliciously cool and refreshing — just as Tamuna imagined it would.

11

Kakheti

"They say Kakheti is the happiest, most easygoing part of Georgia," Marika said. "There is a joke revealing the character of those who live here. An American tourist is walking through its countryside when he comes across a local man asleep under a tree. 'What are you doing wasting your life asleep under a tree —' he asks him, '— when you could be out using your time more productively?' 'How?' asks the Kakhetian. 'You could be working, or studying, or planting . . .' 'Why?' asks the Kakhetian. 'So you could be rich and then do what you always wanted to do,' replies the astonished American. 'What do you think I'm doing right now?' asks the Kakhetian and turns over, pulls his cap back down over his eyes." Marika smiled. "I don't know if it's a completely fair indication of character, but it's where our best wine comes from."

Either way we would soon find out. The bus already hummed its way through the Tbilisi suburbs. To our left the rows of white 1970s tower-blocks followed the city's eastern ridge like a counterfeit Greater Caucasus, followed by the huge Red Army barracks (where the Soviet tanks of April 9th had returned to their deceitful slumber) and on towards this hot south-east corner of Georgia.

Minutes later the bus sailed up over a ridge and suddenly the landscape made another of those abrupt Caucasian about-turns. The colour green was sucked out of the ground, and in its place the arid Samgori steppe stretched away to a hilly horizon. An almost treeless panorama, but unusually for the Caucasus, encircled not by sparkling white peaks, but just peaks. This was my first glimpse of the eastern Lesser Caucasus, the lower deck of the mountainous sandwich that is Georgia. At the end of this valley lay the border with Muslim Azerbaijan.

Yet the brown lifeless vista gave off a false message. The huge valley is in fact one endless, well-irrigated, lovingly tended grape-vine, sprawling across dozens of kilometres in either direction.

A little further on at Ninotsminda, the bus pulled to a halt beside a perfectly walled fortresses, surrounding a church.

"This site here is fifth century, with a 17th century brick bell tower. It's worth a quick look," Marika announced. We descended from the bus. But no sooner had the heavy fortress gate swung open, than a large group of local school-children appeared from nowhere and poured into the citadel all around us.

Dressed in well-starched uniforms of white shirts and vivid red sashes crossed loosely around their chests, these little anarchists immediately found a new and far more fascinating focus for their history lesson: us. Every time I raised my camera at the tower's elegant brickwork about 20 leaping, grinning boys' faces bounced up and down in the viewfinder, with the girls racing up behind holding hands and shouting *"Wee luv yeeu! Wee luv yeeu!"* at the top of their lungs. Finally I gave up on the monument and turned the lens on them. This produced immediate squeals of delight and sent the teachers into a frenzy, arranging them all together in terms of height for an enormous group photo. The organisation of this misbehaving throng took up the rest of our visit and running for the bus I concluded Georgian schoolchildren were no different to all the other millions of joyful hooligans the world over.

Back on board, we hurried on towards the wine press of Georgia, as vine

Ninotsminda (Kakheti) church and fortress, with schoolchildren

after vine flicked by. Every so often the view slotted in another fully intact castle, perched either on a sylvan mountain-top or, as in the case of the Manari Fortress, on a hillock beside the road — a kind of set-designed landscape.

"We have an organisation in Georgia called the Society of David the Builder," Marika explained, "named after our famous 12th century Georgian King. Its members often repair these fortresses now."

I remembered the Heritage Societies in Estonia, one of the most powerful movements towards independence before the arrival of the Popular Front. Groups of citizens fiercely seeking out and restoring their pre-Soviet buildings as if the walls themselves contained their stifled national identity.

As the altitude increased eventually the Gombori mountains closed in around us: a minor range dividing Kakheti into two sections, inner and outer. At the small mountain market at Bakurtsikhe the bus halted again and I found myself staring at a large shop declaring in bold English letters, 'Half Finished Product.' It turned out to be a Georgian translation for bulk purchase shop.

The shelves stood almost empty, and apart from an elegant spear-shaped bread called *shoti*, the market outside showed similar absence of supply, its sellers as morose as in Kazbegi.

But from here on the road descended down into the more genuinely cheerful valley of the Alazani river: Kakheti true. Plantations of roses, geraniums, basil, various fruits and wheat soon skimmed past the window, as the valley extended away to the Daghestan mountains rising up in the east. In this new fertile region the fields began to stitch themselves together with the endless pegs and wire of vines. Village after village passed by; many well known throughout Georgia for their distinctive wines. Inner Kakheti is cherished for bearing many, if not most of the best: Mukuzani, Tsinandali, Kardanakhi, Tibaani, Napareuli, Manavi, Sameba, Akhmeta, and others, not forgetting the brandies like Eniseli and Gremi.

The plethora of cultivation showed no sign of the brutal history associated with this valley.

The Imam Shamil, from a 19th century Russian postcard

The invading Persian armies had marched through it many times from the south, and from the north that 19th century rebel and scourge of the Russian Army, the Imam Shamil, relentlessly harried the Caucasian army and this valley, only to melt back invisibly into the Daghestan Caucasus now just a few kilometres beyond the final row of vines. In 1853 he mustered an army of 10,000 mountain-men and surged down into the valley in a valiant attempt to oust the infidel Russian invaders once and for all. The Russians squarely defeated him. But the Turkic tribes of Azerbaijan (Russia was then in the process of conquering large tracts of northern Turkey) sought their revenge so fervently, he tried yet again the following year, only to be routed again.

Looking out across this blissfully productive valley, my ears still ringing with the cries of the nationalists, it suddenly seemed a very fragile place again.

Not far from the village of Tsinandali (famous for its wine) came another of our scheduled stops; the elegantly shaggy manor house of the poet and Prince Alexander Chavchavadze, the 19th century founder of the Georgian romantic movement. This proudly preserved Georgian stately home, visited by Lermontov and the Russian playwright Griboyedov (the poet's son-in-law), mentioned by Alexander Dumas, stood inside a beautiful ornamental garden, that included a small zoo.

At the entrance I, lagging behind the group as usual, encountered a stubbornly cantankerous Georgian police officer. In spite of my obvious foreigner's clothing, camera and accent, he simply refused to believe I belonged to the tourist group he'd just let through. All attempts to reason were met with glowering *"ara!"*s followed by some strange, dismissive hand gestures — or so I interpreted them — towards the ticket office (now closed). I retreated, waited until he returned to his guard's hut, then quietly sneaked by.

Half an hour later, walking out of the house (now a museum) I saw him standing in the centre of the drive staring straight at me. He beckoned, and in a stern Georgian accent said: *"Idi syuda!"* ('come here!' in Russian). Prudence told me to obey. He escorted me back to his guard's hut and told me to sit down at the small table. As I contemplated the likely results of my crime I saw him reach down to the floor and grasp something shiny hidden beside the door. He then turned round and, beaming ear to ear, held up a bottle of Tsinandali. "We drink!" he exclaimed.

To my astonishment he then filled two glasses to the brim — I noticed the bottle was already half empty — and breaking into fluent Georgian proposed a toast. He gestured for me to stand. When the oration finished — I understood none of it — both our elbows lifted in the air and down the delicious liquid flowed. A look of deep satisfaction entered his eyes. My crime, I realised had been absolved.

Watching him fill the glasses again, I contemplated the sublime difference between the Novgorod police and those of Kakheti. Both arrests stemmed from imaginary crimes. In Novgorod, 1987, I'd committed an act of psychological warfare against the state by using a camera unescorted. In Kakheti I'd simply turned down police hospitality (of the genuine sort). In reality I'd misread his original series of gestures at the gate. Rather than asking for a ticket he had in fact been inviting me into the hut for a friendship toast. This non-Soviet local policeman stuck inside a Kakhetian guard hut still managed to blend work and pleasure. But for those officers in Novgorod, the two remained eternally separate. As the second gush of liquid raced down my throat, I reflected that here in this hut I experienced the vital difference between life in Georgia and that in the Soviet North. In spite of all Stalin's attempts to institutionalise fear, the Georgians never forgot those crucial moments in life that say "the rules be damned," right down to the last police officer.

After the third glass I made some noisy excuses in English, which he in turn couldn't understand, and gestured urgently toward our bus. Finally he nodded and sternly held out his hand. As I stepped out the door his severe look quickly disappeared to the sound of one final *"gaumarjos!"* — "cheers!" For punishment I had received friendship.

A selection of Georgian wines wearing their Soviet-era labels

Within seven years this international friendship was to bear some fruit as the Kakhetian wine industry would attract some of the first foreign investors into Georgia, who started up three joint ventures in the valley. By March 1997 Kakhetian wine could be bought regularly in London, the excellent Saperavi retailing at £4 a bottle.

But according to Giorgi Arsenishvili, the governor of Kakheti — in a speech given at the 1997 Georgian Studies Day, held at London's Lloyds Building — 43 million litres remained in Kakheti still waiting for a buyer.

As for Alexander Chavchavadze, hero of the romantic age, I discovered almost nothing about him then, save he would almost certainly have approved modern Kakhetian police methods. His renown had been massively eclipsed by another Chavchavadze, of no relation. Prince Ilia Chavchavadze, also a 19th century poet (dying 51 years after Alexander in 1907, by assassination), had founded the popular nationalist newspaper *Iveria*, which flourished until the end of that century. Now the Georgian nationalist movement had elevated Prince Ilia to dizzying heights, granting him not only his own society, political party and shrine at the Sioni Cathedral, but canonisation by the Georgian Church in 1987.

As the bus hurried forward up the valley I reflected on this quest to create the perfect Georgian man. An invisible, holy, Georgian leader to aim their country and themselves forward. During all those years of Communism, identity had been attacked furiously by the artificial idealisation of the globalised materialistic, Soviet man. The experiment had failed. Now identity needed to reconstruct itself again from the roots up before any recollectivisation — like the West's attempt to generate an intercontinental 'Green' Man.

Meanwhile the bus completed the last leg of the journey into the heart of Kakheti, by climbing up the gentle Gombori slopes to the town of Telavi. As former seat of the kings of Kakheti, Telavi retains today's administrative throne and local council. As the bus wound its way up towards the sunny town centre and its splendid fortified citadel, so I began to notice a huge oblong shadow intermittently falling across the road. The bus crossed and recrossed it as we climbed the hill. Peering up through the window I caught glimpses of an enormous, ruler-like tower-block next to the citadel, blotting out the sun. But unlike most Soviet tower-blocks, this one stood entirely by itself, rearing up above the quaintly tree-lined, wooden-balconied town, in an act of supreme architectural machismo. The Soviet planners, having restrained themselves and preserved Telavi's amiable, low-lying skyline, obviously felt obliged to make up for their sensitivity by spiking the town through the heart with this monstrosity.

I asked Marika what kind of people inhabited this desecration of all the principals of town-planning. She looked at me and exclaimed with more than a touch of irony: "People like you! It's the Intourist Hotel."

Up on the 14th floor, unwillingly transformed into one of its sinister denizens, I decided there could be but one person who could find positive advantage in this tower of domination — the photographer. With evening already well with us I hurried for the lift.

Over the years I'd discovered that in most Soviet hotels (as with the accompanying political system) the further one strayed from the centre so the more backward management became. With the main 'Service Bureau', usually on the first floor, the top floors of the higher Intourist hotels appeared rather like the extremities of the Soviet empire — neglected. Carpets would expose more threads, rooms show the most signs of wear; the service desks remain unmanned for longer, if at all. But, most important of all, the doors to the roof invariably flapped open in the breeze. The Telavi Intourist proved no exception.

Standing on top of that Kakhetian Empire State, surrounded by a circus of swifts diving and swooping in the wind currents, I squinted through my 600mm lens at the city below. Not large, only about 30,000 inhabitants, its main feature (apart from my 14 storey tripod), appeared as the walled, Persian-style palace of King Irakli II. Built in the middle of the 18th century it contained a church, a basilica and elegant landscaped garden. The whole city seemed to spread out around it trying to copy the character of this successful and much admired monarch, who reigned for 54 years and united Kakheti with Kartli in 1762.

Although a Christian king, Telavi's museum carries a portrait of Irakli wearing a turban, due to his friendship with his Persian enemies. A few years later when Georgia's civil war transformed the Intourist Hotel into a refugee camp draped in washing, and reduced Telavi to two hours of water and electricity a week — with hindsight one felt the Georgians might have taken a leaf out of this Kakhetian's king's book; remembered their old technique of 'making your enemy into your friend.'

Meanwhile the setting sun sent out a fantastic suffusion of evening light settling down onto the southern flanks of the Greater Caucasus. The multiple layers of clouds seemed to melt into each other like a sea of lifting crimson waves. Dotted across the blackness before them, the tin roofs of the city reflected back like silver rafts on a lake of ink.

One roll of film later, I descended to the dining room for what was left of dinner. Our group, it turned out, had been waylaid by locals. A couple of drunken Georgian men, spotting the foreigners had wheeled fearlessly over to our table first applying their attentions to the women.

"Dance!" they'd declared in a gruff, grinning English. The women instantly clamped themselves to their seats. Realising this road thoroughly blocked, they then turned to the men.

Telavi sculpture by Merab Berdzenishvili, celebrating the Kakhetian grape harvest

"Come and join us at our table," they insisted again and again, as our Intourist guide nervously assured us the tradition of Georgian hospitality fully encompassed such random invitations. Yet as far as I could tell the tradition of honouring the guest also seemed to include 'owning' him or her. Our refusals just wouldn't be heard.

I spent a good 20 minutes sneaking in mouthfuls between variations on the negative reply: "*Ara, nyet, nien,* never!" as an enormous Georgian hand gripped my arm as if to drag me off to their table. Finally the sound of angry shouts at their host table, distracted everyone's attention, quickly followed by the sound of a fist smashing on the table-top, and glasses smashing on the floor.

I saw several dark hands immediately grab bottles by the neck. From the intensity of the black looks flashing across that table, it seemed certain a terrible fight would begin. This put an end to the assault on our group, as our kidnappers returned to help restore the peace (which they did).

This sudden and impetuous passion belied a dangerous streak in the Georgian character. One I would encounter again as the long history of inter-ethnic struggles continued to flare in Abkhazia and Ossetia.

It is a mistake to take at face value the wide-eyed Georgian claims that until the Soviets arrived their many tribes and internal nationalities always managed to live harmoniously amongst themselves. After the grand unification of Georgia shortly before Queen Tamar's reign the country had de-unified again and split into squabbling princedoms. Full scale battles had probably only been prevented by outside invasions from the Persians, Turks, Russians and of course the Red Army.

The next morning I ventured out onto the streets, past the Telavi police-station, where three prisoners weeded the front garden as their guard, a single

Bird's-eye view of Telavi from the former Intourist Hotel roof

16th century fortress walls and cathedral roof at Alaverdi (Kakheti)

police officer, chatted idly with his back turned. Beyond it came a charming 'hang out' café with large shady patio and ice-cream fountain. I stopped there to buy the *Morning Star* (on sale at the nearby newsstand) and read that "the British inflation rate had risen to eight per cent," then walked on into the central Irakli Square with its enormous National Theatre and high citadel walls.

Within minutes I realised the reports of the relaxed Kakhetian atmosphere had been accurate. As somebody with TOURIST emblazoned all over his body (camera, clothing and uncertain direction), Telavi turned out to be the only part of Georgia nobody ever asked me to change money, where women and men often smiled at me when passing on the street, and several of my photographic victims actually said *"madlobt!"* (Georgian for 'thank you,') when I grabbed their pictures.

Deciding one of the distinctive black Kakhetian felt hats (still widely worn) might make a good souvenir, I found a shop and asked to try one on. As I aligned it in the mirror I noticed a portrait of Stalin staring back at me from a corner of the glass, as if to say *"I think it suits you."*

It turned out a suitable marketing ploy for Telavi as his picture seemed to re-occur everywhere: on war memorials, shop windows, even in the taxi home, this time pasted against the dashboard. I realised how much this provincial capital lagged behind Tbilisi. It resurrected the last Georgian Big Man into rural daily life, like a kind of absent king. To the locals he still appeared as the biggest, jolliest leader of all time, one who corrected their sense of smallness — his international fame serving as a kind of adrenalin drip to the remoteness of this valley.

A year later back in England, I heard a song to Stalin sung at the Kakhetian festival of Alaverdoba on a BBC Radio 4 programme. Recorded beside the nearby cathedral of Alaverdi, several male voices emitted wild, eagle cries of hysterical praise to the glory of the great general.

In the afternoon our bus took us on a brief tour of the northern valley. We raced over to the magnificent 11th century Alaverdi Cathedral (claimed by Georgians as the tallest building in the world when it was built) then on up into the deep green hills near Daghestan and, to my mind, one of the most beautifully set of all Georgia's churches, the Ikalto Monastery. Surrounded entirely by woods and tall, wistful, cypress, the tower of the eighth century church rises above the ruins of a former 11th century academy, the place rumoured to have enrolled Shota Rustaveli as a student. Now the academy's only earnest Platonic arguments engaged with the encroaching undergrowth, but the place itself remained as enchanted as ever.

Inside the church it came as no surprise to find a 19th century line engraving of Rustaveli's hero knight wrestling with the almighty panther of the poem. It hung on the wall like any other religious icon. During our short visit I caught a tantalising whiff of that spirit of rural poetry pursued by Georgians like Akaki Tsereteli, Alexander then Ilia Chavchavadze (for whom Kakhetian wine was a favourite allegory), and later by Giorgi Leonidze whose Kakhetian idyll *The Wishing Tree* (1956) was used as the basis of Tengiz Abuladze's fine film of the same name.

Sitting beside the petite sixth century Sameba Church I began to feel the roots of a culture whose main survival technique had become hospitality — which to succeed required performance that later developed into its modern poetry, song and dance; a culture that had persued the arts from the earliest times, whose brides learned chunks of Rustaveli's poem to recite to their

Ikalto church and academy (Kakheti)

husbands. Furthermore a nation whose language, as the British scholar Donald Rayfield points out, in the 12th century AD probably had the same number of speakers and readers — and the same prestige among its neighbours — as the English language at the time of Shakespeare.

In these carefully designed rural shrines like Ikalto lingered the kind of tranquillity enabling a man like Rustaveli to sit down and create a 1,600 verse poem. I took my place on the grass and pictured easy summer's days here picnicking with bottles of light Kakhetian wine, strings of local *churchkhela* and soaking up the presences of these imaginary spirits of Georgia. The kind looked to by Ilia Chavchavadze and his fellow 19th century dreamers, as well as Pushkin, who pleaded nostalgically in a 1828 poem:

> *I beg you please sing no more,*
> *the songs of Georgia,*
> *for their mournful sounds*
> *recall for me*
> *a distant life*
> *a distant shore.*

But for me, not on this occasion. The bus summoned me back with a rude blast of its horn. Clambering on board I found myself greeted by the frosty stares of my companions who patiently waited for my daydreaming to end.

Then off we flew, like a petrol-fired cannonball, back to the electronic age.

Drinking shrine, Svaneti, for
passers-by to toast the life of a Svan
who drove off the road (often drunk)

12

Svaneti

The rusted sign beside the road read: 'For The 12th Five Year Plan You Need To Maintain Good Speed And Rhythm.' From my place in the front seat of Ilia's Lada I watched our driver smile at this quaint tribute to Communism, now used only as target-practice by passing locals. Beyond the car bonnet stretched a glorious sight: a hobbit-green valley, rich with pastures, vines and citrus, leading the eye up to a sudden eruption of mountain-side and snowy peaks — our destination.

There would be no problem in maintaining speed and rhythm, our driver Temur had but a few years earlier been Formula Three champion of Georgia.

"Eighth in all the USSR!" put in Ilia from the back seat. I pulled discreetly at the Lada's seat-belt: would it make any difference? This bonding between myself and the hurtling Lada added only a commitment to faith. A faith I feared might grow to a full-blown religion in the yawning canyons ahead.

Before us lay the most notorious stretch of road in all Georgia — the 117 winding kilometres up to the much-talked-about region of Upper Svaneti. A road eternally at war with the elements: blocked by the huge snows of the winter and washed out by flash floods in the spring. Yet the remoteness gave a hefty clue why Georgians revered this distant corner of their mountains beyond all others, why too Svaneti is frequently declared the most Georgian part of Georgia. The language is said to be similar to the Georgian language of the fourth century AD. The churches still contain many of their original crosses and icons (most other regions have lost them either to thieves or the state Art Museum in Tbilisi). The people are fierce and suspicious of foreigners; a reputation they've maintained since before Christ, when Strabo the Greek geographer, described the Svans as "foremost in courage and power. They have a king and a council of 300 men; and they assemble, according to reports, an army of 200,000; for the whole of the people are a fighting force."

"The Svans are traditional and very proud," put in Ilia. "They are also armed. Many weapons in Svaneti, we must be careful." He smiled widely.

For a traditional Georgian (by Western standards) to describe other Georgians as "traditional" implied more than merely parochial. It still shone with nobility. To these men from the capital, Svans embodied something they'd lost, or feared losing. An idealisation of character, a cultural independence — factors well attested by the Svans' survival through the very centuries in which their lowland cousins had to watch Georgian cities

Murkmeli village, the first in the Ushguli complex at about 2,300 metres above sea level. Most towers are still maintained, to defend against avalanches and vendettas.

repeatedly sacked and looted. Furthermore, they are a resiliently religious people. Nothing tells more of the modern Georgian ideal of temperament than those wide-eyed bronze icons gazing up from the 10th century in the Tbilisi Art Museum, their all-seeing, righteous expressions full of purpose as they spear the dragon, trample the non-believer. Svaneti possessed more icons than any other part of Georgia.

A few kilometres down the road came the first signal of our entry into the land of the severe Svans. I'd been remembering the horrified expressions I'd seen in Tbilisi listening to descriptions of Svan driving; particularly Marika's account of their roadside drinking houses — where rather than stopping their journey to drink and relax, they'd drink the better to continue. But was it possible to be any worse than in Tbilisi? The first hint of verification came with a peculiar metal object standing by the side of the road; rather like a mailbox without a door. As the Lada jerked to a halt Ilia identified it.

"Svan religion," he said ambiguously. I gave him a puzzled look. "A shrine," he elaborated, "a Svan drove off the cliff here."

The back wall of the black box carried the photograph of a young man and next to it messages from friends, a few burnt out candles, then to my astonishment a collection of empty glasses. Below that, halfway down the tubular steel post came what could only be described as a miniature bar. A square metal platform stocked with bottles of local wine, vodka and the legendary (and horrible) *chacha* — a locally brewed spirit — all in varying degrees of fullness, ready for the next passer-by.

The irony dial flicked deep into the red when I considered that drunken driving is the primary cause of fatality on this road. Yet true to tradition, Svans still encouraged drivers to stop and drink a hefty toast to the memory of one, almost certainly dead due to drunken driving. I managed to smile wistfully. But the smile wore steadily thinner as the kilometres mounted up and more of these grim tributes to road-death flashed by. A young Svan could be stopping at every one of these shrines, on his way down towards us . . . I thanked Providence for the current petrol shortage and miraculous absence of cars on all Georgia's roads.

The way continued to rise, climbing from sea-level toward its 1500 metre goal, Mestia, the administrative capital of Svaneti. The dense fir and deciduous forest on either side never thinned — a clue to the lushness of the Alpine landscape waiting ahead. I remembered my journey to Vardzia just 100 kilometres to the south; those barren brown mountain-sides of an entirely different climatic zone. What a difference to this dripping green chaos of leaves, fallen branches and ferns.

It added another tiny notch of credibility to the possibility that Jason and his Argonauts may well have visited this same valley many years before Christ. That Georgia was indeed that fairytale, multi-faceted land of Medea and the Golden Fleece. Adventurers like Tim Severin devoted years of their life attempting to prove this. He sailed a reconstructed *Argo* from Greece up the

Bosphoros to Poti on the Black Sea coast and discovered evidence that small quantities of gold still found in these mountains by Svans sifting water through sheep's woollen hides staked into the rivers — hence the link with a golden fleece.

The car switched back and forward up to the long, silting-up artificial lake created by the huge Inguri dam — source of a good portion of Western Georgia's electricity. After this the valley closed in suddenly, the river Inguri periodically disappearing and reappearing at the bottom of a deep, guttural chasm. Occasionally the road surface vanished completely, replaced by landslide mud and stone. By now Ilia had taken the wheel, swerving us blithely round the fallen rocks and doling out more information on the dangerous Svans.

"They have a big problem of vendettas between families, but only in Svaneti. The Svans have customs like in the Middle Centuries."

He explained how the local newspaper frequently reported inter-family murders, then began telling stories of his own experiences with other Georgian mountain-people — once, in particular, when he joined a group of doctors in a nearby valley town.

"At night at one in the morning, we have urgent telephone call from village up in the mountains. 'Very sick, come quickly,' they said." He employed a variety of dramatic hand gestures, each one temporarily abandoning the wheel. "So we find driver and drive for two hours, *two hours* up this little road to the village, and when we get there, do you know what it was . . . ?" his eyes shone. "You know what it *was*?" he repeated again, turning to look at me, completely forgetting the road. ". . . A pig! It was a big pig. We couldn't believe it!"

To emphasise his point, he took both hands off the wheel and jerked them emphatically in the air at the great God of Absurdity, much loved by all Georgians. I waited for the crashing sound as the car hit the rocky verge, then plunged into the ravine . . .

A few kilometres later it almost did. Negotiating another mudslide amidst more heartfelt storytelling, there was suddenly an almighty thud under the car. It stopped the engine and narration dead. The front wheels of the car reared up then thumped down, accompanied by hideous scrapings and crunchings shuddering down the length of the chassis. When the car finally ground to a halt we looked at each other in stunned silence, praying the damage would not be as bad as it sounded. Plainly Ilia, in his love of Absurdity, had driven us straight over a large boulder.

But this time the prayers failed. A quick inspection revealed the car's left-hand rear wheel locked solid. We couldn't continue. A major transmission problem in the High Caucasus, 40 kilometres to the nearest village in either direction, on a road almost traffic-free, with night approaching . . . But my companions took the situation boldly in hand. Without a moment to lose they'd removed the offending wheel, and finding nothing but the frozen drum, began trying to free it by hitting the casing with a tyre-iron.

The sight of these two earnest Georgians thrashing this innocent piece of metal induced a moment of speculation on the national character. Some instinct drove them to activity at any cost, as if an antidote to the years of lassitude following the Stalinist terror — that uniquely Soviet paralysis where doing nothing was always the safest. Here it seemed, action came first and thought all too frequently second — following Scott Fitzgerald's immortal maxim 'action is character.'

As the clanging grew more desperate it seemed our journey had almost certainly ended. The nearest, properly-equipped garage lay down the road not up. The inevitable hitch-hiking direction would take us away from our goal, back toward Zugdidi on the plains below. All those frantic preparations, time taken off work, searching for petrol in Tbilisi — for nothing. But perhaps I, the mere guest should take another glance under the car? Might it be something as simple as a handbrake?

"No!" came a sharp reply from the other end of a tyre-iron. But a brief scrutiny revealed this to be the case. The rock had merely bent one of the brake cable supports. Surely if we just disconnected the handbrake the wheel should free? The banging halted and wearily the driver/mechanic consented to look. Then suddenly came an amazing change of heart.

"Yes!" — followed by more instantaneous action. None of those self-deprecating "oh I'm sorry you're absolutely right"s, to be expected from the English. These Georgians simply switched from angry and frustrated to the opposite, without the bothersome intervention of apology. Action certainly was character.

Hamlet in Upper Svaneti. The sleigh, foreground, is used the year round.

Mestia, the administrative capital of Svaneti

It brought to mind another puzzling reaction. A month after the terrible April 9th slaughter of Georgian demonstrators, the nearby School No. 1 on Rustaveli Avenue re-opened only to find many of the children mysteriously ill. Fearing residues of a toxic riot gas, the authorities immediately closed the building and an international delegation of doctors, already in Tbilisi, began an investigation. They found that once home the children quickly recovered, symptom-free. They reached a unanimous verdict that the illnesses were psychosomatic, picked up from the teachers' and parents' constant anguish at the original gas poisoning. The illness even possessed a specific medical name and etiology. But not one of my many Tbilisi friends (including the well-educated intellectuals) held any truck with these findings — though they trusted everything else from these doctors. They preferred their own interpretation, that the Soviet gases held properties unknown to Western scientists. That their ugly effects were specifically selected to deter future separatist protest among the Georgians. I found it impossible to find anyone not holding to this deep-felt conviction.

The wheel repaired, we soon bumped cheerfully along as if nothing had happened. Below the Inguri river changed colour from muddy turquoise to boiling white, and the road's course took on an increasingly desperate air. It crossed forwards and back across the Inguri, at times swinging out over the angry glacial water propped on spindly concrete struts, or slunk nervously under huge hanging bulwarks of mountain-side. Occasionally it disappeared altogether into unlit, roughly hacked tunnels into the cliff, with water steaming aggressively from fissures in the walls.

Although the road seemed empty, every so often a furious, horn-honking Lada suddenly butted up against our rear bumper, a young Svan driver wearing the traditional grey felt cap, gripping the wheel determinedly. Seconds later he would roar past, bouncing and swerving between the pot-holes as if Armageddon had just been announced. Even our racing champion smiled and shook his head in admiration.

A few years later I met a British art student who decided (unwisely) to hitch-hike up into some mountains nearby. He was picked up by a similar mountain-man driving a Lada who immediately insisted they drink together — as he drove. The Englishman, having seen the drinking shrines, politely refused. But the driver insisted. "You drink!" he said forcefully. The Englishman declined again, until he heard a clicking sound. He turned to find himself staring straight down the barrel of a loaded pistol. "You drink!" The driver repeated. He drank and the journey continued very amicably.

Eventually the switchbacks relaxed, the forest eased off and the occasional long-haired pig sniffed its way beside the roadside — the sure sign of human habitation. Then came an open field, then another, with more space overhead, glimpses of brilliant white snow between the clouds and a growing sense of achievement. We'd made it, finally, amazingly, up into the high mountain grasslands of Upper Svaneti.

And very quickly the atmosphere changed. The landscape opened out into one huge, deep green valley, flanked by jagged peaks. The earth showed an unexpected level of husbandry. Fields of wheat, maize, livestock, inserted a patchwork into the universal greenness. The eye picked out tiny brilliant specks of colour dotted across this giant billiard cloth. The specks slowly crossed the hillsides and were obviously women dressed in their traditional colours. As we came closer we saw flashes of silver from the scythes as they sliced down hay for winter fodder. Closer in and snatches of their songs drifted in through the Lada's windows. Stone walls popped up at the roadside and occasionally we passed some of these women, their foreheads bound with black head-scarves like nuns. In a farmyard beside the road a couple of bullocks pulled a crudely made sledge across the concrete — a reminder of the long, cruel winters never far away.

Then rounding a corner came the startling sight for which Svaneti is renowned. A sudden row of tall stone towers reared up out of the landscape to heights of 20 to 25 metres. They loomed over the first village of Upper Svaneti like a squad of alert warriors, awaiting the next invasion, and seemed to announce a completely new civilisation. I found myself transfixed. These monuments seemed so distant from our own time, yet there they stood dapper and well maintained.

Most Svan towers date back to the 12th and 13th centuries, although a few originate as far back as the first century BC. In Europe only a handful of such family towers still remain in Tuscany, but Svaneti possesses over 200, most still used by their owners. They serve as defence against avalanches and enemies (foreign or, more usually, neighbours). They carried a top-floor family room equipped to last out a long siege or many snowbound weeks. Around these ancient keeps the modern family homes clustered under their tin roves, clinging like temporary lichen to these rocks of the past.

The Lada pulled to a halt and we stepped out, the better to receive this first impression. Then, as I reached for my camera, a sudden shaft of orange sunlight sliced through the clouds and ceremonially knighted the tower-tops with a golden blade. Desperately I fumbled for my lenses, images of Crusader-like inhabitants rushing into my head. Under that unearthly spotlight time seemed to bend back on itself; surely our Lada had driven through a time tunnel, landed us 400 years in the past in some virginal, medieval epoch.

Such enchanted moments are the stuff of travel. They seem to lean over the rim of our world with hints of something completely alien, filling the landscape with the luminous, unexplored events familiar to all children, and forgotten by most adults.

Fanciful thoughts abruptly bought back to reality by nearby electricity pylons and a rusting Soviet caterpillar tractor left in the middle of a field. Suddenly I wondered about my role as ambassador from their future. The Svans held a reputation for distrusting visitors. Could this vendetta-troubled people be right to suspect me and the culture I represented — now taking over where the Soviets left off? Might I conceal even more devious transformations? In places like this one could not trust even one's best intentions.

Directly ahead stood one of the first villages of Upper Svaneti, Latale, its clean towers now standing out crisply against the dark valleys beyond. As we drove toward it giant Soviet-built tractors thundered past us on the road, their trailers piled high with cut hay, spilling across the tarmac. These two epochs of man seemed to cohabit crazily side by side. In this land where the wheel and television arrived in the same human lifespan (sledges were, and often still are, used instead of carts), its people had simply grabbed hold of the modern machinery and used it as an extension of their own primitive system. When the diesels broke down the Svans simply abandoned them right there in the field, like another old sledge. Only, unlike a sledge, they didn't rot.

A few kilometres later we arrived in Mestia, not so much a town but a large village of some 3,500 inhabitants, its centre one of those architecturally dead, Soviet impositions: a large characterless square, but refreshingly absent of cars and brazenly grazed by pigs. On arrival my companions left me behind as guard, embarking on a search for accommodation.

Sitting in that car the only sound came from a wedding party taking place under a large, clear plastic tent directly ahead. Out of this mountain marquee a series of amplified ballads drifted nonsensically up into the evening air. The songs, occasionally punctuated by gunshots, lifted upwards like wisps of jangling smoke into the huge mountain stillness. The tinny noises of this human celebration were quickly mopped up by the huge, skimming clouds, as if by a celestial blotting-paper. High above everything, poking occasionally through those drifting wet wads, the peaks glimpsed down with chilling indifference, like a distant heavenly government. In the face of so much infinity, of what concern humankind? On the street a couple of girls strolled towards the music, their faces plump and pretty, hair blonde, eyes light-green, cheeks apple-red due to the extra haemoglobin at this altitude. Again, an unusual sight as most Georgians are now dark, well mixed with the Turkish and Persian cultures to the south. Yet, according to Georgian lore, this blond blood of the Svans is the sign of truest racial purity, achieved only by their centuries of privileged isolation.

Our residence ended up as Mestia's Intourist hotel, placed on a hillock overlooking the town. Like most modern buildings in Svaneti it jarred

Chased icon of St Georgia, 13th century. Mestia Museum, Svaneti

uncomfortably with the old stone architecture. Inside our room we discovered the obligatory ready-playing radio and both fridge and TV. Ilia was deeply impressed.

"A fridge here, my God! A TV!" he grinned at us. "But don't work — and don't work." He seemed to know by instinct, for quite correctly neither worked. Anything Soviet, like this hotel, was in his eyes automatically damned. At reception we met a couple of East German tourists being turned away from the virtually empty hotel because their visas failed to mention the word 'Mestia.' Ilia couldn't resist poking fun at such regulations.

"My God, it's so serious! No word in their visa! They are *spies*! Yes, I can tell they are spies!"

I couldn't help siding with this cheerful Georgian mockery. What a situation for these holidaymakers, as if Mestia held any military secrets! Georgians quite rightly followed their instinct for natural law and ignored as much of the outdated legislation as they could. Most regarded Soviet authority as a rather stupid, blunt-headed schoolmaster, his heavy discipline all the better to encourage disobedience and delinquency. When Georgia subsequently elected its politically inexperienced, non-Communist government headed by Zviad Gamsakhurdia, some observers described the ensuing disasters as the result of putting the students in charge of the school.

Out on the hotel balcony the small town stretched away below, its rows of towers sticking up out of the earth like the fingertips of the long arm of Svan tradition reaching down beneath the soil. They dotted themselves randomly across the valley, like big signposts to the bottomless historical presence of this race. Archaeologists have found evidence of Svan communities from the second millennium BC and theories abound as to their connections with the great early civilisations. Two Svaneti villages bear the name of the Sumerian water god Lakhamu, and other links have been made between the languages. The pagan Svan sun god Lile is often paralleled with Enlil of the Sumerian sun cult, and today villagers still sing songs opening with the words *"Oh Great White Sun!"* In today's Svan churches one finds Christian crosses adorned with

rams' horns, and several with pagan animals built into their walls, wholly out of kilter with their Orthodox Christianity. For a nation as invaded, conquered, intermixed as Georgia, this small community's direct link to its ancestors of 5,000 years ago is indeed a remarkable feat.

In those distant centuries the Inguri had served as a lifeline up to this mountain sanctuary for the many escaping persecution below. The region's inaccessibility — almost completely cut off in the winters until this century — proved an impregnable defence and thus the villages and language survive. The only nationality to redirect the culture with any permanence has been the Soviet Russians, who bought the road (the first car arrived in 1935), the gas-pipeline, the television transmitter, the airstrip, and the wheel (not needed before as carts are useless in the deep snow) — all since the 1920s.

Marlen Tamliani, our 'tamada' and Matskvarishi Church Protector at Latale

Over a crude supper at the Intourist restaurant — operated by the same girls that made the beds and ran reception — we discussed the problem of depopulation threatening the community. With the arrival of the road and television, young Svans inevitably gathered a taste for the wider world beyond their valley, beautiful though it may be. Furthermore the severe winter of 1987 bought down a number of terrible avalanches, over 70 died, most of them children at a school high in the mountains. This left a bitter scar on this superstitious people, and helped invoke the largest exodus of young in the region's history. In 1988 an estimated 4,000 left, dropping the population to around 12,000.

The total number of Svans living in Georgia is estimated at 45,000 — another indication of their lowland migration over the decades. Today teenagers ask themselves what they can achieve remaining so idyllically cut off, a fact that seemed to worry Ilia from Tbilisi.

"It's important the Svans keep one child, one brother only in the valley. The Svans feel this too. It's very important to preserve the tradition."

Then the meal arrived: a bowl of murky brown soup concealing (for me) hideous lumps of sheep's stomach. As unappetising a sight as I'd ever seen; but the vegetarian's palate was saved by a delicious spicy bean dish (*lobio*), bread and, of course, many full glasses of vodka and wine.

Soon Ilia was telling stories about the shortages of alcohol up north, "in Russia," as he often called the rest of the Soviet Union. "The Russians have a new favourite — I read it in the newspaper. Three shots of insecticide, one of eau de Cologne in their beer — delicious!"

His tone of voice reminded me of a Georgian friend at Leningrad TV, who in one moment of exasperation said to me: "There are three types of logic in this world. Logic logic, women's logic, and Russian logic. *That* is Russian logic!"

The next morning the search for Svaneti true began. The trail led first to the doorstep of a cheerful, ruddy-faced official from the Mestia Museum, called Shadur. Contrary to my expectations of the Svans, he greeted us with a burst of heady Georgian good nature. This soon evolved into violent enthusiasm for our visit. He led me into his office, sat me down at a desk dominated for some reason by a giant green apple, then asked me my official business.

"So you've come to discover Svaneti," he said factually. "You've seen Ushguli yet?" He looked at me earnestly.

"No," I answered. Noticing my eye straying toward the huge apple, he suddenly reached over thrust it into my hand. Not knowing what to do and in a fit of embarrassment, I took a bite. The moment I revealed my awkwardness, his eyes lit up.

"We go today!" he announced. "Ushguli are the highest villages in Europe. You cannot visit Svaneti without visiting Ushguli, impossible!" Under such force of determination we surrendered willingly.

Ushguli

Back in the car, after some unsuccessful attempts at finding lunch, Shadur inquired if I had any specific questions about Svaneti. I asked him about the reports in Tbilisi of Svan snow ceremonies in the winter. Tall pagan towers built out of snow to ascertain the direction of the best harvest from the direction of their melt.

"Yes it happens in Latale and Lenegeri villages, two days at the end of February." Then as if purely on impulse he said: "We go now!"

So with Ushguli placed on hold the car was redirected back down to the village of Latale, the third village up from the border of Upper and Lower Svaneti.

As we drove up the track to the house of the 'protector' of Latale church, Shadur turned to me and with some pride said: "Latale is an important village. *Latale* means 'guard.' This is where the feudal system of Lower Svaneti used to end. Upper Svaneti has always been free. Svanetia is pure Georgia, no Persian influence, no collective farms."

I began to wonder if a method lay behind his apparent impulsiveness. We would begin my tour right at the base of Upper Svaneti, and then proceed in ever deeper and deeper. Or was it simpler yet, that to begin at someone's home in Svaneti would, of dire necessity, involve a major dose of hospitality — in our case, lunch.

At the gate of the house Shadur introduced us to a moustachioed man of about 60. "This is Marlen Tamliani, he is the head of the family," he said with some gravity. The institution of the family stood at the centre of Svan life, and at its centre stood the proud figure of the father. But this hierarchy also applied to the village. The family entrusted to guard the church, the village's most holy place, ranked close to the top. Furthermore, with the recent epidemic of thievery, most churches could no longer leave their icons inside. Svaneti's unconquered valleys meant the churches still possessed many old and highly valuable icons, that anywhere else would end up in museums. It also meant the guards' families would have to be well armed — to the extent that Svaneti's police force played a secondary role to these 12th century guardians.

Before lunch Marlen produced several of Latale's icons and allowed me to photograph a beautiful tenth century silver processional cross, inserted with cloisonné enamel faces. Ilia whispered to me: "Pete, you are lucky. This is very valuable, maybe we are trusted."

At the table several plates full of cheese, tomatoes, cucumbers, and meat quickly appeared. I also noticed three jugs of local wine, one of vodka and another of the dreaded *chacha*. Before I had a chance to line my stomach with any protection the toasting began. First, as was traditional in Svaneti, came "the Great God," second "the Archangel Gabriel," and the third "to St George." After that they resumed Tbilisi-style, "to friendship," "our nations," "Independent Georgia." Marlen then introduced the topic of World War II, speaking about his own role in the battle against the Nazis in 1942 when their southern front advanced towards the oil-fields of Baku, to be stopped just over the mountains from Svaneti. Making the point he took off his felt Svan cap and shook it in the air as he spoke. Thus a toast was called for, partly to diffuse the emotion, partly to enshrine it in the halo of this great victory. He rose to his feet, we all stood with him.

"To Stalin our great General!" he said. By then I simply raised my glass with everyone else. Ilia then explained that Stalin's severe mother had never let him forget his Georgian roots, and he'd always carried a soft spot for the Svans.

Meanwhile Shadur and Ilia began to toast earnestly to their new friendship, and it came to me that in Svaneti this ceremonial descent into drunkenness amounted to a formal treaty between strangers. In the valley of vendettas, trust — for a stranger like me interested in their priceless icons and treasures — could hardly be more valuable. As Ilia was to say later: "Pete, Svaneti is Wild West, nobody protect you. If we disappear, God save us!"

After this, in the end largely liquid lunch, we stumbled our way up the adjacent hill to Latale's Matskhvarishi church. The picturesque chapel is renowned for its 12th century frescoes, but tragically all I remember are a number of magnificent alcoholic blurs, plus a pagan-like cross covered with rams horns. Far too much vodka and *chacha* swam between me and any discerning faculties. I managed to photograph Marlen in his splendid traditional dress, then we stumbled back down the hill and into the car.

With Shadur, Ilia and I, unashamedly drunk, the driving fell to the faithful Temur. He steered the Lada at Shadur's directions, back to Mestia then on up onto a dirt road heading straight for the massive but invisible 5,007 metre shoulder of Mount Tetnuldi at the head of the valley.

"Ushguli, this way!" Shadur pointed drunkenly toward the cloud concealing this snowy giant. But, as we found out later, the upward angle of his finger hardly exaggerated.

As the fields rattled by I tried to make conversation with Temur, asking him about his life and profession as a psychiatrist in Tbilisi. However I experienced serious alcohol-inspired language difficulties. Noticing my problems Ilia helped out: "Temur is a *Tatar*. A Tatar from California!"

The car splashed through fresh puddles, crunched through gravel, dipped and lurched into potholes, in another severe test on the Lada. As the damp valley passed by, the landscape appeared not unlike Switzerland before the arrival of tarmac: fields laced with dirt tracks, in turn leading to balconied and well-eaved houses, politely dotting themselves across the

Tenth century processional cross with embedded enamel faces — Latale Church

hillsides, each one a self-supporting unit, with meadows that in the spring could be found carpeted in wild bluebells, cornflowers, pink caraways, and anemones. But all comparisons with the Alps instantly evaporated with the sight of another Svan village with its remarkable cluster of medieval towers. Such an intact 12th century presence, returning kilometre after kilometre, could belong to only one region, even within the Caucasus. The towers of other districts, like Ossetia just over the mountains, were now mostly crumbled and of a different design to the crenellated Svan tower.

Meanwhile the road began to climb steeply, up out of the valley and toward the next. At the top we looked down into another deep green gully containing a small village, a few towers, some more raggedly cultivated fields, all dominated by a church sitting on a hillock. With no more obvious Soviet-built buildings, the road began to fulfil its promise of winding us back through time.

"Nakipari," Shadur said to me indicating the church. "The Church of Saint George, 12th century. We will see it now."

We arrived in the village at the same time as a violent mountain downpour and an East German film-maker called Rolf. Rolf had heard about our mission and decided to tag along in his own jeep in the hope of filming opportunities. Meanwhile Shadur hurried off, seemingly undaunted, into the torrent and returned dripping head to foot with a man clutching an enormous bunch of keys.

"This is David," he introduced the man. "He is the Church Protector." I looked at the keys, some at least 15 centimetres long — not only pre-Revolutionary but possibly pre-Russian as well. He spent a good 15 minutes sorting out how to undo numerous chains, locks and devices barring thieves from the church. While we waited I asked Rolf about his luck trying to film the suspicious Svans.

"It's been very hard," he admitted. "I've been coming here for four years and still need more."

He said gaining permission to film often involved long drinking sessions, that it could be undone on a whim. "In one village they wouldn't let me take the St George icon out of the church because they said it would rain for a month."

We walked round the building and he pointed out the pagan symbols of a stag's head, deer and a mountain goat carved prominently onto its outer walls; symbols most other Christian churches had long since removed. There could be no denying that here the two religions thrived side by side, with Christian gods doubling as their

(Above) Fresco of St George being tortured on the wheel, Nakipari Church — traditionally, the frescoes were cleaned with bread.
(Below) Pagan symbols on the outside wall of Nakipari Church.

pagan predecessors. St George also spoke for the Moon God; St Barbara the sun god Lile; and the archangels, the protective spirits of the mountains.

Finally the doors gave way and we stepped into an almost completely dark chamber. As my eyes gradually acclimatised to the gloom, holy figures in strange colours loomed out of the blackness. First I noticed a spread of silver halos dancing across the firmament, then slowly the saintly faces filled in beneath. Finally the figure a huge seated man, dominating the entire dome of the church — the Great God — gazed down at us from his heavenly chair like a mountain king. Dressed in shadowy greys and burgundies he held up one hand for attention, while the other spread open a copy of the Bible. Behind his head the numerous haloed saints receded back toward infinity.

For the first time in a Georgian church the totality of the art struck me. For here, unlike in other fine centres of fresco art, as say Vardzia, the paintings remained virtually unmolested since their day of creation in 1130. The images stood faithful to the vision of their creator, Teodor, the court painter of Georgia's celebrated King David the Builder. I saw again the vivid depiction of the tortures of St George; the image of a human body stretched across a wheel in grim illustration of the torments of faith, his psychological persecutions elegantly represented by an imperiously robed Diocletian commanding his torture. Next to this came two wonderfully fluid portraits of St George and St Teodor heroically slaying both Diocletian and a dynamic looking dragon — the symbolic vanquishing of wild pagan emotions. But in this church, I couldn't help but feel the stern overhanging presence of non-Christian mountain gods. The background colours of the frescoes were a primitive dark green and black, outlined by red and white arabesque geometric patterns. These frescoes matched the influence of the distinctly pagan ceremonies still held outside the church at weddings, funerals and some saints' days.

Looking at it made me think of my childhood churches in England. There the iconography had refined itself away deep into the walls, presenting a far too remote, adult image for my childish mind to grasp. But here in this mountain church, the forces of nature glared back full of resolution and purpose. Here I felt God had not yet been tamed by man. Something Almighty clearly hung over life in the mountains. God was indeed still 'great.'

As if to prove it David then unlocked the church safe and pulled out a solid golden chalice along with a bottle of milky liquid. He poured this ominous fluid into the chalice, then pronounced a long toast in the Svan language "to the Great God," praising his power and dominion. With a sense of foreboding I began to realise what would come next. Finally he stopped speaking, lifted the chalice into the air, and gazing at the great figure in the ceiling, downed the liquid in one gulp. With eyes rekindled, he filled it again and handed it straight to me.

Holding the solid gold chalice, staring at the terrible liquid (bearing an eerie similarity to a British floor-cleaner), listening to another long toast in the strange, soft-sounding language, my mind raced through every possible excuse to avoid this refreshment. Take a sip, not swallow, then hand it back . . . faint? The demons of invention span in hopeless circles, and too late, for he finished his speech and immediately two sets of fierce Svan eyes glared at me. A swift glance at Ilia's anxious face bought back memories of vendettas, the easily offended Svans. I had no choice. Lifting the chalice briefly toward the Great God, I tipped the contents into my mouth and gulped. My throat roared out as burning red-hot knives seemed to shoot down to my stomach, then fire out tiny missiles and bomblets throughout my abdomen. With eyes bulging and watering I concluded it also tasted like floor-cleaner. Then to my horror David refilled the cup and handed it straight back. Accepting defeat, I closed my eyes, prayed for deliverance and knocked this one back too.

Perhaps the Great God heard my prayer because David then turned to Ilia, who, with the dedication of a true friend took over my duties as guest. Quickly I pleaded the excuse of photography and, stepping outside the church, found myself instantly drunk — again. Dimly I noticed the rain bouncing off my head in joyful splashes but realised, like a true Svan, water didn't matter any more. I'd lost all fear for my health, which was just as well, for the damage had already been done.

Back in the car, I asked a noisy Ilia how many gold cups he'd drunk in the end.

"Five," he shouted then grabbed my Walkman, slotted on Miles Davis and began thumping his feet loudly on the Lada's floor. A couple minutes later he removed the headphones. "Pete," he said with a look of sudden enlightenment, "I think that liquid was also 12th century."

Nevertheless he survived it, while I, two days later came down with a mysterious, gut-gripping fever — for which I hold this supercharged holy water wholly responsible. Several years later, after Georgia's brief but horrible war with Abkhazia, I heard further foreigner's stories with this terrible liquid. The United Nation's observers (UNOMIG) patrolling the Svanetian Kodori Valley renamed their patrols the '*chacha* patrols' because all too frequently their military vehicles were stopped by armed Svans inviting them in for a drink. On a couple of occasions when they spurned hospitality, pleading they were "on duty," they had their tyres shot out "accidentally." While they were waiting for repairs they, well . . . might as well drink. Like me, they also learned to accept Svan hospitality.

Night approached, and the Lada splashed on through heavy rain up the valley to the village of Lalhor. Here we pulled into the drive of a large private house with balcony. "We stay here," said Shadur emphatically.

"But they're not expecting us," I whispered to Ilia.

"Don't matter. This is Georgia. No problem," he replied, then added more quietly: "I think."

I'd already detected a hint of anxiety in this boisterous doctor from the capital. Even for him, Svan customs were a little strange.

At the house we were greeted by a number of children's faces peering round door-frames, up over window-sills. As far as I could judge the building housed a family including at least six children, plus attendant relations. Inquiries into the size of Lalhor only produced the answer, "Fifty three families." Stepping into the ground-floor kitchen area the senses immediately filled with the rich smells of baking *khachapuri*, emanating from a metal wood-fired stove in the room's centre.

In the corner I noticed a Soviet television tuned to the Moscow Channel, its picture snowy and its sound turned down. The Soviets had been quick to give this other electronic miracle to Svaneti, mounting their transmitter on Svaneti's prominent Queen Tamar's Tower as "a gesture to symbolise the link between epochs." What, I wondered, did this new generation of Svans think when they looked at me? Was this what came after the transmitter?

At table that evening came more brimming jugs of *chacha*, more cucumbers, mutton soup, 'serpent's cheese' — a long braided cheese special to Svaneti. I sat next to a young man of 24 with pale skin and red cheeks. He shook hands firmly and sat down next to me, eager to practise the few words of English he learnt during his schooldays. But more than this, I soon discovered, he wanted to find out about the lifestyle of another young man like him.

"How old are you?" "Do you like Georgia?" Where is your wife?"

The questions came thick and fast. I told him I wasn't married. He just nodded.

"So when will you marry?" he asked.

I explained marriage wasn't always necessary in our culture, that a man and a woman could live together without it.

"I feel the same way," he said earnestly. I could tell he'd thought about the issue, probably via TV programmes.

When I asked what he did for a living, he said simply: "Work."

It seemed he just did everything needed to keep

Musical instruments in a Svan home — the 'changi' (miniature harp) and 'chianuri' (with bow), along with modern heroes

the village running. But our conversation was interrupted by an emotional toast from Ilia — roaring drunk for the third time that day — directed to "Independent Georgia!" At the end of the speech my young neighbour lifted his glass, looked at me fervently and said: "I'm ready to die."

His tone left no doubt of it. The freedom of his country was as important as his own life. Any declared threat would be met with the fullest sacrifice. Yet no sooner had he lowered his glass than the emotion was forgotten and the intensive interrogation into my life continued.

"You can choose a woman when you want, not have to marry her?" "You too decide when you have children?" "Why did you come here to Svaneti?"

I could sense the earnest comparisons with his own life. What was this other culture that allowed a single young man like himself, to travel alone all

A family in Nakipari village

Svan towers at Chajashe village, the second in the Ushguli 'temi' ('community')
— permanently inhabited since before the birth of Christ

the way to his village just to look around then return? To choose a woman and not have children.

At the end of the meal he stood up, shook my hand firmly and said: "You the first foreigner I've spoken to. Thank you!" with a look of intense gratitude.

The memory of that look, haunted me for some time. What had I done? How had I affected him; had my presence planted some irreversible seed into the community?

I argued with myself that if not me then somebody else. That my good quality boots, windcheater, Walkman spoke as many volumes as anything I said, that a bachelor lifestyle was simply the fruits of natural human evolution.

But still the questions wouldn't go away.

The next morning arrived to the sound of a crashing mountain river and the tinkle of cowbells on the road. From the balcony I saw a scattering of houses and towers hemmed in by two enormous mountain-sides disappearing into the cloud. Around about collapsing stone barns stood like battered old rooks, their stones falling back to the earth like spent feathers: a clear sign of Svaneti's depopulation. On the main street a couple of cows strolled nonchalantly toward new steep green pastures, old car pistons tied round their necks as bells.

After breakfast the owner of the house offered to take us the final ten kilometres up to Ushguli in his jeep and we accepted.

The higher we climbed so the snow line descended. Trees fell away converting to shrubs, then finally vanished altogether replaced by the monotonous green turf of a landscape accustomed to deep snow. Then, just as I began to wonder how anything more than a few itinerant sheep could possibly live up here, I spotted a tower high on a hilltop, hundreds of feet above the valley. It seemed to scratch the bottom of the clouds like a ragged guard-house to heaven itself. The jeep continued under its gaze, switch-backing to and fro up a steep incline until finally we crept over the rim and into a shallow, treeless valley.

"Ushguli," Shadur announced emphatically.

Directly ahead of us stood three battered, Stone Age-looking villages; their haggard towers clustering together like old men before their gaunt leader — another solitary black tower standing on a hilltop. The four villages of Ushguli (the furthest, Gvibiani, lay concealed beyond the hill), still contained about a thousand inhabitants. The villages then had electricity (coming and going at random), but little else belonged to our time. The roofs of the towers were spread with shaggy black slates, while below their rendered skin flaked off to show the dark granite flesh beneath. Unlike the towers of Mestia that seemed to rise up as something apart from the earth, these belonged to it, as if strange rocks whittled out by a centuries-old wind. At 2,300 metres, these were not only the highest villages in Svaneti, they were among the oldest. Archaeologists dated the bases of some Ushguli towers to the time of Christ

— another possible explanation why these stone uprights command almost the same respect among Georgians as the mountains themselves.

The villages followed the course of the Inguri river as it approached its source. The dominating black tower stood over the second village, Chajashe, which also contained Ushguli's famous museum and not so famous new hotel. Ushguli's school also used to stand at its foot, but now the site lies as a ruin, after the terrible avalanche of 1987 that buried so many children. They say not a single family in Ushguli remained unmarked that terrible winter.

As for the hotel — I asked our jeep driver, through Ilia, how much it cost for a night, and whether it had been constructed to encourage a new industry in the region.

"It's closed," came the brusque translation from Ilia as they all chatted on among themselves.

Occasionally I detected a reluctance in Ilia to translate some of my questions, as if worried I'd upset the carefully constructed house of cards balanced around our visit. Later on, during a lull in one of the drinking parties he admitted as much. Clutching a beaker full of sloshing vodka ready for the next toast, he said: "Pete, I too am working now like you. I'm working hard. The Svan mafia is terrible, like Columbia! You know someone said you are English mafia — I deny that for you!"

I realised his primary concern was for me, since I was his guest first. On this count he certainly 'worked' to make up for my own unguest-like moderate drinking. On one occasion I watched him down a two litre bottle of wine (the equivalent of one of the enormous Svan drinking horns) in a single, endless gulp. An action to be followed by his taking up residence in 'the hospital' as we renamed the Lada's back seat. About half an hour later, wailing to Leonard Cohen's song *Everybody Knows*, with the words "Everybody's nose . . ." he suddenly ripped the headphones off his ears.

"Stop the car!" he shouted.

"Whats the matter?" Temur asked, driving on.

"Stop the car!" he shouted again, then added: "I'm dying!"

Then he leaned forward, grasped me by the wrist and said pleadingly: "Help me, I'm dying."

We kept asking him what was the matter; but all he would say was "I'm dying, the pain, I'm dying!"

Temur stopped the car; whereupon Ilia flung open the door and staggered to the roadside just in time to release most of the two litres back to the soil. After this he slept like a child, his work complete.

At Chajashe, the jeep skidded to a halt in the mud next to the museum. Shadur and our host then disappeared to hunt down the museum's guard.

With no sign of their return I strolled around the village photographing the buildings and people. After about an hour Ilia suddenly hurried up to me and said: "We go to lunch, now."

I asked where and he pointed to a nearby house underneath a tower. The woman of the house had spotted us wandering around, and simply invited us in.

"Your feet bless our house," said our host with a solemn nod to me at the first toast. "You are the first foreigner to enter here."

I acknowledged the honour and the meal commenced with a quite delicious fresh *khachapuri* the Svans called *teeshdvar*, baked with fresh local cheeses and spices. Eventually word came that Shadur had returned. And so, taking our leave, we walked back to the museum to find him there standing next to a small, steely-eyed man.

"This is the museum's guard, Pridon," said Shadur. "Shake hands."

I took hold of his hand and shook, only to find this stern man refused to let go of my hand. I remained trapped before him at arm's length as he stared back at me, scrutinising my every reaction. Like Shadur's apple, I seemed to be undergoing another test, and a pristine dose of the legendary Svan suspicion. But they did have something to protect. Rumour had it that many pieces in the Ushguli museum rivalled those in Tbilisi's Art Museum. The Svans had lost so many of their treasures they now refused to let them leave their valleys, trusting no one, and barely themselves. Intuition still played a major role in their defence.

Finally he released my hand and turned to Shadur saying in Georgian, "The museum will open—" then qualified it, "—when the priest arrives."

My heart sank, surely a diplomatic refusal. But to my surprise I noticed a tall, bearded man strolled up the road in full robe: the priest, looking ready to conduct a service.

After more formal introductions and speeches during another downpour in which the Svans never moved, as if standing in full sunshine — Pridon finally unlocked the museum door. No sooner had we stepped onto the dirt floor of the tower's first level, than the door swung shut again and I heard the sound of the lock being turned. He put the key into his pocket.

Before us under a single dingy bulb stood two giant bronze processional crosses, a 19th century wooden crossbow and pike. The priest then intoned a long prayer before the cross. Plainly we'd not entered a museum so much as a Holy of Holies for the icons of most of the Ushguli churches. The prayers let everyone know that entry amounted to a privilege. I later discovered how true this was, meeting several tourists who'd travelled all the way up to Ushguli only to be refused entry by Pridon. The objects here were still treated as if they maintained their rightful positions — back in their churches.

After the ceremony we climbed up to the main first floor chamber. Poking my head up through the floor it felt like suddenly being propelled back to the Tbilisi Art Museum. The room was plush, carpeted, the exhibits on its burlap lined walls well laid out, the cabinets standing before them as predicted, full of magnificent icons. As we walked round so the hushed, reverent atmosphere followed, and I noticed many new faces in the crowd — locals who'd heard of the museum's opening just before Pridon locked the door. They stood before the icons, crossed themselves, or just gazed privately, resuming their relationship with these objects. Among the exhibits I saw an 11th century icon of Mary breastfeeding Jesus, a particularly fierce Svan-looking Jesus from the 11th century, a collection of European altar cups given to Svaneti by visitors — one with a man carrying an axe climbing up the stem. "He cut off all the branches of the tree of life, including the one he was sitting on," I was told proudly. Up on the top floor the cabinets displayed some graceful pieces of ancient Svan jewellery.

As we made our way back down the ladder the priest spoke to me. "Fifty per cent of Ushguli's treasures have been stolen," he said, and I began to understand the grudging will of the villagers to show it off. As if by so doing they not only lost some of their power, but also risked losing them altogether. Yet the alternative now was to place them in the new museum being built in Mestia — its intention to protect all Svaneti's religious wealth. I could see them asking what good would come of allowing more foreigners in to photograph? In the end it just added another security threat and belittlement to their holiness. (I'd heard several Georgians express doubts that God could still properly exist in Europe and America.)

Georgian refugee from Abkhazia, holding up her picture of her family's escape over the mountains into Svaneti — part of the War Child 'Children of the Caucasus' therapeutic art project, 1997-98

As we stepped outside I noticed a sonic alarm system, tacked up against the 12th century stone, silently blinking to our departure — working I assumed whenever the electricity did. Once outside the door we met the enigmatic figure of Rolf the film-maker again. Hoping for another filming opportunity he'd shadowed our progress all the way up, but Pridon had forbidden him to film in the museum. He waited outside the locked door thwarted again, and I noticed he gazed with a certain longing up into the snowly flanks of Tetnuldi where a "rich Tatar treasure" was reportedly buried.

"This English friend of yours," he said cheerfully to Ilia, "has seen as much in one day as it took me a year to see."

A hearty compliment to Ilia, his relentless good humour and Svan-like drinking. Certainly I had now received a whirlwind tour right into the heart of the Svan culture. Yet walking to the jeep, looking back at these walls sprouting grass and lichen, sturdily built towers with their slow moving, hospitable inhabitants, I knew I'd missed most of it. In these rare places where antiquity walks the streets, and culture has remained stable for two thousand years; for all their vendettas and drinking, the Svans had still achieved something we in the West hadn't — permanence.

I wondered about this luxury of mine — travel. Had anyone ever really taught us how to use it? It seemed to me these moments should be employed carefully, tacked down. Such rich experience should not just be consumed, but somehow emplanted in active imagination. In Ushguli, at the end of that ragged road under mossy, bending towers, I began to realise the process of travel created a kind of private country of its own. The individualised domain of each voyager, its site loosely pegged out, ready for those adjustments of 'self,' the psychological insight we hope might step up to greet us in such far-flung outposts.

When I shook hands with Pridon to say goodbye, he gripped my hand and stared back as long and determinedly as before. It seemed to say he had given me his trust, now it was up to me to honour it. I vowed I would.

But as fate would have it the tourist boom everyone expected for Georgia and Svaneti never came. With independence Georgia sank instead into civil war. Three years after my visit Svaneti experienced a different kind of influx when over 100,000 Georgian refugees fled from Abkhaz reprisals up the Kodori Valley and over the high passes to safety in Svaneti. An agonising exodus documented by a sole British photographer Mike Goldwater. His pictures show whole families, grandmothers, children and dogs, clutching a few precious belongings, struggling through the snow. Many hundreds of people died on that journey alone.

Four years after this I returned to Georgia working on a project for the charity War Child. As a part of its art therapy we asked those refugee children to make paintings of anything on their minds, and to our surprise nearly all presented us with detailed and loving pictures of Sukhumi beach with palm trees and themselves playing on the sand. Several also painted the scene of escape, clutching their parent's hands, hair blowing in the wind, as they tried to make their way along the snow. I never forget one 12-year-old girl presenting her picture to me with an expression that seem to say "why?"

After the high passes, they arrived in the Svan valleys, like so many thousands of Georgians in the past fleeing persecution in the lowlands. As before the Svans welcomed them in.

It took another three years after that for tourists to gingerly make a return. When they did they reported little change in the landscape. But one friend, working for the Norwegian Refugee Council told me she had encountered the 'New Svaneti.'

"I read your chapter," she said, refering to most of the above paragraphs, "and arrived expecting to to be assailed by wild drinking, shooting and hospitality. But in fact we stayed in one of the new pioneering Svan guest houses. We had to pay $40 each per night, were never invited to a single drinking party. When we entered Mestia Museum, we were told to pay one lari (50 US cents) for every photo we took, and 20 lari in the treasury!"

I received other reports of this new commercial consciousness from Marika whose friend has just returned from Svaneti, making restoration work in the churches. "Now the Svans watch their televisions," she had said grimly. "They are told that to be modern you must charge for everything. My friend said they asked him to pay to enter the church to work on its frescoes! He could see they felt strange doing it, because it was against their nature, but they felt they must copy what they were told."

But just when I starting worrying about the end of an era, I met the UN representative who had experienced UNOMIG's *chacha* patrols in the Kodori Valley. She told me she thought Svan culture was changing, but only in pockets; that essentially it remained the same. Then a thought seemed to strike her.

"The best toasts I've heard in Georgia have been from the Svans," she said decisively. "Recently at one dinner in Lower Svaneti, a Svan *tamada* gave a toast about the Abkhaz War. I will never forget it. Many Svans were killed by Abkhaz in the war and the subject was a Svan woman who during the most intense period of fighting sent her three children to a helicopter for evacuation, only to then watch it shot down by an Abkhaz missile. It took her four terrible days to find out her children were safe. After telling this story the Svan *tamada* raised his glass and said very firmly to all his fellow Georgians, 'I drink this to Abkhaz children.' Everyone drank; most had tears in their eyes."

13

Sukhumi

I decided to take the night train from Tbilisi to Sukhumi. Ilia, with a group of friends, came to the station and gave a final word of advice as I stepped into the carriage. "Have you ever been on a Soviet train before . . . ? Be warned!" The implication was, as with all things Soviet, it might not make it. Or if it did, would be late, uncomfortable, unhappy, and every other negative attached to the Soviet world.

Yet I wondered how the purified, technicolour trains of Independent Georgia ran in his imagination. To my eye this Soviet-built train running on Moscow time (the timetables at stations across the USSR operated according to centralised time) presented itself as clean and well supplied. The crisp, new sheets, pillow-cases, and blankets, matched anything British Rail could produce. But I thanked him for his warning — Ilia had been a true friend.

As the train juddered out of the station, I watched the smiling faces and waving hands, shrinking away on the platform. Who could not feel affected by this time-honoured sense of concern for their guest? It may have been a Georgian tradition, it may simply have been the thing to do, but either way it showed a respect for the stranger, now long forgotten in Europe. I felt sorry to go, and as they all disappeared around the bend in the platform that phrase from Schopenhauer returned — "in every parting comes an image of death." I wondered how these Georgians would survive their newest battle-cry of nationalism? As one Georgian friend had put it: "While it's difficult for anyone to survive the 20th century, here in Georgia we embrace it like we embrace everything we fear — too passionately."

But I worried about their gallant quests for 'freedom' blotting out the sun of long-term planning and political strategy. It seemed they skated across the thin ice of political inexperience, that this potential for mistakes held true right down to its most mundane actions, like driving across town. Indeed within a year, two of those faces on the platform were involved in serious road accidents — the mother of one was killed.

Finally the lights on top of Tbilisi's TV tower slid away into an engulfing night. I acclimatised myself to that mournful grunting, creaking, companionship of railways the world over, their moments of stretching time, placing gaps between life's bigger moments. I always look forward to these strange in-between times, the shuddering journeys along two metal shafts of no-man's land, with all their extra time to catch up on one's sadly neglected inner life.

Sukhumi pier, in that happier 'before the war' period so often referred to by Abkhazians

I felt Tbilisi receding away behind me into the night like a giant Gothic cathedral, shot with bright emotional light streaming through stained glass windows. Out of its doors citizens came and went in full-blooded worship of the past. From inside one heard those religious chords full of nationalism, disguising their fear for the future. A kind of shout of alarm at the approaching new world.

Now I headed toward West Georgia, the traditional outer limit of the country with its wide open border of sea. My spirits lifted. At the other end of the line lay Sukhumi, Georgia's first city on the Black Sea coast. I imagined sub-tropical heat, acres of light and relaxation. In the morning I would wake beside the sea from where Jason and his Argonauts arrived in search of Colchis, King Medes and the Golden Fleece, where many of the Soviet Union's privileged arrived in search of holidays or dachas (Gorbachev owned one at Musera).

But the Sukhumi I approached also contained a curfew and Soviet armour patrolling its streets. Tomorrow morning I would also wake in the modern Autonomous Republic of Abkhazia, home of the then newly reviled Abkhazians. Earlier in the summer the Stalinist deep sleep had finally declared itself over with the first inter-ethnic flare-up within Georgia's own borders since the 1917 Revolution. None of us had any clue of the terrible conflagration that lay in store, just four years down the road, resulting in 250,000 Georgians being ethnically cleansed from their homes in Abkhazia.

Some months had now passed since April 9th, and Georgian (and Abkhazian) blood had flowed again that following July as the two sides fought over the territory's sovereignty. But to say Georgian had fought Georgian, would now be unacceptable for the Abkhazians. They regarded this violence as an indigenous population resisting a colonial power (Georgia), since Abkhazia had spent many centuries fluctuating in and out of the Georgian federation. A humiliating and ironic rebellion for the Georgians, whose own complaint against the Russians found a carbon copy within their own borders — this time with themselves as the brutalising central power. A conflict soon duplicating itself more violently in the bloody Ossetian uprising of 1991.

In Sukhumi I wanted to try and understand why this emotion suddenly reared its head in another ancient nationality who, like the Ossetians, could also live relatively peacefully within or beside Georgia — as they had for many centuries.

In the two-berth sleeper sat a powerfully-built man in his late thirties. When one of my Georgian friends sat briefly on his bed at the station, he'd responded with an instant "get off!" His eyes had glared back as if the territory of the bed was his alone and had been violated. Yet the moment the train left the station his mood changed. No longer aggressively dominating the small space between the beds, he behaved with absolute civility. Discovering I spoke only a few Georgian words, his face lit up with pleasure. I realised instantly, I shared my compartment with 'the enemy,' an Abkhazian.

Via a mixture of Russian and several European languages he told me he lived in the town of Novy Afon, just up the coast from Sukhumi; a former Greek community; that he had come to dislike the Georgians who he felt behaved like bullies.

"Georgians hate Abkhazians," he said. "They shout 'Abkhazia is ours' and treat us like property."

I'd been curious to hear the other side of the story ever since the day a liberal Georgian friend sneeringly described the Abkhazians as "Russified Turks, with no culture of their own" (patently untrue).

"We're tired of being 'ruled' by Georgia," he said. "We want to rule ourselves and maintain a friendship with Moscow. We're not crazy separatists like the Georgians."

Yet statistics pointed to a serious problem here. The half million or so population of Abkhazia stood as 44 per cent Georgian and only 17 per cent Abkhazian. At the same time the Autonomous Republic remained one of the most (if not 'the' most) rich, luxurious, and profitably cultivated areas of the Soviet Union. The sub-tropical strip running along the western end of the Greater Caucasus caught plenty of sun and rain. A land of rich alluvial soil and long sandy beaches. On top of this, its coastline stood at the heart of the 'Russian Riviera,' the 800 kilometre strip of coast from Batumi, in Georgia's south-west corner up to Novorossiysk in the Russian Federation.

In his angry expression I felt that same tirelessly rising sap of 'independence,' the sublimated quest for individuality then saturating most of the Soviet bloc. To the outsider, watching it inflate the veins of a tiny autonomous republic within a republic, it seemed like madness. But then I'd not spent all my life penned down under Stalin's bludgeoning attempt to homogenise almost every aspect of public and private life.

After the lights were shut out, I lay back on my bunk wondering how on earth to solve this problem of self-definition. Here, surely, lay one of those terrible dilemmas of identity that, as Jung put it, could never be "solved," only "outgrown." I racked my brain for anyone I'd met in the Soviet Union who'd outgrown or stepped beyond this peculiar need for aggressive self-redefinition? As the train climbed toward the dark, invisible vales of the former West Georgian kingdom of Imereti, the mental screen remained quite blank. But just as sleep threatened to slip in its place, suddenly a name flicked up: Sasha Bashlachov.

Yes, here stood a powerful alternative to the ideas of 'self' resurrecting themselves in the post-Soviet world; one that during his tragically short life he announced as widely as possible. In the fashion of men like Maxim Gorky before him, Bashlachov had become a poetic vagabond, abandoning his work as a journalist on Cherepovets' newspaper *The Communist* to become a poet and singer.

I'll never forget our first meeting one wintery afternoon on Leningrad's Nevsky Prospekt back in 1987. He'd stood there a fierce, blue-eyed, gap-toothed poet wearing a Jim Morrison badge, speaking no English yet brimming with manic enthusiasm and passion. I asked, via a Russian friend Alec Khan, what he thought about the psychological 'system' imposed by the Soviet government. He looked back half smiling and asked: "Which system?"

I gestured to the buildings and streets all around.

"Oh that . . . ," he replied. "I've got nothing to do with it. The word 'system' is a dead word for me — it's their word not mine."

Coming from anyone else I might have logged this as wishful thinking; but the zest of his speech, the intense burrowing look in his eye, the delight on Alec's face as he translated, somehow made it utterly believable.

I suddenly felt myself in the presence of the kind of imaginative freedom easily capable of withstanding any political system — except perhaps its own. He spoke intelligently with a wide-eyed fervour that sometimes placed his face inches away from mine, his fingers grasping the air to make his point.

I asked him about the struggles of self versus nationality in the USSR.

"We go to war, fight each other, kill," he'd said. "But it's like being with a woman. It's impossible to understand, so we fight in our frustration. For me the fight has turned to singing. To me this is like searching for a woman's voice. You hear it when you're wrapped in the womb, then suddenly you're born into bright lights and noise. And you hear her screams, which were a part of you. You think they're delightful for her and you spend your life looking for that scream again, that is music. You come out of the womb with the question, how to find this voice again. But then you realise it's a mistaken question, birth itself was your answer and you mistook it for a question."

"And nationality?" I repeated.

"It's another cry — is the same!" he exclaimed.

He grabbed my notepad wrote down two almost identical looking Russian words.

"The first word, *strach* means 'fear,'" he said with great purpose. "The second word *trach* means 'to make love.' You see the connection?"

He stared back at me, full of a terrible, urgent, laughing need for me to understand.

"Death is in between both. To me it's also like a woman. Only a woman can really kill you, because only a woman can really love you. Death itself is just a brief physical event — it's easy. I try to die now every day . . ."

If his songs hadn't been so marvellous, even in translation. If some of the USSR's greatest singers and writers hadn't praised him rapturously — Alla Pugacheva (the Soviet Barbra Streisand) had burst into tears when she first heard him sing, declaring him a genius — these may have sounded like the words of a madman. But everyone who came into contact with Sasha reported the same sense of genius, and bursting, impossible divination — in many ways too powerful for the world around it. This made it all the harder to accept his choice to indulge his curiosity towards life's biggest emotion of all, with his suicide in February 1988.

I woke to the sight of fields of tea, sweetcorn and tobacco, outside the window; to the jagged white peaks above Lower Svaneti to the east. The temperature and the humidity had climbed dramatically during the 1,000 metre drop from Tbilisi; an entirely new climatic zone had been entered. The train now rattled through the hostile fields of Abkhazia.

As the dense undergrowth, flannel-green leaves, occasional bending palm, drifted peacefully by, I wondered about this nationality within a nationality now resisting the Georgians. A culture just as ancient, with a distinctive language linked not to Georgian but to the tribes of the Northern Caucasus like the Circassians. The Kingdom of Abkhazia had merged with West Georgia many centuries ago for the sake of a collective Georgian strength to repel Abkhazia's historical enemy the Turks. Now, along with the rest of Georgia, identity seemed more important than strength. The train passed a cemetery with an extraordinary memorial — a garage-like shrine rising over a hideously crumpled car. A grim example of how the strength of modern technology can be ignored by Caucasians. I hoped these peoples wouldn't race down the road to independence in the same way they did to the shops (unfortunately they did).

Suddenly a huge space opened out in the left-hand window, and with it the smooth millpond of the Black Sea, its sky and water melting sublimely together at the horizon. Before it a long sandy beach followed the course of the railway, spreading unendingly north and south like a yellow bracelet wrapping around the sea. Yet in spite of this balmy atmosphere the September

Views of Sukhumi, 1989 (clockwise from top left) — Amra restaurant on Sukhumi pier; downtown Sukhumi; beachside cafe; the sea front leading to the Ritza Hotel (formerly the San Remo — in Trotsky's time); Sukhumi beach

crowds had not arrived. I counted perhaps 30 holiday-makers along a two kilometre stretch of sand, only ten in the water. Sukhumi might have been the Blackpool of the southern USSR but it remained a pleasant far cry from the fearsome thrusts at entertainment so characterising the British seaside.

From the station I asked the cab to drive me straight to the seafront. Like a pilgrim to open space, I had first to soak in all this emptiness, to relax. I prayed for a secluded bench on a wide, carless esplanade, facing the water, and Sukhumi, like all good seaside resort towns, provided exactly that. I sank down onto the seat close to the Hotel Abkhazia, and under some gently rustling palms, inhaled my first health-restoring gulps of Black Sea air.

Ahead spread the lazy landscape of gently rippling water stretching away to the place where the Soviet Union finally ended. The extraordinary calm of the sea's surface swept out before us like an enormous living movie screen, running a permanent feature of borderlessness and uninhibited water. I could feel its energising message breathing back over all the ambling holiday-makers. Tideless, the Black Sea behaves more like a lake than a sea, its sinister depths (below 180 metres nothing lives) almost registering on the surface. Some say the sea takes its name from a lining of dark sediment and hydrogen sulphide, occasionally stirred up by storms, others say its from the rusty black sand found on its southern beaches.

On either side of me rows of chairs were filled with more blond heads than usual, a sure sign of the heavy Russian presence in this far-flung corner of the USSR. All eyes seemed to drift southward out towards the Muslim region of Ajara, Batumi, then the Turkish border — a border much trafficked by Georgians, with relatives (supposed or real) in Northern Turkey, and plenty of items to sell to the currency bearing Turks.

I closed my eyes and tried to remember my background reading on Sukhumi's history. According to archaeological evidence the city had thrived as a population centre right back to the Stone Age. In the ancient kingdom of Colchis it flourished as a focal point of local trade. When the Greeks arrived they changed its name to Dioscuria, and the town into an international port which, by the second century BC, even minted its own coins. But the eroding advance of the Black Sea was to claim most of the original port, then a few centuries later the Romans saw to the rest. By the second century AD it evolved into their fortress town of Sebastopolis, which subsequently fell to the Byzantines then the Turks, and so on with the usual Caucasian ping-pong of conquest and reconquest, devastation and rebuilding, right up to our present century (in 1867 its population was reduced to 412 by the Turks, during the Russo-Turkish War). During the Soviet period the city restored its status as capital, and climbed back to a population of 120,000 — then of course to lose two thirds of that again in 1993-94 during its separatist war with Georgia (at the time beyond my, and most people's wildest imaginings).

Opening my eyes, I looked down the esplanade to see men and women wearing T-shirts emblazoned with slogans like 'Buggy' or 'Disco,' children eating ice-creams or clutching buckets and spades. The fully normalised image of modern sea-resort life. Yet I also knew that not far out under the water of Sukhumi bay lay an acropolis, a contemporary of the Parthenon and still standing.

Directly ahead the focal point of the sea-front was its pier, with its entrance of neon-lit dolphins diving through a hoop. Beyond them stood the Amra Restaurant striding out into the bay on stilts, with its breezy upstairs café and the word 'restaurant' written in Russian across the front. At first I mistook it for Abkhazian, as it uses an extended Russian alphabet, but then noticed none of the peculiar 19th century bulges on its letters.

Around me I watched the dark eyes and eagle-like noses walk past along the esplanade, asking myself which were Abkhazian, which Georgian? A few minutes later a dark-haired Georgian came up to ask me the time in an aggressive, rough Russian. I smelt alcohol on his breath. When I held up my wrist for him to look, he spat on the ground and walked away. He wished to make the point that we Russians (the wine made him mistake my blond hair as Slavic), waving our cameras as if nothing were going on, should not feel welcome in *his* seaside resort. Many Georgians resented the Russians in Sukhumi for what they saw as their support for the Abkhazian cause, believing the Russians put the Abkhazians up to their rebellion to deliberately sabotage the Georgian call for independence. During the taxi ride from the station I'd passed several Soviet Army armoured cars manning road-blocks, searching vehicles for weapons. Yet more targets for Georgian resentment.

Sitting amid this blend of the murderous and the happy, I noticed a boy of about eight on the beach playing a new game with his enormous Russian grandmother. She threw stones and he dodged them. I watched fascinated as sport grew steadily more determined. He shouted at her to throw the stones harder. She laughed but did as she was told, until after a few minutes I could tell she genuinely tried to hit him and he genuinely had to leap hard and wide to dodge these phoney bullets.

Could this have been the game now played throughout the city; provocation and counter-provocation as the two populations threatened to pull the city apart — which of course is exactly what they did . . .

It made me remember a scene in Fazil Iskandar's *Sandro of Chegem*, where a character implores Uncle Sandro not to say he was a Menshevik. "I'm just myself," came Sandro's wise reply. One laments the absence of such tact today.

My home in Sukhumi turned out to be a room in the 15th Congress Holiday Home on the Tbilisi Road. This miniature Soviet Butlins, comprised two tower-blocks, a large communal eating hall, outdoors dance area, and public address system, surrounded by a high metal fence and gates. On the other side of the gates, just across the bustling Tbilisi highway, the Black Sea lapped amiably against the sand.

That evening, fearing the 11pm curfew lock-out, I leant against the alcohol-free bar and watched the organised entertainment. First a dance. A smartly dressed band played ballads and polite rock and roll, as a group of reserved couples swayed on the floor. This unemotional mixing of men and women took place in a camp dotted with noticeboards exhorting inmates not to drink, to follow camp rules and Congress ideology. Watching the dance I remembered George Orwell's term for love-making in *1984* — "our duty to the party" — knowing here was one point he sorely mispredicted. Soviet Russia had evolved as a highly promiscuous society in which sex had become more "our only escape from the party."

This camp, virtually unchanged since Brezhnev's day, conveyed with impeccable authenticity the good clean atmosphere of obedience of the last 70 years, right down to the distance between the dresses and nylon brown trousers on the dancefloor. But now, just outside the perimeter fence came an awakening. The compliant Caucasian tribes were beginning their war dance, threatening to break in.

Clutching my paper cup filled with cherry juice, I engaged in a conversation with a schoolteacher from Moscow, who spoke a quite passable English. I noticed his cup full of wine. I asked him where on earth he bought it.

"Here." He smiled and lifted the bottle from beside his feet, then taking hold of another cup filled it for me.

"They don't care," he said, throwing a glance to the staff behind the bar, "because they didn't serve it. They won't get in trouble."

"But you will," I suggested.

He smiled sweetly. "What are they going to do, throw me out? There's a curfew! Besides everybody here is drunk."

At first I didn't believe him, having watched those stiff, restrained dancers. But he proved absolutely right. The alcohol, rather than liberating people, simply sunk them deeper into their introspection. Confirmation arrived with that night's organised entertainment: 'The Love Competition.'

The band stopped playing and a camp attendant clutching a microphone stepped forward to explain the rules. "First of all we need an attractive young woman . . . ," she said and walked straight over to a blonde girl in the audience, took her by the arm and positioned her at the front of the dance floor. She asked the girl her name.

"This is Tanya, she's from Minsk," she said into the microphone. "Now which men would like to have a date with her?"

There followed a moment of terrible silence, as the sodden introversion compounded in on itself. Finally a couple of isolated hands rose sheepishly out of the crowd. Seeing this a few other men gingerly lifted theirs.

"OK, you, you and you," said the compere, pointing to various hands in the audience and beckoning them to step forward. She then positioned these male suitors at the opposite end of the floor from the girl.

"Now you must take a step forward and tell the girl just how much you like her . . ."

She told the girl at first to encourage the men, listen to each entreaty, then cut it off when she felt she'd heard enough and pass on to the next. For every ten seconds of speaking, the suitors could take a step toward her. Thus she produced a staggered line of applicants, frozen in their headlong rush towards their feminine prize.

The compere handed the microphone to the first man, who introduced himself as Serge from Kiev in very slurred speech. He took his step forward then dried up completely. The compere tried to help.

"Tell her how beautiful she is, how much you would like to meet her, what you have to offer her."

Serge held the microphone to his lips, opened his mouth but no sound emerged. He just stood there open-mouthed, either too drunk or too shy to say more than his name. The microphone was quickly passed to the next — a tall, tanked-up Czech who took several huge strides forward amid a torrent of soulful promises, claims and gross flattery until he too was stopped, a good two yards ahead of the Ukrainian. After this the microphone was handed to a casual, smooth-talking Georgian from Tbilisi who, focusing his attention on the girl, walked forward speaking in the most charming and persuasive tones, as if not playing a game at all. He was allowed two good strides beyond the Czech.

My companion from the bar made a wry observation: "Russian women always seem to like Georgian men — why, I don't know!"

"Perhaps they're more charming?" I suggested.

"I don't call their love of Stalin very charming," he replied gruffly.

But his words turned out to be prophetic because on the third round the Georgian went on to win convincingly. I asked my companion what he thought about the Georgian charm in relation to the Abkhazians, and the problem now closing in on the camp gates.

"The Georgians are crazy," he said with some distaste. "They're trying to force the Abkhazians to speak Georgian. They put forward a new programme at the university only in Georgian, so the Abkhazians would have to learn. This led to the fighting. Because you see the conflict is really only because the Abkhazians won't join them in their plans to separate from the Soviet Union. Their refusal made the Georgians furious, and they started shouting 'Abkhazia is ours,' that the Abkhazians are devils, collaborators with the evil Russians."

He smiled briefly then shrugged his shoulders.

"They're crazy," he repeated, "like little Stalins. They have, what do you say . . . inferiority complex. Give them power and overnight they become capable of great cruelty, like Stalin."

I thought it strange that Stalin had suddenly become nothing to do with Russia, a purely Georgian phenomena. Then came a metallic sound behind us. Two Ministry of Interior soldiers had appeared clutching Kalashnikovs, as the public address system came to life.

"It is now 11 o'clock," announced a stiff school-mistressish voice. "Due to

the extraordinary situation will you all now please return to your rooms."
From her tone I almost expected to hear her add: "and wash behind your
ears." We obeyed.

The next morning I walked out onto my room's balcony and looked down at the
camp's wispy pines and palms, the speakers tied to the trees, the glimpses of
Black Sea beyond. I inhaled the sweet fragrance of Asmantus now floating
across the city. All signs of any curfew or trouble in the nation of Georgia had
disappeared. The sea breathed in and out with the same deep tranquillity as it
had for a million years. Would the inter-ethnic problems of these mountains
just fade away — as easily as the arrival of this soothing dawn after last night's
curfew? Instinct even then told me 'no.'

I walked into the town and searching for a short-cut to the beach accidentally wandered into a large private holiday camp for Party officials and Army officers. On the beach at the end of an elegant palm-lined walkway, a couple of junior officers stood stretching on the sand, another dried

*Photographs of a claimed 150-year-old man and a 147-year-old
(Sukhumi Museum)*

himself with a large red towel. I watched an old military man jogging along the
sea front at walking pace, his bleach-white belly wobbling in the morning light.

Later that day at the Abkhazian State Museum I saw a photograph of a man
looking remarkably like that jogger, with a caption beneath it reading '150
years old.' Next to it came another picture of two dozen centenarians dressed
in Caucasian mountain dress, with *papakhi* wool hats, *masra* cartridge belts,
moustaches, and daggers lying across their knees. The museum also filled
itself with numerous fossils, palaeolithic finds, and collections of stuffed local
animals. In one display I saw a Caucasian aurochs, an imperial eagle, an ibex
and a bear; clues to the huge range of wildlife still found in the Caucasus and
still, even in 1998, attracting little interest from Western naturalists and film-
makers.

Outside the museum's entrance stood a large dolmen reminding visitors of
Sukhumi's imponderable history, dating way back into Palaeolithic times.
Many of these antiquated tombs could be found scattered among the nearby
hills, as well as (so we were told) some remarkable six-foot tall stone penises
— not on display in the museum — although I once discovered one hidden

away from embarrassed Intourist guides, at the bottom of Tbilisi's Architectural Park.

Later, at the State Institute for Gerontology, I asked the resident professor for more scientific proof of these claims of Abkhaz longevity. He replied casually but clearly: "We've found that Abkhazia averages 38 centenarians per 100,000 of the population, while the rest of the world averages about 15 per 100,000."

And how did he arrive at these figures?

"In this institute we've studied about 1,500 cases in depth since 1974," he said. "We've learnt to be very careful because our research shows that 56 per cent of old people give a wrong date of birth, and generally once over 80 feel they've earned the right to add on a few more years to their total."

Young and old — 75-year-old wife of an orchard owner holding a Caucasian sheepdog puppy

Still not entirely convinced, we asked how they verified age?

"The most accurate method of dating them is by their teeth," he said then smiled. "But most have already lost them."

"What about the photographic evidence," someone interjected. "Like the two dozen centenarian men and the two 150 year olds in the museum?"

"A good example of exaggeration," he said calmly. "It's interesting to remember there are twice as many women centenarians as men, and how many photographs of women did you see in the museum?"

I didn't remember seeing any, and suddenly I found myself inclined to believe this scientist.

"The oldest properly documented age we have living here in Abkhazia at the moment is 107. But if you ask him his age he'll tell you he's 140. I personally don't believe it's possible to age beyond 120."

From here the conversation grew steadily more fascinating and I found my notebook filling up rapidly. Under the 'advice' section my remarks ran as follows: *Centenarians rarely smoke; they eat a wide variety of vegetables; prefer maize bread instead of wheat, like yoghurts, cheeses, beans and natural wines — they drink two to three full glasses a day. Honey seems to play a part in their diet. Never been a fat centenarian. All are slim, active, and have usually lived a full married life, not many bachelor centenarians. They hunt or pick the fruit, they drink coffee only for medicinal purposes. The world's oldest man liked to drink half a pint of hard liquor before going to bed every night . . .*

Then came the bad news. *They all lived in villages most of their lives where the air is clean.*

He then gestured to an old woman sitting quietly in the corner who for some reason I'd assumed to be the cleaner. "This woman is 90," he said "and she's still very active and in good health. Ask her your questions if you like."

At this moment her face suddenly came alive. Her eyes sparkled with as much vitality and sensitivity as a teenager. The muscles tugged and relaxed around them like delicate bell-ropes as she listened, more to the tone of our questions, than the words.

How long do you sleep? Do you read the newspapers? Do you drive a car?

The professor interrupted: "Not one of our centenarians has ever driven a motor car." In Georgia this didn't surprise me in the least.

"Do you have any tips for a long life?" someone finally asked. She replied matter-of-factly through the translation of our local Abkhazian guide.

"I think you should eat a good diet, and be well respected by your family," she said simply. Then, raising her voice just a trace she added: "And, most important of all, you must do only good to people, you must live with a moral purity."

There followed a moment of animated discussion between our Abkhazian guide (a fierce supporter of the Soviet regime) and the professor. He seemed to have spotted a mistranslation — even though I thought he couldn't speak English. The professor then asked the group's Leningrad guide — a far better representative of glasnost — to retranslate the last line.

"She says you must live with a *clear conscience*," she corrected, and the professor agreed.

At last, I thought, the habitual old lies and mistranslations of the last 70 years, are being spotted. I noticed the old woman also showed the glimmer of a smile. I looked at her delicate features, trying to guess at the stock of natural philosophy inside those last two words. This face had grown up in Tsarist Georgia, had watched the Revolution slowly ferment, arrive, then with all its own apparent glasnost and perestroika, be followed by Georgia's Menshevik government. Her fingers would briefly have used the new rouble of Independent Georgia, before the Bolsheviks snatched them away and replaced them with the roubles of Soviet Russia. She, like everyone, would then have felt the grip of Stalin steadily tighten around daily life, culminating in the terrible purges of 1937. Now once again she saw her nation close in on a new *fin de siècle*, amidst more revolution, perestroika and the arrival of an Independent Georgia. No wonder this old woman had asked, with a certain degree of determination, for a clear conscience. The behaviour of the humankind she'd witnessed so far had shown little evidence of it.

*

The next afternoon, the bus took me up the coast in the direction of the luxurious resorts of Pitsunda and Gagra. Following the winding Black Sea highway for half an hour we arrived at another balmy, palm-studded resort, the former Greek colony of Novy Afon (translating as New Athens). Here swans decorated the roadside 'water gardens,' and an enormous 'tourist attraction' cavern lurked deep inside its holy Mt Iveri, awaiting coaches like ours.

As the bus wheeled round the coastal hairpin bends, past the numerous citrus and persimmon orchards, walnut and cherry groves, so we began to see

The water garden, Novy Afon, in the more orderly, pre-war days

the red flags of Communism hanging from house windows, instead of the purple and black of Independent Georgia. Sure signs of leaving the area of the Georgian majority.

"This is the road that Maxim Gorky helped construct," our guide interrupted my thoughts. I remembered how the young Gorky returned to the Caucasus several times as the 1917 Revolution fermented itself among these very same houses. He'd lived as a virtual tramp, paying his way from job to job, priming his imagination with its deeply romantic supercharge. I imagined the young writer digging out these very embankments along the Sukhumi Military Highway, now permitting us our air-cushioned race between tourist resorts. Toils that also permitted the Bolshevik Red Army (that he supported like many young writers — only to swiftly decry after the Revolution) to attack Georgia in its three-pronged assault, bringing down the more liberal Menshevik government in ten short days.

I remembered his over-the-top descriptions from *The Birth of a Man* sitting near here, recovering from bee-stings, triumphantly dipping bread into a pot of honey. When he looked up he saw Georgia as a kingdom full of "jewels, silk and happy children," "sowing it with kaleidoscopic treasures," and the Caucasus mountains as a "magnificent church" built by sinners "to conceal their past from their own conscience." Chekhov also had passed through Abkhazia declaring "the scenery is maddeningly beautiful . . . every little bush, every shadow in the mountains, all the delicate shades of the sea and sky offering me a thousand plots."

Finally we arrived at the caves, only to find them locked.

"Must be a strike," said our guide. "Part of the troubles." We descended from the bus milled around the closed-up reception centre, with that so near and yet so far feeling. Then I happened to glance across the valley where, to my astonishment, I saw a genuinely 'magnificent church' perched on the opposite hill, not once mentioned by our guide. A huge building consisting of silver tipped pastel blue domes bubbling up out of the mountain-side, its walls painted in rich yellows and red, and crowned by spires. What, we all asked her excitedly, was *this*?

"It's the old Novy Afon Monastery," she said, adding casually: "It's not interesting."

She seemed greatly surprised by our desire to visit it.

"It's just been repainted," she said. "It only looks good on the outside. There's nothing there."

Monastery of St Simon, at Novy Afon (at the time a Soviet holiday camp)

But she convinced no one. The bus was turned round and driven to the bottom of the hill. "Well if you really want to visit it, you'll have to walk up the hill," she said unhelpfully. But to her surprise, everybody did just that.

And not in vain, for at the top came my last memorable experience of unified Georgia, before the trauma of independence in late 1990 and its splitting into pieces. For this majestic monastery built in 1875 on the site of the chapel of Saint Simon the Canaanite (said to have bought Christianity to Abkhazia in AD 55), with its courtyard surrounding an enormous, cathedral-sized church, had been converted into a Soviet holiday camp. But not the high-class, executive Communist Party palace one might expect; instead a down-market 2-star workers' accommodation. Walking around the converted, decaying dormitories, trying to peer in through the locked church's windows (then a museum), one tasted again how functionalism had triumphed over imagination — to everyone's detriment.

I reflected how Gorky's "mighty church" of the Caucasus had in fact been built right here, only to then have its conscience publicly stripped naked by the Communists a few years later. In the place of what they saw as a wasted human belief in God, they imposed an even less convincing belief in man — dressed up as the dictatorship of the proletariat. The monastery had become the atheists' heavenly reward (no longer hidden away in the after-life of the devious capitalists) but back on tangible earth.

Yet the untidiness of that inner courtyard, the caravans standing in a haphazard row, the obvious lack of organisation, told that a point was still being made. This fine old building still needed to be shamed.

I walked up to two enormous six-metre high doors and, pushing gingerly, found to my surprise they swung open. I found myself stepping into what used to be the refectory, now the camp canteen. This once magnificent room — capable of feeding 720 monks, with tall stained glass windows, paintings of the saints and apostles and its huge fresco of the Feeding of the Five Thousand — had been converted into a self-serve caff. The frescoes of the apostles surrounding the eaters had been partially painted over and defaced by the new regime, just as the frescoes at Vardzia had been attacked by the Muslims. Electrical conduits ran straight through the patriarchs' faces, a plug had been positioned on an apostle's stomach, and connected to it, just below where the serene face had looked back from under its halo, an old plastic speaker. Walking by I heard a faint music trying to crackle out of its dirty grill. Stopping to listen, I suddenly recognised Vivaldi's *Dixit Dominus*.

Instantly that sense of unconscious theatricality, then so common in the dying Soviet world, was back. Here was a society so blind to its own ironies, it never noticed how its own collective intelligence insisted that it crumble. There inside that wall, the voice of a religion held captive for 70 years, now struggled to re-emerge.

Eight years later in 1997, I returned to Novy Afon to find the monastery a monastery again. The *Dixit Dominus* was back, but with it a new set of problems.

★

Part II

INDEPENDENT GEORGIA

Chased icon of St George killing the Emperor Diocletian
(Nakipari, Upper Svaneti — 11th century)

14

The eve of independence

D uring the last months of 1990 and the start of 1991, changes lashed across the Georgian nation of a magnitude unknown since the Bolshevik invasion of 1921. First the name went. The Soviet Socialist Republic of Georgia became the Republic of Georgia. The Communist Party lost power in the USSR's first democratic election in November 1990 and a new government formed by Zviad Gamsakhurdia quickly locked itself in a separatist battle with Moscow as the republic tried to shake itself free from its Communist past. For a few months the bird of Georgian independence sang loudly within its Russian cage — and then suddenly the cage was gone.

Heading south again, trying to keep pace with events I met a Georgian woman at the Aeroflot desk at Moscow's Vnukovo Airport. As usual she stood in the midst of a furious battle with airline officials. Due to our similar plight — the flight had been delayed eight hours, until 4am — that instant friendship, capable with most Georgians, sprang up. After a highly frank discussion on Georgia's 'war' with Ossetia, the collapsing politics of the USSR, the various government personalities, I finally asked the profession of her father.

"He's with the Ministry of the Interior," she said cheerfully (Ministry of Interior was tantamount to saying KGB).

"Oh no." I couldn't stop myself. She smiled.

"Don't worry, now it's the *free* democratic Republic of Georgia!"

"You mean even the KGB is for Independent Georgia?" I joked.

"Yes it is," she said. "It's officially separated itself from Moscow. Now it's the Georgian KGB.

Not certain how to take this, I decided to keep my ear close to the ground on arrival. Boarding the Tupolev I wondered why the old edifice of fear had changed its name . . . and if many other organisations with roots now deep in Caucasian soil would also simply redesign their frontispiece?

At the other end of the two and a quarter hour flight, I found a capital city offering up a good deal more than a face-lift. First came the sight most Georgians never expected to see in their lifetimes — the magenta, black and white flag of Independent Georgia flying on the Stalinist Government Building on Rustaveli Avenue. Then came a sight I never expected — Lenin Square without Lenin. In his place a small, cheerful patch of grass — today covered with scrawny roses. Lenin Square had been rephrased into Freedom

Square. In the shops too, progress displayed itself: formerly black-market goods (Western cigarettes, videotapes, cassettes) were now openly on sale for roubles.

As for the 'democratic forces' replacing the rapid decline of Communist power — clearly they had exacted a price. On that first evening, trying to catch a taxi on Rustaveli Avenue, came a dilemma never encountered before in Georgia — the taxis no longer stopped. Dozens of people lined the roadside, leaned out ever more eagerly towards the hurtling Ladas — in vain. They drove on empty, occasionally stopping to pick up women. But single men standing alone . . . never. What had happened? At the house of a Georgian friend that night I received the answer.

"The streets aren't safe like they used to be," he said. "Taxis are being held up, people are being robbed, many have guns now. The situation is not good."

In spite of the tendency for Georgians to overdramatise, I'd already felt a change in the psychological climate. The new independence had encouraged a new individuality. But this combined with a weapons free-for-all created a dangerous cocktail — resulting in steeply rising crime statistics.

My friend told me the weapons-per-capita ratio had climbed drastically — due partly to the war in Ossetia, with the arming of the new

End of empire (Soviet) dining-room at the Tbilisi Hotel, just before its destruction in the 1991 civil war

Georgian National Guard, and partly due to the many disaffected Red Army conscripts in Russia's army bases across Georgia, selling weapons into a proliferating black market.

"For you, a Kalashnikov will cost $250.00 . . . if you want," he added politely (I would subsequently be offered one for a tenth that price), then went on to explain.

"The situation in Ossetia, in Tskhinvali is bad. Many houses have been burnt and people killed. Moscow is supplying the Ossetians with weapons, and the Georgian National Guard were fighting them. Now the Red Army are there in force protecting the Ossetians."

When Southern Ossetia (in Georgia) had declared its intention to unify with its Northern part in the Russian Federation, the new Gamsakhurdia government declared Georgia would no longer recognise South Ossetia as distinct from Georgia and blockaded the region.

At the same time some Georgian intellectuals, who previously called for uncompromising collective action against the Soviet regime, were starting to backpedal now this fierce anti-Sovietism had become Government policy. They saw it threatening to spill over into pointless fanaticism and confrontation. My friend (who preferred to remain anonymous) added: "It was one thing for our leaders to pump up emotions in cries for 'independence,' quite another to convert them into serious strategies for reform. Our new government hasn't learnt the second stage yet; they're still stuck in the habit of confrontation."

Gamsakhurdia then unleashed some crazily nationalistic ideas on his parliament. He proposed Georgian citizenship would only be conferred on those with family roots in the country before 1801 and the Russian takeover. His former liberal support

The Paliashvili Opera House, Tbilisi

quickly ebbed away, some even suspecting him of encouraging the Ossetian war, which he always portrayed as a Russian plot using the Ossetians simply to capture more Georgian territory. Then came more worrying signs of clinical paranoia when he started referring to the Kremlin as 'Satan,' and 'anti-Georgian tendencies' massing in society around him — a fact expanded in his book *The Spiritual Mission of Georgia* (1991) which claimed outright the Holy Grail resided at Gelati Cathedral. When in August 1991 he appeared to support the authoritarian Moscow putsch, his allies in the Georgian National Guard abruptly switched allegiance to the opposition National Democratic Party and Georgia's civil war began.

That night I found myself again stranded on the street trying to stop a car. My concerned hostess had insisted the Tbilisi streets were no longer safe to walk at night (although subsequently I had no trouble), and accompanied me outside at 2am, to wave furiously at the traffic. When a car finally stopped for her (not me), she bundled me into the back and, hardly glancing at the occupants, shouted the name of my hotel. Stepping back, she then slammed the door and waved a cheery good-bye from the kerbside.

As the car lurched forward I saw two members of Tbilisi's swarthy, wild-eyed youth in the front seats. The one in the passenger seat asked in an alcohol-tinged, mafioso voice,

"Hotel Tbilisi, *da?*"

The words were spoken aggressively from the corner of his mouth, with as much distaste for the Russian language as the Moscow regime. Did he know I was English? The driver swerved round a corner and reaching down to steady myself, I placed my hand straight onto the snub barrel of an Uzi machine-gun. Noticing, the driver reached round and grabbed the weapon up to the front.

As the car raced on I realised I'd stepped into the very chariot of anarchy now steering Tbilisi. These two night-cruising heroes had won back Georgia from Russia, now they patrolled it with their toys of death. I guessed from that earnest glint in his eye, this kid (19 at most) had seen combat action (veterans call it the 1,000-yard stare). I asked if they'd been to Tskhinvali.

"*Da,*" came the stark reply.

I realised these boys, initially expecting to pick up a woman, drove on confused by the alternative (me): what should they do? In Tbilisi at 2am, they were the law. Then the hotel loomed in the windscreen.

"Cigarette!" demanded the driver.

For the privilege of releasing me unscathed he at least required Western payment. But I'd no cigarettes left — given all to my evening's hosts. Also I had no dollars, leaving them all behind in my room. Digging deep into my bag, I found a lone pack of chewing-gum and handed it up front. They took this limp gesture without a word and when the car drew up level with the hotel, instead of slowing down it accelerated.

Not a good sign. A couple of weeks earlier a friend had been driven out to the suburbs, robbed then abandoned. I tried another tactic — the friendship technique. Reaching forward I offered my hand in the gesture of sincerest friendship, thanking them for taking me home (although the hotel was already several hundred metres behind). Miraculously it worked.

Both faces instantly lit up with smiles. The brakes were applied, an illegal U-turn effected, and the car screeched to a halt on the pavement outside the hotel door. They both then shook my hand vigorously, wished me well and squealed the tyres off into the night.

Stepping back into the grand hallway of the Hotel Tbilisi I realised the fine old Caucasian tradition of 'honouring the guest' had probably saved me. What I didn't recognise was how these beginnings of Georgia's new gangster culture would dominate the country until Eduard Shevardnadze's first assassination attempt in 1995. Here were two of the young shoots of war that later would form Georgia's many irregular militias. The following evening I walked up the Avenue again, this time towards the yellow and red-walled Paliashvili Opera House. Outside it a large gathering of Georgian faces clutched banners reading 'Free our Political Prisoners!' Slogans now directed against the increasingly paranoid government of Gamsakhurdia and his

Round Table Alliance — who had arrested the leaders of two 'anti-Georgian' opposition parties.

I began to fear the 'new democracy' might simply replace the old dictatorship with a new one. Talking to members of that protest, several strongly criticised Gamsakhurdia. One described the Round Table Alliance as the victory of the "shouting party"; another expressed a fear that Zviadist nationalism came close to a self-fulfilling prophecy of hatred against Russia rather than constructing the positive alternative.

Then he added: "Real democrats don't imprison their rivals, no matter what they say."

I asked about the alternative parties. He said they were temporarily losing their way. And the Communist Party?

"They came up with a new title—" he said half smiling, "—the 'National Socialist Party.' Then someone told them about Hitler!"

I felt the re-creating Georgian nation all around me, beginning as observers predicted, in a blaze of impulsive zeal, confusion, mistakes, good and bad intentions. The hard rock of united hostility against the Soviets had begun to split into competing factions, with the long established scapegoat of blaming "the Kremlin" as the source of all Georgia's problems, failing. Moves toward political pluralism were establishing a deep split in the population, that by the end of 1991 would create crude government censorship and running street battles.

Walking on I noticed the interior of the Opera ablaze with light. Had these feelings transferred themselves into the arts? I stepped up to the front door and encountered a babushka demanding my ticket.

"What no ticket!" she exclaimed then suddenly smiled and waved me through, as if tickets, like Communism were now an old joke.

For the next 15 minutes I wandered around inside this reconstruction of a Moorish palace. Founded in 1851 during Georgia's emergence as a European centre of culture, burnt down mysteriously and then rebuilt in the 1970s, its walls were stuffed with beautiful Arabesque mirrors, turquoise mosaics, gold reliefs, and chandeliers.

I pushed open one of the balcony doors and to my astonishment found myself looking down on a plush velvet 1,100-seat auditorium, where a full cast and orchestra were mid-scene in *Aida*, playing to an almost completely empty theatre. I counted 70 costumed performers on the stage, outnumbering the audience about five to one. I watched as the soprano reached the climax of an aria then sank down on her knees in a passionate plea to the empty rows of seats. What had happened to everyone? Had a nation of drama lovers found a performance more vivid than anything in the theatre — outside on the streets?

I decided to catch up on the lives of my former Tbilisi friends. Phoning Manana first she told me her marriage had passed off as planned.

"Now I'm eight months pregnant," she said. "I'm taking a break from my career."

Next Ilia told me he now planned to educate his children in the West — (which he subsequently managed). Marika, who in between times had visited London, remained the same as ever, absorbed in her love of Georgian art. Tamuna's phone didn't respond any more.

Putting down the receiver I realised the blue touchpaper I'd watched fizzling two years earlier was now blasting up into space. With a zeal the Bolsheviks would have envied, the new government set about taking over, transforming or abolishing every institution, organisation and structure of the Communists' era. The chaos had begun and already some Georgians expressed serious doubts. Around this time I heard one ex-pat Georgian in London utter a burst of nostalgia for those 'lazy days' of Communism. The period when everything fun was illegal, caviar-plentiful, when nobody had to work hard, earn money for rent, the phone bill, etc, as they do in the West. The years when rebellion was pure, noble and simple against the wicked Russians.

The inevitable explosion of frustration came in December 1991 — when I was back in England. After the National Guard switched allegiance to the Opposition group, its leaders, the sculptor Tengiz Kitovani, the theatre critic Jaba Ioseliani and Georgia's former prime minister, Tengiz Sigua led an insurrection against Gamsakhurdia's government. For three weeks everyone's worst nightmare materialised as hand-to-hand fighting raged up and down the elegant Rustaveli Avenue. Buildings used by snipers drew relentless fire and several were destroyed. The entire northern flank of Freedom Square was reduced to rubble and had to be pulled down along with the hospitable Artists' House on Rustaveli Avenue. The Tbilisi Hotel became a burnt-out ruin. By Christmas Day 1991, Gamsakhurdia was trapped in the Government Building with his last 300 loyal troops.

From my London living-room the drama was heart-rending to follow. All those dreams secretly harboured for an artistic nation restoring its international presence, blew itself to pieces across the world's television screens.

When in February 1992 the Kurdish street sweepers returned to Rustaveli Avenue to clear up the debris, we all began remembering the early warning signs. I recounted the words of a Georgian friend describing the moment Lenin was finally removed from Tbilisi's Lenin Square: "A great cheer that rose up across our city as the monstrous statue was finally uprooted. But you know there was a funny moment in the ceremony. When the crane tried to lift Lenin away . . . ," she looked a little uncertain, ". . . his feet stuck themselves inside the base, they wouldn't free from Georgian soil."

Just 16 months later Georgians were shooting each other not a hundred metres away from those feet. Gamsakhurdia, ended up like Lenin's shoes, stuck underground in a Government Building bunker. Having fulfilled his role as blazing nationalistic figurehead leading Georgia free from Communism, political inexperience let him down. With calls for help increasingly unheeded, on January 6th 1992 he fled Tbilisi, only eight months after his election with a 87 per cent majority as Georgia's first president.

The seeds of nationalism he represented had sprouted, blossomed and now dropped him to the ground, like a shiny, inflated and spent fruit. Two years later he was dead, dying during his ill-advised return to Zugdidi hoping to garner support for a march on Tbilisi. The circumstances of his death are disputed to this day.

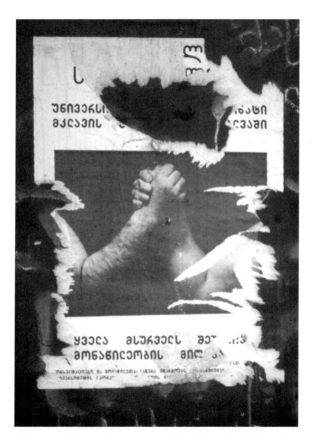

"Open to all comers" — a poster advertising a local Georgian arm-wrestling competition (a popular sport among Caucasians)

15

The young shoots of war

F or over a year commitments in Britain prevented my return to Tbilisi. During this time I received news of the changes from Georgian emigrés arriving in London, with growing apprehension. They reported, with typical cheerfulness, "well at least life in Tbilisi can't get any worse." Then of course it did. When the war in Ossetia dwindled to a stalemate, the battle for Rustaveli Avenue erupted. When that ended, the new Abkhazian debacle began — as if the ending of one only generated the next, or some diabolical force merely redirected tragedy, region to region. Meanwhile the story of modern Georgia became a fairy tale in reverse as the economy collapsed. In 1992 gross domestic product fell in real terms by 40.3 per cent; in 1993 by 39 per cent; in 1994 by 35 per cent (European Bank of Reconstruction and Development figures).

As the bad news kept on coming, I began to wonder about some terrible logic within this catastrophe. Might a nation in some perverse, unconscious way be trying to teach itself a lesson? In his book *Fear of Freedom*, the psychologist Eric Fromm describes the process generating nationalism as a cultural demand for individualism in societies with nowhere to place it.

Perhaps Georgia's independence had come too quickly for its own good, and Shevarnadze's return in March 1992 too late? Severed from all economic assistance and with no market economy to nurture individualist dreams of wealth, young men with soaring expectations roamed the streets sustained by the bright metallic glint of their own AK47s. With nowhere else to turn finally, they resorted to a social institution known well to Georgia from its Soviet days — the mafia.

It was a damp, drizzly evening on Rustaveli Avenue that greeted my next return. This time not a joyful reunion. Very un-Georgian thick metal bars had appeared in shop windows and I had just seen an extraordinary sight — the Iveria Hotel, where I'd stayed so many times in the 1980s — no longer a hotel but a refugee camp. All 20 storeys of its exclusive balconies now decked out with refugee washing and listless, depressed figures. Although I'd followed the Abkhaz War in the British press, read about the hideous act of ethnic cleansing in which 250,000 Georgians were forced to flee Abkhazia — seeing the evidence rising up 70 metres into the air in the centre of Tbilisi, stuck the knife in deep.

Dazed, I continued on down the avenue to halt again before the burnt-out hulk of the Tbilisi Hotel. The Ladas hissed past it in the rain, their headlights

Rustaveli Avenue 1992 — the destroyed School No 1, Art Institute and KGB headquarters (opposite the Tbilisi Hotel)

flashing off its broken window panes like memories of the gunfire bringing on its ruination. During the three-week battle for Rustaveli Avenue, the Tbilisi had been the Opposition forces' main gun position for shooting at Gamsakhurdia's Parliament building.

I stood there feeling a city around me gritting its teeth. Its tone was acid-grey, the same colour as the cartridge smoke clinging to its walls; or the memories in the faces behind the windows. Most families were touched personally, some marriages split down the middle, one side (often the women) siding with Gamsakhurdia, the other with the Opposition. Georgian young men, steeped in Caucasian romanticism, had taken weapons to "defend their country" more eagerly than any youth culture I'd seen. The eagerness belied large gaps in foresight, which led to many very real ones in the architecture — a madness compounded by the fact that right after this debacle Kitovani's troops went on to invade Abkhazia, provoking the psychological inevitability of defeat. So often I still wish Georgians would listen to the advice found within their own infallible war hero myth, Amirani (mentioned earlier).

Instead to my right lay the wide empty space that a year earlier had been the Artists' House — a large art gallery and coffee bar directly opposite the Government Building. A thin board disguised a huge hole. Just down the avenue the School No. 1 was now a ruin. Directly behind me lay two other airy non-presences — the old KGB headquarters and Art Institute. The latter, having saved many superb icons during the Soviet period (like the beautiful seventh century Kachaghani Cross), then had to watch their destruction during the first hysterical moments of 'freedom.' Marika told me she and her colleagues risked their lives running in and out of the building carrying priceless icons. "I saved the 11th century icon of St Theodore and St George that's in your icon book," she had said later with more shame than pride. I began to feel all these holes in the walls and culture like the lost teeth in the welcome smile that was once Tbilisi.

But there were other gaps too. The Avenue itself was virtually empty and a petrol shortage had reduced the traffic by two thirds. Many citizens now locked away their cars as too much trouble, no petrol, street theft, hijacking, vandalism. Guns were now everyday objects and their prices kept falling. A few months later a new publication *The Georgian Business News* would offer only two commodities on its 'Prices' page: arms and black market gold and silver. The list read exactly as follows:

PRICES TO ARMS (IN DOLLARS)

		One bullet
AKM	400	0.5
AKS	300	0.5
Makarov	400	1
Nagan revolver	600-700	2
'TT'	500-600	1.5
Woman pistol	150-200	1
'Stechkin'	800	2
Limonka	10-20	—

Private inquiries revealed these prices as highly inflated. Below the gold and silver prices it stated:

IN PAWNSHOP ON THE SECURITY 14 CARAT GOLD $3 FOR GRAM
AND 24 CARAT GOLD $5.

But now the time was 9pm, when the Tbilisi Dr Jekyll turned into its Mr Hyde, its streets undergoing an invisible takeover by a new generation of car-roaming, gun-toting youth. Darkness had descended accompanied by the occasional crack of distant gunfire; sometimes a streak of tracer-fire flashing straight up into the sky from in the hills — not in anger but an eerie exuberance. In the air I started to feel a direct link between this youth-assisted descent into anarchy and the Cult of the Young Man — forged in the last century by the likes of Lermontov and Byron.

I hoped very much my next meeting, with Manana, would take me to the heart of this modernised Cult and its engine of destruction. Earlier that morning I'd made a surprise phone call.

"Peter, you're here!" she exclaimed. "I have a great life now. Come to the Parliament Building in one hour. Say my name at the door."

The young shoots of war

Intrigued by her sudden link with government, I obeyed. Two years earlier I'd seen Manana as one of the 'New Georgians,' but instead of a business environment she'd received a war zone. Also I detected a slight change in her voice — a harder, more instructive tone; less of the bright girlish timbre that once sung so sweetly around the table.

I arrived at the Parliament Building — the former Institute of Marxism and Leninism, as the Government Building underwent repairs — and duly pronounced her name. After a bustle of confusion at Security, I heard the word "Jaba" mentioned. A few minutes later a well-groomed young man arrived to escort me up to Manana's new office. He avoided the metal-detector due to a pistol tucked ostentatiously inside his belt.

The word Jaba alerted me to Manana's new position in the government.

  'Jaba' abbreviated Jaba Ioseliani — the charismatic leader of Georgia's main mafia group, the Mkhed-rioni ('horsemen'). Some claimed him more powerful than Shevardnadze. Indeed it was he, Kitovani and Sigua who all jointly invited Eduard Shevardnadze to return to Georgia as Head of State, in 1992.

(Right) The seventh century Kachaghani Cross, before the 1991 civil war. (Left)The Kachaghani Cross after the civil war — photo taken October 1997 at the Art Museum

I met Manana briefly in Jaba's office positioned, some say deliberately, right above Shevardnadze's in the same wing. Her job was one of his 'assistants.' She'd put on weight, but her eyes flashed as brightly as ever. Round the desk three or four AK47s leaned against the wall like abandoned brooms. The phone rang incessantly, and after a few minutes we decided to meet again that evening on Rustaveli Avenue — where I now stood.

Waiting under the dim lighting I noticed a couple of youths across the road, aged 20 at most, staring at me from the open window of a tinted glass BMW. They wore that wounded-but-noble stare of their new Wild West. The driver dragged on his Marlboro, flicked the ash disinterestedly onto the tarmac. Dressed in a black polar-neck with beret to match, he sported the Western cigarette in the same way men wore gold chains in London. Inside his look I felt a smouldering envy towards us globe-trotting foreigners — the very few daring to visit Tbilisi. In the back of the car the silhouette of a Kalashnikov rose ostentatiously between the seats.

Clearly the Mkhedrioni, after their successful battle against the Zviadists (Zviad Gamsakhurdia's supporters), had no one else to save but themselves. Since my last visit their numbers had increased dramatically, absorbing many of the former irregular militias. Some estimates put them at 2,500 in Tbilisi alone.

I watched one of the new police Ladas drive by looking right through the illegally-parked BMW. Everyone knew the Mkhedrioni outgunned the police — who were rarely issued weapons due to corruption. The BMW bought to mind a conversation with a journalist friend here — about how the vendetta diminished in Corsica with the arrival of the car.

Member of the Mkhedrioni ('Horsemen') displaying identity medallion and authority

"Men no longer needed to kill in blood feuds to display their prowess—" I had remarked, "—they out-accelerated."

"Georgian men don't need to just out-accelerate," he replied. "This is the country where bullets are the main part of the national dress (the *chokha*). The BMW is a kind of new *chokha* on wheels, and still needs its bullets."

Minutes later the squealing of tires announced the arrival of a brand-new Lada Riva, Manana behind the wheel.

"Get in!" she shouted joyfully, and we sped off. The BMW across the road flicked on its lights and followed. Inside our car sat two young men in their early twenties, dressed in black — one apparently 'owned' the car. How a 19 year old came into such riches was greeted by a shrug from Manana. His friend muttered, "from the Zviadists."

First we sped up to Tsqneti, the Beverly Hills of Tbilisi, to one of the government dachas, commandeered by Manana and her friends.

"You like my new home?" she asked, then before I could reply rushed off to deal with her new baby. The flat was spacious and untidy, overlooking an empty swimming pool. The 'maid' came in and opened champagne for me. But before I'd drunk a sip, other friends arrived and decided to take me back down to Tbilisi and another 'house' in the Vera region.

This second mafia base looked like the former home of a rich artist. The comfortable living room sported a grand piano, several expensive chairs and sofas, a widescreen Sony, and a totally out-of-place poster of Sylvester Stallone. Lounging among these young, unshaven men, pistols jammed in belts, cigarettes in mouths, talking in husky tones, their sentences usually beginning with the word *bichi* ('boy' in Georgian slang), I told Manana I wanted an interview. Immediately she shouted *"Gocha, modi!"* ('come here, Gocha!') at a swarthy, pirate lookalike with a double-clip Kalashnikov slung over his shoulder. He ambled over. As an opener I asked him how much he paid for his weapon.

"Nothing," he said with a certain pride at this Russian-made weapon now under his command.

Manana explained that after Gamsakhurdia had initiated the policy of popular rearmament in 1991, the new free market was taken very literally and guns were supplied 'free' to 16 year olds and upwards vowing loyalty to the correct militia. I asked how much it would cost me.

Captured weapons on display at the Tbilisi Police Headquarters, 1992

"You want?" he asked, his eyes suddenly narrowed. I told him no, but as a foreigner how much to buy an AK?

"Maybe . . . ," he looked around for help, but his friends just grinned, saying nothing, ". . . maybe $100." I suddenly realised the Mkhedrioni were not used to paying for things, especially guns. "If you want, we take you to shop," he added.

Noting my confusion, Manana explained: "A Russian army base."

It turned out customers

would be driven straight into Red Army bases, as they would a car showroom (Georgia still had some 40,000 Russian troops). I wondered about this disturbingly close relationship between Russian arms manufacturers and their customer base. Later I heard a story confirming it from the Chechen War. When Chechen fighters ran out of weapons and ammunition during the battle for Pervomayskoye, money was paid on the outside for a resupply. Apparently a Russian brigade was hired to launch a phoney attack on the village. The Chechens fired over their heads then the Russians retreated leaving their weapons on the ground — for the Chechens to collect.

I noticed a bronze medallion of St George slaying the dragon, hanging against his gun barrel.

"Membership medal," Manana explained. Gocha turned it over. On the back it bore a Christian cross, its bottom curled into the Georgian letter 'J' — standing for the Mkhedrioni's poet-leader Jaba — the former bank-robber turned theatre critic.

"We take an oath not to leave the group — or we die," he said with a pride belying the incandescent need for individualism in these boys, whose filial ardour for Jaba elevated him to Christ-like proportions. Below it were some letters and numbers.

"Blood group," Gocha said, then added with a grin, "like in Vietnam." After this unexpected smile his expression quickly returned to the deadpan warrior.

I'd seen that expression before in combat veterans, one seeming to look out from a point beyond all causes. Somehow all he wanted was peace, but like the Stallone and Bruce Lee posters everywhere in Tbilisi, the only means he knew to achieve it was war.

The next day, looking for more words behind the deeds, I visited the home of a former militia leader, who had subsequently joined the Mkhedrioni. Like Jaba, he was a former university lecturer and fan of T. S. Eliot. He lived in a flat with his family, the main feature of the living-room was a gleaming AK47 left leaning against the kitchen wall like any household item. He spoke very matter-of-factly about his role as partisan.

"Our first group formed very quickly in late 1991 to help fight Gamsakhurdia. It had about 100 members, mostly students, academics, artists, writers. The oldest was 43, the youngest 16. The average age was 20. Then, there were many other groups like ours. After Gamsakhurdia left, it half-disbanded, some joined the National Guard, some the Mkhedrioni."

As he spoke his young son walked up and handed him his loaded pistol, as naturally he would his pipe.

Surprised, I asked him why he needed it.

"Always ready," he said flatly, making a shielded reference to the inter-mafia rivalries springing up across Tbilisi, accounting for much of the gunfire heard at night. I asked him how it felt to use a gun in his city.

"Once you use it a few times it has an effect on you. You feel you belong to

Tbilisi policeman with new Lada squad car. Note the cocked cap, a carry-over from the Soviet era of disrespect for authority, even in the police.

it, you owe it something. You start to want to take it with you, feel naked without it." I suggested there was a danger in encouraging young men to use weapons without sufficient thought of their consequences.

"This is the Caucasus," he replied simply. "We're always surrounded by enemies."

He said it in a tone of voice that seemed to make a direct link to that long anchor-line of identity stretching deep down into Georgia's rich, non-Soviet past of 'horsemen,' Queen Tamar, the 12th century Golden Age. For these 'new democracies' the first act of freedom had not been economic (as the West, with a typical lack of psychological insight expected), but nationalistic — in aggressive 'self-defining' lunges towards the past. For the great majority, the only reliable 'self' they knew existed not in some hazy, free-market future but in the memories, iconography and borders of an independent, *individualistic* past. The consequences had been dire.

A few days later a teacher friend of mine, Ilia Noladze, opened his garage only to find his Lada had been stolen (the second in two years). Reporting it to the police he received only the usual shrug and a "what do you expect us to do?" So he returned the next day with a 'friend' of the police chief. This time over a brandy and a pleasant chat he was asked: "Would you like to meet the criminals? Might 3 o'clock tomorrow suit you?" Astonished, he agreed and a meeting was set up at Tbilisi's main hospital.

"I arrived at a bedside and met a man with five bullet-holes in his stomach," said a bemused Ilia. "I told him my problem and he seemed very friendly, offered me cigarettes, took my phone number and said he'd see what he could do."

Three days later a stranger rang to say he had found the car in an underground garage 300 metres from his home. "The car was fine, but of course the police rang asking if everything was 'all right.' I think their price was about the same as your car insurance in the West."

Shortly after this the mafia started trying to go legit, by opening businesses. Signs saying 'Commercial Shop,' 'Economic Firm,' 'Many Branched Bank,' 'Joint Stock Company' sprang up across Tbilisi — with inevitable casualties. A friend of mine's 21-year-old daughter saw a TV ad for a new bank calling itself "The Golden Cup Trade Industrial Company." She decided to invest everything she had ($50).

"I bought my shares for $1.30 each," she said pointing to a pile of colourful, Monopoly-style certificates. "Two and a half weeks later they were worth $2.65, so I went down to the office to sell. When I arrived the door was closed with a small note pinned to it saying just 'good-bye.'"

With no official records or traceable registration the amount drained out of the Golden Cup is anyone's guess. Estimates put it at "several million."

Later I discussed this road to semi-anarchy with my journalist friend in a bar at Tbilisi's 4-star Metechi Palace Hotel. As we spoke, pop videos played loudly on the bar top and dark-eyed waitresses drifted between tables taking orders in husky pidgin English. He glanced at the TV playing the old *Thriller* video.

"The imagery they see is as much ours as theirs," he said wistfully. "Their Sonys, JVCs, BMWs play our rock 'n' roll fantasies. Teenagers are fascinated by the real emotions of combat in an increasingly unreal, fashion-conscious world. In the Gulf War I saw young British soldiers photographing each other thrusting knifes into Iraqi corpses, posing around the dead, bragging, experimenting, to the astonished horror of liberal journalists." He gave me a serious look. "I think these events of war have to happen *because* they are so odious. Youth is always drawn into areas shunned by its society."

He raised his glass. "But this is just the conversation we have in a mafia bar deep in the Caucasus, during a war. It won't always be like this here," he smiled grimly. "These gangsters are too hospitable. Cultures go through phases just like people."

We clinked our glasses, drank to hospitality. I told him I prayed he would be right, although it seemed unlikely. Upstairs, the Metechi's Piano Bar was now the domain of Mkhedrioni, and a man at the next table clearly packed a weapon.

"OK," he said simply. "You buy our Piano Bar drinks in two years time. You won't see a single gangster, I guarantee it."

Two years later I did buy the drinks. He was absolutely right.

16

Batumi

My next visit in November 1994 seemed to coincide with a watershed in Georgia's period of shame. The moral decline appeared to be ending — at least the fighting. But then, as if pre-ordained by that perverse God temporarily assigned to the Georgians, came a completely new set of problems. In my region of Tbilisi, Saburtalo, they began one evening at 8.30pm. The lights went out.

"Is anybody in the lift?" came a first voice in the pitch darkness. "Did you buy candles like I asked?" came another. Although power cuts had happened before, nobody was to know the mother of all power cuts had arrived. Turkmenistan had shut off Georgia's gas for non-payment.

The next day bad went to worse — the phone died. The dial tone in our 36 prefix exchange (then the only good exchanges began with 9 or 22) started literally to 'wail,' as if crying for help. Soon this yowl was followed by a spluttering, burbling sound, like a death-rattle, as power drained from the cables — then complete deadness as the system finally expired. The disease affected the whole city in varying degrees. At the Metechi Palace Hotel the operator told me she could connect me to Paris, New York, London, but as for Tbilisi . . . "perhaps you'll take a taxi."

In that one day everyone's life transformed and for me Tbilisi became a third world city. My life reshaped itself into an eternal quest for a socket that offered a slight spark or fizz (the current fluctuated between about 70 and 300 volts). Every evening I would scour the skyline for signs of domestic lights then try to think of anyone who might accept me and my computer in their living-room. Power cuts, spanning a day in the city centre, lasted several in the outskirts. Then, just to rub it in, the water failed, as power was shut off to the pumping stations.

My new morning ritual became wake up, flip the light switch and sigh — invariably nothing happened. No power meant no shower, no shave, no wake-up tea, no heat, and usually no phone. So it was off to light the kerosene heater in the kitchen, and setting the kettle on top. It would take about an hour to boil, which meant half an hour until the ancient razor could offer a halfway decent shave with the water saved up in the bath (in severe winters bathtubs would often freeze solid, making the day's first task an assault with ice-pick). The dried-up water pipes meant washing, toilet flushes — the taken-for-granted events of civilisation were now luxuries.

When light did return, or a distant gurgling announced water struggling back up the pipes, I discovered a strange new joy — along with the general population. Cheers would erupt from all floors of apartment buildings. Immediately showers would be occupied, buckets and baths filled, the electric heater, TV and radio switched on in pure celebration — which of course only further drained the supply.

For all of us, walking upstairs became the new exercise, nobody trusted lifts, even when they worked — power cuts struck at random (unlike in Armenia, where by then people had schedules). And exercise it was, especially if you had to carry water as well. Once I met a Georgian man on the 11th floor of a 1970s Soviet-built highrise, carrying two buckets in his hand, his young son following obediently behind with a brimming kettle. "God is punishing us!" he smiled cheerfully, and plodded on whistling a song for his son.

The Georgian coupon — interim currency (1993-95). After 18 months the bill on the right (500,000 coupons) was worth roughly the same as the older one on the left (1 coupon)

Again I remembered why I liked Georgia. Indefatigably cheerful in adversity (Georgia's history provided ample practice). That first evening a group of us went out to one of the new restaurants — determinedly staying open by cutting back the menu, serving Eniseli brandy instead of hot drinks. Dinner became a genuinely candle-lit event, with live music. After our supper of very little food — disguised by low light, we danced simply to keep warm. After several swirls one Georgian woman said to me: "Peter — and you think we Georgians need electricity to be happy?" I told her we English usually did, but could learn.

However, the electricity merely indicated another more serious problem — the Georgian economy. The treasury was overwhelmed by the burden of 250,000 refugees — most now crammed into Georgia's empty tourist hotels. The middle-class intelligentsia suffered terribly as academies and institutes closed. Professors could be found driving buses, architects labourers, oncologists hustling in cross-border trading, if they were lucky — unemployment or a token state salary ($10 a month) being more common.

After the rouble-zone collapsed in 1993 Georgia introduced its infamous 'coupon' — quickly a candidate for the world's most worthless currency. Introduced in the summer of 1993 at 700 coupons to the dollar, two years later it traded at 2,200,000. People avoided it like the plague, preferring Russian roubles and US dollars. One friend, David Rowson, from the British

Council, said when he first tried to use the coupon near Telavi, locals refused to believe it could possibly be money. In September 1995 it was replaced by the inflation-free lari and today the coupon has found its greatest value ever — as a collector's item. The one coupon note illustrated cost me one lari (80 cents) in Tbilisi's flea market in November 1997.

Georgia's economic collapse had been the most dramatic in all the former Soviet republics and international aid agencies had already arrived. The United Nations, Oxfam, Médecins Sans Frontières, the Red Cross and a clutch of others set up offices to begin employing local staff, ironically becoming the first major foreign investors in Georgia's new economy.

But as for commercial investment, nothing happened save a few self-illuminating advertising hoardings sprouting mysteriously from the Rustaveli Avenue tarmac. Like an invasion of alien mushrooms, they glowed in the evenings with strange confidence, radiating messages from planet Marlboro, Fanta, Nivea, products often not yet existing in Georgia. The result was to engender a mixture of hope and envy — which would set the tenor of the new Georgian market for years to come.

It was in the midst of this new winter deprivation (to become seasonal) that I set out to find a lift to the one area of Georgia I'd so far missed — Ajara. Picking up the phone, my luck was in.

"Meet me outside the Ajara Hotel tomorrow," announced the crackling male voice — a friend of a friend of Marika's called Soso. "We'll take the Istanbul bus, get off at Batumi."

I felt a sudden rush of excitement. Batumi was the capital of Ajara, the 'Muslim' south-west of Georgia and celebrated by several poets. According to my Soviet guidebook the city "had one of the warmest winters in the Soviet Union." I'd never forgotten Mandelstam's 1920 description of Batumi (also called Batum) during its transition from Turkish backwater to European boomtown:

Batum in its entirety resembles an object easily fitting in the palm of your hand. You never experience its boundaries or distances. You can move around it as you would inside a room, and what is more, the air in Batum is always as steamy as inside a room. The mechanism controlling this tiny toy-like town, raised by the conditions of our times to the status of a Russian-style California gold-rush city, is extraordinarily simple. It rests on one mainspring — the Turkish lira. The exchange rate of the lira alters by night when the town is fast asleep. In the morning the inhabitants wake up to a new exchange rate, no one knowing quite how it happened. The lira pulses in the blood of every Batumian. Indeed it is the bakers who announce the morning rate with the morning bread.

Galaktion Tabidze had also written a book of poems on Ajara, while Bulgakov, Chekhov, Gorky had all chosen to stay there.

I arrived at the Hotel Ajara to find Soso standing beside a bus with Turkish

Eduard Shevardnadze as Head of State in his office at the former Institute of Marxism and Leninism, before his election as President in 1995.

plates — the (then) $25 run to Istanbul, the cheapest route to Georgia. He was a snappily dressed, 'new Georgian' of about 35, with a nose for money and healthy taste for the absurd (I always think a love of the absurd is the only quality Georgians genuinely share with the British). He spoke reasonable English and within minutes proved himself a good companion. When, after sustained arguing, we were turfed off the bus by the Turkish driver for refusing to pay full price to Istanbul (we were only going one fifth the distance), Soso just smiled, remarking casually: "Don't worry, it's just talk."

It hadn't looked like "just talk," but he was absolutely right. A minute before leaving, the driver ambled up to us, slipped our six dollars into his pocket and nodded at the door, gruffly instructing us to "stand." We sat of course, and as the kilometres passed Soso introduced himself in that constantly cheerful, attentive Georgian way, impossible not to like — in spite of his own obvious skill at "just talk."

"I'm in the oil business," was all I ever received about his work, apparently linked with aid agencies in Western Georgia. He switched his talk to his family's dacha on the Black Sea coast.

"We will see it. It's beautiful, on the beach in near Kobuleti, Georgia's Malibu." Then he smiled meekly. "Unfortunately the bandits came, so now only the walls are beautiful. We have no furniture."

His smile seemed to imply visits from bandits in empty holiday homes, were now routine in the Caucasus.

Within an hour he had introduced himself to most of the other passengers, particularly two Russian girls who, until he arrived, worked on a never-ending crossword by the window — between penetrating stares at the richer-looking men on the bus. A few minutes later Soso returned.

"They're going to Trabzon . . . ," he said, nonchalantly adding the word "Natashas," then gazed out the window.

"Both called Natasha . . . ?" I queried.

"Na-ta-shas!" he said louder, but not so they could hear. "They're on a *business* trip." He held my eye just long enough for the penny to drop, then added: "They're everywhere in Trabzon. They earn more in a weekend there, than a whole month in Perm. Mostly they fly down, but these two had friends in Tbilisi. Soon they'll be at work." He winked at me, as if with a word he'd fix up everything.

A flash of colour out the window caught my eye. We were passing through Guria, along the flanks of the lesser Caucasus — the lower row of teeth in the mountain jaw that grips Georgia. Autumn had now established itself across the region, a time when you feel pressure of this jaw gently tighten. To the north the jagged molars of the Higher Caucasus gleamed freshly white in the sharpened air. To the south, the Lesser Caucasus had closed in too, showing off their first dusting of winter snow. Both ranges combined to form the devilish grin that is late autumn in the Caucasus, with its shiny ice eyes focusing down on the valley below. Between them, in the gardens beside the road, persimmon trees had lost their leaves, the yellow-orange fruit dangling on the bare branches like baubles left hanging on deserted Christmas trees. A strange, otherworldly sight, giving the impression we had just gate-crashed a huge party held in secret by nature. Through the middle of it, on the tarmac road, we humans hurried by unnoticing, mostly as intermittent convoys of trucks with Turkish, sometimes Iranian plates. Our main mission was carrying in the new cargo of kerosene heaters now catching premium prices in electricity-starved Tbilisi.

"Soon we'll pass Shevardnadze's village," said Soso. I took the opportunity to ask what he thought of his Head of State.

"Our White Fox . . . ," he noted, his face seemed to show wily approval. "He's clever, which is good for Georgia. Georgians need someone who can think ahead, because mostly they don't." He grinned. "You know they have a saying about Guria: it has only two exports, persimmons and intrigue."

'The further you are . . .'
by Galaktion Tabidze (1891-1959)

The further you are, the closer a dream of you caresses my soul, as untouchable as rays of the sun, unassailable as Eden. If you are now not the one I think you are, then let my damaged heart be wrong, for it needs you like the white angels need heaven. Allow my love to burn this strange pleasure that fills a sea with waters of sadness. Allow a belief in this delirium which is a miracle of love, a holiday from truth.

—TRANSLATED BY P. NASMYTH & N. ANDRONIKASHVILI

Tangerine and apple orchards appeared as the road surface deteriorated — the new holes in Georgia's unmaintained roads were proving far more effective as lifesavers than speed bumps. I began to feel the exotic mix that has always been the Caucasus: Turkish bus, Russian girls, the gleam of white mountains, men and women en route to Istanbul to buy then sell in the Tbilisi market. Our modern bus followed an ancient route, the old Silk Route which even in the era of air cargo refused to die. Indeed airlines today now talk about the 'Silk Flight Path' with the Caucasus as a significant stop en route to India and the Far East.

Shortly after this, the Black Sea appeared, a livid orange strip running across the horizon as the sun dipped down under its waves. Then the bus stopped and armed guards climbed on board checking passports.

"Ajaran border," Soso remarked under his breath. "Not a real border, it's to keep the Georgian mafia out," then he smiled, ". . . away from theirs."

As they took my passport outside for a long inspection, Soso continued: "In the war they used to say Ajara would secede from Georgia. But that was just talk." (Soso often used the phrase, underlining this key element in Caucasian communication, which has two distinct stages: the first tests the water, or tries it on; the second, not instantly recognisable, is "real talk"). He continued. "Aslan Abashidze, the ruler, is also a clever man. It's what you English call p . . . , p . . ."

"Posturing . . . ?" I suggested.

"Yes. He made this check-point to stop the Mkhedrioni coming in. It made Ajara the safest place in Georgia. Here all the guns belong to one man."

Passports were cleared and on we drove into the darkness. I'd heard about this 'Aslan' in Tbilisi, a few people pronouncing his name with distaste; claiming him a giant mafiosi who made a fortune out of controlling the Turco-Georgian border. But they all grudgingly admitted Ajara had been the safest place to live during 1992-3. About an hour later we stopped abruptly again. Outside was pitch dark.

"Quick get out!" Soso insisted. "They've stopped for us!"

Amazed I looked around. "Why here in the middle of a field?"

But he just grabbed my arm, shoved me out the door, shouting: "We're here!"

Standing on the road I squinted into the darkness. A car drove by and in its headlights I saw windows, pavements, old, ornate buildings — the kind found in capitals or ports. Soso was right: this carpet of darkness concealed a large, dead city, completely without electricity. We had arrived in Mandelstam's 'gold-rush city' — Batumi.

"They're having a power cut," Soso said off-handedly.

A slight understatement — confirmed by my rechargeable shaver which I left plugged-in for the whole five days in Batumi. It remained flat as a pancake.

When daylight arrived I found myself in a modern, Soviet flat, with no water, electricity or gas. My shower was a British Airways towelette. But once outside the door, the morning walk became a sheer pleasure. Suddenly a new kind of air pressed against my face. Fresh, tingly, full of messages from 500 kilometres of open sea. A hazy sun wrapped around my arms and seemed to swathe itself around the bell-jar of zesty light hanging over the city. By the port, palm trees waved casually in a breeze that glided off the miles of empty water. On the quayside puddles from overnight rain gave evidence of natural street-cleaning, and I remembered Mandelstam's words: *"Winter rain in Batum resembles a warm showerbath lasting several weeks."* Luckily it had stopped. I slung my jacket on my arm, wandered among the early 20th century streets, counting only four Soviet tower-blocks in the centre. I ended my journey at the sea-front in full shirtsleeve order. (Since then I've sunbathed on the Black Sea coast as late as mid December.)

At a harbour-front cafe on Gogibashvili Street, I ordered a Turkish coffee standing under the coloured umbrellas and watched a huge Russian military transport ship load with mandarins. Sipping the sweetened liquid I glanced out to sea. Turkey herself was just 18 kilometres to the south, across the border at Sarpi. You could feel the closeness. The spire of a mosque rose up not two hundred metres to the left, standing like a beacon to the fact that Ajara had spent 300 years in Turkey (between the 16th and 19th centuries) — the occupation only ending in 1878 when, after the Russo-Turkish War, the Congress of Berlin gave it over to Russian control.

This had been a crucial moment for Batumi and the Caucasus. The Baku oil-fields were being developed (see Appendix) and a period of strong Europeanisation and investment began almost immediately. By 1888, 21 per

Melting-pot Batumi centre, with mosque, Soviet mural and pre-Revolutionary balconies

cent of the world's entire oil production passed through Batumi — then the railhead of the new Caspian-Black Sea rail link. A few years later a pipeline terminus and large refinery (funded by the Rothschild family) were added. But not only oil investment. By 1892 Georgia produced 38 per cent of the world's manganese — passing through Batumi and its sister Black Sea port, Poti, 100 kilometres to the north. The trade expanded and by 1917 it was said Baku had more millionaires than Paris or London — most had villas in Batumi.

But Batumi was to receive a curious link with Britain. After the Russian Revolution the Turks briefly retook the city, but the Germans (then their allies) persuaded them to leave. After the German defeat in Europe the power-vacuum was filled by the British (worried about their oil investment), making Ajara a British protectorate with an English military governor and 20,000 troops. The troops left mid 1920 after lengthy arguments between Lloyd George, Lord Curzon and Winston Churchill — then the minister for war. As a result I would hear the rumour that some modern-day Ajarans carried traces of British blood. Indeed today the British Military Cemetery in Batumi contains 79 non-combat war graves.

My walk to the sea-front took me past elegant turn-of-the-century mansions displaying a fascinating blend of Art Nouveau, Art Deco, Neo Classical, Italian baroque, mingled with the Caucasian balcony — which some now call Caucasian Art Nouveau. As one Georgian architect told me: "The mansions of Batumi display more styles of architecture on one street than anywhere in Europe. In London I'd always get lost because the houses are the same."

Gazing out over the flat Black Sea waves, I considered this period of rapid development. Russia's

Georgian hospitality — invitation to a passer-by from a Batumi balcony. Batumi architecture combines a number of European styles.

victory transformed the city within 20 years, from being "not very attractive
. . . [with] absolutely nothing to attract the stranger's attention," as Oliver
Wardrop described it in 1887, to an elegant European port and third city in
the Caucasus region. European hotels and mansions made Batumi a lure for
Russian society — the 'dangerous kiss' near the Islamic frontier that
Pyatigorsk had been a century earlier. It built a theatre, an opera, opened a
British consulate, and flourished under Russian rule, where it had faded under
Turkish.

Intellectual life also revived. The young Joseph Stalin or 'Koba' (his
revolutionary name — *koba* means 'indomitable' in Turkish) continued his
socialist education in Batumi jail between 1902-3, a time when the Tsarist
prisons were regarded as the better 'universities.' Noe Zhordania and the
Menshevik government fled from here, making it the last independent city of
Georgia in 1921. Later in the Soviet period, Yesenin, the Russian poet who
briefly married the American dancer Isadora Duncan, found solace here for a
few months in 1924-5. Mandelstam, who was arrested (ironically) as a
'Bolshevik,' describes its gold-rush atmosphere then as alternately:

> . . . *a filthy cauldron of exploitation and treachery; a dubious window on Europe*
> *for the Soviet nation . . . [and] an enchanting semi-Oriental Mediterranean*
> *port with Turkish coffee bars, courteous merchants and Russian traders . . .*

Impatient to see the evidence for myself I drained my cup and headed for the
centre. Very quickly Batumi lived up to its reputation for varied architecture —
in every way except one. For virtually all its fine old buildings, former banks,
merchants homes, Italian/French shops, were neglected. Four years of war and
poverty had shut down all maintenance. Walls were cracked, balconies sagged,
windows broken. On the streets some manhole covers had even been stolen,
then sold as scrap across the Turkish border, leaving gaping holes. (In Tbilisi
whole streets lost their trams because thieves stole the copper conductor wires.)

Walking through it, I felt a strange mixture of euphoria and tragedy. This
was the city Mandelstam later returned to after his happy *Journey to Armenia*
in 1931. He came to the Caucasus then in a very different mood — fleeing the
"watermelon emptiness" of Bolshevik Russia, seeking "the splendid intimacy
with the world of real things." That day on former Stalina Prospekt I
encountered its modern alternative first as Ajaran 'Securicor': a group of six
ordinarily dressed men, AK47s dangling casually at their sides, one man
walking in the centre holding a small grubby plastic bag stuffed with small,
dollar-shaped objects — obviously Aslan's private police. Was this the new
world of real things? None of the passers-by showed any concern about the
weapons — now obviously an everyday occurrence.

Either way, clearly Aslan's formula — outgun everybody to such a degree
nobody would consider trying — worked, at least for now. I heard no gunfire at
all during my stay in Batumi and wandered around at all times of day and night.

A few minutes later I encountered one of Batumi's better known buildings, the Art Nouveau bank on former Mikhailovsky Street, now April 9th Street. Built in 1903 it showed a sorry modern face. The grey facade of elegant Art Nouveau swirls and curves were flaking off, above the roof was broken. A fabulous building that in the West would be feted and treasured, here weeping down onto the street with neglect. I turned round. Behind me stood the old London Hotel — built at roughly the same time, with no roof at all. I felt that instinctive urge to do something — but what? Couldn't I convince somebody, somewhere to invest?

I reconnected with Soso that evening, at a sea-front restaurant. Over to the

The Art Nouveau bank on former Mikhailovsky Street, Batumi, built in 1903

side two men wearing expensive Italian clothes sat with their wives and immediately beckoned for us to join them. I asked who they were.

"Very important people," Soso said under his breath, accepting with an ingratiating smile.

"Is one Aslan?" I asked.

"No!" he said much louder, adding: "Of course not!" As if everyone should know who he was.

During our introductions I discovered that I too had become "a very important person" — as Soso's newest calling card.

The meal proceeded and, as is often the case in Georgia, the younger of the two wives spoke excellent English — language study being more popular among women than men. Her perfume, I guessed, was French, and her company, the new merchant class growing up around the Western-funded pipeline soon to be constructed between Baku and Supsa, its Black Sea terminal. After a polite but mundane conversation I asked her about Britain's old connection with Batumi. Suddenly emotion flicked into her eye.

"You know we had 15,000 British soldiers here," she said pointedly, then hesitated. "My grandmother spoke very good English, her sister had an English passport. I still have it with its red cover."

Her voice trailed off as if entering the territory of an uncomfortable memory. She changed the subject, but a few minutes later, as if unable to resist any longer, returned to it.

"You know about the Georgian wives when the English left Batumi?" she looked at me intently. I told her "no." Then she leaned forward and giving each word an individual weight said: "When your soldiers were leaving on the ship, all the Georgian wives were put in a ferry to be pulled behind it. When they started to go out of the port somebody said Fascist planes were coming to attack, so to save the wives the rope was cut." She paused, glanced out toward the open sea, now a gaping black space beyond the window. "The ship sailed away and the Georgian wives were left behind in the harbour."

The last sentence was said so bleakly, it could have happened yesterday. I felt the strange link between this modern woman and an event 40 years before her birth. That image of a taut rope flying loose, the rear end of a large troop ship shrinking away into the distance. What could be a more symbolic end to freedom in Georgia and the start of Bolshevik imprisonment? For 75 years these two women had preserved that passport, no doubt as a memorial to the life that never was. Now I noticed she wore a pearl necklace — wealth, they had discovered, was the new red passport to the West for post-Soviet Georgians.

Lilo tangerine juice. Possibly independent Georgia's first home-manufactured product

During a lull in the conversation I asked about the chances of meeting the real Aslan.

"Just go to see him," said one of the VIPs simply.

Back in the flat I asked Soso about this apparent lack of a need for appointments. He gave me a wide-eyed look.

"Aslan is unpredictable," he said. "Nobody knows what he's going to do. The other day he kept the American ambassador waiting for three hours. He is a king. Pasha Aslan! Everything depends on his mood." Then he beamed at me. "But first we go to my house!"

So next afternoon, obediently, I walked up to Freedom (formerly Lenin) Square to rendezvous with Soso's minibus. The route took me along streets with Caucasian balconies running the whole length, dangling bunches of grapes over the road, past the synagogue, an abandoned Armenian church, then the grand Catholic cathedral, recently requisitioned by the Georgian Orthodox Church. I finally arrived in a large open space flanked by various markets, shops and tree-lined avenues.

Browsing through a stall in the square something caught my attention; a pair of shoes with the words MADE IN GEORGIA printed on the sole. I experienced a tiny thrill. The first product manufactured by independent Georgia . . . ? Certainly I wouldn't see another clearly indigenous product for a year — then a carton of tangerine juice stamped PRODUCED BY LILO COMPANY TBILISI, GEORGIA.

A historic moment, as with these shoes a new pattern was established for my every subsequent trip. The first inquiry into Georgia's progress began at the supermarket shelf — with every new locally-made product feeling like a major triumph. After the collapse of the Soviet Union I'd seen whole fruit crops lying on the ground rotting — their industry gone. Slowly, a few daring businessmen were starting to fill the gaping hole left by the Soviet system. Several excellent Georgian brandies then appeared with redesigned bottles, then a whole range of Dutch-bottled wines and a Georgian plum jam.

Driving to Soso's beach house we climbed up into Mandelstam's "gentle Japanese hills" overlooking Batumi with their villas surrounded by camphor, laurel, mulberry, bamboo, and every so often the eagle-wing tips of banana palms. Then came the neat green rows of tea plantations (during the Soviet period Ajara had 11 tea factories) and the sight of the Lesser Caucasus finally dipping down under the waves, carrying their load of tall silvery eucalyptus (planted at the turn of the century to drain the Batumi marshes).

We arrived at Soso's home, a convoy of one minibus and several VIP Mercedes and BMWs. It stood, as predicted, right on the beach and without a stick of furniture.

"Don't worry, the neighbours will lend us," he said cheerfully, hurrying round carrying crates of wine and Coca-Cola. True to his word, within an hour we had a table and enough chairs for 30 people. Georgians are duty-bound to help their neighbours' feasts, even to their last scrap of food. As the writer Kurban Said described Caucasian hospitality in his fine novel *Ali and Nino*:

> *If a guest enters your house holding the severed head of your only son in his hands, you must still receive him, offer him food and drink.*

Within an hour, a long banqueting table had been stocked with food and drink. Outside the sun set and another moonless night descended. In the gathering gloom Soso suddenly exclaimed: "We need candles!" Someone was immediately dispatched back to the neighbours.

Two hours later, with the toasts and songs in full flood (the dinner even included a 'choir'), I escaped to the balcony to try and find a moment's peace. I glanced out over the waves at the black space where Batumi, a city of 150,000 should have sent a dazzling burst of light across the water. Now all that showed was a couple of flickers from mast lights on ships in the harbour.

Between the shouts and songs I could just hear the lapping waves and tried, as a respite, to imagine the smooth white

Georgia's local tea on sale at Tbilisi main market

sails that bore Jason and his Argonauts past this spot two and a half thousand years earlier.

"What are you doing?" A woman's voice addressed me from behind.

One of the local girls had been 'sent' to find out why the Englishman missed the toasts. She had dark hair, oval eyes; a face probably similar to those the Greeks encountered when they landed just up the coast in Colchis. I asked what she used

Oriental sweet shop — Lenin Street, Batumi

to think about when she gazed out over this water during her childhood.

"The West," she replied instantly, looking out over the waves as if she still did. I asked if she'd been there.

"Only Turkey," she said as if it didn't count.

A loud drinking toast sounded from the house, followed by the few chords of a song. I asked her what it meant.

"That song was *Mravalzhamier*," she said livening up. I will translate it." (The following is the translation gathered by British musicologist Gerard McBurney):

> *Let us sing brothers*
> *Till we see each other.*
> *We will have time to grieve*
> *When we are lying in the black earth*
> *And the chunks of black earth*
> *Fall lightly down on our hearts.*

It was followed by a long sonorous toast, which slowly climbed up to a hysterical, party conference-style climax.

I told her it reminded me of the story of an English friend who once remarked to a Georgian that the early sessions of the Georgian Parliament resembled long toasting sessions, not debates — to which the Georgian replied: "British toasts more resemble debates."

She laughed. "Our oral tradition isn't like it was. But a good toast should be like poetry, like a good song." As she said it a song started up again. She listened for a moment then said: "This one is from Guria."

I listened as the male voices started a chorus that two years later I would hear at London's Royal Albert Hall, sung by the Rustavi Choir — to two encores and a standing ovation. But there, emerging from the chaos of toasts and drunkenness, by an electricity-free Black Sea, the sound came across as pure and ancient as the sight of Jason's white sails. A new song started, this time including the extraordinary dissonant yodelling from Guria — *krimanchuli* — that so fascinated Stravinsky and Gyorgy Ligeti. I had received my respite and returned to the banquet.

"What about Aslan?" I asked Soso the next morning.

"Let's go now!" he exclaimed and immediately led the way out the door, past the mirrored oriental sweet shop on Lenin Street to his 'palace,' the Government Building just a few doors up.

"He's in," he remarked, pointing to the large black Mercedes parked out on the street — number plate BBB 001, then added: "Bomb-proofed."

Inside, waiting to hear if Aslan would see us, we were shown some plans for the new Batumi by the architectural department, who vowed "to make our city like it was 100 years ago."

I noticed the design included a marina, several huge international hotels, a vast new opera, not unlike Sydney. I was about to ask about plans to renovate the old architecture, when a dapper young man stepped in.

"He will see you now," he announced proudly.

Everyone in the room seemed to jump, and suddenly the presence of this hidden king, filled the air. We were hurried through one giant antechamber, the size of ballroom, to a security desk where they took my camera, then the door opened into a second vaster chamber, lit by a sparkling Venetian chandelier. Underneath it, a parquet floor bore a single desk at the far end beside a TV playing Sky News. About 20 metres away at the near end stood a couple of neat, French sofas and a low table. Soso and I sat down and waited expectantly. A minute later the door at the far end opened to reveal a small, beady-eyed man wearing a light-blue checked jacket and black trousers. He bounded across the parquet and greeted me warmly, his eyes bright and watchful. Aslan (like most major Caucasian politicians) had narrowly escaped at least one assassination attempt and lived in expectation of the next.

"Welcome to Ajara!" he announced and beckoned me to sit back down on the couch. "Do you like it here? Safe isn't it?"

I told him it felt unusually safe.

"So what can I do to help your stay here?" He seemed to beam out a kind of intelligent intensity, like a man ever vigilant in a whirlpool of intrigue. This alertness reminded me of that other great Caucasian charmer, George Gurdjief (who once tried to open his institute in Tbilisi). Gurdjief had captivated many a Western seeker by pinpointing what he called "essences" in people. A state of perpetual alertness of the kind found, he once said, in mountain bandits who spent most of the day concentrating attention down their gun barrels.

To break the ice I asked if he knew anywhere I could find the famous *acharuli khachapuri* — an egg floating in a bread and cheese boat — as no café could serve it due to the power shortage (no ovens). Alsan immediately sprang to his feet.

"You shall have it now!" he declared and disappeared back into the doorway, returning a minute later saying it was on its way. I took my cue to ask him about the electricity problem in Ajara.

"We may not have very much, but I at least control what we have!" He grinned then stood up and, extracting a portable phone, dialled a number to speak a few words. Ten seconds later, to my complete surprise, the palace was plunged into total darkness.

Sitting in that impenetrable gloom I realised what Soso meant by unpredictable behaviour, but also sensed a method in Aslan's madness. He had just displayed absolute control over all forces of Ajaran energy, human or otherwise — and far more vividly than if he'd summoned in a brigade of crack troops.

With light restored, I asked him about his relations with the Russians. Some Tbilisians mumbled he had sold his soul to Russia because he allowed a strong Russian troop presence in Ajara and the Russian border police to set up their 'false border' between Georgia and Turkey — in effect the CIS frontier. This was to produce another act of theatre. He stood up, strode over to his desk, extracted a book from a drawer.

"This," he announced boldly, "is Russia's *Who's Who*! And who do you think is on the first line of the first page . . . ?" He smiled widely and handed it over. I saw his name printed in Russian at the head of the page. "That is our relationship!"

I couldn't help but like him, even though many Ajarans complained of corruption and no electricity. I knew this was only a half royal display; the other half was to gauge my reactions. Politically, Aslan's position was not easy: maintaining a delicate balancing act between two loaded guns. Muslim Turkey lay on his southern flank, Orthodox Russia the north, with numerous Georgian inter-tribal rivalries, feudal ambitions and mafias in the middle. Political analysts (living outside Georgia) generally believed he managed all these conflicting elements adequately — keeping his goal as stability and wealth for himself, rather than expansion.

The huge Dynamo Tbilisi stadium at the start of Georgia's epic European Cup qualifier against Wales, November 1994 (Georgia won 5-0). Note the electronic scoreboard still fighting with the low voltage — theoretically 220 volts, in effect fluctuating between around 70 and 300.

The *khachapuri* arrived, along with delicious Ajaran tea, with a hint of lemon. We chatted on in a civilised way, my listeners's eyes occasionally narrowing, still trying to out the motive behind my visit. A spy from Britain or Shevardnadze . . . ? But in the end I left the palace feeling refreshed and made very welcome.

Stepping outside we were immediately engulfed by the inky blackness of a Batumi night. Stumbling down the street, praying for no open manhole covers, I glanced back over my shoulder. The golden shafts of light streamed out of Aslan's windows, as the only visible illumination in the whole city.

A couple of days later I returned to Tbilisi to witness an event that would prove as significant to the new independent nation as any. Georgia had entered the European Cup for the first time in its history and would play Wales at home. It came in the wake of Dynamo Tbilisi's disgrace a year earlier — caught trying to bribe the referee in a UEFA Cup match, for which they were promptly suspended. Georgia the nation had yet to win a match.

By chance I had met the only Welshman in Georgia the day before in Batumi. Although he professed to be "only a rugby fan" he made the seven-hour journey to Tbilisi for the game. We arranged to meet outside the ground, but the vast Dynamo Tbilisi stadium — the size of Wembley — defeated all my attempts at finding not only him but an entrance. Finally I accosted a couple of youths who promptly escorted me (and themselves) through a gate shouting *"Ingliseli zhurnalisti!"* without paying.

Inside the vast, concrete amphitheatre I studied the sea of perhaps 20,000 dark male faces for another blond head — but failed. To my left a large electronic scoreboard tried its best to produce the words GEORGIA and WALES (succeeding only by half-time), its circuits battling valiantly with the low voltage.

The atmosphere in the stadium was more curious than electric. For me it was a strange moment to see the familiar British faces of Ian Rush and Neville Southall step onto the pitch then gaze nervously around at the wild Caucasian turf. Their minds had obviously been primed with tales of guns and mafia. I say 'obviously' for something had to explain what followed.

The game was like few I'd ever seen. Not only did Georgia win 5-0, Temur Ketsbaia (since taken by Newcastle United) scored Georgia's first ever goal as a nation in a major competition (until then Georgians had to play as Dynamo Tbilisi in the Soviet league). Although I theoretically supported Wales, when the ball curled into the Wales net, something lifted me from my seat and made me cheer out wildly with the other 20,000. I sat down again hurriedly.

Perhaps I'd intuited that this single event would put Georgia on the map as no other. Suddenly the British press started remembering the Dynamo Tbilisi from 1981 that beat Liverpool and went on to take the Cup Winners Cup. Indeed, a few weeks later Georgia made its first significant export to the West — as Giorgi Kinkladze, one of the goal scorers — who signed to Manchester

City. 'Kinky' as he became known (for his style of dribbling) was to raise Georgia's profile significantly in Britain, regularly out-polling Shevardnadze in the popular press.

Since then Georgia's sporting prowess has drawn more attention — including a memorable project run by Christian Aid (which I helped). During the Georgia–England World Cup qualifiers (1996/7) they organised children from the Dzegvi Orphanage near Tbilisi to meet Glenn Hoddle, then play with their heroes in Georgia's national team. The children were so moved by the experience they produced some splendid drawings of both sides — at the time of writing still touring British cathedrals.

A lesser known fact, kept strangely quiet, is that the Georgians remain world leaders in women's chess. They monotonously retained the Olympic championship since they first entered

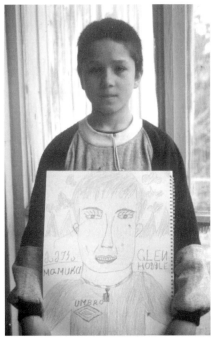

A Georgian boy from Dzegvi orphanage paints Glenn Hoddle, the England coach — exhibited in Britain by Christian Aid

the bi-annual competition in 1992. They also held the women's World Chess Championship for 29 years after Nona Gaprindashvili took it in 1962 — to be beaten in 1979 by the 17-year-old Maya Chiburdanidze, who lost it in 1991. I remember discussing this combination of competitiveness and concentration with a Georgian friend.

"You know of course that Madam Petrovna Blavatsky was also educated in Tbilisi," he said suddenly. "Her powers of concentration reached even into the next world!"

I asked what he meant.

"What I mean is that here our lives are not so separated, specialised as yours in the West. I think sport, religion, politics are all similar. For instance we Georgians play football like we play our politics. We're all great individualists. We dribble the ball too far, won't pass and finally run out of space. But watch out for when we learn team work!"

Giorgi Kinkladze (right), Georgia's football sensation at Manchester City, with co-player Misha Kavelashvili

17

Khevsureti

I t was a strange feeling, boarding the Landrover Defender with Union Jack fluttering on the bonnet. Strange because after a 74 year gap of Communism, then civil war, a British diplomatic mission had finally returned to the Caucasus. Until then I had enjoyed being one of the few Brits in Georgia. Now I found myself royally upstaged, sitting inside the vehicle of Britain's first ever ambassador to Georgia, Stephen Nash. Appointed in October 1995 he, with the aid of his deputy Michael Hancock, had now established a diminutive home base in a suit of rooms at Tbilisi's Metechi Palace Hotel.

Sitting up inside this mini four-wheeled Britain, about to set off for the remote mountain district of Khevsureti, I tried to adjust to this brief umbilical reconnection to our islands. I'd become so used to isolation from the West here; the Soviet/Russian visa and Aeroflot battles, to finally arrive in a universe of Ladas and Nivas. Now a smooth-running English diesel, new tyres and spare parts direct from the UK — the world had turned upside-down.

Added to this came an uncertainty about our destination. Khevsureti is one of the wilder frontiers of Georgia, historic flashpoint with the Muslim foe, and lies right up against a now hostile-to-foreigners Chechenia (two British aid-workers had been kidnapped a few weeks earlier). The relationship between these remote mountain valleys has always been ambiguous — properly understood only by the locals.

Recently the two centuries-old enemies had renewed their friendship. When Stalin forcibly removed the Chechens from their lands after World War II, as punishment for allegedly siding with the Nazis, they returned to find the Khevsurs, who had been moved into their Jariakhi glen homes, vacating the houses willingly and leaving gifts and cattle as presents. More recently during the Chechen war against Russia, the Khevsurs had resisted all Russian pressure to betray their Muslim neighbours. How friendly were they now? Friendly enough to help kidnap an ambassador?

The feeling was complicated by the fact that Stephen Nash decided to travel not in the official vehicle but with our Georgian hosts in the Niva ahead. It left myself and fellow Englishman Andrew Murrey considering the option of who would pose as ambassador for the day (in the front).

"A decoy ambassador," I remarked, "should be useful near the Chechen border and kidnap zone."

But Andrew, alert to my ploy for gaining the better-view front seat,

An original, hand-painted map of the Khevsureti region, with illustrations of traditional dress

declared he doubted the Khevsurs sheltered Chechen bandits, and would gladly make the sacrifice for his country.

Outplayed, I sat back and considered Britain's late diplomatic return to Georgia. The Germans and Americans had landed in strength two years earlier (receiving diplomatic plates 001 and 002 respectively, 007 going to the UNHCR, 017 to Britain), bagging two of Tbilisi's finer properties for their embassies, then pouring in aid and influence. America even managed to negotiate the splendid former House of Friendship on Antoneli Street, where during the Communist period I'd sipped glasses of mineral water, trying to spot microphone positions.

As we pulled away I began to wonder how much the memories of nations behave like those of people. Had Britain's delayed return to Georgia made any subliminal link with her previous departure? Many Georgians believed the withdrawal of British troops in 1919-20 sent the Bolsheviks a green light to invade (a fact disputed by historians, who mostly follow Winston Churchill's reasoning — then Britain's Secretary of State for War — who saw the Bolshevik ambitions on Menshevik Georgia as too zealous to stop).

Either way we were back, although the Union Jack still lacked a proper flagpole at the Metechi Palace Hotel — just a small six inch pendant perching on Stephen Nash's desk. But, perhaps as important to Britain's resurrecting relationship, were the two 19th century portraits hung on the wall above it — of Britain's last representative in the area, its former chief commissioner of the

Caucasus, Oliver Wardrop, alongside his sister Marjory.

If Britain had planted any lasting diplomatic seed in Georgian soil worthy of resurrection, it had to be Oliver and Marjory Wardrop. As a young Victorian making his Grand Tour Oliver had visited Georgia in 1887 and wrote a book on his experiences — *The Kingdom of Georgia*. A few years later his highly educated sister Marjory, who at the time described herself as "only a horrid woman instead of an independent man! (who has) to stay at home and do nothing . . . ," took it on herself to learn Georgian and diligently produced the first English translation (or, as she put it, "attempted close rendering") of Rustaveli's *Man in the Panther Skin* (the title differs according to era and country).

Such literary dedication was rewarded when she wrote a letter in perfect Georgian to the poet Ilia Chavchavadze. He published it on the cover of his newspaper *Iveria* — after which Oliver wrote back to his sister: "My only *raison d'être* here is that I am related to you. Your popularity is enormous and . . . everybody is clamouring to have you out here." She came with her mother on a fairy-tale visit in 1894, to be greeted by large crowds and choirs at the stations. Oliver's subsequent appointment as British chief commissioner in 1919 had proved a much needed, if brief, diplomatic success — cut short by the brutal Bolshevik invasion of 1921.

Stephen Nash rightly promoted the memory of the Wardrops and is generally regarded as restarting the relationship well, especially via his attention to the arts. Kutaisi, I'm told, currently plans to name one of its streets after the Wardrops.

Michael Hancock also encountered Britain's literary associations, when one of his first meetings as deputy head of mission was with a local Armenian insisting his parrot Gocha be placed in the *Guinness Book of Records* for speaking the most

19th century Georgians dressed in Khevsur chain mail. Photo taken in a Tbilisi studio — collected by Oliver Wardrop (now part of the Wardrop Collection, the Bodleian Library, Oxford).

number of words in the world (mostly Russian and Armenian).

Now, as the Defender blithely sailed past Georgia's new clutch of drive-in petrol stations, I wondered about the esteem held for Khevsureti by other more famous wordsmiths like Vazha Pshavela, Ilia Chavchavadze, Grigol Robakidze. All had written hymns of praise to its people and culture (along with Pshavi and Tusheti) — where it was rumoured locals still held poetry competitions, keeping the oral tradition hanging on by fingernails. What, I wondered, might be so elemental to the modern Georgian self-image, lurking up here?

Our destination Shatili, the main village of Khevsureti, lay not a great distance from Tbilisi (about 120 kilometres) but the mileage belied the condition of the roads. Although now mid-July, some doubt existed that the road was yet open. A sturdy 4-wheel drive, seven hours and sturdier-yet driving were required.

But as we picked up the Mtkvari embankment, my spirits lifted. The images of strange-patterned tunics and an almost purely pagan culture had been planted in my mind back in 1988, during a tantalising conversation with a Khevsur woman called Lela. Perhaps here lay my first clue.

During those clovered Soviet days, she told me that every winter more Khevsur families were abandoning their frosty northern villages in favour of the then centrally heated flats in Tbilisi. They returned for the summer months, but with every departure their traditional family residences took a step closer to the holiday home.

Lela had been a child of this new Khevsur double life. Her intellect had matured down in the capital, care of a stolid Soviet schooling, including philology and literature at the State University; her soul received a soaring education during those four summer months in the mountains, staying with her family's relations (her village had been abandoned). Thus she imbibed two sets of values, the custom, language and ritual of her Khevsur ancestors, against a background of the strict educational disciplines of a Tbilisi faculty. As a direct result she tried to combine both worlds by teaching Khevsur theory of weaving and embroidery to students at the university — exactly the same skills she'd learnt as a girl from her mother. Her driving purpose had become to keep these old skills and ideas alive in any way possible.

"In Khevsur culture," she had said in a voice seeming to indulge a secret pleasure, "there existed something very unique . . ."

She followed this with a searching look, as if hunting a way to convey her ideas to an Englishman. "Perhaps like the eternal values stored in Shakespeare — because, you see, we too had our own way of recording it, in our embroidery."

She'd reached into her bag and pulled out several pieces of finely embroidered black cloth, and laid them carefully out on the table. "You can read it here, right on our old clothing. You can find everything in these patterns."

She'd said the words with such emotion I found myself gazing intently at the cloth, trying to divine a meaning from the rows of tiny squares, coloured crosses and angular pattern.

"If you understand these, you can restore the religion and character of their culture. I see it as a kind of writing. These colours and shapes represent the essences, both of the people who made them and the tribe they belonged to. They're like banks of ideas or information stored here in code."

She'd run her finger down the intricately sewn rows. "These patterns are so important, because you see the Khevsur religion allowed no icons, no images of God. This is all there is. It's not a Christian religion. They have an invisible God, a kind of mathematical harmony that's hard to explain. But you can feel it here, sense this harmony they worship in these colours and motifs."

I'd looked closely at the hundreds of tiny interlocking crosses and geometric patterns flowing across the cloth. I'd never seen designs quite like these, yet at the same time found them attractive, each motif somehow preparing you for the next. Back in London a specialist in Near Eastern carpets told me this style was unique to this area of the Caucasus.

"If you look at the crosses," Lela had said carefully, "you can see how they seem to emerge out of the star motif. The starburst is an early symbol for the sun."

I knew the worship of the sun had been put forward as one of the earliest religions in the Caucasus. She picked up one of the embroideries covered in the small, multi-pointed crosses,

"These are perhaps closer to the original cross. See how its many spines are like the sun's rays. Later they simplified it down to four."

Noticing my interest, she then reached into her bag and extracted some battered photographs showing men and women wearing this traditional dress. They stood before a primitive, fortress-like village, its old walls growing out of the rock like a ragged brown crystal. Their embroidered shirts and dresses were covered with these same crosses and stars, large and small, none of them the Christian Latin cross, but the so-called pagan (also Greek) cross with each of its arms equidistant from the centre — a symbol similar to those adopted by some early Christians, then the Crusaders and later by the Nazis in the 1930s. They stood out in brilliant whites, reds, or in yellow outline, sewn across the black tunic, or worn across the foreheads of women. In the centre of some larger crosses, coins had been attached, flashing back their bronze CCCP lettering like new cult symbols.

"These people are from the village of Shatili," she said. "The crosses are created over areas of the body they want to protect, both physically and psychologically."

I pictured a human back criss-crossed with points of light, drawn in from the sun by the crosses; for the first time making a connection with this motif as a symbol of health, used by organisations like our Red Cross.

I asked her about the reports from foreigners in the 1930s who spoke of

Khevsurs walking round Tbilisi dressed in chain mail and the large red crosses of the Crusaders.

"It's not true that the Crusaders bought this design to Khevsureti." she said firmly. "It's simply when the Khevsurs saw these crosses on the soldiers' armour they copied the design because of its similarity with their own. This is why Crusader crosses used to be found up here, even in this century. The design still shielded people."

Khevsur tunic with its distinctive pre-Christian crosses, not to be confused with the Crusader crosses of a later period

Meanwhile the Defender cruised past the Lego-style Ministry of Roads, taking the Gudauri-Vladikavkaz road, then after 45 minutes swung right onto a heavily potholed road and bridge over the Aragvi bridge then up past the Zhinvali Reservoir. We dodged and climbed steadily upward past rows of beech, walnut, elder, alder and surprisingly few houses. The air became cleaner, sweeter; trees thick with moisture, the atmosphere in the car gathering expectation.

None of us had been to Khevsureti before, including four of the five Georgians in our two cars. As we talked about our destination I discovered my knowledge was equal to theirs, simply from my conversation with Lela all those years earlier.

When we stopped a few hours later to eat lunch in a smooth green pasture of wild poppies and daisies, overlooked by distant snowy peaks, I re-read that conversation with Lela about the Khevsur embroideries back in the 1980s.

"If you look at them *closely*," she had said in a tone implying only a fool wouldn't, "you'll see how the Khevsur character is in fact a great synthesis. On one side, they follow a very strict, severe way of life and habit, and on the other, contain a very poetic, lyric, romantic nature. The Khevsurs are known as wonderful poets, they have a strong oral tradition and are among Georgia's best. You can see it in the dark cloth and then the sparse but brilliant coloured patterns.

"You can see the character there too. If you look at the pattern on these leggings—" she lifted up an elegantly woven tube of blue swirls, geometric spirals and crosses set against a black-knit background, "—you know from the austere, rich feel to this design it's from Khevsureti. But this other design—" she picked up a fragment of brighter, more cheerful embroidery, "—is from Pshavi, the next valley over from Khevsureti. You can see it here, the lighter, less severe style."

I noticed how its brighter, cleverly intersecting white and yellow crosses did indeed convey a different mood.

"You see," she'd continued, "if you look at these dark Khevsur colours, you get a feel for the Khevsur woman who wasn't even allowed to cry if she lost her child. It would be a shame; it would show lack of strength. Because of their hard life they also tended not to get married until 28 or 30. Then immediately after their marriage she wasn't allowed to sit near her husband, or on their first night even sleep on the same floor as him. Here life was very severe, strict."

Then suddenly she'd smiled. "But you know even within all this austerity they allowed freedoms. Due to their late marriage they were allowed to have what you might call 'boyfriends.' These would be official and formally accepted by the village. Couples could behave like lovers in every way except, of course, make children, which only happened after marriage."

Then she picked up the Pshavi embroidery. "But in Pshavi the same system operated much more freely. And you can see all these things in the colours and patterns. The Pshavian colours are more bright yellow, happy. You can find this illustration of character throughout all Georgian traditional dress."

Vazha Pshavela (1861-1915), regarded by many as Georgia's second poet — most of his work is set in the Khevsureti region

She'd looked at me curiously. "You may also have noticed that traditional Georgian dress doesn't have pockets."

I'd confessed I hadn't.

"Well this is because before we didn't like to keep money with ourselves, to be always thinking about it. Even today money isn't the main thing for us. We're not mercantile. We're very romantic in this matter."

Although the new free-market Georgia was now eroding this side of the character, up on that hillside, eating fresh tomatoes and delicious organically grown apricots (as is nearly all produce in new Georgia), I suddenly felt a lot closer to this romanticised past.

I remembered how Tamuna had hinted as much without ever being able to say it, feeling herself haunted by 'fairy tales' she couldn't define. Lela too had seemed touched by the same undefinable sense of loss, but unlike Tamuna it fuelled her way forward.

Romanticism has always played a central role in the Georgian character. The highly praised poet Vazha Pshavela (1861-1915) had come from this region

The High Mountains

by Vazha Pshavela (1861-1915)

They were standing and waiting, waiting outside time like the limitlessness of a sea. Their thoughts hid behind stone faces that said nothing, save that enmity itself awaits with them. That a fire boils in their summits, craving escape. But they have no voice. They stand and wait.

Mountains, for whom do you wait? A lover perhaps — not seen for an age? Or a child, brother or mother, so distant you have to bend a rocky ear to the sky — then hear no answer? How can you stand so motionless in this water that is the past, present and future? Is your waiting really as old as the sea, as great as limitless God?

Do you wait for a time when every flower, insect and breeze will sleep, allow your huge exhalation, release your hidden cry of stone? Are you like those men never admitting the rocks of sadness clamped to their breasts?

Mountains, why don't you sing? Why should I die without hearing this sweet sound? Why not laugh? Or just a tiny smile for your friends? Why a slave to this granite of time, with all life locked in your cliffs? Sometimes I think you only pretend, that a happiness hides in your precipices. Does not just one small candle light in your flanks when the eagle circles your summits, rests a wing on your shoulder? How exquisite you are together! He who you formed leans a head on your own. How handsome, how obstinate he is! He is your messenger from God, for it is he who informs God on you. Surely with him on your skin dreams flow through your rocky mind. Of course they do! See all those bright flowers nodding gently on your slopes — these are your hopes.

But why then cover yourselves with mists? Perhaps you must hide as you think. When you decide to deliver grass to us on your skin, to drop down a cold stream, the avalanche, a prancing stag. Sometimes I think you might lie my friends. Am I right? And to whom do you lie?

They are standing and waiting. Rain beats on their heads, thunder plays in their eyes, lightning burns at their fringes and their hearts. Does it matter if avalanches fall, if they bring down skulls and stones? Flee all you who fear life under these heights of sky. Go hide quietly down the valley.

Now it snows. The mountains are covered with ice and cold. The stones are drunken faces stuck to the slopes, covered in their shroud. They play dead, they cry 'Bury us!' as we wait to be buried by them.

They are standing and waiting. I can feel a heartache under those faces; a longing that never dies, that cannot die. For whom, for what do they wait? Perhaps it is something invisible to us . . . A possession that when they have it will simply demand more and more. Could their wait be insatiability itself? Yes surely that is it: insatiability is all they really are.

— *1895,* TRANSLATED BY P. NASMYTH & N. ANDRONIKASHVILI

NOTE: *Osip Mandelstam, who translated Pshavela (the pen-name of Luka Razikashvili), said of Pshavela's work in 'A Word or Two about Georgia Art': "His imagery, almost medieval in its epic majesty, contains an elemental force. It seethes with the concrete, the tangible, with everyday reality. Every utterance inadvertently becomes an image, and yet the word does not suffice — he must rip each word to pieces as it were, with his teeth, making the most of the passionate temperament of Georgian poetry. Wine ages — therein lies its future. Culture ferments — therein lies its youth. Preserve your own art; those narrow clay jugs buried beneath the earth."*

and wrote what many regard as 19th century Georgia's finest poetry. His poem 'The Snake Eater' is set in Khevsureti's mountains which, as he put it:

> *. . . bless the heavens with their gracefulness*
> *in cool breezes that swirl and moan around their peaks.*

Here certainly lay another clue to the link with the Romantic era. The poem tells the deeply animistic story of a man, Mindia, captured by wizards, who eats snake's flesh to then discover he understands the language of birds and flowers. Pshavela's poetry works even in translation (in spite of Robert Frost's missive "the only thing you lose in translating poetry is the poetry"). Most of his poems are set in Khevsureti and vividly convey the atmosphere of this region before its depopulation. The following is my version of the opening lines of his poem 'Host and Guest':

> *Behind the buried gloom of night*
> *icy, pale to the eye*
> *Chechenia is a bare, rocky throne.*
> *In a gorge below the river roars*
> *its seething, inward wrath.*
> *The mountains bend down*
> *wash hands and faces in the spray,*
> *the souls of dead men*
> *living on their flanks . . .*
> *. . . in the distance appears a Chechen village*
> *perched like an eagle's nest*
> *and as beautiful to observe*
> *as a woman's breast.*

Back in the Defender we continued on toward the same rock throne, the road now doubling as an assault course. Potholes, gravel patches, cracks, gushing streams attacked its surface. We began to follow a series of rusting Soviet pylons that in turn followed the boiling, muddy Aragvi river. Why did Soviet planners choose to put electricity pylons in the middle of a river? Was this the Leninist answer to built-in obsolescence? From his ambassador's seat, Andrew remarked he'd once seen a sign in Red Square declaring 'Socialism is Communism plus Electrification.'

Half an hour later came a potent symbol of what had happened to electrification without Communism. A huge pylon lay spread out across the Aragvi flood plain like a dead stick-insect, its black limbs splayed, its wires like crumpled antennae, long since shorted out. Most of the villages of this lower Khevsureti district had been without power for a year. We passed the village of Barisaho where, to confirm its gap from civilization a sign stated flatly: 'It is prohibited to drive buses from Barisaho to Shatili.'

"Why?" I asked our driver.

"They never arrive," he said simply, with chilling ambiguity. But as he spoke, something small and colourful shot past the window.

"A tourist shop . . . ?" said Andrew in a tone doubting his own eyes.

We skidded to a halt, reversed back

Khevsur tourist kiosk at roadside with Shota Arabuli's paintings for sale. The first shows a visitation from the Archangel Gabriel.

and discovered exactly that. A kiosk offering the usual ancient bars of Snickers, bottles of Coca-Cola, but also an old Khevsur shield, an embroidered dress and two locally made paintings. As we marvelled at this mountain merchandising, a short, bright-eyed man of about 40 walked out of the adjoining cornfield.

"Fifteen lari," he answered our queries about the paintings, then admitted he painted them himself. We promptly paid up. Then he said: "You want to see the museum?"

We looked round but could see nothing remotely museum-like. He pointed to an ordinary house above the cornfield. We followed him into the two-storey wooden structure which, as we climbed the stairs, seemed to bend and moan under our collective weight. I feared the whole thing might collapse if more than four adults stood upstairs at any one time. We passed a small 'library' made up of sagging shelves, then entered a room stuffed with boxes below rows of beautifully embroidered dresses and everyday Khevsur tools. There were sheep combs, hide-tenderisers, wooden butter churns, jewellery and a necklace

Khevsur cribs carrying the 'everlasting spiral' motif, thought to be an adaption of the ancient sun symbol. It appears frequently in modern Georgia. The Round Table Alliance party adopted it, and it appears on Georgian tetri coins.

Spring flowers in Lower Khevsureti

made up of short Khevsur crosses and old Russian kopeks. Everything seemed to be coated in a thin, grey film of antiquity, as if scooped up out of the earth and hung on the wall. I saw several examples of the 'everlasting spiral' carved on wooden boxes and cribs, a sun symbol dating back to Sumerian times, making Khevsur origins yet more mysterious. As we admired the collection our host told us his name, Shota Arabuli.

"Yes I am a Khevsur, and a painter," he said in a quiet voice. "I came back up from Tbilisi in 1986 during peristroika." He gestured at the tunics and artifacts. "They are from my family and friend's families."

I spotted a pile of paintings stacked under a table, and leafed through. They showed a remarkable range of themes — from Khevsur village parties, visitations from the Angel Gabriel, to scenes from *100 Years of Solitude* by Gabriel García Márquez. I asked how many visitors his museum received a year.

He thought for some time, then said: "About ten."

I noticed how different his slow, thoughtful tone was to the Svans, who as soon as we'd met invited us to drink. I remembered Marika once talking about these two tribes. "It's very interesting. They're only a few valleys apart but their cultures are completely different. The Svans have wonderful paintings in churches, but an undeveloped oral tradition. The Khevsurs have virtually no paintings and no churches, but a wonderful poetry and oral literature."

I wondered if Shota's attraction to Márquez was perhaps part of this literary tradition, a link to the solitude of the Khevsurs, the tribe of the past . . .

By now the ambassador had returned, which meant our party nearly doubled his museum's annual gate. I feared for the groaning floor-joists but Shota refused our offered entrance fee. His face seemed to radiate a kind of joyful disbelief. When Stephen was introduced as the *elchi* ('ambassador') from Britain his expression never changed. I felt that if we'd said "an invader from outer space" it would have been the same.

Back in the shop we bought embroidered leggings, maps, calendars (printed on torn rolls of cheap Turkish paper), then drove off up toward the tantalising cracks of snow and rock, disappearing between the clouds.

As we climbed our guide, Rostov, said many Khevsurs had come down to Tbilisi from their villages in Soviet times but never felt themselves at home in anonymous city life.

"Up in their mountains they were somebody. Down there they were nobody. During our Civil War (1992-94) some started returning because life was better up here. The population of Khevsureti has now increased slightly."

Then the road took a steep turn upward. We laboured past giant hog-weed, azaleas, docks, then suddenly entered a wide-open green mountain slope. Graceful, velvet-green fingers of grass reached down for the Aragvi, their surfaces shaved down by grazing, beside crevasses crammed with wild rose, cow parsley, the white dashes of streams. By 2,500 metres the mountains had turned into a vast, unkempt flower garden. Kilometre upon kilometre of blue, yellow, white, with sudden scarlet slashes of poppy. In the distance acres of daisies gave the mountain-side a silver sheen: flowers that in 'The Snake Eater' Vazha Pshavela described as "glittering like Queen Tamar's very eyes."

We stopped the car, took pictures in an air charged with the fragrance of a million flowers. Wading out into the now knee-high blossoms I wondered if centuries of looking at these patterns had inspired the Khevsur women in their embroideries.

A shepherd encountered close to 3,000m on a Khevsur pass

Finally we reached the summit at 2,885 metres and looked down on a new landscape in which patches of snow added a polka-dot to the everlasting green. Over to the north-east, the mountains of Daghestan looked sternly down — to the north, so did the dangerous Chechen highlands. In the distance, the valley narrowed to a crack which led through a gulley to the village of Shatili. Looking down on this emptiness I remembered the words of a Georgian friend talking about the stories she had heard of the Gods underlying this landscape.

"I don't know if it's right," she had said, "and I keep hearing different versions, but the Khevsurs still have a wonderful mythology.

"The way I understand it is that before the Gods arrived the Khevsur land was ruled by *devis*, evil creatures who used them as slaves. That one day a Khevsur appealed to the main god, Morige, who sent down his sons, the warrior-gods, Kopala and Kviria. *Kvira* is the Georgian word for 'Sunday' and is associated with the sun. You can see a slight similarity with Christianity although this was much earlier. There was a big battle, the *devis* were defeated, and the land became holy. The Khevsurs have several gods who sometimes come down to earth. They can move freely between heaven, earth and the underworld. Gudani is another and when the Christians came he became associated with St George. The 'churches' of the Khevsurs are the places where the sons of God descend to earth. They build *khatis*, small covered areas over these places, put objects in them like those bought back from the underworld by a Khevsur man who once accompanied a son of God through one of their doorways into the land of the ancestors. If you go into certain *khati* today, occasionally you'll see some of these items: a bell, a cup, a sieve, a plough, a banner of a woman. The territory of each *khati* is supposed to be the distance you can hear its bell. Many *khatis* are now empty because the treasures have been stolen or lost. The Khevsurs believe treasure has a mystical power that makes you either good or bad — purifies your soul or turns you into a *devi*."

With these words turning through my head I surveyed this land of the Sons of God. Certainly a captivating myth, no matter how accurate. I could feel how it bound these people to their land before the arrival of Christianity. But who kept it going now? A couple of kilometres later came a first clue: a shepherd walking with his horse and dog. We stopped to talk and encountered

Abandoned fortresses beside the Argun river, on the way to Shatili. The Khevsur gods were said to descend to earth in the shafts of sunlight cutting through the clouds.

a wonderfully wind-sculptured face sprouting long white whiskers from his spending weeks at a time up here. When he smiled, his face transformed into a dramatic contour map, with two shiny blue lakes for eyes. The warmth it radiated made us linger, asking questions.

"I've always been a shepherd and always lived up here," he answered us politely. "Yes, the mountains have been overgrazed but the herds are smaller now."

"Don't you get lonely?" Andrew asked.

"No, and I'm 70 years old!" he laughed, giving us a wide engrained smile, then added for no particular reason: "I love the mountains."

I felt that he really did, and, as we drove on, reflected on Lela's words on the style of Khevsur embroidery. Certainly you could feel a softer, less severe character in these men. Their valleys were lower than Svaneti, the winters milder — Shatili itself stood at 1,400 metres. Also perhaps, due to their remoteness, the Christianisation of Highland Georgia in the 12th century had never really stuck. It vanished almost completely when, at the start of this century, Soviet Communism inadvertently assisted the return to the former nature religion.

About 500 metres lower we met the new river that would serve as our guide to Shatili — the Argun. We drove on until two ruined fortresses suddenly appeared over to the left, swirling in and out of clouds like a scene painted by Caspar Friedrich — a first hint at the long history of human settlement under these hills. The castles seemed to challenge us to believe they existed, then suddenly faded away completely into the mist as if the wizard's spell creating them had failed. I started to feel that enchantment so possessing the 19th century Romantics, which increased five minutes later when another look-out tower reared up directly beside the road, like a frontier marker into the past. From here on, it seemed to say, you obey the law of the mountains. After this the road plunged downward along with the Argun into a new world of trees, avalanches and mudslides. It brought back the warning given by Caucasus Travel — that the road may not yet be clear, having been closed just five days earlier. "You'll be the first vehicle to make it through in eight months," they'd said, wishing us well.

Eight kilometres later their warning proved prophetic — the road abruptly dead-ended under an angry white hill of dripping snow and earth. It felt like the mountain had blocked our way deliberately, by laying down the fat arm of an avalanche. A third of the way up, a yellow bulldozer laboriously carved a snow road, watched by a team of men. We stopped the car and joined them feeling beaten and rejected.

In frustration, I raised my eyes to see yet another castle looking down from a dizzying 100 metre cliff, so ragged it appeared to grow from the rock itself.

"Seventh century," Rostov answered my query as he hurried off to speak to the workers. I began to understand the animism in Vazha Pshavela's work — particularly his 'Snake Eater' where the hero Mindia listens to the words of nature then predicts the behaviour of men. Here rocks and man seemed to have finally merged, explaining perhaps why Pshavela himself wrote poems directly addressing mountains, as if they could hear him back (see page 230).

I asked one of the workers the distance to Shatili.

"*Erti*," he said holding up a single, leathery finger (Georgian for 'one'). I assumed he meant kilometres. And how many hours to cut a road through?

"*Ori*," he held up a second finger (Georgian for 'two').

We all looked at each other. Experience taught me to double most estimates of time in Georgia (in the end the road took six more hours). With little other option we decided to try and walk in.

We scrambled up over the avalanche, walked a couple of kilometres, rounded a corner and suddenly confronted what at first looked like a strange

Shatili, the old town, now abandoned — the 16 families live in an annex just round the hill

black rock formation. As we approached so the rocks began to gather signs of arrangement, then possible human construction. Only about 300 metres away did I finally click this was it — we'd arrived at the mournful black citadel of Shatili.

"Now *this* is desolate," remarked Andrew. The place looked less a village, more a series of slate slabs stacked together, a few windows tapped in at the top, as if a flock of ragged crows had landed on the hill then turned to stone. A closer look revealed a cluster of towers knitted together to make a single, tall defensive wall at the base — the object the Sufi Chechens hurled themselves against for centuries, feeling spurred on by sacrifice to their own, great invisible God.

Stephen Nash, Britain's first ambassador to Georgia, trying on a 'papakhi' hat

As we entered the fortress, rain began to beat down determinedly, rapping against the black stone alleys. Images from Pshavela's poem 'Aluda Ketelauri', returned. Set in Shatili, its hero is banished by his fellow villagers for refusing to hack off the right hand of a vanquished Muslim foe (a Khevsur custom), out of respect for his courage.

Looking at the inky slate blocks slotted together over a thousand years ago (Shatili was built between the seventh and 13th centuries), I could easily imagine the severed hands tacked over the low door-frames. Above them the four-storey towers had windows only on the top floors (out of reach of invaders). Hanging over the doors were slots for pouring boiling oil. Everything about these stones spoke of the threat to human survival, now bought up to date for us with the Chechen presence just six kilometres to the north, with their new reputation for kidnapping foreigners instead of Khevsurs.

We knocked on some doors hoping to find a resident who might know about us, or at least point to someone who did, but received no reply. On one tower we found a plaque registering the capture of a Chechen general in 1843. Peering inside the tiny window revealed a perfectly preserved Khevsur home. A fire with a hanging spit dominated the centre below a smoke-charred roof. Embroidered Khevsur gowns decorated the walls beside all the everyday utensils encountered by the French writer Odette Keun in her book of the early 1920s *In the Land of the Golden Fleece: Through Independent Menshevik Georgia*. But to us it appeared as if everyone had just upped and left on our approach.

"These stones don't want us," I remarked.

"I'm not sure I want these stones," replied Andrew.

With no reception committee, we climbed on feeling as abandoned as the towers of Shatili, my mind beginning to fill the windows with ambassador-snatching Chechens. Our next encounter, aptly enough, was a graveyard, its stones like miniature black-slate tower-homes, each with a white crystal placed on the top instead of a cross.

Overwhelmed with a heavy mountain gloom and considering returning to Tbilisi — an eight hour drive, by then much of it in the dark, Stephen suddenly spotted a first sign of something beyond the 13th century (apart from some border-guard dwellings by the river). A single military satellite dish standing on a generator (used, it turned out, only for TV reception), and beside it two swarthy young men. They walked up and greeted us in Russian.

"How is your home?" — the traditional Chechen greeting. Just for an instant I thought my worst fears were about to come true. We asked them what they did. "We're shepherds," said the one with penetrating eyes, adding: "but we don't have any sheep." When we asked why, he just smiled, saying in a tone implying it should be obvious: "Because of the war." Before they could ask us who we were, we hurried on and arrived at what can only be described as a 'main street' — a row of 20 or so houses, either side of a street. We had finally found Shatili's 16 families.

With this, life suddenly returned. Spirals of smoke lifted out of chimneys, children played in the front gardens and, most surprising of all, electricity lit up bulbs in the windows (Shatili had just installed its own mini hydro-electric system).

Two hours later we sat inside the Khevsur home of the head of the local Georgian border patrol. A family-embroidered tunic was mounted on the wall and the smell of baking *khachapuri* drifted in from a communal stone oven out in the street. I visited the kitchen where his three young daughters helped mother and grandmother fold up *khinkali* (the large Georgian ravioli, originating in Khevsureti). When I asked the row of three big-eyed faces *"Ra kviat?"* (Georgian for 'what's your name?'), I received three silent stares as if *I* had become the invader from outer space. I offered sweets, accepted just as silently — they obviously had met very few foreigners.

Eventually our host arrived at about 10pm. Fortyish, wearing full battle-dress and AK47, he warmly shook the hands of the ambassador, not noticing the gun pointed straight at his midriff. The meal consisted of normal Georgian fare, with the addition of a bowl of Khevsur butter. We drank glasses of Kakhetian wine and fortunately no *jibitaururi* (the Khevsur *chacha*, rumoured to be as deadly as its Svan brother-liquor).

The next morning we accompanied our host Irakli into the old town where he unlocked the door of the museum tower, and said without any pride in his voice: "I was born in this tower."

Inside, the everyday objects of a Khevsur childhood greeted us, including the large central fire, metal spit and a small wooden cradle. Stephen asked if the cradle had been his.

"Probably," Irakli admitted, adding: "We left the tower in the 1960s. Most of my life has been where you're staying."

We asked when the last person left the old town.

"In 1985—" then he smiled, "—in a coffin. He stayed as long as he could."

I tried to picture those poetry and story-telling evenings described by Lela inside this darkened, sooty place. A home as lightless, threatening as the mountains round it. I asked him about the Khevsur and Pshavi poetry competitions. Festivals in which rival verse-smiths from different valleys harangued each other to and fro across drinking tables — not unlike New York rappers of today.

"It's not the same now," Irakli said with a slight reluctance. "We have television and electricity." Then his voice lightened, as if trying to be helpful. "But they have poetry competitions at school."

To me, the tone of that last sentence announced the death knell of this tradition more clearly than a state proclamation. Irakli went on to say that in its heyday Shatili housed about 350 people, that the tower's lowest level was for cattle, the next for sheep, the third for the family and top for guests. I wondered if the culture, as well as the town, had become a museum-piece.

A member of Georgia's new border patrol — which comprises the majority of Shatili's current population

We followed him on into a medium-sized, open-ended hut, filled with huge blackened vats, their interiors a bright, cheerful copper. "This is our 'beer house' — we are brewing for next weekend's festival." He pointed to one of the larger copper vats. "This one was made in the 18th century."

I had heard these drinking festivals were one of the last vestiges of Khevsur religious-social culture — vaguely reminiscent of Navaho peyote ceremonies, when tribe members gather together united by a semi-religious sacrament.

"Could we try some?" Stephen asked. My stomach made an involuntary contraction remembering that Svaneti encounter with sacred distillation.

"It's holy beer, nobody drinks it until the festival," Irakli said firmly, and I relaxed. "We call this ceremony *sadaka*. People come with silver bowls, they light candles and pray to the Angels. Sometimes they bring victims."

"Victims?"

"Sheep," he said quietly. My friend told me these festivals used to be more elaborate, but today some people still wore traditional costumes. However, Irakli seemed more keen on the conducted tour. "Here is where we made gunpowder," he announced, pointing to a mortar and pestle, explaining they once distilled it out of sheep's urine owing to its high ammonium content. He then pointed to a long, low bench beside it. "This is where the Khevsur Parliament sat." But amid all these collapsing buildings, grown over with weeds these artifacts seemed only the mere echoes of a former culture. Depopulation, relocation, inaccessibility and a dialect too similar to Kartvelian Georgian had sealed it for the Khevsurs.

Continuing the tour, he took us to the Shatili's first, but never completed hotel in one of the towers, then at my request to one of the 'praying places' or *salotsavi*.

"Shatili has four praying places," he explained. "One to St George, one Mary, one the Unnamed Angel (or Invisible God), one the Angel of the Door." I asked if I could see it. "Yes," he said, but wouldn't accompany me, saying: "It's not the right day."

It turned out to be little more than a roof placed between two overhanging rocks and a front wall. The area was protected by a fence surrounding a small field of stinging nettles growing to shoulder-height. Plainly this one hadn't been used for some time. But, although with nothing more than a few candle stains around the slab of rock on the cliff-face, an atmosphere remained. I vividly felt the object of worship was Nature herself — the slab of rock possibly being one of the Khevsur Doors through which the Sons of God passed en route between Heaven and the Underworld.

Religion, it seemed to me, was always the attempt to speak to death. Here ringed by snowy mountains, gushing rivers, thickly wooded escarpments, nature demanded to be addressed, entreatied, as Pshavela had attempted. Perhaps this was why Georgians still so idolised this now desolate region.

Afterwards walking on up toward the Chechen border, we passed tall lime-stone columns rising up out of the adjacent cliffs like the sculptures of these Sons of God. Beside them the river frothed ever more wildly. The haunted atmosphere increased as we passed the ruin of a Chechen military helicopter from the recent war, some of its pieces now used as stays in a highly rickety bridge across the river.

How did it crash? Rostov consulted a Khevsur accompanying us. "Carrying too much cheese," he answered gravely.

"Cheese . . . ?"

"They were carrying supplies up to one of the mountain villages," he said flatly. "The altitude was too high."

Although said in all seriousness, I noticed they seemed to enjoy our smiles. Deciding not to pursue this and ask if 'cheese' might be a codeword for weapons, I chatted with one of the locals accompanying us, through an interpreter, about the Chechen Sufi sects (such as the Naqshbandi) now just across the border — a religion whose quest to purify the heart involved a total surrender to a cause, in which death became an honour, hence the Chechen reputation for fearlessness in battle and mafia operations.

"Today modern people live in a world in which we're told to believe in ourselves," he said emphatically. "But up here we have a private world in which we also believe in our 'not-selves.'" He gave me a penetrating look, then added: "It is our religion, and when we believe it fully, we cannot be defeated. Russia keeps forgetting this."

"We?" I queried.

"I'm a Chechen!" he grinned at me. "Didn't you know?"

I glanced anxiously at the ambassador, now engrossed in conversation with Irakli. Suddenly my fear of kidnapping vanished. Up here we all walked together as guests of the Khevsurs and Chechens combined. They would all defend us with their lives against any hint of kidnapping. The code of friendship bonding these two enemies lived on, growing — at least for now — out of the land itself. For the moment the land decreed companionship, hospitality — and in the High Caucasus one learnt to count one's blessings.

18

Georgia's war:
a return to Sukhumi

I t was a foggy morning in Samegrelo (also known as Mingrelia), Western Georgia, when I began that long put-off mission — to investigate the psychological landscape of Georgia's civil war. The sun rose forebodingly over the white Caucasus to the east and struck the water tanks of Zugdidi, converting them into silver bubbles floating on a lake of mist. Cockerels crowed, a distant bandsaw made use of the hour or so of 'wake-up' electricity before it disappeared for the day. I climbed out of bed, stepped onto the veranda, inhaled the damp air on what was to be one of the most surreal days in my history of visiting the Caucasus.

Standing on that balcony I felt these traces of the six years of war hysteria that had been a plague across the whole region. Now, for the most part, it had petered out. In its place an invisible quarantine flag hung over these mountains in the eyes of the world. While the pellets of lead ceased their thudding into street walls, the peace in many of the former battle zones returned to an uneasy stalemate — the kind sometimes seen between drunks down by the Tbilisi sulphur baths after indecisive punch-ups. They'd enter a muttering, kept-apart-by-friends stage, usually on either side of the street.

When the electricity abruptly shut off, I could almost hear the muttering begin again.

In a mood of anxious anticipation, I swallowed a cup of mild local tea and climbed into the waiting Oxfam car. Ten minutes later we were driving through a pleasant low-lying city full of welcoming vined homes, to the city centre where knots of unemployed men hung out beside the empty plinth that once held up Lenin. Several of the kiosks carried portraits of Zviad Gamsakhurdia — giving a reminder of his 1993 return to Zugdidi, trying to raise an army among the Mingrelians (traditionally resistant to Tbilisi with their distinctive language and names ending in '-ia' or '-ua' rather than '-dze' or '-shvili') to march on Tbilisi. It had failed dramatically.

Our driver, a former academic turned employee for any aid agency that would have him, pointed to one of the few Soviet tower-blocks in Zugdidi's centre. "Here we liked Soviet corruption," he said enthusiastically. "Those eight storeys there should have been 13 . . ." His sentence trailed off, as if he need say no more.

Finally I had to ask: "What about the other five?"

"Here!" he gestured at the passing avenues of pleasant, self-contained dachas.

Grunts of acknowledgement came from the other Georgians in the car. A few minutes later the giant SUKHUMI 91KMS sign appeared above the windscreen and a shadow seemed to fill the car. I remembered it clearly from my trip to Abkhazia in 1989. Apart from being older, more battered, it appeared the same as when the M27 tarmac beneath it thrummed with car-fulls of Georgian/Russian/Armenian tourists hurrying for the Sukhumi beaches one hour up the road.

Now the road was deserted. Apart from our car, the only traffic amounted to a solitary cow ambling down the centre and one old woman pushing a pram converted into a cart.

Our driver hooted at the cow then swerved irritably round it and hurried on. So many emotions now clung to the sign's neglected paintwork — for all of us: pathos, anger, absurdity and the unmistakable presence of weapons. It seemed to hang there like a fixed empty smile, cut off from the real world.

"The Abkhaz border is about six kilometres," the driver remarked darkly, and again I tried to picture this extraordinary fact. The last time I passed that sign my skin tingled from afternoons swimming in the Black Sea, drying in the tropical breeze on Sukhumi beach. A refreshed, purified feeling uniting all bodies and faces by that becalmed flat plate of water. Although the city carried ethnic rumblings even then, the rustling palms, smoothing air overwhelmed

Lenin replaced by St Nino's cross in Zugdidi town centre, Mingrelia

the primitive emotions of nationalism and ownership. I still couldn't believe all that tranquillity had so brutally ended, converted itself into a hell.

Beside me in the car sat an English worker for Oxfam, there to help the 40,000 Georgian refugees from Abkhazia currently repatriated in Zugdidi. He added to the driver's comment: "I've supplied aid to Abkhazia for two years and never been there."

I sensed a curiosity as deep as mine. We had to *see* the landscape of this invisible, irrational human force that needed suddenly to create a new frontier where none existed before, to then defend it with its every last breath.

Because of ongoing terrorism, only a few Western aid agencies had set up offices in Sukhumi — not Oxfam. As a result, my host could only take me to the border, like a tourist. Twenty minutes later the car drew to a halt before the Inguri river.

"Don't take any pictures," he said quickly. "We had trouble here recently; our mission chief was held at gunpoint." We peered through the windscreen at a view that seemed to hit me in the stomach. Directly ahead stood the Inguri bridge blocked by heavy anti-tank defences, camouflage netting, sandbags, gun-positions. The last time I crossed it the only resistance had been wind. Now it bristled with hostility. I strained my eyes at the forbidden zone across the flood plain. The lamp-posts and trees looked just the same as in 1989; so too the painted backdrop of snowy mountains, luscious foothills. Nature had at least remained the same — but, since then, something invisible had changed in the heads of its most dangerous creation, ourselves.

I told myself that over there existed a completely new country, with its own constitution, flag, legislature. A country recognised by no government in the world and abandoned by two thirds of its population. I could see its flag, a single hand held palm-up, ringed by seven stars, like a 'stay away' signal to the Georgians across the river. I was told the previous Abkhaz flag carried two hands, one to welcome friends, the second forbidding enemies. Now only one remained — nicknamed by Georgians as the "hidden hand of Moscow," due to the way Russian military influence dramatically ended Georgia's misguided adventure in Abkhazia.

I tried to picture the moment of impetuous invasion back in 1992. Young, undisciplined fighters, blazing with the myth of noble Caucasian-banditry, streaming across this bridge to 'sort out' the Abkhazians — an attack that provoked a fierce Russian-backed counter-offensive a few months later that ethnically cleansed nigh on the entire Georgian population (44 per cent of the total), some 250,000 people, leaving Abkhazia a ghost region.

The driver's expression darkened as he peered toward the Russian 'peacekeeper' positions across the bridge. For him Russia was to blame again — deliberately keeping the Caucasus unstable to maintain their influence. He had grown up just 15 kilometres across that river in Gali town. I asked him if he now regretted the Georgian invasion.

"No . . . ," he said a shade too quickly. Later, after a few drinks and some earnest prompting he did admit: "OK, not all our troops behaved well, but Shevardnadze didn't properly control Georgia then. But he does now and their leaders are in jail. It's time the Abkhazians let us go home."

He pronounced the last sentence bitterly. One could understand his frustration. The leaders of Georgia's December 1992 incursion, Tengiz Kitovani (National Guard) and Jaba Ioseliani (Mkhedrioni) were both behind bars. Additionally the Gali region never carried much of an Abkhazian presence or claim and remained mostly deserted when the new border arrived.

That night I sat with a group of aid workers round a table in Zugdidi's only bar open after 9pm, discussing what we'd seen. Drinking Western beers (at Western prices) I spoke to a Spanish aid worker and another Georgian driver. The Georgian, like many drivers, proved remarkably well educated. He spoke English learned during his economics degree — as he put it, "in a country without economics."

"The psychology is simple—" the Spaniard said, "—projection. Georgia was squeezed by its neighbour Russia for 70 years. It needed to squeeze someone back, so it attacked Abkhazia."

"How can we *attack* our own country?" the driver replied coolly. "Abkhazia is in Georgia. Our languages come from the same group."

The Spaniard, by now a little drunk, bypassed the old discussion on which language came first in the Ibero-Caucasian language group (in which Abkhaz and Georgian are grouped geographically — not genetically).

"Russia subjugated Georgia, so when independence came Georgians turned against their neighbours the Ossetians. The Ossetians in turn then attacked the Ingush, and so on down the line until you reach here — Abkhazia."

The Georgian gave him a stern look.

"You forget one thing in your 'line,'" he said flatly, "you forget yourself." The Spaniard looked alarmed. The driver continued. "Foreigners never follow it to the top — to include themselves. The West had a huge effect on us. In fact you started it all."

The Spaniard's alarm turned to annoyance. "You're blaming us for all your problems?"

"No . . . ," the driver said more calmly. "I'm just saying you started it by squeezing Russia in the first place."

The Spaniard looked puzzled for a moment then said doubtfully: "You mean in the Cold War?"

"No," the driver replied. "With your Walkmans, videos and cigarettes. Your existence squeezed us." He pointed to the Spaniard's Heineken. "That's a day's wages here in Zugdidi. Look at your clothes, your watch, your shoes, your car out there on the street . . ." He gestured at the new Nissan Patrol parked deliberately within eyesight, in case of break-ins.

The annoyance in the Spaniard's eye seemed to retract momentarily, then suddenly lit up again. "You're saying the hysteria of nationalism in the Caucasus was just the cry of frustration because you couldn't have our living standard?" He pronounced the words dryly as if quoting from a book. "That our Walkmans and videos provoked your inferiority complex which then drove you to each other's throats?"

I felt he half-addressed this statement at me, hoping for back-up.

There was an awkward silence, then the Georgian leaned forward and suddenly clapped the Spaniard on the shoulder.

"Don't worry my friend," he said with a generous smile. "Everybody blames everyone else in the Caucasus. I think it's time we drink. We're here together, we are friends."

Then suddenly he stood up and in a loud voice addressed the group. "I want to drink to friendship, to my friends from Europe here," he gestured to me and the Spaniard. "They have come all the way from Madrid and London to help us. To friendship!"

The Spaniard looked relieved. We raised our glasses.

A few minutes later I talked to him alone. He worked in his organisation's Sukhumi office and, unlike many aid workers, had seen both sides of the border.

"This isn't Georgia or Abkhazia," he said swallowing a fifth or sixth beer. "It's Caucasia. A lot of small nations with big histories, mostly as victims. Small nations are just like small people, they dream of becoming big. When they're crowded together in mountain areas it's worse — they're more quickly threatened." He swilled back another mouthful. "The Abkhaz and Georgians have fought and made up before. In 1919 they felt exactly the same. They'll make up again."

I mentioned this emotion could easily be played upon by unscrupulous politicians wishing to keep things stirred up. "Yes," he said gravely. "Caucasians are pretty hot-headed. Stalin knew that. He shifted boundaries, whole peoples, planted nationality time-bombs here. Now they've been going off."

I remarked on a curious link with real time-bombs now sunk into Georgian soil — in the form of mines along the border (being patiently extracted by Britain's Halo Trust).

He grinned. "You know after big storms in the High Caucasus, the Inguri floods and carries the mines down to the sea at Anakalia, which is where our staff swim in the summer. We sometimes see them lying on the bottom."

I decided to ask the question I'd been holding back all evening.

"Could you take me to Sukhumi when you return tomorrow?"

I held my breath, but a hard look appeared in his eye.

"Sorry," he said flatly. "You're too high risk, we don't take anybody."

"High risk?"

"In case of injury. The road in is sometimes mined by Georgian partisans, keeping the pressure on the Abkhaz."

His expression took on that glazed, 'agency official' distance — the kind he had to show Abkhaz supplicants every day at his office. He continued impassively. "A Russian APC (Armoured Personnel Carrier) was blown off the road recently. Before that a civilian had died setting off a tripwire on the Sukhumi highway near Gali. We're not insured to take you."

For about the eighth time in the last five days I experienced disappointment and frustration. Every international agency had refused me — with the same excuses. A few weeks earlier a prominent British politician received the same treatment, finally having to cross the bridge on foot.

I trecked home grimly, but the next morning my luck turned. A letter I'd carried for a local NGO (non-governmental organisation) in Sukhumi, then given to the UN to deliver, produced results.

"Your invitation has arrived," said the UN officer on the phone. "The Abkhaz Department of Foreign Affairs sent it. If you write us a disclaimer — we can take you in tomorrow."

"And out?" I asked.

"Perhaps," he said, "but I can't guarantee it."

I put down the phone with that blend of excitement and apprehension when a sealed-up doorway abruptly swings wide open. The old Caucasian 'friendship system' had triumphed — as it had so many times before. But getting out . . . ? My hand hesitated reaching for the pen to write the disclaimer — but only briefly. If friendship could prevail once, surely it would again . . .

That evening I sat out on the veranda watching the sunset lay out a row of livid orange ribbons out across the sky. A warm breeze blew in from Imereti to the east, stroking a scented hand across the city. In the neighbour's house a young girl's voice shouted out the name "Alissa! Alissa!" repeatedly like a musical refrain. All around Zugdidi settled down to watch its local TV lottery. My landlady had bought five tickets at ten tetri each (eight US cents). I'd left her staring at the TV where a dandyish young man prepared to withdraw ping-pong balls from a goldfish bowl in what looked like a family living-room.

This time tomorrow I'd be in the land forbidden to all these displaced people; the land they would probably dream about that night, like their lottery win . . .

The next morning a white Nissan Patrol with blue UN flag arrived at the door. Twenty minutes later we cruised up to the Inguri bridge fortifications where, to my astonishment, we found ourselves waved through all the check-points, without a glimpse at my hard-earned papers. How simply the insurmountable barrier lifted — to me a fine argument in favour of the UN.

On the other side the first sight was unexpected — several dozen Georgians walking through the fiercely independent territory of Abkhazia. They pushed prams converted into carts, or lugged sacks of vegetables, bags of nuts on their shoulders. Our driver, an Armenian, answered my curiosity.

"Local refugees persuade, bribe border guards to let them in. The price is about $3.00. If the name on the passport is Abkhazian it can be free. Before they used to risk the minefields to visit their deserted old homes, make repairs, tend their plots of land and cattle." He gestured to a man on crutches at the roadside. "They or their cows sometimes are minesweepers. Recently some have started bringing over their children."

It seemed the Georgians who crossed the bridge were allowed no transport and had to tramp along the verge beside the odd destroyed fuselages of cars, blown up by mines. I pointed to a crumpled Lada.

"What are our chances of ending up like that?" I asked.

Wild horses and war-ruined buildings at the Ochamchira turn-off, on the periodically mined M27 between Gali and Sukhumi

"Little . . . ," the Armenian replied, then added ominously: ". . . here. North of Gali they had a few mines, but UNOMIG (the United Nations observer force) stopped running their armoured car escort last week, when you had to follow in the APC tyre tracks. They think it's safe now."

The UN had a token garrison of 60 to 70 unarmed 'observers' stationed in Sukhumi and occasionally escorted foreigners, but the real work of 'peacekeeping' was left to 2,000 Russian troops. On the post-Communist world stage Georgia remained within the Russian camp — as it had for the last 200 years.

A few kilometres later, on a better stretch of road, we shot past a newly restored church and school. "The UNHCR," the Armenian said and gestured toward it. "After we restored it, it was blown up again by Georgian partisans before the local elections, but has been repaired. It's good to see children here again."

His voice showed its first hint of enthusiasm. But for me the whole experience was utterly surreal. I felt we'd arrived in a completely different territory to the one I'd known eight years earlier. As if someone had swapped the real Abkhazia with a beaten-up, second-hand replacement.

The first main settlement was Gali. The Russian writing on the store-fronts had decayed terribly. A few lethargic Georgian returnees walked or pushed produce-prams along the open streets. Obviously no one wanted to repair the old buildings lest they had to be re-abandoned. After this came more checkpoints, then an eerily empty road. The Armenian glanced at me.

"Here are the mines."

I noticed he didn't smile and kept his eyes fixed on the road surface. Wrecked car fuselages reappeared, but this time flanked by an unkempt landscape — plenty of opportunity for partisans to take potshots at aid vehicles then melt back across the Inguri. On the right, the High Caucasus closed in kilometre by kilometre. In the clear sunlight their white summits looked down like a row of schoolboy caps attending some celestial lesson beyond human comprehension.

I reminded myself here was one of the more dramatic mountain eruptions in the world. The nearby Mt Elbruz rose from sea-level to 5,642 metres in just 90 kilometres.

But again, a deceitful beauty. In 1993 these mountains claimed many Georgian lives as they fled Abkhaz reprisals into Svaneti — whole families perishing in the high passes.

Soon huge tea plantations and orchards flashed by, all overgrown with weeds, their branches spreading wildly, peaches, apples, tangerines, dropping to the ground to lie in rotting piles. The Armenian sped on, his eyes gripped to the flashing white lines.

"Six months ago one aid vehicle was strafed. The partisans don't like us helping the Abkhaz," he said as we passed a plume of steam spurting out of broken pipes from the abandoned natural hot-water springs.

Every so often he slowed down to lurch round blown-up bridges, then came a stretch of empty rows of homes and overgrown gardens many with roofs — just no owners. Every kilometre made it abundantly clear; history had played a cruel trick on Abkhazia. After defeating the invading Georgian army in 1993, the Abkhaz expected Russia, its military supporter, to step in and resurrect its economy. But instead its northern neighbour, with typical unpredictability, enforced the Georgian embargo against it. Now its southern border permitted only a trickle of hand-luggage-only pedestrians. To the West its sea was blockaded and its northern frontier with Russia wore the dubious fame of giving women and not men (under 60) the rights to cross.

Thus for four years this green paradise

The Alouisi villa on the flanks of Sukhumi mountain, as it was in 1905

Dilapidated Caucasian Art Nouveau on a Sukhumi villa

remained imprisoned in its own victory; ridden with poverty and crime, abandoned by much of its population, most aid agencies and even journalists.

Beyond Ochamchira, a large colonial building flashed by with a headless statue — obviously a former school, now with roof collapsing, weeds overrunning the fields.

I had to ask: "Why won't the Abkhaz let the Georgians return to these homes, just so they don't collapse?"

The Armenian smiled thinly. "Officially the Sukhumi government has agreed to let them back into Gali. Unofficially they resist it. They fear Georgian reprisals against the Abkhaz reprisals . . . ," the thin smile deepened, ". . . which were against former Georgian reprisals and so on back to the 11th century." He gave a heavily ironic look. "The Abkhaz are trapped. When you corner a Caucasian cat it will scratch the most fiercely."

Then the Kelasuri River appeared in the windscreen. "Sukhumi . . . ," the Armenian said in a way redolent of Martin Sheen's pronouncement "Saigon . . ." at the start of *Apocalypse Now*.

So this was it. I put my head out the window and received a blast of that familiar fruit-laden scent of Abkhazia: verdant, welcoming, tinged with sea air. It seemed cleaner than before (Sukhumi has seen an enormous decrease in car use), and suddenly I remembered the Botanical Gardens, its luxurious scents that carried all the way to the sea-front. Yet looking at the overgrown hillsides it was obvious most of the gardeners now tended weapons. In Tbilisi I'd been told nearly all men carried guns, either on their person or in their cars.

"Sukhumi is like Tbilisi in 1992, only poorer," Georgian friends had told me. "There's a 50 per cent chance of being mugged at night." They also warned I'd be regarded as a Georgian spy and shouldn't go at all.

But the delicious Sukhumi air seemed to purge all fears. Besides, I was

The former Communist Party Headquarters, Sukhumi

seeing what had been kept from the West for too long — hardly a single photograph of Sukhumi had appeared in a British newspaper for three years.

A glint of water to the left announced the Black Sea, and soon we were flashing down a deserted Tbilisi Highway. I caught a glimpse of the former Fifteenth Congress Holiday Home — my hotel back in 1989 — then a few minutes later we stopped before a large, heavily defended gateway.

Eight years earlier this had been a Soviet Army holiday camp where I'd risked life and freedom to take a snap of old Russian generals exercising on the beach.

"Where are we?" I asked the Armenian.

"The Russian Army headquarters."

Now was I really surprised? After eight years and a war, Russia still retained its prime beach-front property. Indeed, bar one burnt-out tower-block, little had changed in the camp, right down to the polished portrait of Lenin by the driveway. We stopped before the beach front and a grand, pillared building, smelling of the same Russian polish as 1989.

An hour later we left the camp and drove into the city proper, seeking lunch. Within minutes I found myself staring speechless at a transformed city.

The lavish European/Caucasian villas climbing the flanks of Sukhumi Mountain, lay battered and dying. Their cupolas, balconies, art-deco reliefs, were flaking, cracking, tracked with bullet-holes. Garden doors stood open, plants and shrubs sprawled unkempt over walls as the properties changed hands with the Georgian exodus and the new owners felt an increasingly insecure tenure as Abkhazia failed to receive its Russian support. Unique creations of the 19th–early 20th century now sagging like sad, old animals abandoned by the herd. They lolled against the hillside with only memories of the time when Black Sea ports stood as trade-gateways to and from the East, and European holiday destinations — the time of Oliver Wardrop, who in 1888 wrote prophetically: "There is no reason why Georgia should not become as popular a resort as Norway or Switzerland. It is not as far away as people imagine . . . It is at least as beautiful as either of the countries just named." Not long after he wrote these words villas sprang up, owned largely by rich merchant families from Italy, Paris and particularly Greece. The city thrived and by 1919 Sukhumi had a British consulate and British Telegraph Office.

Now their vines were unpruned and sprawling, their outhouses caving in. These buildings, the pride of the Caucasus, were giving up the ghost. The area had become a hospice for a particular architecture.

I spotted the grand double-cupolaed Alouisi family villa of 1905, that I'd photographed on my first visit. The roof was thick with rust, huge chunks of plaster dropped from the walls, large cracks

(Top) Soviet-era post card of the Ritsa Hotel in its heyday, circa 1975. (Bottom) The hotel in September 1997, without domes or roof.

sent jagged lines down the sides. The structure seemed to have avoided the war, but not its aftermath and its terrible illness of neglect — now the hallmark of Sukhumi. Later I heard the building's pre-Revolutionary owners sent representatives over from Paris to see if it could be saved. They had left shaking their heads.

These fine 80 to 100-year-old villas had reached that stage in life requiring constant attention. Neglect now meant rot seeped into the cracks, infected the structure core. Short of a massive investment this one would die, and probably soon. Even the squatters had now fled. Here was the full tragedy of war without real victory: loss for everyone. The only winners in Sukhumi were the oleander and magnolia now multiplying out of their garden confines.

After lunch I walked out alone into the Sukhumi streets. I, the so-called 'Georgian spy,' wanted to imagine how this city might feel to a returning Georgian. Was it now an 'enemy' city?

Within a few blocks I realised it would never be. Although bullet-holes climbed walls, statues were shot, a whole block of Lakoba street had been reduced to ruins (and subsequently erased), I could detect no direct threat from these frontispieces. In spite of the war, Sukhumi itself didn't intimidate — it couldn't. The streets were low-lying, tree-lined and friendly. The Botanical Garden still radiated its perfume, every vista to the sea-front welcomed the visitor — helplessly.

I turned a corner and my mood suddenly changed. For there, standing up like a huge white fist, stood the tower-block of the former Communist headquarters. Thirteen storeys of bureaucratic culpability for the years of pent-up hostility. All its windows were broken, smoke stains climbed the walls like black fingers, a shot-up Lenin plinth fronted it, without Lenin. It was as if all the poison, anger, resentment stored within its walls had suddenly burst through the windows, exploded out onto the street and the defenceless old buildings. Now the fist had lost its power, transformed into a dead white tooth stuck in the soil at the end of ragged triumphal gardens. I pulled out my camera — unwise when alone in a weapon-saturated population with an average monthly pension of 2,000 roubles (50 cents) — and snapped it. In so doing, I effectively made myself a target as well and began to feel all that sublimated fear, anger, hostility in the air that had turned into an 'ethnic war.' The frustration, of course, had many hidden sources. But I'd just heard of a new one from a cheerful Russian lady at lunch, that day.

"You know when Georgia began its anti-Russian propaganda in Gamsakhurdia's time, and the Russians stopped coming to Georgia . . . ," she said thoughtfully. "It also meant that the Russian girls stopped coming . . ." She paused, gave a wry smile. "It meant that the Georgian men had so much frustration building up inside them, of course there had to be a war!"

We all laughed, but later I tested her theory in Tbilisi, asking Georgians what they thought about the idea of Russians returning to Georgia for their holidays. Georgian men invariably said "Great, no problem . . ." The women always expressed doubts.

I turned onto the former Lenin Street (now Tsar Leon) and headed for the sea front, my old haunt beside the Hotel Ritsa. Eight years earlier I had eaten my best restaurant meal in Georgia there, spending many hours in the nearby cafés, or on the pier.

About halfway down, I spotted a bookshop and deviated. Very little sat on the shelves. A few embargo-beating Turkish exercise books, pencils, pads, several old Soviet books, then a large section of beautiful, second-hand European art books — being sold on commission by Sukhumi's newly impoverished intelligentsia.

The girl behind the counter gave me a strange look. My clothes radiated the word 'foreigner' — but what kind? I pointed at a postcard set of Abkhazia on the shelf.

"How much?" I asked.

"One thousand roubles," she replied flatly, but her eyes remained sharp. It was as if price hardly mattered. Far more significant was that I should want them. But one thousand Russian roubles — about 20 cents (US) for a set of 18, high quality, gold-embossed Soviet era cards of Abkhazia . . . absurdly cheap. As if tourism now belonged to a bygone age. But I'd seen similar sets of Soviet cards selling on Tbilisi's Rustaveli Avenue for three lari — two dollars fifty. A clear indication these terrible times could change.

I reached into my wallet, pulled out a 5,000 rouble note. As I did a Georgian one lari stuck to the bottom and fluttered to the

Sukhumi esplanade in 1989 . . .

ground. She reached down, picked up the enemy currency, studied it closely before handing it back. I could tell she'd never seen a lari before, with its attractive rendition of Pirosmani's deer. She looked at me curiously, then excusing herself, promptly disappeared out to find change for the 5,000 roubles. When she returned I held out the lari.

"A present," I said, curious to what levels of resentment filtered down to street level. Would her Abkhaz pride allow her to accept the 'enemy' currency, as a foreigner's gift?

A flicker of suspicion returned, but only fleetingly. She looked at the note again, her curiosity obviously not satisfied. Then, with a nod to me, not the money, she took it.

"*Tank yu,*" she said in English, and smiled shyly.

In that gesture I suddenly saw how wars could end, even between fiercely independent Caucasians. In spite of all the TV and radio indoctrination (for a while Georgian TV ran what some foreigners called "two minutes hate" footage on Abkhazia between programmes), not every Abkhazian hated every Georgian implacably — by a long chalk, nor vice-versa. Indeed they seemed to hate each other only at certain times. Most ordinary people needed just to get on with life — without the nationalism. It seemed trade might prove a good route to reconnecting embittered neighbours — necessity being the mother of much political invention. Indeed it had already begun between Abkhaz and Georgians in the Gali market.

I left the shop feeling cheered, only to encounter another grim sight, the now roofless Ritsa Hotel. Fortunately the café on the esplanade facing the sea-front still existed, along with the pier. I ordered a Turkish coffee — again no problem avoiding the embargo — and began flipping through my post-card set. Suddenly my head span. For there was a picture of the very spot where I sat at the Ritsa in the clean 1980s. What a change! The card

showed the two elegant silver cupolas, formerly on the Ritsa roof — which I'd completely for-gotten. Below them children walked by eating ice-creams, a liner snoozed out on the Black Sea. The tarmac was smooth, unpitted, the palms pruned and healthy. The

. . . and in 1997

Ritsa itself seemed to gleam with fresh paint, its ornamentation proud, untatty and included the famous balcony where Lev Trotsky delivered a speech when Sukhumi was a Russian/European resort and the Ritsa, the San Remo Hotel.

I looked up from the card at the real Ritsa. Trotsky's balcony remained but he wouldn't stand on it now. The rooms inside, like those in the Hotel Abkhazia across the road — were destroyed. Much as I tried to be hopeful in that warm sun, life as I knew it in Sukhumi had departed. Existence had, for the most part, become survival. The city showed almost no signs of repair. A crane hung listlessly over the Hotel Abkhazia, as inoperative as the building it served.

Late afternoon I returned to the pier with an Abkhaz man of about 30. His name was Koba and, like most Abkhazians, he lived an only partially employed existence. Also, as with most Abkhazians, our conversation very quickly turned to the war.

"My best friend died fighting the Georgians," he said, glancing bitterly out to sea towards Georgia. "Now I don't want to be a part of that terrible country."

I asked if he felt the two sides could yet learn to live together again, perhaps in separated districts of Sukhumi.

"Maybe in Gali it would be OK, but here . . ." He paused as if considering something too painful. "For me it would be difficult. My mother was beaten up five times by Georgian soldiers. She is a 65-year-old woman."

He stared at me long and hard with that grim fixation of one whose independence had been achieved at the cost of freedom. His whole persona seemed to radiate the classic siege mentality, with its pressure of three years isolation and non-communication with the outside world. A bitter punishment for the Abkhaz, who are every bit as hospitable as their Georgian neighbours — as indeed the architecture of their capital declares. But sealed borders, cut phone lines, closed roads and airports, forbade these Caucasians their best cure — to play host.

I asked if the Abkhaz victory, with its current isolation and political abandonment, amounted to a defeat. He glared at me.

"No," he said firmly. "We see

'Taking-the-air' shelters on Sukhumi beach in 1989 . . .

this as a lesson. It teaches us to be strong. If we can survive this, then Abkhazia will always survive."

In his words I felt the echo of all those small Caucasian nations: Armenians, Azeris, Chechens, Georgians, Ossetians, Ingush. Neighbours that down the centuries fought each other, only to find themselves suddenly pressed into alliances against huge invading neighbours. Abkhazia had been conquered by the Ottoman Turks in 1578, forcibly converted to Islam and used as a source for slaves and cattle. During the 18th century, in alliance with the Georgians, they repeatedly tried to expel the Turks, but only when the Russians arrived in the early 19th century, and Abkhazia's Muslim highland tribesmen had re-patriated themselves in Turkey, did it succeed — at which point Abkhazia was promptly annexed by the Russian Empire.

I asked Koba if he could take me back to ITAR, the compound, I was told, where most foreign nationals stayed. To my astonishment he drove me straight back to the 15th Congress Holiday Home on the Tbilisi Highway — the very holiday camp where I'd stayed in 1989 and watched the Love Competition.

Even more surprising was that, but for the row of Nissan Patrols and Nivas painted with aid agency insignia, it hadn't changed at all, right down to its strutting peacocks and lack of bath-plugs. A clear message that life, given half a chance, could easily continue as before.

That night my dreams were full of fighting and disturbed faces. I woke early to the sound of the restful waves breaking on the Black Sea shore across the deserted Tbilisi Highway. I persuaded the gate guards to let me out, then wandered down onto the pebbles.

The light was grey, and the concrete 'taking-the-air-shelters' with their new bullet marks and cauldite scars bought me smartly back to the present. Nothing restful about the beach now. The retreating Georgian army had fought its way out of Sukhumi along this route. Shrapnel and shell casings, metal debris and rubbish had desecrated the paradise.

. . . and in 1997

I decided to walk into town using my 'Tbilisi '92' tactics, wearing a gangster's black woollen hat and my right hand pressed heavily into my pocket — as if holding a gun. As always, it worked, and I passed the new 'drug addicts' park' under the railway underpass amid a group of other men doing the same.

That afternoon Koba drove me up the coast, starting along the Sukhumi esplanade. We passed rusting, abandoned children's playgrounds and the hulks of half sunken ships lying in the harbour or driven up onto the beach then left to rust like expired whales. I was amazed to see abandoned luxury beach-front homes, some with swimming pools, not even squatted — and kept remembering the 40,000 Georgian refugees, just across the border, crammed into huts and hotels.

Six months later I returned to the nearby Novy Rayon to find young artists during the children's painting project I'd set up for the charity War Child. We provided therapeutic art for children in five former war zones across the Caucasus, as well as an exhibition and postcards to encourage trans-border communication between those who would inherit the region.

I'll never forget climbing up one of the bullet-hole-pitted high-rises to meet a boy artist and his family. The whole living-room wall was covered with his paintings.

"During the fighting we had to live in the cellar," his mother explained.

"Each time we came up we found more bullet-holes in our living-room wall, so we started using Sasha's paintings to cover them up. Only then did we start noticing what a good painter he was. Everyone encouraged him."

On the outskirts of town I recognised the Gumista tourist camp beside the river. I'd spent my first night in Abkhazia there eight years earlier. I asked if we could make a brief deviation.

"It's a minefield," Koba said flatly. "Nobody goes in except teenagers looking for mines to rebuild then use as bombs to stun fish. Often they just blow themselves up." Then suddenly his eyes were sad and for the first time in our meeting he seemed to let down his guard. "Sometimes I think we won the war and lost the peace," he said simply.

We stopped at a roadside stall to buy 'aid food' — tins of cheese and biscuits donated free by international agencies, then sold into the black market. Afterwards we drove up to the house of Koba's friend, an artist. His balcony offered a splendid view of St Simon's Monastery — now re-inhabited by Russian monks.

"Why didn't Abkhaz monks take it?" I asked.

"We're not such a religious people in that way," replied Koba. I asked why there were no mosques in Sukhumi; did it mean the Abkhaz were more Christian than Muslim?

"We're not more anything," Koba said. "We Abkhaz don't have churches we have 'places.'"

I looked at the artist; his eyes seemed more thoughtful.

"One of the best 'places,'" he said speaking slowly, "is right here, in these caves," he pointed to the ground beneath our feet. "Many are still undiscovered." He poured us all a small glass of *chacha*. "You know when I was depressed during the war, I would go down inside and live in the darkness, sometimes ten, fifteen days. Afterwards I would feel better."

I pictured his retreat down under the mountain, away from the human madness of tanks, bullets, Kalashnikovs racing by overhead. A solitary man living in a huge dripping chamber, surrounded by wet rocks, water-carved sculptures and stalagmites — finding a faith restored in the slow growth of nature, away from his own species.

I wondered if here was someone who defied the traditional 19th century Cult of the Young Man, with its fascination with weapons, heroism and extinction. His encounter with 'death' came as an aesthetic experience, as a guide in the high mountains or in the blackness of caves rather than in battle. I decided to ask him why he thought men had to fight.

"Men like to fight wars because they need to understand emotions in themselves, usually about death," he said glancing grimly away toward the coastline. "They think this is the 'place' they will learn, but usually they or their friends die first."

I felt in his voice that "condition of melancholy" described by Vladimir Nabakov as the essential well-spring from which all great artists had to draw.

In my years as a journalist I had seen this expression before, following combat, and always felt this kind of sad, melancholic wisdom a secret ambition of war. Indeed, the emotional breakthroughs, the humility discovered facing death seemed almost unconsciously sought. I'd seen it in England on the BBC *Nine O'Clock News,* when families from Northern Ireland, after the funeral of their murdered fathers, said they "forgave the people who killed him." Extraordinary turnarounds of emotion after years of sectarian bitterness and vengeance.

But as for the Caucasus, perhaps the last words on this should come from the former Soviet cultural attaché in Britain, the Georgian Niko Kiasashvili, just before his own death in 1996. "Dear Peter," he had said with that warm smile of the Shakespeare and James Joyce scholar, "how much humility do you expect from us proud mountain peoples? You can't tell us to drop our pride. It's like telling us not to breath. *However* . . . ," and his eyes lit up, ". . . perhaps you can make us *forget*. You can encourage our music, dance, literature, toasting, drama. Because often when we forget, we forgive."

19

A religious revival

Bodbe

"**P**eter *darling!* You must come tomorrow! We're going to the most wonderful place, to aid the nuns at Bodbe Monastery!" Sometimes in Georgia you find yourself swept up by a powerful, irresistible force, then pulled off toward unknown destinations. These words belonged to one such force — Keti Dolidze, theatre producer, founder of the White Scarf Organisation, and soon to be general director of Georgia's first international arts festival — GIFT.

She spoke with such enthusiasm, I had to glance at my friend Tamriko from the Metechi Palace Hotel, who just nodded. "You should go," she confirmed in a tone that implied something important waited there.

Perhaps she also sensed that, for me, this latest unknown destination also hid a second. Not only was Keti playing her part in Georgia's new-found religious revival with her White Scarf Organisation, she had also just proposed another revival event, the GIFT festival — a major two-week festival of artists, set for the following October. Perhaps, I thought, if I followed her to one destination, it might offer clues to the outcome of the second.

Keti continued to explain: "They've just re-opened one of the most important monasteries in Georgia — made it a nunnery with 35 nuns. It's run by a wonderful person: Deda ('mother' in Georgian) Teodora. We're helping her, bringing the nuns supplies."

So the following day I sat on a bus, an ageing Intourist 40-seater, that no longer chariot-raced down the highway as in the days of Soviet Georgia. Rather it trundled along sedately between speed limits and potholes, the driver obeyed traffic laws with an eerie un-Georgian zeal. One result of independence was that state-owned property (like buses) had been privatised, which meant privately maintained. Unfortunately this also seemed to apply to police income — on-the-spot traffic fines becoming the newest traffic hazard. Meanwhile Keti continued to describe our destination.

"Bodbe is the burial place of our Saint Nino. Her cross has been Georgia's main symbol since the fifth century. It's made of entwined vine branches bound by her own hair." She held one up and for the first time I connected its famously sloping arms to their means of attachment. Keti continued earnestly: "It's our most holy icon. Once our King Bagrationi gave it to Tsar Alexander II of Russia as the symbol of unity between the two nations (St Nino is also a saint in the Russian Church). The Tsar returned the cross to the Caucasus in a ceremonial journey across Russia, to be blessed at every major church. Now we are opening all our churches and monasteries again, making our own ceremonial journeys . . ." But her explanation was cut short by the bus stopping, then a police officer stepping on board.

"Where are you going?" he asked bluntly.

Keti began explaining our charity mission to Bodbe. The officer frowned, making his disbelief very obvious, then asked: "So what are you taking?"

Keti turned and pointed to a pile of 35 jackets stacked up in the back of the bus. The officer walked over, lifted one up to find it covered with camouflage markings. Our aid, it seemed, would be 35 flak jackets.

"For nuns?" he asked incredulous. Then sensing a lucrative afternoon he straightened up, announcing: "You can't continue. This is military equipment."

As baffled as the policeman, I watched in fascination as another surreal Georgian scene played itself out.

"They're a charity gift from the Minister of Defence himself!" Keti declared. The others on the bus (mostly artists and writers) joined in. But the officer made it clear he didn't believe us.

"Three of the nuns have tuberculosis," Keti said with increasing emotion. "It's their third winter without electricity . . ."

Soon arms and voices were being raised, wide, dramatic hand-gestures flourished in the air, fingers as important as the words. I heard loud *"aras!"* from all sides, followed by heavy name-dropping, imploring,

Bell tower of St Nicholas church at David Gareja monastery

frantic waving, until finally the policeman pushed up his hat in a gesture of non-comprehension and, shaking his head, stepped off the bus.

As we drove on I wondered about this need for drama in Georgia. This scene had felt almost deliberately created; Georgians loved absurdity so much, it was as if they used it to create that release valve for their huge ideas of self. In those grand hand gestures I began to understand the roots of Georgia's excellent theatre tradition — regularly impressing the English with Shakespeare. (Peter Brook, the English director, also a GIFT Festival

Sighnaghi, Kakheti — a Silk Road trade centre in the 18th and 19th centuries

director, described the *Don Juan* by Tbilisi's Tumanishvili Theatre as the best he'd ever seen.)

Later I discussed this 'inspirational' nature of the Georgian character with a British businessman working in Tbilisi. "Georgians admire actions carried out with what they call *guli* ('heart')," he said speaking from hard experience. "This means much is done on the spur of the moment, usually in great gusts of inspiration — whether right or wrong hardly matters. They feel if they are wrong with 'heart,' they at least can be forgiven."

I asked if this linked in with that much-quoted Ingush proverb from the North Caucasus: "He who thinks of the consequences, cannot be brave."

"I'm sure that proverb is Georgian," he grinned, then added: "However I've also found that, given the right incentive, they can think ahead as well as anyone."

The bus followed the road to Sighnaghi, but turned off just before reaching the picturesque hilltop town. When we arrived at Bodbe the mood in the bus changed completely. We stopped beside a large, battered, 19th century monastery on a mountain-side, with an older three-tiered bell-tower and older yet church. All were set inside a copse of tall, wistful cypresses and, like most Georgian religious centres, offered a stupendous view. Directly below spread the wide and fertile Alazani valley, following the glittering thread of the Alazani river south. The scene was given a delicious icing by the row of snow-capped Daghestan Caucasus to the north.

Facing all this stood the diminutive St Nino's church with its foundations dating back to the fifth century. The first chapel was built on the instructions of King Mirian himself, shortly after his conversion from Zoroastrianism, when according to legend a fiery cross appeared in the sky over Mtskheta, the old capital, surrounded by a crown of stars. Two of the stars then flew off to different parts of Georgia, one hanging over Bodbe, where Nino asked a cross be erected.

Standing by its entrance were two darkly robed figures. Keti, whose mood had become almost reverential, hurried over to shake hands with the first — a demure figure draped in black from head to toe, covering all but the front of her face — Deda Teodora. Beside her stood the local metropolitan at Bodbe — Bishop Atenasa. Under the old stone bell tower I felt how these two religious figures represented Georgia's secret of survival down through the centuries.

Deda Teodora shook my hand with all the simplicity and self-possession suited to her role, then led us into the church and its small stone shrine-room containing St Nino's tomb. Lit solely by candles (the nunnery received only two hours of electricity every four days) and surrounded by walls of elegiacally fading frescoes, fragments of Old Georgian script and icons dedicated to the young fourth century 'slave girl,' she lit a candle of her own. The sight of her motionless, habit-covered face standing before those antique images seemed to resurrect St Nino right up into the 20th century.

Outside Keti Dolidze explained Deda Teodora's story.

"Many young people are returning to the church now. They come not only because of poverty, they also want to build something up again. Deda Teodora is only 30. When she chose her vocation her parents were very disappointed. She was so beautiful, full of intelligence, ready for marriage and a career. But instead she came here. Now, of course, everyone is proud of her."

After the service Deda took us to the monastery building. We walked past

Bodbe Monastery, 3km from Sighnaghi in Kakheti

broken windows, subsiding balconies and general dereliction — so much so that when England's Archbishop of Canterbury visited Georgia in May 1993, his request to visit Bodbe was turned down. I felt the full spartan life of those centuries before electricity, with its requirement to rebuild the constantly destroyed churches. The nuns slid around us in the corridors, now struggling to repair both the building and the icons.

In her private quarters Deda Teodora presented us with the traditional Georgian hospitality — saying grace staring straight at the face of St Nino on the wall. We all felt the living link between this modern young woman and the fourth century saint. I also began to feel the connections between the church's liturgy, songs and fresco painting with modern Georgian literature, song, table ritual and modern art. Perhaps, I told myself, this slow, determined rebuilding of the monastery augered well for a festival of arts . . .

Deda ('Mother') Teodora, the founding Mother Superior of the new nunnery at Bodbe, the burial place of St Nino

After the meal, as a gift perhaps from both traditions, Deda Teodora presented me with a hand-painted icon of St Nino made by one of the Bodbe nuns. At first I felt embarrassed, undeserving of the object of so many hours' devotion, but she had insisted.

Back in London it sat on my mantlepiece for three months, looking down with those calm, hooded eyes of the fourth century until finally one evening I found myself compelled to write an article about its and Bodbe's resurrection. The piece was published in an American magazine and, to my surprise and delight, many readers sent in donations — all of which made their way back to that fifth century chapel overlooking the Daghestan Caucasus.

David Gareja

There is an interesting, if controversial, theory about an underlying strain in Georgian culture. Controversial because it blurs the lines of distinction between two supposedly conflicting religions — Orthodox Christianity and Orthodox Islam; interesting because within the subtleties of this blur resides some of the most interesting art and religious 'feeling' in both worlds.

The theory suggests that Christian Georgian culture carries a hidden vein of Sufism (a generic word for the persecuted Muslim mystical tradition). As mentioned before, a case can be made for Rustaveli's *Knight in the Panther Skin* with its hero Tariel presented in a panther (sometimes tiger) skin — a practice formerly found among Sufi dervishes. Furthermore the period of the poem matches well with the great flowering of Sufi literature and culture in neighbouring countries, especially northern Persia, in poets like Omar Khayyam (1048-1142), Nezami of Ganja (1141-1203), Rumi (1207-73). Rustaveli's declarations on perfect love in the prologue, with his self-annihilating adoration of his Queen — all point to a concealed spiritual path within the state of so-called love-madness.

Bishop Atenasa of the Bodbe diocese

The roots of Sufism, the religion of divine love, are mysterious — some say evolving out of oriental Christian monasticism (which pre-dates Islam), then localised and reshaped within the Muslim states — evolving into the specific Sufi orders after the 12th century.

The idea had always intrigued me but been impossible to prove either way. It seemed my invitation to the cave monastery of David Gareja, in the desert highland, right up against the Azeri border, might be as good a place as any to chew it over. At one time the largest monastery in Georgia, its caves date back to the sixth century and on a clear day would almost have been within sight of the Sufi poet Nezami's home, down the valley in Azerbaijan.

Mary icon hanging directly over St Nino's tomb, in Bodbe

I travelled there in a jeep driven by a young seismologist called Gia, working at the monitoring station near the main monastery at Lavra.

"I only work here because of the caves," he said, reeling the Niva wheel around the potholes in the deteriorating road south of Rustavi. "Lavra re-opened just two years ago. Now it has four monks and four not-yet-monks. In Communist times it had no monks — just one 'watcher.'"

I asked if he himself might be a not-yet-monk. He grinned.

David Gareja monastery in its sandstone desert — inhabited since the sixth century AD

"Maybe . . . but I'm married," then continued to speak about the monastery: "Gareja is Georgia's most holy place but it's been forgotten. Just a few years ago the watcher found local shepherds making fires out of the ancient monastery books."

I had the sudden feeling Gia had appointed himself a new kind of watcher — guiding the foreign visitors to make sure they respected the site.

As the landscape progressively emptied itself of all features (helped by the Turks who once felled a large forest here) I considered the monastery's history. Founded in the sixth century by the monk David Gareja, one of the 13 Syrian Fathers, it grew rapidly. As the landscape converted to barren scrub, I wondered if he could ever have guessed that by the 12th century well over ten thousand monks would have followed his footsteps to these remote caves on this rocky, snake infested promontory. They would create a complex covering 24 kilometres and incorporating 12 separate monasteries. Eight hundred years after this, many of the elegant pastel frescoes would still radiate their messages of angels and apostles from the rock, to those who could commandeer a Niva, Lada or minibus and drive down from the hooting capital, an hour and a half to the north.

As the road deteriorated into dirt-track through a highland wilderness, Gia helped fill in the history. "In the ninth century the monastery had buildings and a church at Lavra. Then in the 11th century it was destroyed by Turks, until David the Builder helped restore it." Then suddenly he pointed to a rusting Soviet armoured-car by the side of the road. "And in the 20th century the Soviet Army tried to destroy it. They used this area as their shooting range."

I told him I'd read they stopped in 1994.

"They did, but now the Georgian Army has started." He stared grimly at the road ahead.

As we drove on he helped me build up a full picture of the site. It seemed after David the Builder had given it royal patronage, the nearby 'Desert Monastery' of Udabno was hewn into sandstone, along with Bertubani (now in Azerbaijan) and Chichkhituri. This had been Georgia's and David Gareja's Golden Age, only to be abruptly ended by the Mongol invasion, then after that by Tamerlane the Great in the 14th century.

"But the monks kept coming back," Gia said proudly, "until Shah Abbas came in the 17th century and killed 6,000."

This terrible debacle of 1615 began the decline of the Gareja complex. Afterwards nothing was ever the same. During the 18th and 19th centuries the monastery continued a life of revivals and setbacks, until the Communists arrived in the 20th century and forbade the bourgeois self-indulgence of monasticism — permitting only a 'caretaker' to oversee the site — until 1988.

A couple of small farm buildings abruptly appeared on a desolate hillside before us. Gia stopped the Niva, shut off the engine, then wound down the window.

Monks' cells carved in the sandstone at Lavra, David Gareja

"Listen!" he said solemnly.

We sat without moving for some time and heard absolutely nothing. The landscape seemed to fill with a deafening, all-embracing silence. Never had I heard such a flawless absence of sound. Combined with that empty space ahead, it seemed to make the air sparkle, its currents filling with an invisible ore. Any sound that did arrive became enshrined in new meaning. The distant bark of a dog seemed to come at our ears out of the canyons of pre-history.

'The Ascent of the Cross' in the north part of the main church at Udabno — 11th century (David Gareja)

On either side acres of golden yellow grass climbed sandy hillsides, interrupted only by the occasional shrub. Not a bird, a tree, a telegraph wire cut the horizon, and the sky seemed to press down against the ground as pure and immense as on the day of creation.

As for human habitation, nothing impinged on this huge solitude in three directions. In the fourth, directly ahead, stood a couple of houses, an unfinished museum, and a few roaming dogs — but the atmosphere remained more or less the same as the day David Gareja arrived fourteen hundred years ago. Legend has it he was accused by a woman of making her pregnant in Tbilisi. He prophesied his denial would be proved when she gave birth to a stone. She did of course, and other miracles followed, elevating David into a much-admired saint.

I began to see what attracted him here. Out across the valley the earth stretched before us in tender pink sandstone strips, as if baring her flesh to the sky. This strange rock formation lay directly in front of the monastery, as if southern Georgia lured the monks here by coyly revealing her calves to those embarking on a long and lonely relationship with God. Backed by a huge sandstone escarpment the monastery blended this silence with acres of empty gin-clear light.

The warrior saint Dimitri at the chapel cave of Dimitri II, Udabno (13th century)

The atmosphere seemed to cast into total irrelevance all discussions about Sufi or Christian roots to Georgian culture. The experience of some kind of universal God seemed to hang in this air — beyond denomination. As a Buddhist once said to me: "The highest form of mystical experience isn't a vision of God, or experience bought on by drugs or fasting — it's just a feeling like pure, clear water."

Inspecting the falling frescos at the main church cave of the Udabno ('desert') monastery above Lavra, David Gareja

As we walked up to the stone door of Lavra, the air seemed to run with it. When I finally broke the silence telling Gia this phrase, he said simply: "There's a spring in the cliff here, called David's Tears. It has given the monastery water from the start."

The Lavra monastery itself also fitted the landscape like a glove. The upper church of St Nicholas was petite and earth-coloured, the lower Church of the Transfiguration delved into the hillside, a cave in itself. The cells of the monks cut neatly into a couple of sandstone clefts, reaching down off the hillside on either side, like the sweep of gentle eyebrows. Their framed windows and bright doors fitted the rock, appearing rather like hobbit holes.

Although no longer in the mood to unearth cultural differences, I had one interview to do. A split had recently opened up within the Georgian Orthodox Church — the first in Georgian Christianity since it officially separated from the Armenian Gregorian tradition in the eighth century. It had sent a shudder through the Georgian psyche, and meant the age-old unity, the steadfast rock to which they always returned, had shown a first crack. One of the rebellious monks lived at Gareja.

But I had also suspected Western influences may have played some part. With independence evangelical groups from USA and Europe had landed in Georgia to proselytise loudly on Rustaveli Avenue. They had offended the usually hospitable Georgians. "Why do they need to do this?" one Georgian friend had politely asked me. "Can't they see we have a perfectly adequate church that is far older than theirs?"

But this persistent bible-bashing had eventually led to a backlash within certain elements of the Georgian Church. A group of monks felt they wanted nothing to do with this 'Western' ecumenical movement — with its creeping, money-sweetened infiltration of their tradition. They had insisted the Patriarch withdraw Georgia from the World Council of Churches — which he did. But they still went ahead and formed a breakaway group describing themselves as "the real Orthodox Church" of Georgia.

Still soaking in the water-clear atmosphere, I climbed up to meet Gareja's supporter of this mission for cultural purity (he asked me not to use his name, but refer to him as 'Mama' ('father' in Georgian). His cell lay at the top of sandstone steps that had softened and curved in gentle shapes over the centuries. Mama greeted me with a friendly and sincere smile then asked that I not take his photograph.

"Some visitors respect us here, others not. We are worried our monastery will soon become a museum, with us the exhibits," he said, his bearded face showed a mixture of warmth and anxiety, clearly starting to feel the pressures of ownership bearing down on his new home.

"Here is a place to find God, everybody feels it here. We like sincere visitors, but not those who don't respect Gareja. Most foreigners are fine, although sometimes foreign women come and walk around showing their shoulders and legs. It's not appropriate. This is a serious place. We want it to stay the kind of place people can come and show respect, because respect contains humility, which we all need to feel God."

As he spoke I could sense his uncertainty for the future mingled with a striving for purity — the kind accompanying Georgia's independence during Gamsakhurdia's time. Clearly he feared the ecumenical link with the West, from what he'd seen of a few of its loud, insensitive and ultimately money-grabbing members. They were even worse than the Soviet regime just shaken off (a fear many of us from the West also share).

He continued: "We had a film crew from America come. They wanted to make a film here. I told them 'no.' This is not a film set. This is a real place. They were very sad, some cried. I was sorry to make them unhappy, but I think they didn't really know what a monastery is."

"When tourists come," I suggested, "perhaps they should be asked to follow a rule of not speaking. That way the silence would be preserved for them as well, saving the atmosphere for you and giving them that new and different experience they crave."

He smiled at the idea but didn't answer — clearly without any knowledge of the dam-burst of international tourism.

Later Gia and I walked up the steep hill to the Udabno Monastery. Arriving at the top was to encounter an even deeper, other-worldly silence than at Lavra. We stood for some time at the crest of the ridge, absorbing its voluminous empty space before a desert valley. This time the view offered no female shapes in sandstone — just miles of emptiness, the very 'void' out of which the gods of most religions appear, then speak to the solitary.

A couple metres below the crest the Udabno ('desert' in Georgian) monastery stretched out for a kilometre of now uninhabited caves, most filled with glowing pastel frescoes painted on the walls and ceilings.

Gia explained that the Udabno cave complex followed the template developed earlier at Uplitsikhe, near Gori. But, unlike Uplitsikhe, here against this desert backdrop the emphasis was purely spiritual. The monks had added scenes from David Gareja's life to the chapel walls, developing that distinctive Georgian hagiographic style outside the Byzantine canonic school — the kind found later throughout the nation's churches and illuminated manuscripts.

As Gia led me into the petite Khareba chapel I had the feeling of stepping into an open museum cabinet, then being allowed to walk unmolested through antiquity. No signs, no fences, no guards intervened between our bodies and priceless images of antiquity. Never before have I felt so close to ancient art, nor experienced its huge defencelessness.

As if in confirmation, many frescoes had been scrawled over with pointless modern graffiti — mostly crude signatures and dates in Russian. I asked Gia why.

"Russian soldiers," he said stiffly. "They came here after their shooting." I pointed to some written in Georgian.

"Our soldiers copied them," he answered gravely.

Most desecrations came at about head-height where the soldiers could reach, but higher up, especially in the chapels, came evidence of eyes and faces systematically gouged.

"Made earlier," said Gia, "by Muslims."

He led me through the caves one by one, to stop in a larger space with a wide variety of images on the wall, including a chariot.

"This one is the main church," he said, pointing at frescoes which, in spite of their defacing and flaking from the walls, let the presences of the saints glow out of the rock, as if living on inside its yellow skin.

We arrived in the refectory to find a lavish fresco of the Last Supper gazing down on sandstone tables where the monks had knelt to eat their frugal desert fare. In the adjoining room a large earthenware vat buried in the sand, displayed that eternal monkish taste for wine. The grapes were obviously supplied by the local villagers — who along with limited cultivation down at Lavra and ingenious water-collecting channels cut in the sandstone cliff, kept the monastery alive.

Mama ('father') Andre — icon painter and part of Georgia's rebellious religious revival

I glanced down at the ground and noticed a number of round holes.

"Snakes," Gia said simply. "This place is dangerous in the spring." Back in Tbilisi I heard Udabno was one of the few remaining Georgian homes of the highly poisonous viper, *Vipera Lebetina*. (According to the publication *Natura Caucasia* Georgia also has two endemic species, *Vipera Kaznakovi* and *Vipera Dinniki*). Several people had died from bites here. But this didn't seem to bother him. Something else did. His face became grave.

"I've one more thing to show you," he announced, and led me to what used to be a small, fresco-painted cave, now with its whole roof lying on the ground, collapsed.

"This happened two months ago," he pointed to the huge broken segment sitting on the earth, adding. "The Mongols, the Persians, the Arabs destroyed Gareja, but not as well as erosion." Beside it lay a pile of fresco fragments in a heap on the sand. Some carried the same elaborate scroll motifs and darker pigment from the angels wrapping themselves round the arched walls.

His eye held mine squarely, but this time he said nothing.

I recognised the look as a silent cry for help. It seemed to say that we in the West, even with our tourists and film crews, would be most welcome to help. That like everything worthwhile in modern civilisation — it just required the appropriate sensitivity.

20

Kutaisi

Waiting for Goga

St David's Square in Kutaisi, Imereti, spread out still and unhurried on a sultry evening. The odd Lada or BMW grazed by in the heat; a traffic policeman idly waved his baton at cars. Summer was here and, in West Georgia, quite a different thing to that in Kartlian East Georgia — noticeably hotter (now cooling from a shimmering 40 degrees) yet sufferable. Altogether, the atmosphere in Georgia's second city was pleasingly calm after the hustle of the newly mobile-telephoned Tbilisi. The central park trees to my left leaned down friendly arms towards the passers by. I noticed the taxis didn't buzz and swarm toward any lonely figure standing by the roadside as in the capital — if indeed taxis existed here in any serious way. Mostly Imeretians would stretch out lazy arms and a car would stop, often because they knew each other. "*Gamarjoba Khatuna, sheidzleba . . . ?*" ("Hello Khatuna, is it possible . . . ?") they would say and step in.

I'd taken a position in the new Bistro on Kutaisi's central square, now named David's Square after the builder of Kutaisi's nearby cathedral, Gelati. I'd come hoping to meet someone called Goga. He, I had been told, was the axis of cultural life for the new generation of Imeretians replacing the Sovietised youth-rebels of the early 1990s.

"He's a 'Mr Nightlife,'" my Tbilisian poet friend Lado told me (something of a Mr Nightlife himself) and wrote down his phone number. "See him, he will show everything. Kutaisi, good city."

Secretly I'd expected to hear traces of rivalry between Georgia's number one and two cities — as you do between Moscow and St Petersburg (among poets no less than anyone). But from the perspective of Lado, vying was only minor. Tbilisians only occasionally looked down on their West Georgian cousins as country bumpkins; generally the banter was good-natured.

But as for contacting Goga — there were problems. His phone number, like many in Kutaisi, proved a lost cause. I'd been told if he hung out anywhere it might be at one of these two prime white plastic tables facing the main theatre and statue of David Aghmashenebeli ('The Builder') riding his prancing horse, recently arrived on the plinth vacated by Stalin.

Watching a constant circulation of traffic round the animal, I felt this statue begin to turn into the spindle on which the city revolved. Cars from all areas drove in to pay circular homage to its rider holding out a baby church in the palm of his hand — then drive off on their missions. This generous offering of a church stood as the symbol of the force unifying Georgia for centuries — here representing the 12th century Gelati monastery — its frescoes the pride of Georgia. But to me it also seemed to stand for the new baby Georgia now struggling to be reborn in every city centre like this. David the Builder was offering out a second attempt at birth — after Georgia's disastrous first, war-torn period of independence.

The Roman Catholic Church and Rioni river, Kutaisi (Imereti)

I had liked Kutaisi instantly. A pleasantly uncluttered metropolis of 250,000, lacking the abrasive noises, the wild horn blasts, display car-alarms and *mobiluri* blibbles found in Tbilisi. I could understand Kutaisi's popularity with poets, how it had spawned two of Georgia's favourites, Titsian Tabidze and Paolo Iashvili. The city never overwhelmed. Its northern suburbs had a way of pressing up into the woods of the Greater Caucasus foothills without intruding, while its centre was wrapped round by a gushing wild Rioni river, now gathering a few admiring bankside cafés.

But I'd come here for another reason too. Kutaisi was also the city giving life to one of this century's most unusual revolutionary poets — Vladimir Mayakovsky. The poet had grown up here, spending most of his first thirteen years not two hundred metres from where I sat — at the Gymnasium School (School Number One during the Soviet period), beside the central square.

Mayakovsky's life had always intrigued me for its blend of what might be described as 'Georgian zeal' (the kind still hurtling Ladas round blind Tbilisi corners) with a blazing Russian imagination. His blood was Russian, but his childhood Georgian. This added to the radical tenor of his day, generated his fervent support of the Bolshiviks — followed by his equally fervent disillusionment, resulting in his suicide in 1930.

I tried to picture the young, burning poet, eyes devouring these same tree branches opposite the Ethnographic Museum; how he imbibed a sense of beauty from Kutaisi's wooded hillsides and backdrop of snow-capped mountains; a boundless hope in man from these easy-going streets and parks. Son of a forester, Mayakovsky was born beside a roaring river at Bagdadi, 20kms south of Kutaisi, and always claimed Georgia as a main understay of his poetic life. I'd often wondered if his Georgian romanticism had produced the curious double strand in his work: the fiercely materialistic, Bolshevik poetry (quoted earlier), then the intensely tender, wounded love poetry.

Letting my eyes cruise across the curved facade of Kutaisi's grand Drama Theatre (directly behind the horse), an idea floated into my head that there had been something highly romantic in Mayakovsky's rejection of romanticism (the Georgian Symbolists and Blue Horns) for Communism and Constructivism. That this also applied to his suicide, which became a poetic act in itself and accompanied one of his finest poems.

With no sign of Goga, I was joined at the café table by a local woman called Madonna — my hostess from the Kutaisi-Newport Association. Although her interest in Mayakovsky was less than mine, when the previous day I quoted Goethe — "To understand the poet, you must go to his country" — she replied instantly: "Then I'll show you Kutaisi!"

With my eyes attuned to those of the forester's son, she had taken me to the craggy 11th century Bagrat Cathedral surveying the city centre from a cliff directly above the Rioni. As the city's most dominant building, its ruined transepts spread out eagle-wings to hover watchfully above the rooftops. It was easy to see how this structure alone shed a fairy-tale cast into a poet's

The centre of Kutaisi, with its large Drama Theatre, statue of David Aghmashenebeli, and Bagrat Cathedral above on the hill

The partially restored Bagrat Cathedral, overlooking Kutaisi, from the Ukimerioni hill.

mind — the kind enabling him to later believe in the psychologically blind castles in the air of Communist ideology. Indeed, with the help of modern floodlights, at night this ghost from the 11th century seemed to float in the sky like a permanent bat-signal from Georgia's golden past.

Standing inside its roofless interior Madonna had said: "You know in the tenth century, Kutaisi unified all Georgia as its capital under King Bagration III. It was only in 1120 David the Builder moved the capital to Tbilisi." Her voice carried a trace of pride, as if a fact not often acknowledged by Tbilisians.

From the nearby cliff-top we looked out over the town with its spread of tin roofs lying across Kutaisi's gentle hills. Directly below the river gushed down from the High Caucasus overlooked by a few once elegant homes. Most were looking shabby, in poor state of repair.

"Our city is poor after the war," she said gesturing to the crowds gathering in the market beside the Chain Bridge. "We have 18,000 refugees from Abkhazia." But to me Kutaisi seemed to manage its poverty well.

In the afternoon we drove to another magnetic centre for all of Kutaisi's poets — Gelati, seven kilometres into the foothills. But first we stopped at the impressive Motsameta ('Martyrs') Monastery, perched on a spur of rock above two sheer cliff faces above the Tskhaltsitela river. A site bearing a church since the fourth century, it had been desecrated and burnt down many times, including by the Cheka in 1923 — the start of the horrors that eventually drove Mayakovsky to his desperate act.

Sitting on a dizzying balcony, jutting out right over the chasm, its caretaker, the 82-year-old Father Gagi, recounted another remarkable tale of defiance in the years following the Bolshevik arrival

"I watched the Cheka take away the Motsameta relics in 1923," he said gravely, the twinkle momentarily leaving his eyes. "I never forgot it. When I grew up I became a religious activist. They sent me to Siberia for this . . . ," he paused again and glanced northward at the snows on Mt Shkara, ". . . for 11 years."

I was about to ask if this was in 1937 — the same year his Kutaisi compatriot Paolo Iashvili shot himself in the Union Building during a presidium session — when Mama Gagi's huge Great Dane bounded onto the balcony to lick all our faces. After he had partially succeeded, Mama Gagi continued: "When I returned from prison I continued my activism. They arrested me twice again, but when I got cancer the authorities decided I'd received my just punishment. I decided to come back and die in my home area—" then he smiled brightly, "—but instead God cured me!" He gestured out at the stunning panorama of the High Caucasus. "So here I am here with you, left on this earth to help others!"

We left Motsameta with our spirits lifted by such a cheerful ambassador from Georgia's grim past. It seemed the perfect launch for Gelati, one of the nation's best preserved centres of religious art and learning.

Indeed when we arrived and stepped into its splendid Cathedral of the

Virgin I was amazed to find the extent of preservation and restoration — for the walls are covered in original artwork floor to ceiling, dominated by one huge, 12th century mosaic filling the altar bay with scenes from the Nativity and Annunciation. The effect was akin to stepping inside the cranium of a wild imagination — almost every inch is filled with coloured faces, images, memories, like the very subconscious of a nation, its saints, royalty and nobility climbing the walls, head upon head.

Georgians are rightly proud of Gelati. From the moment the building was founded in 1106, artwork charted the cathedral's development and rebuilding right up to the 19th century. Like all Georgian religious art, it followed the

Portraits of St Constantine and St Helen — north arm, Gelati cathedral (16th century)

Byzantine School (it is said the creator of the giant mosaic of two and a half million stones studied in Constantinople), several of the fresco faces wearing dramatic, mountainesque expressions. The north wall's 16th century portraits of a severe row of nobility beside David the Builder hint at the time's religious determinism, which in the 20th century found a political/artistic expression.

I imagined a young Mayakovsky gazing round this temple to the imagination, drinking in the opulent history of Georgia's visual heritage. Indeed some speculate the geometric patterns surrounding Gelati's frescoes inspired his abstract Constructivist designs in posters. The same theory also suggests that Georgia's remarkable per-capita ratio of painters and poets (in lectures, I sometimes describe the country as the "artists' colony" at the base of the former Soviet Union) grew from this rich vein of religious painting, originating in the illuminated bibles and manuscripts in the caves of Vardzia and David Gareja.

Outside Madonna pointed to a building with an open book carved above its portal.

"This is the 12th century 'Academy of Learning.' It is modelled on Plato's. David bought Neoplatonist scholars here to teach after they were forbidden in Constantinople (like Ioane Petritzi). They had a painting school and studied astronomy, geometry, philosophy." Then she smiled. "Now they've opened a new academy down in Kutaisi."

I asked if this meant that Kutaisi maintained its institutions dedicated to literature. She thought for a moment then said: "We have our university of course . . . ," then added suddenly, as if an afterthought: ". . . and Mayakovsky's museum at Bagdadi."

The road to Bagdadi followed the same as that to the Imeretian mountain resort of Sairme. I wanted to go partly due to another interesting fact in the history of rewriting. Five years after Mayakovsky's suicide, he was suddenly resurrected by the

16th century portrait of David Aghmashenebeli ('The Builder') — Gelati north wall

Party as the Poet of the Communist Revolution in 1935 — one of several that Pasternak later described as being "propagated like potatoes." I knew the main tenor of the museum would Sovietise every part of his life, but often the more far-flung museums in the former Soviet Union squeezed more truth past the censors.

Bagdadi lay at the foot of the Lesser Caucasus, and just beyond it, at the base of a mountain gorge, stood the wooden forester's hut of Mayakovsky's childhood. Idyllic and rustic beside a grassy riverbank, we found it surrounded by pear trees. I could think of no better place for any child-poet to grow up.

Nearby, a large concrete museum building had been constructed. Its caretaker, Niko Kuchukhidze was found and he hurried over brandishing keys and a smile at finally receiving a foreign guest. I looked at his sixtyish face wondering how he could feel now. After so many years supporting the Soviet state he found his world turned upside down. His museum was dedicated to a poet, once publicly loved (1915-29), then loathed (1930-35), then loved again (1935-86), only to be reviled again (1991-). Not an easy position. I asked what he thought of the present-day regime. His answer was that of a tactful historian.

"The new capitalism we have in Georgia today is like that in Mayakovsky's time," he said in a factual voice, then proceeded to talk about the need to preserve the museum's 2,000 exhibits.

"He's been under pressure recently," noted Madonna quietly. "Some local people say the museum is redundant, they want to make it into a restaurant."

I asked him about attendances. His face dropped.

"We used to have 100,000 people coming every year. Yeltsin even visited in 1986. But now we have perhaps 4,000."

Stepping inside the entrance we encountered the usual problem — no electricity. Ten minutes later, by some miracle, a few lights were encouraged to glow a dim yellow. It meant we could at least see where the exhibits were, even if

Detail from an altar icon at Kutaisi Ethnographic Museum

their content remained less than clear. I was pleased to see it contained many of Mayakovsky's poems in their various published forms, often with illustrations, as well as some of the Constructivist posters. But I had to focus

North wall interior of Gelati Cathedral

the beam of my pen-torch and examine details piece by piece.

"Mayakovsky illustrated about 3,000 placards," Niko said, "and wrote the words for some 6,000." I asked just how Georgian he thought Mayakovsky really was, since he spent most of his life in Russia.

"Four generations of Mayakovsky's family lived in Georgia. He had a Georgian temperament." Then he said enigmatically, "They put Mayakovsky's brain in an institute in Moscow."

I couldn't decide if this was just part of the patter he must have given hundreds of times over the years, or he now made some specific point? Indeed did he now know what information to give — with the museum's allegiances switching so many times? Mayakovsky's hero status had disappeared (unlike Stalin's at the Gori museum) during Georgia's fanatically anti-

Russian period in Gamsakhurdia's rule. Indeed his statue near Gudauri had disappeared shortly after Georgian independence (rumoured to be sold as scrap in Turkey).

I signed the visitor's book and took my leave, feeling another vital piece of Georgian history teetering on the brink of more rewriting. Niko looked worried as we drove away past the pear trees, and again I had that feeling of abandoning someone — all too common in my journeys round Georgia.

Back in Kutaisi we dropped in on the reception of an Imeretian wedding, held in the sweltering canteen of the local tractor factory. With my mind still piecing together the images of Mayakovsky's long poetic adolescence, I found myself sitting next to a young local woman with light green eyes and European style of dressing. Our conversation quickly revealed her as decidedly poorer than her Tbilisi contemporaries, yet her choice of clothing didn't show it, indicating a temperament closer to what I knew in Western Europe. Her voice, too, seemed more at ease with itself. Indeed if it hadn't been for the language I might have judged her poise and sensitivity French.

Imeretian cuisine at a Kutaisi wedding

"Some Kutaisi people like to say our city is the most ancient in the world," she answered my introductory questions with a half-smile, indicating doubts at such boastful statements.

I asked if she believed the sorceress Medea had lived here, when Kutaisi was reportedly the capital of Colchis.

"We learned at school that Kutaisi had been the Greek city Miletus in the seventh century BC — so probably. Would you like some more wine?"

Our conversation moved on to the Imeretian cuisine filling table before us — clearly more varied than East Georgian, with its salads spiced with apples and hazelnuts — then to wine. I asked about local claims that Georgia had been the birthplace of wine culture (due to archaeological evidence of grape-pip accumulations around 7,000 BC).

"You have to be careful about boasting in Georgia," she smiled.

But after we left I found her presence lingering with me. Those calm, unexaggerated gestures, thoughtful eyes and a natural elegance. Like the city itself she seemed unhurried, contained within herself, beside its wild mountain river and men.

Back at the café, sipping a local Vartsikhe brandy and no longer waiting for Goga, I allowed the impressions of the city to meld in my mind. If Mayakovsky had stayed — allowed this ambience and its women to sink in

(Left) Vladimir Mayakovsky; (right) Constructivist era, anti-capitalist poster
— both at the Mayakovsky Museum, Bagdadi

under his skin — might the force of the Revolution have lost one of its brightest flames? Was this green-eyed woman's delicate and natural refinement indicative of what lay forgotten in West Georgia?

I ordered another brandy. The floodlights of the Bagrat Cathedral flicked on, and the great orange eagle spread its wings over the city. All around me the evening felt delicious and invisible, the soil of Imereti radiating up the heat of day, quietly ripening the fruit and grapes — as it had for a million years.

21

New Georgia

*I*t was another first night back in Tbilisi, after a memorable 'supra' (a feast completely covering the table surface) I walked home with a new Georgian friend Nanuli, along Gamsakhurdia Street, named not after the failed president, but his father, the novelist Constantine Gamsakhurdia. The city had changed again — but this had been expected. Indeed the copy of *Georgian Economic Trends* borrowed on the plane over, had predicted a 14.7 per cent growth in GDP for Georgia in the last quarter of 1997 (in early 1998 the IMF would place Georgia at third position for the most rapid GDP growths in the world).

Although mentally prepared for modernisation, I still found myself shocked at the number of new, marble-fronted shops and restaurants, shining out onto the run-down pavements. Marlboro, Pall Mall, President cigarette posters winked back from formerly blank walls, as if those disappearing in anti-smoking Western Europe, were being simply re-hung here. The major tobacco companies had begun an aggressive marketing strategy for Georgia (later I would encounter the notorious 'start-smoking girls': teams of baseball hat-wearing nubiles, patrolling Tbilisi at night offering free cigarettes to anyone seen not smoking). I remembered the phrase of a Georgian from several years earlier: "Georgians embrace everything too passionately." Did this now apply to the marketing techniques of the West?

I was almost expecting it when, reaching the Polytechnic Metro station, the whole region, streetlights and all, abruptly plunged into almost total darkness. I glanced at my watch — just after midnight — shut-off time for the Saburtalo area. Georgians, notoriously bad at saving electricity, still had the state to do it for them, as the government struggled to meet the world-market fuel prices for its power stations.

Walking on, guided by the beam of a never-be-without-in-Tbilisi pen-torch, there seemed a certain inevitability to this darkness. Georgia, in its love of impulsive, symbolic thinking seemed almost to have provided these city-wide black-outs deliberately. As if the city needed its daily reminder of the unobserved gloom of unconscious forces propelling its impulsive behaviour. Looking around, Gamsakhurdia Street had converted to pure third-world sootiness. The shadows loomed like muggers among the unlit Soviet-built 14-storey cliffs, as the forgotten, Asian otherworld of Tbilisi seemed to take a step forward. A compelling feeling, yet experience told me the greatest danger

Consumer culture crashes into the Caucasus — individual artistic expression arrives on Gamsakhurdia Street, Tbilisi in the early 1990s

lay not in any Caucasian bandit, but in the lurking pavement potholes and occasional open manhole cover. Then, as if summoned by this other personality of a city, the wind whipped up out of nowhere, cut round the buildings to make personal attacks on our bodies, thrusting icy hands through clothing, wrapping round necks and ears. It bought on images of its wild Caucasian journey, down from the perma snowfields to the north by Mt Kazbek, along the icy Aragvi riverbanks, through the canyons to strike the city with that trumpet-blast reminder of the high, hostile mountain-scape just 50 kilometres away. Nanuli remarked that the wind reminded her of the atmosphere in Vazha Pshavela's poem 'Host and Guest.'

"Pshavela makes you remember the mountains," she said almost proudly, and I realised she actually enjoyed this chill, hostile wind, as if it stirred an ancestral part of her character still lingering up in those high, wind-blasted villages.

Buttoning up, I glanced round and noticed how some of the shop-fronts now had their own private power supply, the signs continuing to burn brightly below the towers of ink-black windows. A few interiors even remained lit, their new marble floors and counters selling mostly sweets, champagne and cigarettes. The city's rich obviously still sunk their money into property rather than banks, remaining cautious after the collapses of 1993 and '94. The other unmistakable change came in the fresh batch of English words adorning the fronts. On one shop door I was surprised to find a poster advertising 'BINGO' at one of the city's former cinemas. I asked Nanuli if she'd ever played.

"No," she said flatly, her expression suddenly became serious. "You know our *kinos* ('cinemas') are suffering. Our film industry hardly makes any films, although in countries like France our directors like Nana Jorjadze end up with Oscar nominations. We've nothing new to show except erotic and some Russian films. Now we have bingo!" (Nana Jorjadze's film *Chef in Love* was nominated for an Oscar in 1997.)

Her face picked up that happy-go-lucky expression typical of Georgians weathering periods of subjugation. It seemed to say "What can we do? Let's enjoy it — whatever it is!" But it wouldn't be the first time I'd hear disquiet at the direction of the rapid commercialisation.

Then, just as we reached a street corner, a burst of gunfire suddenly erupted directly ahead.

Modern Georgian painter, Merab Abramishvili, at a recent exhibition opening

"What's happening?" I asked in alarm, memories flooding back of those bleak Mkhedrioni days of 1992.

"Probably bandits," Nanuli replied casually. "Let's go this way." She steered

Hand painted advertisement, Plekhanov district, Tbilisi — one of the few outlets for Georgia's many talented, unemployed artists

us off onto a side-street as calmly as if we'd encountered a detour sign. I glanced at her face. It showed no concern at all, as if bandits would always exist in the Caucasus. "Bandits and hospitality," I repeated a friend's description of Georgia in 1992, then asked her if she knew any. She smiled wistfully.

"Recently I heard about some . . . A car belonging to one of your Western charities UMCOR was stopped by drunken bandits near Gori. First they took the car, then decided to kidnap the people inside. But rather than tying them up and demanding money, they took them to a Georgian feast, made them eat

Tbilisi wall-hoarding in 1989, illustrating the old Georgian alphabet
— which was in use as late as the 11th century

and drink. The next morning the bandits decided they had all become such friends they delivered them and the car back to UMCOR . . ."

I encountered the same easy-going tone a few months later in February 1998, after Eduard Shevardnadze's second assassination attempt. Many Georgians, while blaming the Russians for trying to destabilise Georgia's bid for the second pipeline, talked about it in casual, 'there we go again,' voices, as if assassination, like vendetta, slotted neatly into human nature. Indeed shortly after this four foreign UN employees were briefly kidnapped in Zugdidi, to be paraded across national television drinking and eating in Georgian feasts. They were released, so rumour had it, in order of their drinking ability.

We strolled on, the wind bit into my face and there were no more shots. Indeed such sounds are now rare in Tbilisi, after the constant popping during 1992 and '93. Generally the capital is judged safer for visitors than most in Western Europe.

"I'm cold," Nanuli said simply and gripped my arm. As we continued, I asked about this casual acceptance of the wild in the human character, quoting that commonly used Georgian word *gizhi* — 'crazy'.

"Yes, most Georgian men like to be slightly *gizhi*," she admitted. "I think it reminds them of their mountain roots." I suggested she might include women here. She looked doubtful until I described Manana's wild gleaming eyes in the car back in 1989, as her husband played chicken down the wrong side of the Mtskheta dual carriageway.

"Yes that's *gizhi*," she agreed, "but normal."

Same hoarding in the mid 1990s, taken over by Western advertising culture
— and upsetting many locals

I remarked that over the years I'd noticed an attraction to hysteria in the Caucasus. Gunfire mixed with romanticism, the kind that "gallops the cliff-edges of terrible truth."

"Or the Mtskheta freeway," she added simply.

The following day I walked down Rustaveli Avenue with a group of Georgian friends discussing the video of the BBC *Travel Show's* first-ever destination report on Georgia, broadcast in June 1997. I'd watched it in London having read several enthusing articles in the British press (invariably punning on *Georgia on my Mind*).

"We didn't like that report," said one of the Georgian men. "It didn't show what Georgia really is. It showed old ladies being friendly in Gori market, not who we are . . ." He frowned. "We are also a modern culture who makes selling-out performances of Shakespeare in your Barbican Theatre, London."

I told him that on British standards the report had been favourable — the presenter concluding her investigation lying on a high Caucasian meadow near Gudauri, giving Georgia "the thumbs up," then adding "but get here soon because it's developing and modernising quickly."

As I repeated that phrase I glanced round at the new Rustaveli Avenue, displaying at least two dozen new shops and businesses. Beside me Kodak, Fanta, Coca-Cola, Samsung, 'Salon' blazed out of the walls. McDonald's was on its way. But New Georgia had started to pick up its own distinctive style. Many of the restaurants and cafes had been created in a very personal style, as if by artists (very often they were). Names like 'Nicola' (filled with Pirosmani copies), the 'Café Vincent' (after Van Gogh), 'Maly' with its richly lugubrious romantic murals, welcomed Georgian visitors with menus written in English and Georgian (the Russian language had almost disappeared in the city centre, right down to the street signs). I began to remember the fantasy I'd had in the late 1980s of Georgia becoming a modern, Europeanised artist colony. A repository for the 'romantic modern' — as opposed to the 'ironic modern,' now so frequently the vogue in London and New York.

Ajaran children dancers waiting to perform at the 1997 Tbilisoba

Next to the opera a snappily dressed 'new Georgian' leant against a new, tinted-glass BMW, chatting on his *mobiluri*. I asked about this new male self-image. Everybody in the group approved. One of the men mentioned he'd just spent $400 on a *mobiluri* himself. As he enthused about its advantages I felt the new Western mould forming around his country — so eager to enter the living-rooms and travel brochures of Western Europe. Indeed in November 1997 Georgia presented itself for the first time at the World Travel Market at Olympia, London. There David from Caucasus Travel would tell me that, "in 1998 we hope to double Georgia's total of foreign tourists to about 3,000." He then added that in 1989 Georgia had 1.8 million visitors, 280,000 from outside the Soviet Union.

The process was clearly just beginning. While Russians were now heading for Tenerife, Western tourists were being told of a destination with a 'difference.' To hurry on down before it too became like us.

But, looking at Rustaveli Avenue, I couldn't help feel a certain irony. The bulk of the Georgian population clearly aimed to eradicate this difference as quickly as possible. The Western chain supermarket (like Tbilisi's memorable Super Babylon) was becoming normal in Tbilisi with astonishing speed. The friendly old ladies in markets selling *churchkhela* (a delicious, phallic-shaped combination of nuts and grape paste) — to West Europeans, adorably 'other,'

Tbilisoba, 1997 — the city's annual festival right at the end of October. The smoke is from the scores of shashlik grills.

to Georgians carried elements of dusty antiquity. Most families would rather push trolleys round Super Babylons — like us.

We walked on, past a couple of police standing at the side of the road randomly waving batons at passing cars to pull over. Most simply drove on.

"Why?" I asked.

"That's very Georgian," everybody laughed. "Those men are our new mafia. The government feels they're easier to control in a uniform as police than in BMWs and black clothes, as in 1992-94."

This hadn't changed from the Soviet times. The UNDP report of 1997 estimated the total number of police in Georgia exceeded 40,000. An interesting figure and one issue of the *Georgia Profile* magazine compared the total police in Georgia (a nation with a total population 5.5 million) against the 10,000 police in New York (total population of 15 million).

Wondering how the group would react, I told the joke about the New Russian who shows off his new $3,000 digitised diamond watch to another New Russian. "You fool!" says the second New Russian, "I just saw exactly the same model round the corner for $5,000!"

Everybody laughed, said that was "very Russian" would never happen in Georgia. But later when I told it to Nanuli she didn't laugh, even seemed slightly moved.

"Yes, it's already happening in Georgia," she said thoughtfully. "We Georgians are proud. We pretend to be heroes when we're insecure." Then she looked at me more earnestly. "For instance I am insecure,

Ceremonial daggers on sale at the Georgian Arts and Culture Centre, Tbilisi — Georgians are traditionally famous metalsmiths

though I don't tell you. You see none of us really know what this Western future is. All we do is copy you then hope. If one new Western-style petrol station opens on a road, very likely you'll have another a month later right next to it."

I told Nanuli of a book I one day wanted to write, called 'Same World.' About the enormous Sameness now spreading across the globe; the kind epitomised by airport terminals everywhere, letting us land in one country only to find an airport terminal selling exactly the Same goods in exactly the Same way as in the country we left. A factor slowly wiping away those essential differences of travel.

I suggested we still needed different standards of behaviour to give us a perspective on our own, adding: "So I hope you won't imitate us completely, eliminate all your maddening differences!"

But Nanuli took issue. "I flew your British Mediterranean Airways a month ago to London," she said. "It was great. Perhaps you don't know how great it is?"

I confessed to my own joyous disbelief watching those world-famous blue-dressed hostesses announce: "Today's flying time from Heathrow to Tbilisi will be four hours and forty minutes."

Until that moment every journey to Georgia had been a trial of endurance. Particularly those involving Moscow's airport from hell, Vnokovo. Without exception each transit through its army of underpaid, over-corrupted officials became a battle of wits and nerves. Arrival on the plane felt more like a reward than a right. I even heard the story of a friend who, sitting triumphantly on her Tbilisi-bound plane, suddenly discovered half the

Women selling 'churchkhela' at Tbilisi's main market — and toasting the photographer

passengers believed it flew to Makhachkala. After independence I'd quickly resorted to the direct, but hit-and-miss Orbi link through Frankfurt. Although shaky, they always worked for me. But a couple of British friends told me they phone-booked from London, flew to Frankfurt only to be told someone more important *(tsnobili)* had been given their seats. I later heard the story of a Georgian pilot having his keys confiscated while literally on the runway, because the airline never paid its insurance. After that I tried the break-down bus journey up from Armenia ($7 and never again); then the 19 hour, four-hours-sitting-at-the-Georgian-border train ride from Baku . . . As a result British Mediterranean had coined the marketing phrase 'Tbileasy.'

"It is almost too easy . . . ," I remarked.

"No it isn't," Nanuli said, giving me a jarring look. I realised my mistake — using my own standards to judge her long-limited freedoms. She, who had just made her first, magical, five day trip to London, experienced the city I constantly needed to escape as a paradise, full of its own 'differences' for her.

I told her I still feared this same global standardisation of ambition, here as much as anywhere.

"My friend was recently in Armenia," she replied more thoughtfully. "He said they've gone for a more American style of your standardisation. Their new shop designs think more of money, less of individuality and art, like ours in Georgia. 'Georgia,' he had said, 'is going the European route.'"

The theme of individuality in the Caucasian character would often return. Later, in another discussion with Nanuli I told the story of a friend who once looked up to see the Daghestani minister of agriculture's Mercedes flying through the air, in mid-delivery by heli-copter to a mountain town. This in order to make a fittingly proud entrance.

"You Westerners say our pride gets in the way, is egoistic, starts wars . . . ," she had responded. "Well, sometimes I think Caucasian pride is just a stage, and we've forgotten what comes next. After pride I think is a nobility that no longer needs to be

A kiosk, Tskhinvali. Immediately after independence Georgia's free market first showed itself as 'kiosk culture' — as in Russia.

admired. A kind of literary or spiritual feeling, the kind we see in Rustaveli's poems, experience in our songs. It's something most people praise but rarely live."

In October 1997, during Georgia's GIFT international festival of arts, the tenor of this conversation resurfaced with my journalist friend at the Metechi Palace Hotel. We discussed the superb Georgian production of *Midsummer Night's Dream* (formerly playing to great acclaim at London's Barbican), directed by the late Michael Tumanishvili.

"Why," I asked him, "do Georgians have a reputation for inspirational, rather than practical organising, when clearly they are very capable of combining the two, as in this play?"

"Because they're still seen as using their old 'friendship economics,'" he said. "During the Soviet period it was the only means they knew of making a profit — short-term, black-market trading. They're still afraid of thinking ahead too far in case everything collapses, like it used to." Then after a moment's thought he added: "But Georgians learn quickly — when they really want."

I told the story of myself and a Georgian friend trying to borrow money from a Georgian bank while attempting to open a bookshop in Tbilisi. They'd offered us a loan at 60 per cent per annum, then said, "but because you're friends, we'll make it 40 per cent" adding that terms were usually only for three months, but in our case could be extended to six (we wanted five years). Short-termism had yet to leave the banks.

"Yes," he agreed. "This longer-view economics and proper loan facilities is what Georgia desperately needs now; and probably will get . . ." Then he looked thoughtful. "But you know, I think we have a few things to learn from them too. Work is gaining such manic, inhuman qualities in the West, we could receive some of their 'romantic economics' back."

I asked what he meant. His eyes searched the walls for a moment. "I've always imagined a more friendship-aware market place; one more aesthetically tuned, human, less frenetic." He spoke hesitantly as if trying to define it. "You see it in the way Georgians insist on enjoying their work before all else."

I asked how this could ever match the West's image of the clockwork and clean economic kitchen.

"I think it does. In the West we're discovering people work better when they're happy. Georgia is a-happy-go-lucky culture. While it needs less of the 'go-lucky' bit, we could use more of both."

A growing economy — note that Russian on public signs of the new Georgia is conspicuously absent

The following night I went to watch Georgia's new Basement Theatre's production of *The Dance of Death* by Strindberg, starring the Georgian actor Ramaz Chkhikvadze. Sitting in the small actor-built theatre I reflected on why the GIFT festival, with its planeful of 160 unpaid Western performers, had turned out such a success — for the performers no less than their audience. Vanessa Redgrave had arrived true to her promise, to be driven into Tbilisi in a red taxi marked 'RED GRAVE.' Like any great actress, she engaged the city on all levels, from its refugees — she opened our War Child exhibition — to its president. Indeed, the following day, she produced the most delighted smile I've ever seen on Eduard Shevardnadze's face, when joining in with the Georgian children's traditional dancing at the Mayor's Palace. Paco Peña then thrilled Tbilisi with his flamenco, and for the next 12 days it felt we were all witnessing the turning point in Georgia's seven years' bad luck since independence. An impression that even survived Shevardnadze's second assassination attempt, five months later.

Back in the Basement Theatre, the lights went down and a fantastic, burlesque production begun — unlike any Strindberg I'd seen. It took about 15 minutes for the slow penny to drop — *The Dance of Death* had in fact been switched, unannounced in the programme, for *The Threepenny Opera*. But the production was so strong, with such a force of caricature acting, I remembered again Robert Sturua's words about the Georgian character having something to teach us in the West.

Afterwards, back in my borrowed Tbilisi flat overlooking the railway station, I listened to a tape of Georgian and European music, wondering if this could be the reason I kept returning — seeking this elusive difference. Indeed the novelist and poet D. M. Thomas, also present at the festival, had just told the story of his first day in Tbilisi.

"A Georgian man came up to me on the funicular railway, asked me what I did. I told him I was a poet. 'I'm a poet too!' he exclaimed and to my surprise immediately produced a book of his poems. 'You must come with me! I'm going to the grave of our poet Niko Baratashvili at our Poets' Church. We're having a ceremony!' So I went and ended up being filmed reciting a Shakespeare sonnet from memory above his grave. This is something that could never have happened in England!"

Meanwhile, on the music tape the Rustavi Choir gave way to Georgian *panduri*, which in turn switched to a series of Faure's luxurious songs. The new, smooth, dark-chocolate tone of the European soprano seemed strangely rich and colour-saturated against the raw, strumming *panduri*. It conjured up images of elegant Paris streets. 19th century London, tinkling fountains, set beside the urgent floods, calamities, rusty pistols of the High Caucasus. Suddenly ours was a galaxy-smooth world of good manners, cultivated charm and deceit — that in the end produced equally disastrous wars as any Georgian emotionalism. Were we not just the flipside of the same coin?

The final song on the tape belonged to the Rustavi Choir who sang the famous male polyphony *'Shen khar Venakhi'* ('You are a Vineyard'). This time the mountain voices seemed to echo straight down from the high cathedrals of rock permanently hanging above Georgia's towns. It seemed as if the very cliffs themselves had found a voice and sang back the long-forgotten message of Nanuli's second level of pride.

Suddenly I felt a twinge of relief. Same World still had some distance to travel before it overwhelmed the modern Caucasus.

*

FURTHER
READING

*Independent Georgia sets sail — cartoon from
'The Devil's Whip' satirical magazine,
Tbilisi, 1919*

1930s poster produced by the Georgian Bolsheviks exhorting the Georgian people to "fight against the kulaks and create a new, Socialist agriculture"

Appendix:
Oil, water & Mensheviks

*I*t would be improper to write about modern Georgia without a few words on the Caucasian oil industry, former and present. Azerbaijani black gold and its transportation, has played a crucial role in the region's fortune, at every level of society — from railway tickets to opera houses. As I write, a new mood of optimism fills Georgia as oil again begins its tentative flow to the Black Sea ports from the large Caspian field (and to a lesser extent local deposits). Yet one cannot help but notice a curious similarity to the former Western oil investment and pipeline project of almost exactly a century ago.

In 1874, Robert Nobel, brother of the Swedish inventor of dynamite Alfred, arrived in Baku shortly after the Russian government deregulated the fledgling Baku oil industry. He came looking for walnut to fulfil an arms contract for the Russian government. But instead of purchasing rifle-butts he bought an oil refinery. Together with another brother, Ludwig, the Nobels radically transformed the few hand-dug oil pits in the Baku area, effectively increasing Russia's total oil production from 600,000 barrels a year in 1874, to ten million a decade later. They also invested in a number of new refineries and, in this short time, successfully forced nearly all the American kerosine out of the Russian market.

Having launched a major new industry the Nobels then needed to expand out into foreign markets, ahead of the American competition — John Rockefeller and his Standard Oil. Thus they initiated major investment into the Caucasian infrastructure. In the mid 1870s the people of Tbilisi still found it cheaper to import kerosine all 12,800 kilometres from America, than transport it the 546 from Baku. Ludwig Nobel ended the dislocation between East and West Caucasia once and for all when, in 1883, he entered into a financial partnership with the Rothschild family and completed the coast to coast railway link between Baku and Batum (Batumi) on the Black Sea coast. With the help of more Rothschild money he funded several other projects including the Batumi refinery. Then in 1889, to solve problems of delay on the painfully slow section over Georgia's Surami Mountains, he constructed a 67km pipeline. Not long after this the pipeline was expanded in both directions to cover the full distance, Baku to Batumi (completed in 1905).

The same problem of transportation from the Caucasus oil-fields was also responsible for the birth-cry of another of the world's biggest companies: Shell. Its founder, Marcus Samuel, son of a shell merchant in London's East End, made his first trip to the region in 1890. He immediately realised the great potential of the Caspian fields and the same year devised a new bulk-tanker design — whose progeny he named after shells — 'Conch,' 'Clam,' 'Cowrie,' etc. Within a mere three years he had ten such ships, which he sailed through the new Suez Canal to the new Far Eastern markets.

Today with curious *fin-de-siècle* coincidence, Western oil investment has again spread itself across Caucasian soil — already to the tune of over a billion dollars (30 billion are promised). Georgia will serve as the first transit corridor for 'early oil,' the first pipeline was scheduled to be finished in September 1998, terminating as a mooring out into the Black Sea at Supsa. It can deliver 115,000 barrels a day for transportation westward through the Bosphoros. The AIOC (Azerbaijan International Oil Company) consortium of companies has halved the political risk by proposing two pipeline routes — the second passing northward through Russia. The danger of terrorist attacks has been calculated into the economics of delivery. The decision was taken to include more, rather than less, of the local states, relying on safety in numbers.

In the 19th and early 20th centuries oil brought significant riches, not only to the Rothschilds and Nobels, but also to cities like Baku, Batumi and, to a lesser extent, Tbilisi. The hope is it will again. In the early 20th century it led to a strong desire from the Western powers for stability in the region (British troops were stationed across the Caucasus). The same international pressure for Caucasian peace is now also expected. Whether it is strong enough to placate Russian and internal Caucasian jealousies over the contract awards remains to be seen — especially after the second attempt on Eduard Shevardnadze's life on the February 9th 1998.

In the 1920s, the West, of course, failed in its quest for calm — although, it has to be said, not helped by the turmoil in Europe itself. Then, as today, Georgia's independence as a nation was preceded by a period of intense nationalistic sentiment — its prime stoker being the poet and banker Ilia Chavchavadze (murdered in 1907, probably by Tsarist agents). With independence this feeling, in both periods, dwindled. However here is the point where the parallels divide.

The intellectual climate greeting the Western investment today is very different to that in the late 19th century. Then the Caucasus, particularly Georgia, was a spawning ground for furtive intellectual and revolutionary activity. Many educated in Tbilisi later became prominent Narodniks, Marxists, Anarchists, Bolsheviks, Mensheviks. Publications that would never have survived the Tsarist secret police (Okhrana) in Russia, emerged from Baku and Tbilisi — like Lenin's *Iskra* ('The Spark'); the Anarchist weekly *Nobati* ('The Toxin'); and the satirical, semi-Menshevik *Esmakis Matrakhi* ('The Devil's Whip'). One young Bolshevik revolutionary codenamed 'Koba' —Stalin — said he owed the sharpening of his skills in 'revolutionary combat' to his early strike-raising experiences in Batumi and Baku. The emerging oil industry provided a perfect Capitalist foil for teeth-sharpening by these early Communists. The conditions of work undergone by the first oil employees were appalling — compulsory 12 to 14 hour days were common. The success of Stalin and others in organising strikes was a main factor in the decline of 'Russian oil.' In 1904, it supplied 31 per cent of the world's total petroleum; by 1913 it had dropped to 9 per cent. Today, after 70 years of Communist isolation, the will for revolution is gone. The psychological climate for re-engagement with the West is very open. However this is accompanied by a dramatic, television-led rise in expectations. Comparisons of wealth will inevitably lead to feelings of injustice and jealousy — which will take every trick of modern marketing and social management to contain.

One other result of that first oil boom and political backlash, was the Georgian Menshevik movement. Noe Ramishvili (who became Georgia's first Prime Minister on May 26th 1918), and Noe Zhordania (who took over until the Bolshevik invasion of February 1921) separated the Georgian leadership from the Russian Bolsheviks and followed the Menshevik ('minority') path set out by L. Martov. The Georgian Mensheviks are regarded by some as the world's first liberal Communist government (1918-1921). They accepted the creation of the Russian Duma after the 1905 October Revolution, and quickly found themselves attacked by the Bolsheviks for abandoning the dictatorship of the proletariat led by a ruling elite (Stalin daubed them "liberal constitutionalists"). They fascinated many prominent Socialists in England, including Ramsay MacDonald who visited independent Georgia with a delegation of prominent European Socialists and future prime ministers, in 1920.

The Mensheviks nationalised the estates of the rich landowners and aristocrats but left the 'bourgeois order' and middle class more or less intact. Georgian was declared the official language of state and Russian was banned in the constituent assembly, courts and army. They also opened the first university in Tbilisi in 1918 and introduced the eight-hour working day. However their rule was frustrated from the start. Ridden with Bolshevik agitation, Georgia was also blockaded on two sides — by the Red Army, as well as the Russian Whites under General Denikin, to the north, and a hostile Armenia to the south. It suffered food shortages, a chronically imbalanced budget and tear-away inflation outdoing even the 1995 coupon. In 1919, the government issued 50 kopek notes (the maximum being 500 roubles) — by the time of 1924 monetary reform under the Bolsheviks, 250 million rouble notes were not uncommon. Added to these troubles came an invasion by the Armenians — repulsed in December 1918.

However, according to the widely respected Georgian scholar, David Marshall Lang, the Menshevik experiment had started off well and, but for the Bolshevik invasion, may have succeeded. The parallels with its policies and today's continue right up to the moment its leaders had to flee the country. In late 1920, the Georgian government sent a delegation to Western Europe which managed to secure promises of loans and concessions from Britain, concerning the Batumi naval base and oil refineries. In Italy they signed a deal for coal extraction near Sukhumi, and in France an agreement for silk production.

Select bibliography

Allen, W. E. D., *A History of the Georgian People*, Kegan Paul, 1932.
Allen, W. E. D. & Muratov P., *Caucasian Battlefields: 1828-1921*, Cambridge University Press, 1953.
Allen, W. E D., *Russian Embassies to the Georgian Kings*, 2 vols, Cambridge University Press, 1970.
Ascherson, Neal, *The Black Sea*, Jonathan Cape, 1995.
Avalov, Zurab, *The Independence of Georgia in International Politics, 1918-1921*, Headly Brothers, 1940.
Aves, Jonathan, *Georgia: From Chaos to Stability*, Chatham House (RIIA), 1995.

Baddeley, J. F., *The Rugged Flanks of the Caucasus*, Oxford University Press, 1940.
Barrett, David, *Catalogue of the Wardrop Collection*, Oxford University Press, 1973.
Bennett, Vanora, *Crying Wolf: The Return of War to Chechnya*, Picador, 1998.
Blanch, Lesley, *The Sabres of Paradise*, Carroll & Graf, 1995.
Braund, David, *Georgia in Antiquity*, Clarendon Press, Oxford, 1994.
Brook, Stephen, *The Claws of the Crab*, Sinclair-Stephenson, 1992.
Bryce, James, *Transcaucasia and Ararat*, MacMillan, 1877.
Burney, C., & Lang, D. M., *The Peoples of the Hills*, Praeger, 1972.

Chenciner, Robert, *Daghestan: Survival and Tradition*, Curzon Press, 1997.

Dubois de Montpereux, *Voyage autour du Caucase*, 6 vols, Librairie de Gide, Paris, 1839.
Dumas, Alexander, *Adventures in Caucasia*, Chilton Books, 1962.

Eastmond, Antony, *Royal Imagery in Medieval Georgia*, Pennsylvania State University Press, 1998.

Farson, Negley, *Caucasian Journey*, Evans Brothers, 1951.
Freshfield, Douglas, *Travels in the Central Caucasus and Bashan*, Longman & Green, 1869.
Freshfield, Douglas, *The Exploration of the Caucasus*, 2 vols, London, 1902.
Fromm, Erich, *Fear of Freedom*, Routledge, 1942.

Gachechiladze, Revaz, *The New Georgia*, UCL Press, 1995.
Goldenberg, Suzanne, *The Pride of Small Nations*, Zed Books, 1994.
Goldenberg S., Schofield, R., & Wright, J., *Transcaucasian Borders*, UCL 1996 .
Gorky, Maxim, *Autobiography*, 1953.

Iskander, Fazil, *Sandro of Chegem*, trans. Susan Brownsberger, Jonathan Cape, 1983.

Jones, Stephen, *Georgian Social Democracy in Opposition and Power*, University of London, 1984.

Kelly, Laurence, *Lermontov: Tragedy in the Caucasus*, Robin Clark, 1983.
Keun, Odette, *In the Land of the Golden Fleece*, trans. H. Jessiman, 1924.

Lang, David M., *The Georgians*, Thames & Hudson, 1966.
Lang, David M., *Lives and Legends of the Georgian Saints*, Allen & Unwin, 1956.
Lang, David M., *A Modern History of Georgia*, Weidenfeld & Nicolson, 1962.
Lang, David M., *The Wisdom of Balahvar: A Christian Legend of the Buddha*, London, 1957.
Lermontov, Mikhail, *A Hero of Our Time*, trans. Paul Foote. Penguin, 1966.
Lermontov, Mikhail, *The Demon*, trans. R. Burness, Douglas & Furness, 1918.

Maclean, Fitzroy, *Eastern Approaches*, Jonathan Cape, 1949.

Select bibliography

Maclean, Fitzroy, *To Caucasus: The End of All the Earth*, Jonathan Cape, 1976.

Mandelstam, Osip, *Journey to Armenia*, trans. Clarence Brown, Redstone Press, 1989.

Mandelstam, Osip, *Mandelstam: The Complete Critical Prose and Letters*, trans. Jane Harris & Constance Link, Ardis, 1979.

Marsden, Phillip, *The Spirit Wrestlers*, Harper Collins, 1998.

Mondadori, Arnoldo, *The Icon*, Evans Brothers, 1982.

Nasmyth, Peter, *The Wardrops: A Legacy of Britain in Georgia*, The British Council, 1998.

Nevinson, Henry, 'The Fire of the Caucasus', *Harpers*, New York, March 1908.

Pasternak, Boris, *Letters to Georgian Friends*, trans. David Magarshack, Secker & Warburg, 1968.

Pereira, Michael, *Across the Caucasus*, Geoffry Bless, 1973.

Porter, Robert Ker, *Travels in Georgia, Persia, Armenia, Ancient Babylonia: 1817-20*, London, 1821.

Pushkin, Alexander, *Journey to Erzrum*, trans. B. Ingemansson, Ardis Publishers, 1974.

Pushkin, Alexander, *The Bronze Horseman: Selected poems of Alexander Pushkin*, trans. D. M. Thomas, Secker & Warburg, 1982.

Rayfield, Donald, *The Literature of Georgia*, Curzon Press, 1998 [2nd revised edn].

Rayfield, Donald (trans.), *Vazha Pshavela: Three Poems*, Ganatleba, Tbilisi, 1981.

Rhinelander, L. H., *The Incorporation of the Caucasus into the Russian Empire: The Case for Georgia*, Columbia University, 1972.

Rosen, Roger, *The Georgian Republic*, Odyssey, 1991.

Russell, Mary, *Please Don't Call It Soviet Georgia*, Serpent's Tail, 1991.

Said, Kurban, *Ali and Nino*, trans. Jenia Graman, Robin Clark Ltd, 1990 [originally published in Vienna, 1937].

Spencer, Edmund, *Travels in the Western Caucasus*, 2 vols, London, 1838.

Suny, Ronald, *The Making of the Georgian Nation*, I. B. Tauris, 1989.

Thubron, Colin, *Among the Russians*, William Heinemann, 1983.

Tolstoy, Leo, *Hadji Murad*, in *Master and Man*, trans. Paul Foote, Penguin, 1976.

Tolstoy, Leo, *The Cossacks*, trans. Rosemary Edmonds, Penguin, 1960.

Urushadze, Venera, *Anthology of Georgian Poetry*, trans. Verena Urushadze, State Publishing House, Tbilisi, 1958.

Vivian, Katherine, *Sufic Traces in Georgian Literature*, Institute for Cultural Research, 1982 [also in *The Georgians: A Handbook*, ed. Nick Awde, Curzon Press, 1998].

Wardrop, Marjory (trans.), *The Man in the Panther Skin*, The Royal Asiatic Society, 1912.

Wardrop, Marjory (trans.), *Georgian Folk Tales*, David Nutt, 1894.

Wardrop, Marjory (trans.), *The Hermit*, by Ilia Chavchavadze, Bernard Quaritch, 1895.

Wardrop, Nino, 'Oliver, Marjory and Georgia', *The Bodleian Library Record*, vol. XIV, April 1994.

Wardrop, Oliver, *The Kingdom of Georgia*, Sampson Low, Marston, Searle & Rivington, 1888.

Wardrop, Oliver (trans.), *The Book of Wisdom and Lies*, Kelmscott Press, 1894.

Wardrop, Oliver, *Catalogue of Georgian Manuscripts in the British Museum*, British Museum, 1913.

Wardrop, Oliver, 'English-Svanetian Vocabulary', *Journal of the Royal Asiatic Society*, July 1911.

Wardrop, Oliver, *The Georgian Version of the Story of the Loves of Vis and Ramin*, Royal Asiatic Society, 1902.

Wardrop, Oliver (trans.), *The Life of St Nino*, Oxford, 1903.

Wolley, Clive Phillips, *Savage Svanetia*, 2 vols, London, 1883.

Yagan, Mural, *I Come from behind Kaf Mountain*, Threshold, 1984.

Yergin, Daniel, *The Prize: The Epic Quest for Oil, Money and Power*, Simon & Schuster, 1991.

Political chronology of Georgia since 1900

1903   Russian Social-Democratic Worker's Party split into two factions —
        Bolshevik and Mensheviks.
1905   October Revolution, St Petersburg. Georgian Mensheviks support
        creation of Russian Duma.
1918   On May 26th, Noe Ramishvili becomes first prime minister of the
        independent Georgian Republic. The Menshevik Noe Zhordania
        takes over on June 24th.
1919   Oliver Wardrop is appointed Chief British Commissioner of the
        Caucasus. Sets up office in Tbilisi.
1921   Bolshevik Red Army invades Georgia in February. Noe Zhordania
        and Menshevik government flee from Batumi.
1924   First purge in Georgia — at Stalin's instruction.
1936/7 Second wave of purges in Georgia, under Lavrenti Beria.
1941   Nazis invade Russia, are stopped in the North Caucasus.
1953   Stalin dies.
1972   Eduard Shevardnadze becomes First Secretary of the Georgian
        Communist Party.
1986   Mikhail Gorbachev's glasnost and perestroika begin.
1990   October: Georgia holds its first democratic parliamentary elections.
        Round Table alliance led by Zviad Gamsakhurdia win.
1991   Zviad Gamsakhurdia elected first President of independent
        Georgia.
1992   January: Two week civil war ends with victory for Opposition forces
        against Gamsakhurdia, who flees.
        March: Eduard Shevardnadze returns to become Chairman of the
        ruling State Council. August: Georgian troops march into Abkhazia,
        led by Tengiz Kitovani.
1993   September: Abkhaz forces with Russian backing expel Georgian
        forces from Abkhazia. 250,000 ethnic Georgians flee Abhkazia.
1994   May: Cease-fire signed in Georgia — Abkhazia stalemate. 2,500
        Russian and CIS peace-keeping soldiers deployed.
1995   August: Assassination attempt on Eduard Shevardnadze.
        November: Eduard Shevardnadze elected President. The lari
        introduced.
1996   Zurab Zhvania, Georgia's new Speaker of Parliament, establishes
        himself as Shevardnadze's possible successor.
1997   Work commences on 'early oil' pipeline — Baku to Supsa.
1998   February: Second assassination attempt on Eduard Shevardnadze.
        May: 30,000 Georgians forced to flee the Gali region of Abkhazia.

Index